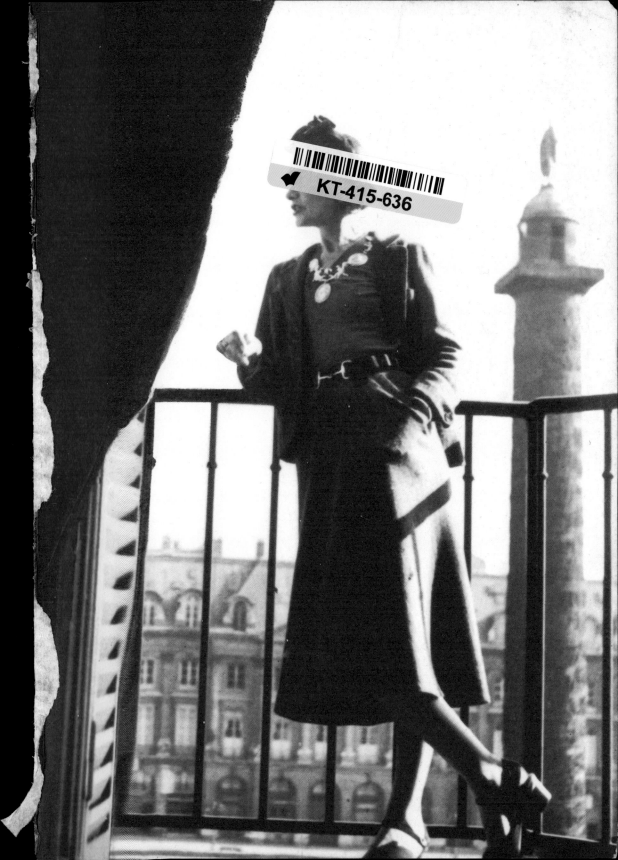

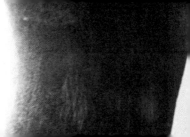

Coco Chanel

THE LEGEND AND THE LIFE

JUSTINE PICARDIE

HarperCollins*Publishers*

'I IMPOSED BLACK; IT'S STILL GOING STRONG TODAY, FOR

BLACK WIPES OUT EVERYTHING ELSE AROUND: Coco Chanel

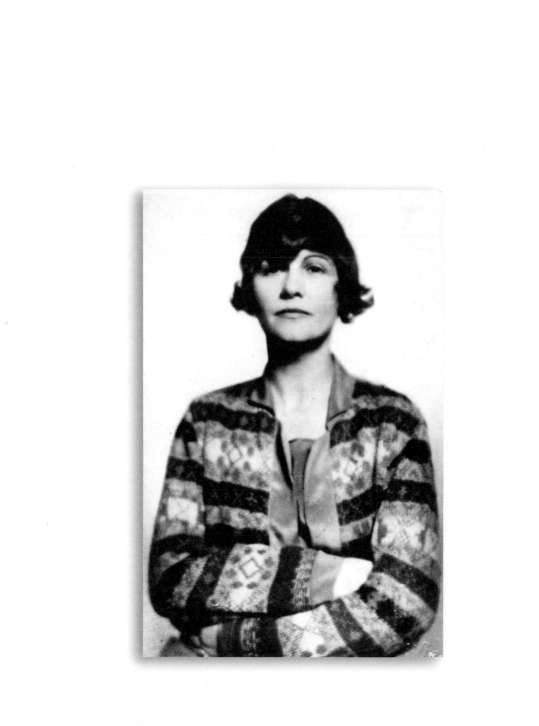

CONTENTS

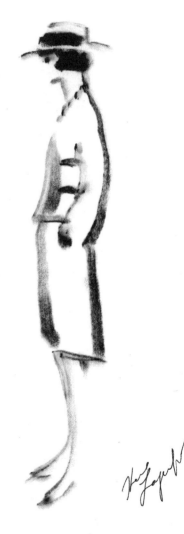

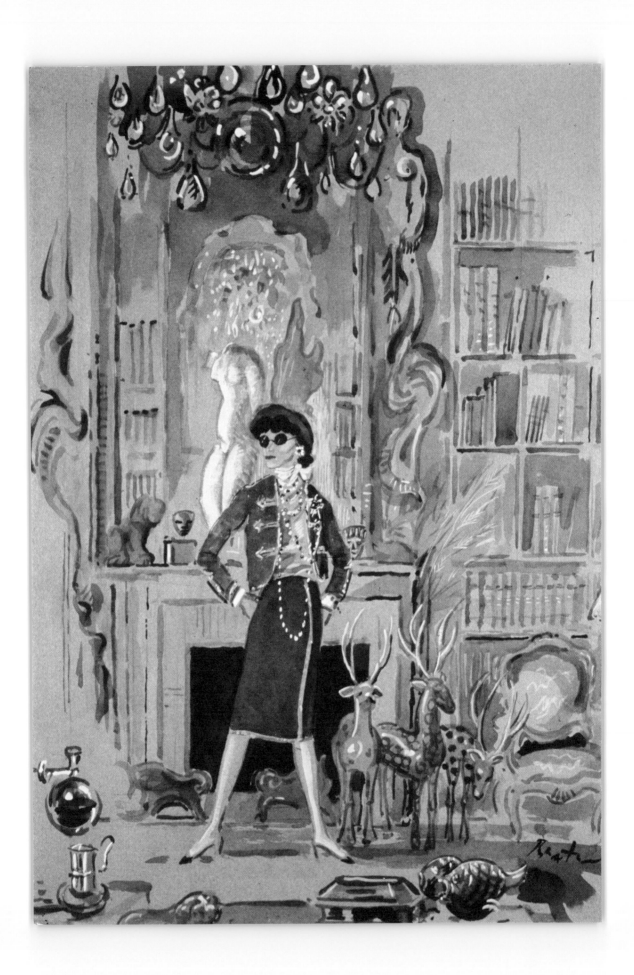

MADEMOISELLE IS AT HOME

'When my customers come to me, they like to cross the threshold of some magic place; they feel a satisfaction that is perhaps a trace vulgar but that delights them: they are privileged characters who are incorporated into our legend. For them this is a far greater pleasure than ordering another suit. Legend is the consecration of fame.'
Coco Chanel, 1935

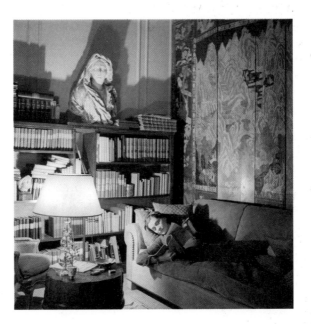

Left: Cecil Beaton's painted sketch of Chanel in her private apartment, 1969.
Above: Chanel, reclining on her beige sofa. Roger Schall, 1938.

The House of Chanel stands at 31 Rue Cambon, a shrine to its dead creator, yet also a living, thriving temple of twenty-first-century fashion, the destination for pilgrims who travel here from all around the world. Outside, dusk falls on a grey wintry afternoon in Paris, the darkness and the drizzle mingling into an early twilight, the shadows of the surrounding buildings lying heavy on the narrow street. Inside, the air is perfumed and warm in the ground-floor boutique, a cocoon of luxury lined with cream surfaces and silvered mirrors, the customers hovering like hummingbirds above glass cases of enticing jewel-coloured lipsticks, or swooping on rails of silk-lined tweed jackets. Their eyes dart towards the film projection of the latest collection, comparing what they see in the shop with what is portrayed on the screen (and perhaps in their mind's eye, a vision of themselves transformed, dressed all in Chanel). You can watch the video reflected in the mirrors, too; the porcelain-faced models riding on a white and gold carousel. But instead of wooden horses galloping in a ceaseless circle, there are the famous symbols of Coco Chanel: pearls and camellias and the interlocked double-C logo, as globally recognisable as the Stars and Stripes or the swastika. As the carousel revolves on the screen, the reflections in the mirrors are also spinning, and for a few seconds everything is in movement; nothing seems solid at all.

This is as you would expect in the heart and headquarters of an international fashion brand, where mutability is integral to its business of selling new stock every season; yet there must always be something immediately familiar, suggestive of an iconography that denotes heritage and enduring value. The contradictions of such an enterprise are unavoidable – it's a balancing act between constant change and constancy – as is evident in Coco Chanel's own observations on the business of fashion: 'A dress is neither a tragedy, nor a painting; it is a charming and ephemeral creation, not an everlasting work of art. Fashion should die and die quickly, in order that commerce may survive … The more transient fashion is the more perfect it is. You can't protect what is already dead.'

And yet Mademoiselle protected her house, and here it still stands. Beside the entrance to the boutique is another doorway, closed to the public by a discreet dark-suited security guard, though not to select couture clients, who ascend Chanel's mirrored staircase when they come for private fittings in the hushed salon on the first floor. Not a trace of dust or dirt marks the floor, dark and shiny as a lipstick case, and the ivory walls are perfectly smooth, as befits a ceremonial space where pieces from the current couture collection hang on rails, veiled in white shrouds like novitiates. Beyond here, the staircase continues to rise through the centre of the house, up to the place where Chanel watched her fashion shows unfold, hidden from the audience below, yet seeing everything beneath her, perched on the fifth step from the top of the spiralling stairs.

Pause for a moment on the staircase, and it gives you the strangest sensation. The mirrors are simultaneously reflecting from all angles; there is no escape from the sight of your body bisected, slivers of face and limbs. So you must watch yourself as you climb the flight to the second floor, to the unmarked mirrored double doors that lead into Mademoiselle Chanel's private apartment. Open the door, and it is as if she has never left the building; for here is her sanctuary polished and preserved, decades after her death on 10th January 1971.

You might call it a mausoleum, yet it feels too alive for that, for these rooms are still filled with her presence, along with her possessions. On the other side of the door is an entrance hall, the walls lined with early eighteenth-century Coromandel screens, their red lacquer patterned with a mysterious Oriental landscape, where women in kimonos fly on the back of white birds, and men are carried by fishes and turtles. There are pale mountains and wraiths of clouds and lakes on the screens, waterfalls and temples and precipices, a world beyond the walls of this Parisian apartment; and the sound of the city is silenced by the softness of thick beige carpet, the view concealed by the mirrors that reflect the Chinese screens.

The hall seems hermetically sealed, the way out hidden by mirrors, but two life-size Venetian blackamoors gesture to go on, past a pair of reindeer that stand to attention on either side of a bunch of gilded wheat in a silver vase. The statues point into the salon, but the reflection of their painted eyes and pointing hands is multiplied in a series of mirrored images, upending all sense of direction, skewing perspective within these looking-glass walls. Another door leads from the hall to the dining room where Chanel entertained guests, six beige suede-upholstered chairs at a walnut table; two lions on the tabletop; two gilt and crystal-encrusted mirrors in the alcoves; the ceiling curved like the vaulting of a Romanesque church. A smaller sitting room is lined with more antique Chinese screens, watched over by a stone statue of the Madonna and Child, his eyes at the door, hers cast down to the ground. But there is no bedroom in the apartment, for Mademoiselle slept across the street, on the top floor of the Ritz, with a view over the rooftops of Rue Cambon. Her hotel room was unadorned

– white cotton sheets, white walls, austere like the convent orphanage where she was educated – but her apartment remains as ornate as it was in her lifetime. The walls are lined in gold fabric; not that much can be seen of them, for they are covered with books and screens and mirrors, conserved like the inside of a holy sanctum, or the final resting place of an Ancient Egyptian queen.

If the mirrored staircase is the backbone of the House of Chanel, then Mademoiselle's salon – the largest of the three main rooms in her apartment – is its hidden heart. The outside world is not entirely excluded, for there are windows reaching from floor to ceiling, overlooking Rue Cambon to the school on the other side of the street, where children still study in the first-floor classroom, just as they did when Mademoiselle Chanel lived here. But did she look out of the window at them, or keep her eyes fixed on the treasures within these walls? There are yet more Chinese screens hiding the doors (Chanel hated the sight of doors, she said, for they reminded her of those who had already left, and those who would leave her again). Look closer, and you could lose yourself within their intricacies, drawn into a landscape of boats and bridges, of graceful women kneeling beside the water; a place where serpents and dragons fly through the air, above unicorns and elephants; where the trees grow leaves like fine white lace, and camellias are perpetually in blossom.

You could spend days in this room and never want to leave, such is the wealth of its riches. Two walls are lined with leather-bound books: antique editions of Plutarch, Euripides and Homer; the memoirs of Casanova and the essays of Montaigne; *The Confessions of St Augustine* and *The Dialogues* of Plato; the complete works of Maupassant and Molière in French, Shelley and Shakespeare in English; and two volumes of a weighty Holy Bible, published in London by the aptly named Virtue and Co. (If you happen to take down Volume Three of Shelley from the shelf, it falls open at a well-thumbed page from the poet's preface to *Julian and Maddalo*: 'Of the Maniac I can give no information. He seems, by his own account, to have been disappointed in love. He was evidently a very cultivated and amiable person when in his right senses. His story, told at length, might be like many other stories of the same kind: the unconnected exclamations of his agony will perhaps be found a sufficient comment for the text of every heart.')

In front of one of these walls of rare books stands Mademoiselle's roll-top desk, where her cream-coloured writing paper and envelopes are still in the compartment where she kept them. Above is a gilt-framed painting of a lion, signifying Chanel's astrological sign of Leo, in commemoration of her birthday on 19th August, although she was less willing to remember the year of her birth, 1883, adjusting it when it suited her purposes; even tearing it out of her passport. 'My age varies according to the days and the people I happen to be with,' she told a young American journalist in 1959, when she was 76. 'When I'm bored I feel very old, and since I'm extremely bored with you, I'm going to be a thousand years old in five minutes …' Beside the lion is a vase of crystal camellias; on the leather desktop is her tortoiseshell fan, engraved with the stars that she constantly reworked into her jewellery designs, and a pair of her spectacles. Try them on, and the room dissolves into a blur of gold and red and shadows; quickly take them off again, to stop the walls from closing in.

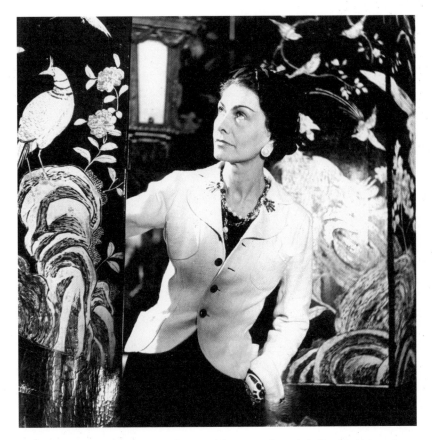

Chanel standing beside her antique Coromandel screens, decorated with white birds and camellia branches. Boris Lipnitzki, 1937.

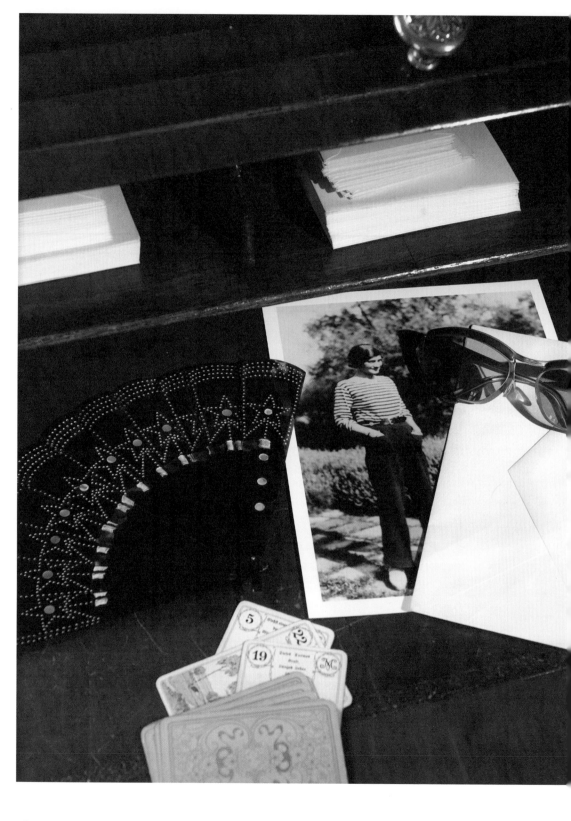

The drawers of the desk are unlocked; two are empty – and much was emptied from here, mysteriously vanishing on the night of Mademoiselle's death; shadowy figures stealing down the mirrored staircase, disappearing with bags of her belongings, including most of her precious jewels (the priceless ropes of pearls and necklaces of rubies and emeralds, her dazzling diamond rings and bracelets). But the right-hand drawer still contains a few of her personal possessions: a pair of sunglasses in a soft leather pouch, another fan, this one even more delicate, fashioned in paper and fragile wooden frets, and a sheaf of photographs of Mademoiselle Chanel. The first is of her in 1937, elegant in a white jacket and pearls, standing beside the Coromandel screen in the hall. Her eyes do not look into the camera lens, but gaze sideways, towards something or someone unseen, somewhere beyond the screen, beyond the white birds and camellias.

There are several more photographs in the drawer: Chanel as a young woman astride a white horse, head held high to the camera, but her eyes hidden in the shade of a wide-brimmed hat. A man stands beside her, her lover Boy Capel, his hands lightly touching her foot in the stirrup; they are dressed in near-identical riding outfits, a boyish tie her only addition to the crisp white shirt and trim jodhpurs. Twenty years on, and Boy Capel is gone, while Chanel is balanced on the shoulder of her friend Serge Lifar, a handsome ballet dancer, his hair as glossily dark as hers. She is wearing her strands of pearls over a black sweater and white trousers, and smiling in the light of a Riviera morning. Sunshine dapples her face again in a picture of a younger Chanel on a countryside road, where she is standing beside her car, nonchalant in a striped matelot top and navy sailor trousers; a reminder of her life beyond Rue Cambon, of her villa beside the sea in the south of France. And then there is the photograph of Chanel in 1920 with her lover, the Grand Duke Dmitri, cousin of the Russian tsar, and one of the assassins of Rasputin. He is as handsome as a movie star; she is more beautiful than any of her models, hair cropped short, tanned skin glowing against iridescent pearls and white satin dress, gazing into his eyes.

But mostly the pictures show Chanel alone: poised by the fireplace, or reclining on the long beige-suede sofa in the salon, studying a book, her hand hovering over a page of cryptic Indian illustrations. You cannot read her expression in these photographs of a solitary woman, the elegant lines of her face impassive, her eyebrows arched, a cigarette in her hand, its smoke rising like a decoy.

Writing paper, envelopes, spectacles, a tortoiseshell fan, photographs
and a collection of Tarot cards, as Chanel left them, on her desk.

And so you go back to searching the room, trying to decode the cipher, looking for clues that might explain its owner's enigmatic face. There are bunches of dried wheat on either side of the marble fireplace, and two more made of gilt-covered wood on the mantelpiece, emblematic of good fortune and prosperity. A golden lion raises its paw to a Grecian mask, a woman's face with eyes as dark as Chanel's; and in the centre of the mantelpiece is a first-century headless torso of Aphrodite, its marble curves reflected in the looking glass, so that it seems to be one of twins. The Baroque mirror above the fireplace is vast, almost reaching the high ceiling, framed by pillars of cherubs and grapes. Its reflections are refracted by yet another mirror, of darker, smokier glass, which hangs above the suede sofa; leaning against the faded gilt frame is a gold crucifix (a double-barred cross, typical of those seen in the Spanish holy town of Caravaca, a former stronghold of the Knights Templar). Beside the cross is a painting of a single wheatsheaf by Salvador Dalí, one of Chanel's many artist friends.

You could go on searching for meaning here, noting the quilted cushions on the sofa (diagonal quilting, the same pattern as her famous handbags); hunting for the lions in the room; counting the pairs of animals. There are the two bronze deer by the fireplace, almost life-size, a buck and doe, their cloven feet sinking

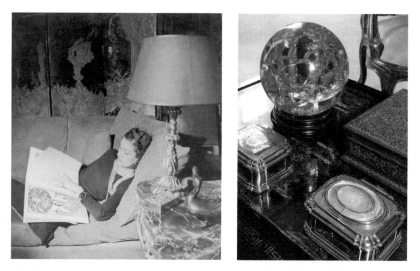

Left: Chanel studying a book of Indian illustrations given to her by her lover, Boy Capel. Jean Moral, 1937.
Right: A fortune teller's ball and two of the gold dressing-table containers that Chanel received as a gift from the Duke of Westminster.

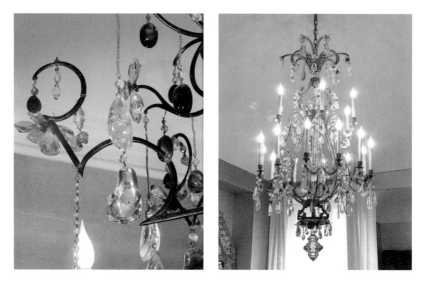

Chanel designed the chandelier in the salon of her apartment: her iconography is hidden in the wrought-iron frame and crystals; G is for Gabrielle, double C for Coco Chanel, and 5, the number which made her fortune. Right: The elaborate chandelier in Chanel's dining room.

into the carpet, and another tiny pair beside the sofa, in painted metal, with vases of pink flowers on their backs. Two camels on a side-table, two frogs (one glass, one bronze); two lovebirds made of pearl in a tiny jewelled cage; two porcelain horses, on either side of the smoky mirror; two golden fire-dogs in the empty hearth. Once you start looking, the doublings are everywhere: a second Grecian mask, staring at its twin from across the room; two Egyptian sphinx; two ceramic bowls on top of a bookshelf, one containing a broken shard of crystal; two clocks, one on the desk, which has stopped at 3.23, on the eleventh day of an unnumbered month, the other suspended, miraculously, on a mirrored wall between the two windows, its hands motionless at 1.18, a winged and vengeful angel of death wielding a scythe above the clockface.

A collection of symbolic objects is scattered throughout the room: a Catholic icon, a Buddha holding a spray of roses in his hand, another Buddha beside a strange mythical creature (part lion, part dog, part man, with an expression on his face of a sorrowful Caliban); a crystal glass cross, a mariner's navigational tool, a single bronze hand made by Diego Giacometti; a pack of Tarot cards (the number five is on top, Chanel's lucky number, illustrated by a picture of a green tree, its roots visible above the ground). There is evidence of great wealth, and perhaps of great love: Chanel is said to have discovered her taste for

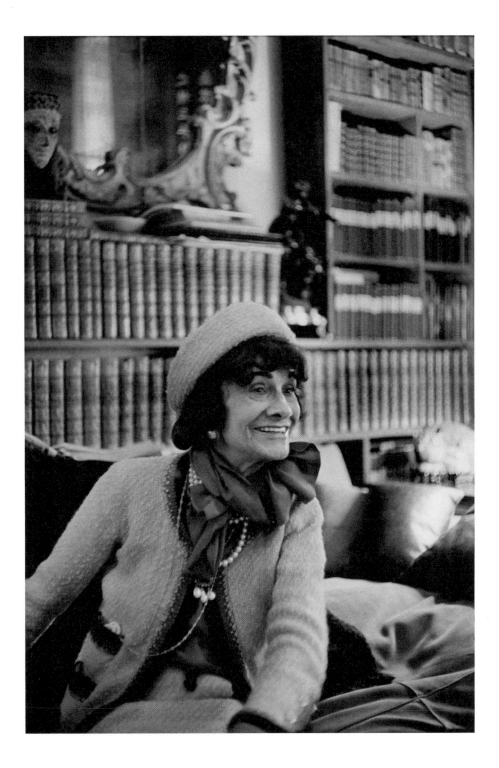

Coromandel screens with the first and foremost love of her life, Boy Capel, the Englishman who also introduced her to theosophy and literature. Then there are the weighty solid-gold boxes engraved with the crest of a crown, a gift to Chanel from the Duke of Westminster, who showered her with jewels during their decade-long love affair, although there is no further sign of him here in the apartment apart from a novel by Alexandre Dumas, borrowed from the ducal library. The boxes stand empty on a low table in front of the sofa, flanked by a pair of fortune-teller's glass globes: one is in white quartz, cool to the touch; the other of gold-flecked resin, unexpectedly warm beneath the hands. Gaze into the glass, and nothing is clear; both globes contain only the faintest reflections of the chandelier that hangs from the middle of the ceiling. It is a magnificent creation – designed by Chanel herself – adorned with dozens of crystal orbs and stars, camellias and grapes; sparkling from a black wrought-iron frame. Look long enough, and the hidden letters and numbers in the frame begin to emerge from the abstract pattern: at the top of the chandelier there are Gs for Gabrielle, Chanel's name at christening; double Cs for Coco Chanel, the name under which she became famous; and fives – the number which made her fortune, as the label on the perfume that still sells more than any other brand in the world.

Walk back to the desk, and dare to sit down on the beige suede-upholstered chair where Mademoiselle used to work; run your fingers over the marks of her pen still visible in the multiple scores and angry scratches on the ink-stained leather desktop. The hands of the clocks are fixed for ever, the room is silent, the cream linen curtains are still; nothing moves across the mirrors, the gleaming light from the chandelier remains caught in time, as if preserved in amber. You cannot see the reflections in the mirrors when you are writing at the desk, only the eyes of the painted lion in the gold frame, the hands of the blackamoors, disappearing through the half-open door; but the hairs on the back of your neck are prickling; and perhaps, if you could turn around quickly enough, who on earth might be reflected in the looking-glass walls?

'Sometimes, when the boutique is closed, we feel her presence,' said my guide to the apartment, on my first visit here, glancing over her shoulder at the sound of a creaking door, the murmur of voices on the staircase, nervous as if she were being watched. 'After dark, even when the lights are on, you might glimpse her in the mirror, or hear her footsteps in the drawing room, very soft and quiet, too quick for anyone to catch up with her ...'

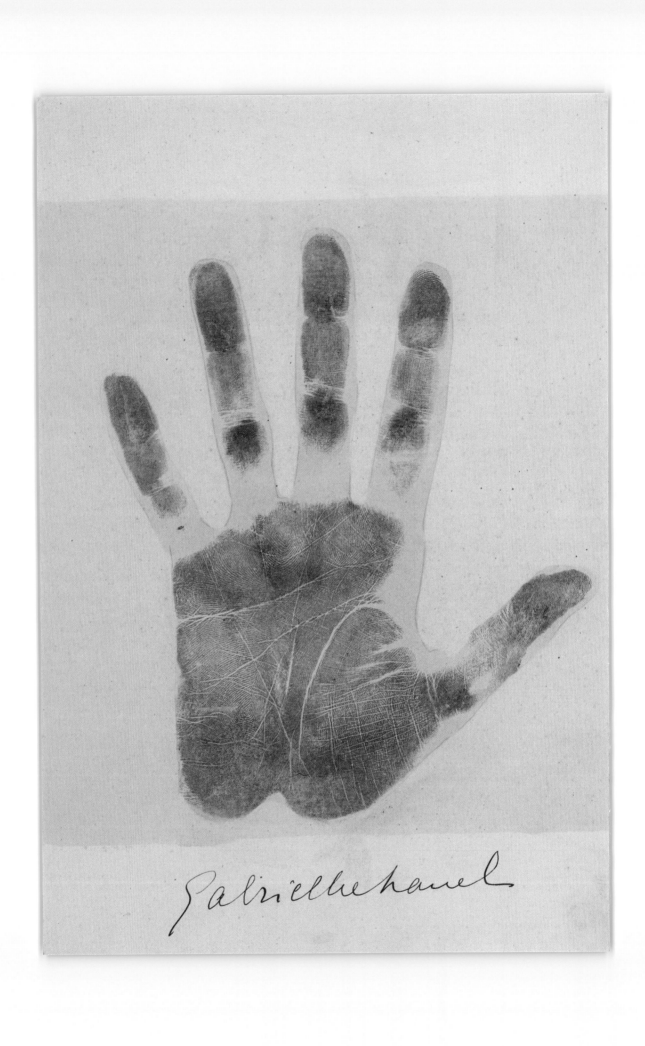

GABRIELLE

'Those on whom legends are built *are* their legends,' declared Coco Chanel to her friend Paul Morand, one of several writers to whom she tried, and failed, to tell the story of her life. 'People's lives are an enigma,' she said to another friend, Claude Delay, not long before her death, when her face had already become a fixed mask to the world, and her myth apparently impenetrable. Delay was a young woman at the time, the daughter of a well-known French psychiatrist, but is herself now an eminent psychoanalyst, and an expert guide to the labyrinth of secrets and lies that Chanel constructed to conceal the truth of her past. Not that there is ever a single truth in a life, especially for a woman who built a career on refashioning women's ideas of themselves; which may be why Chanel recounted so many different stories about herself, as if in each version something new might emerge out of her history.

'I don't like the family,' she told Delay, in one of a series of revelatory, rambling conversations in her final decade. 'You're born in it, not of it. I don't know anything more terrifying than the family.' And so she circled around and about it, telling and retelling the narrative of her youth, remaking history just as she remade the sleeves of a jacket, unfastening its seams and cutting its threads, and then sewing it back together again. 'Childhood – you speak of it when you're very tired, because it's a time when you had hopes, expectations. I remember my childhood by heart.'

If Chanel's memory did survive intact, she nevertheless obscured her past from others, reshaping its heartaches, smoothing away the rough edges. Even her birth certificate is misleading – her father's surname, and hers, were misspelt due to a clerical error as Chasnel. But she could not keep all the details hidden: her mother's maiden name was Eugénie Jeanne Dévolles, and despite attempts by Chanel in later life to erase the date, the official record shows that her mother gave birth to Gabrielle on 19th August 1883 in the poorhouse in Saumur, a market town on the river Loire. Eugénie (known as Jeanne) was 20, Henri-Albert (known as Albert) was 28, and listed as a *marchand*, or merchant, on Gabrielle's birth certificate. They were not yet married but already had one daughter, Julia, born less than a year previously, on 11th September 1882.

'I was born on a journey,' Chanel told an American reporter in answer to his question about the exact location of her birthplace. Although this was an evasion – she was born in a hospice for the poor, run by an order of nuns, the Sisters of Providence – her parents were generally on the move, itinerant market traders selling buttons and bonnets, aprons and overalls, travelling between towns, just as her paternal grandparents had done. Gabrielle's father was the son of a peddler, and like her, he had been born in a poorhouse (in Nîmes in 1856); his surname had also been misspelt on his birth certificate, but on this occasion as Henri-Albert Charnet. The mistake was not corrected in official records until over

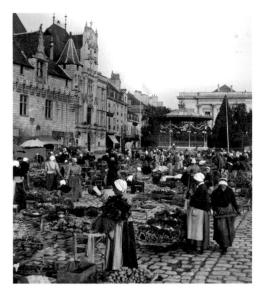

The marketplace in Saumur, Maine-et-Loire, France; Chanel was born in the town on 19th August 1883, the illegitimate daughter of itinerant market traders, who sold buttons and basic haberdashery.

two decades later, in 1878, when a court decree stated that Charnet be replaced on the certificate by Chanel, 'which is the true name'.

'My father was not there,' she explained to another journalist, Marcel Haedrich (editor-in-chief of *Marie-Claire*, and a man who had spent enough time with Chanel to regard himself as her friend, drawing on his conversations with her in a biography he wrote soon after her death). 'That poor woman, my mother, had to go looking for him. It's a sad story, and very boring – I've heard it so many times.'

Thus she dismissed the beginning of her story, and never told it with any accuracy herself; never acknowledging that the truth was far from boring, but too troubling to reveal. Gabrielle's father was not present at her birth, setting a pattern that was to be repeated thereafter. A man who often appeared to be on the run from his family, he had already vanished when Jeanne became pregnant with their first child, and refused to marry her when he was finally tracked down, a month before she gave birth to their daughter Julia. Consequently, both the girls were born illegitimate; it was not until Gabrielle was 15 months old that her parents eventually married, in November 1884. Soon afterwards, her mother was pregnant again, and on the move through the Auvergne in south-central France, an isolated region where Jeanne had been born into a peasant family in the village of Courpière. She would have found little refuge there: both Jeanne's parents were dead by the time she had met her elusive future husband, and although her brother had done his best to protect her interests when she fell pregnant, her illegitimate babies did nothing to soften the weight of local disapproval. A boy, christened Alphonse, was born in 1885; another daughter, Antoinette, in 1887; a son, Lucien, in 1889; and the final baby, Augustin, who died in infancy, in 1891.

Chanel rarely talked about the circumstances of her birth, but she did occasionally mention a train journey that her mother had undertaken just beforehand, in search of the elusive Albert. 'What with the clothes of that time,' she remarked to Haedrich with her customary, circuitous vagueness, 'I suppose no one could see that she was about to have a baby. Some people helped her – they were very kind: they took her into their home and sent for a doctor. My mother didn't want to stay there.

'"You can get another train tomorrow," the people said, to soothe her. "You'll find your husband tomorrow." But the doctor realized that my mother wasn't ill at all. "She's about to have a baby," he said. At that point the people who had

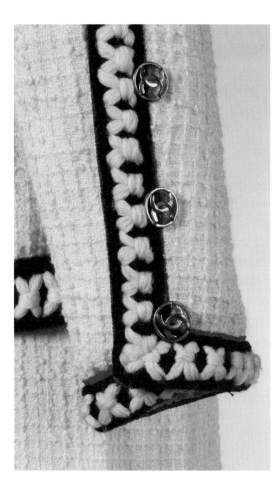

Chanel's signature buttons were adorned with a variety of symbolic motifs. The collection featured here, all designed by Mademoiselle Chanel, include a lion, the interlaced double Cs, a camellia, stars and chains.

been so nice to her were furious. They wanted to throw her out. The doctor insisted that they take care of her. They took her to a hospital, where I was born. One of the hospital nuns was my godmother.'

The name of this nun was Gabrielle Bonheur, according to Chanel, 'so I was baptized Gabrielle Bonheur Chanel. I knew nothing of this for a long time. There was never any occasion to check my baptismal certificate. During the war I sent for all my documents because one was always afraid of the worst ...' In fact, the name Bonheur does not appear on her baptismal certificate, but perhaps Gabrielle felt the right to make it her own in later life; to lay claim to its meaning, which is happiness.

In yet another version of her birth, told to a different friend, André-Louis

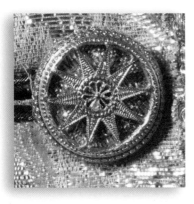

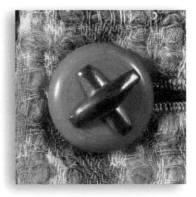

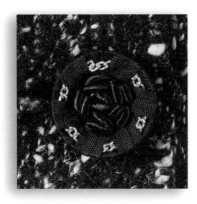

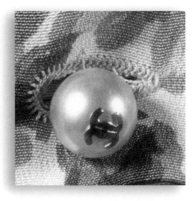

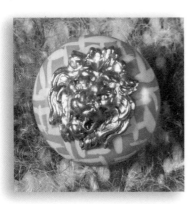

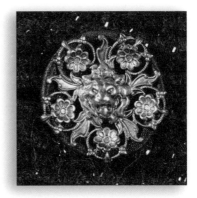

Dubois, Gabrielle mentioned a train again, suggesting that her mother went into labour while travelling on the railway. 'She talked constantly about trains, sometimes even claiming to have been born on a train,' said Dubois, remembering Chanel to a French journalist soon after her death. 'Why this obsession with trains?' One possible answer is that she had an uncle who was a railway employee, but even so, trains seemed to have a deeper significance for Chanel than that; as if they were a connection to a past that was always on the move, yet ran along fixed lines, to a destination of her own choosing.

Whatever her association with train travel, she was also a child of the poorhouse, plain Gabrielle Chasnel. And Gabrielle she stayed throughout her childhood – Coco was a creation that came later – although she invented a story that is revealing in its untruths: 'My father used to call me "Little Coco" until something better should come along,' she told Haedrich. 'He didn't like [the name] "Gabrielle" at all; it hadn't been his choice. And he was right. Soon the "Little" drifted away and I was simply Coco.' It may be that her father was complaining that he didn't like Gabrielle herself; that he had not chosen to have children; for soon he left them, discontented with marriage and fatherhood, always on the lookout for something better.

At times, Gabrielle declared Coco to be an 'awful' name; and yet she was proud of its recognition throughout the world, evidence of her indisputable presence, despite the lack of acknowledgement or recognition by her father. But still it was a cipher, a name that her father had never known, even though she declared otherwise. 'If anyone had told me before the war that I'd be Coco Chanel to the whole world, I'd have laughed,' she said to Haedrich. 'Mademoiselle Chanel had four thousand employees and the richest man in England loved her. And now I'm Coco Chanel! Nevertheless, it isn't my name … People stop me in the street: "Are you really Coco Chanel?" When I give autographs, I write "Coco Chanel". On a train to Lausanne a couple of weeks ago, the whole carriage paraded past me. In my own premises I'm called "Mademoiselle"; that goes without saying. I certainly don't want to be called Coco in the House of Chanel.' (These seemingly disconnected sentences are as Haedrich transcribed them; the fleeting references to her name and the train exactly as he recorded them.)

In truth, no one knew for certain what name Gabrielle answered to in childhood, nor where exactly Coco came from. In old age, Chanel told Claude Delay that her father spoke English – 'that was considered something diabolical in the provinces' – which seems highly unlikely, but it is possible that the story formed a link in her mind with the English-speaking men that she loved in adulthood (Boy Capel and the Duke of Westminster, both of whom were to prove unfaithful to her). She also told Delay that her father gave her a present when he returned from one of his numerous trips away: a penholder made of a knucklebone, with Notre-Dame depicted on one side, and the Eiffel Tower on the other; and that she had dug a hole for this re-tooled bone in a cemetery, and buried the gift, as an offering to the dead.

If Chanel's own account is to be believed, by the age of six she was spending as much time as possible in a graveyard. 'Every child has a special place, where he or she likes to hide, play and dream,' she said to Paul Morand (who set down her memories in his book, *L'Allure de Chanel*). 'Mine was an Auvergne cemetery. I knew no one there, not even the dead.' And yet the dead seemed to become alive for her there, although they remained as silent as their graves.

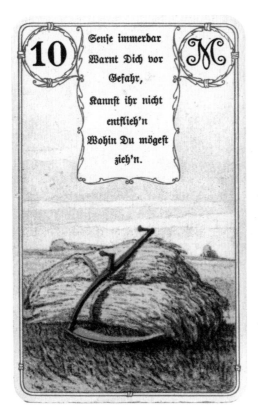

Chanel's number 10 Tarot card – one of the many symbols of wheat which she kept in her Rue Cambon apartment. It reads: 'Always a scythe around / Will warn you of danger, / You cannot ever escape it / Wherever you may go.'

'I was the queen of this secret garden. I loved its subterranean dwellers. "The dead are not dead as long as we think of them," I would tell myself.'

She became attached to two unnamed tombstones, decorating them with wildflowers – poppies and daisies and cornflowers – bringing her rag dolls to the cemetery; her favourite dolls, because she had made them for herself. 'I wanted to be sure that I was loved,' she told Morand, 'but I lived with people who showed no pity. I like talking to myself and I don't listen to what I'm told: this is probably due to the fact that the first people to whom I opened my heart were the dead.'

Her mother figures only as a shadowy invalid in Gabrielle's memories; though there are a few splashes of crimson that stain the blank pages within Chanel's shifting narratives – her stories of the blood that a sick woman coughed onto white handkerchiefs, and an interior which bears some resemblance to the sinister red room where Jane Eyre was incarcerated as a child. Chanel, in later life, was a fan of the Brontës, returning repeatedly to *Jane Eyre* and *Wuthering Heights* (stories of near incestuous passion, of locked doors and unhinged minds). But her description of the red room is also reminiscent of another nineteenth-century novel, *The Yellow Wallpaper* by Charlotte Perkins Gilman, in which a woman goes mad after the birth of her child, and peels the paper from the walls of the room that imprisons her. In Chanel's story (as told to Paul

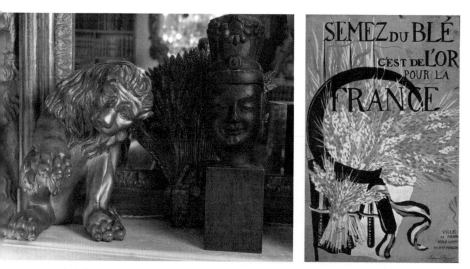

Left: One of the gilt-covered wooden bunches of wheat on the mantelpiece in Chanel's apartment, alongside a golden lion and a limestone carving.
Right: A French First World War poster. 'Grow Wheat, It is Gold for France.'

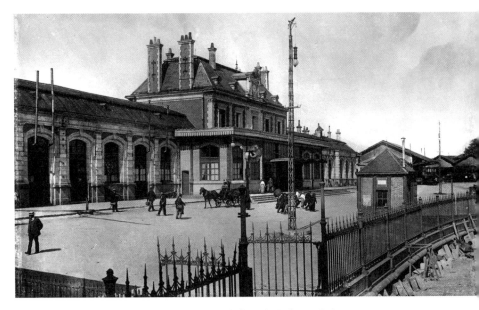

Brive-la-Gaillarde railway station. Chanel's mother died nearby in the market town, while her father was travelling.

Morand), the wallpaper was red. She was five, and her mother already very ill, when she was taken with her two sisters to stay at the home of an elderly uncle. 'We were shut away in a room covered in red wallpaper. To begin with, we were very well-behaved; then we noticed that the red wallpaper was very damp and could be peeled off from the walls.' The girls started by peeling small pieces, then climbed onto chairs, and stripped the entire room down to its bare pink plaster: 'the pleasure was sublime!' When their mother came into the room, she was silent, saying nothing to her daughters, simply contemplating the disaster, and weeping without making any sound.

Chanel was to claim that her mother died of tuberculosis, which was not necessarily an accurate diagnosis of what killed Jeanne; poverty, pregnancy and pneumonia were as likely to blame. In her account to Delay (subsequently published in *Chanel solitaire*), the family lived in a large enough house for the children to be kept in isolation from their sick mother. In fact, they were crowded with her into one room in the market town of Brive-la-Gaillarde, while their father abandoned them for the road. But the story Chanel told Delay had her father present, kissing her sister Julia and her on the head as they were eating lunch (no mention was made of the other siblings). 'He hated the smell of hair and always asked how long it was since we'd had ours washed.' Who knows how often the Chanel children were able to wash their hair, while their mother lay sick in bed, and their father was gone; but in Chanel's memory, she would answer to her father that her hair was clean, washed 'three days ago, with yellow soap'.

She also imagined herself as her father's favourite. 'I didn't so much love as want to be loved,' she told Delay. 'So I loved my father because he preferred me to my sister. I couldn't have borne for him to feel the same about us both.' But she also claimed to have had a rival, a servant who she believed was poisoning her. 'I knew she slept with my father – that is, I didn't know, I didn't understand anything about that sort of thing, but I guessed, and I used to frighten her by saying I'd tell my mother.' Once upon a time, in this dark fairytale, her parents went away together, and Gabrielle and her sister set out in search of them, to escape from the evil servant. When they finally reached their parents, Gabrielle fell asleep on her father's shoulder, and the next day he bought her a blue dress.

In another of her confessions to Delay (narratives in which the truth may or may not be unravelled from the fictions), Chanel said that as a child she was frightened of ghosts and what lay hidden beneath the bed in the darkness. Gabrielle's graveyard offerings were not enough to protect her, and in the night the dead seemed more sinister than they did in her daylight games at the cemetery. But in the story as she told it – one of a series that could have been designed more for herself than for her listener – her father came to her; he was there to soothe her fears. 'Don't be frightened,' he said to her, as every good father should. 'No one is going to hurt you.' Even so, she was still terrified of a man under her bed, throwing wheat at her. 'But wheat is very good,' her father said, taking her into his arms. Ever since then, she explained to Delay, she had always kept a bunch of wheat close to her: in her bedroom at the Ritz, and in each room of her apartment in Rue Cambon.

Yet all the goodness of the wheat could not keep her mother from dying. Gabrielle maintained that she was 6 years old at the time; in reality, she was 11. Her father was absent again, travelling away from home, when Jeanne was found dead in her bed in a freezing room in Brive, on a bitterly cold February morning in 1895. History does not relate if Gabrielle watched her mother die, or for how long she and her siblings remained alone with the corpse; and Mademoiselle Chanel never revealed the truth, either.

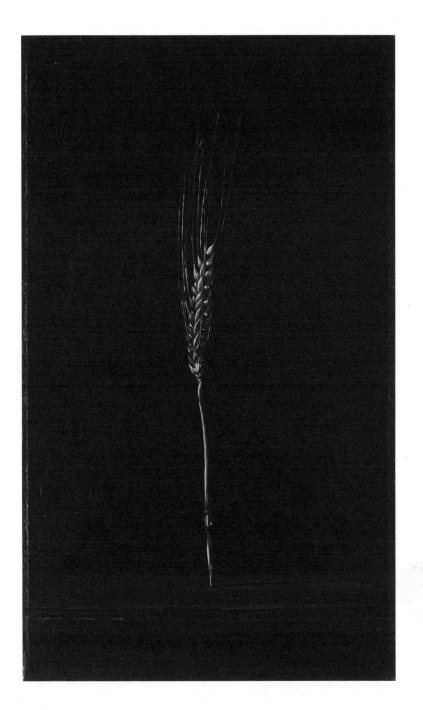

Salvador Dalí's painting of a single ear of wheat, which hangs in Chanel's apartment.

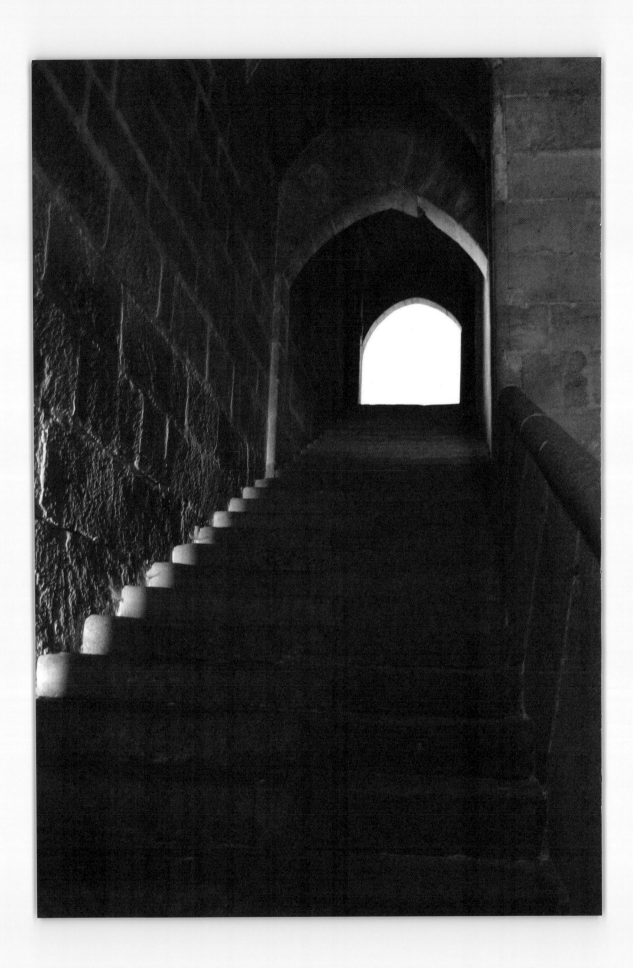

IN THE SHADOW OF THE CROSS

Brive-la-Gaillarde is a traditional railway town, a junction on the main line from Paris to Toulouse, occupying a central position in the vast heartland of France; as good a starting point as any for a pilgrim in search of Chanel. Take the road eastwards from the station; it runs through the centre of the town, then follows the curves of the river across a flat plain, towards forested mountains in the distance. After a few miles there is a narrow turning off the main road, climbing in serpentine twists, apparently coiling in on itself up the steep ascent. But at last it leads to Aubazine, a medieval village dominated by the dark bulk of a twelfth-century Cistercian monastery and abbey, founded by St Etienne in 1135.

This is the place to which Gabrielle's father drove her in a cart from Brive, along with her two sisters, Julia and Antoinette, soon after the death of their mother. The boys were left elsewhere – deposited with a peasant family; foundlings used as unpaid labour – and the three girls were handed over to the nuns who ran an orphanage within the abbey walls, the sisters of the Congregation of the Sacred Heart of Mary. The children's father promptly disappeared. Gabrielle later claimed he had gone to America in search of a fortune in a promised land, the New World, far away from the ascetic cloisters where he had abandoned his daughters.

Not that Gabrielle ever described it as abandonment; nor did she use the word 'orphanage'. Instead, she told a number of embroidered stories about being left with her 'aunts', while her sister (she was vague about which one) was sent to a convent. There were two 'aunts' in her various narratives: black-clad, cold-eyed, stern and always nameless. 'Actually, they weren't my aunts, but my mother's first cousins,' she once remarked to Marcel Haedrich, adding that she lived with them in 'the remotest corner of Auvergne. My aunts were good people, but absolutely without tenderness. I was not loved in their house. I got no affection. Children suffer from such things.'

Then, in a longer outburst, she gave away something of the misery she had felt, in a denial that also serves as a kind of confession: 'People say I'm an *Auvergnate*. There's nothing of the *Auvergnate* in me – nothing, nothing. My mother was one. In that part of the world, though, I was thoroughly unhappy. I fed on sorrow and horror. I wanted to kill myself I don't know how many times. "That poor Jeanne" – I couldn't stand hearing my mother talked about in that way anymore. Like all children, I listened at closed doors. I learned that my father had ruined my mother – "poor Jeanne". All the same, she'd married the man she loved. And having to hear people call me an orphan! They felt sorry for me. I had nothing to be pitied for – I had a father. All this was humiliating. I realized no one

From left: Chanel's mother's death certificate. The Calvary, Aubazine. French Carmelite nuns at prayer. The monastic buildings of Aubazine.

loved me and I was being kept out of charity. There were visitors – plenty of visitors. I heard the questions put to my aunts: "Does the little one's father still send money?"'

But there were no visits, and no money, and no stern aunts. Gabrielle spent seven years in the orphanage, until she was 18. Her father never returned to see her or her siblings, although she created a version for Marcel Haedrich in which he did visit; but even in that fantasy he did not rescue her: 'When my father came to visit, my aunts did themselves up for him. He had a great deal of charm, and he told many stories. "Don't listen to my aunts," I said to him. "I'm so unhappy – take me away …"'

Like her father, Gabrielle told many stories, and she used them to protect his memory, identifying herself with him, rather than her sickly mother. It was as if she felt her father had been right to leave his wife and children, and sought to portray his flight as an act of youthful strength. In this version of her past, Gabrielle reinvented him as a far younger man – 'not yet thirty' – and the father of only two daughters, rather than a man approaching 40, who had cast off five children, along with a dead wife. 'He'd made a new life,' she said to Haedrich. 'I understand that. He made a new family. His two daughters were in good hands. They were being brought up. He had more children. He was right. I would

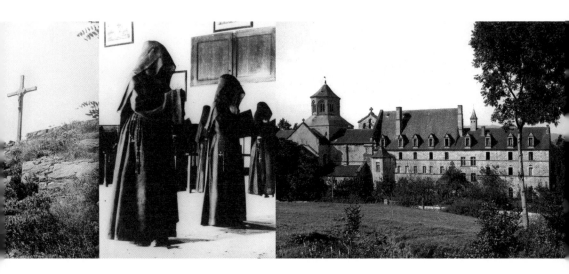

have done the same thing. No one under thirty could have coped with the situation. Imagine, a widower with two daughters! He really loved me. I represented the good days, fun, happiness …'

In reality, happiness was scarce in the orphanage, nor was there much love there. Gabrielle Chanel went to live in Aubazine soon after her mother's death in February 1895; over a lifetime later, at the same time of year – a season when winter has not yet loosened its grip on the mountains – I came to stay in the abbey myself. Little has changed in the last century: only the orphans have disappeared. But you can still see their bedrooms in the original monastery building that adjoins the abbey, the simple iron beds lined up against whitewashed walls hung with crucifixes. Each of the rooms has the name of a saint on the door, and when the wooden shutters are open, a view of the forests that surround Aubazine. Beyond the forests, far away, is the railway track out of Brive, but you cannot see a trace of it from here; only the groves of chestnut trees and the mountains wreathed in a pale, frosty mist.

Visitors seldom come in winter, and the dwindling community of nuns spends much of its life in silence: silent prayer, silent meal times, silent contemplation of God. If ever there was a place to feel close to God, it should be here, high on the hill, nearing the sky; yet somehow, sometimes, the walls that enclose the monastery seem to get in the way. Inside the abbey is darkness, the stone floor as cold as the unadorned walls, a chill rising from the ground that feels as if it has been frozen since St Etienne walked here. A few shafts of light pierce the shadows through the opaque grey and pearl-white windows; there is no figurative stained glass in this Cistercian abbey, but the panes form geometric patterns, knots and loops that look eerily like the double C of Chanel's logo.

Did Gabrielle gaze through these windows? Did she stare up at them, when she should have kept her eyes down to the ground, her head bowed in prayer? Towards the end of her life, Chanel told a story of sitting with other children in a wooden pew in church. A nun poked her with a stick when Gabrielle sang 'Ave Maria' too loudly; meanwhile, alone on another bench, was a hunchback. 'I'd have liked to sit down beside him and touch his hump,' she said to Claude Delay, 'and tell him that it didn't matter, he could still be loved.'

The abbey is empty when I walk through its pews, my steps the only sound in the silence. To the right of the altar is the stone tomb of St Etienne, a shrine where his sacred relics are preserved; to the left, a Madonna and headless Child. Along the walls are wooden misericords, ledges for the monks to rest against during the long night vigils, with strange leonine creatures carved into the ends (and in their faces you can see something of the lion that watches over Chanel's apartment from above the fireplace in her salon). On the far side of the church, so shadowy that it takes a little while for one's eyes to make out the detail, is a stone staircase that leads up to an ancient wooden door, heavy and blackened by the centuries. This is the staircase that Chanel walked up and down every day on her way to and from her prayers; 36 steps from the orphanage to the abbey, from Vespers to Matins, from dim morning to dark night, over and over again.

Climb the stairs, and push the black door open. It leads into a long corridor on the first floor of the monastery; on one side are more doors, into the sober bedrooms and offices of the nuns; on the other side are high windows, their frames painted beige, overlooking the central walled courtyard and the fountain in the middle, carved out of a huge boulder by the followers of St Etienne. The corridor is paved with an intricate mosaic, thousands of tiny pebbles formed into patterns of stars and a moon; a bishop's mitre and a Maltese cross; flowers with eight petals each; and another, more cryptic pattern (of loops and a square formed of circles and triangles) which the current inhabitants of the monastery cannot decipher. But the nun who acts as my guide accepts it as a holy symbol of God's plan, a creation that leads to the Creator. 'All we know is that it was made by the monks, like everything else here,' she says, 'and it has a special meaning.'

'Of what?' I ask her.

'Of the language of numbers, the mystery of the Holy Trinity,' she says. 'The meaning of God, which we cannot always understand, and yet we know to be the truth.' There is no more that she can tell me about the magic or the logic of the mosaic, and by now it is time for prayers again, so I follow her down another stone staircase, the steps worn into hollows by legions of faithful feet, to the chapel on the ground floor where the nuns gather for the six o'clock service. They seem to lose themselves in prayer – their eyes remain closed, as darkness falls; they kneel in silence, motionless, even though it is icy cold – and I try to concentrate on the mystery of the Holy Trinity. But my mind and my eyes wander, counting the windows, searching for the geometry in the stones, 12 stones in an arch around each window. (Do they represent the 12 disciples, or the 12 tribes of Israel; or am I searching for significance, seeking a pattern that does not exist amidst these random stones?)

Here is the place that Gabrielle prayed, and sewed, and slept; here is a world contained by high walls, where the hours are divided into devotions. How did she

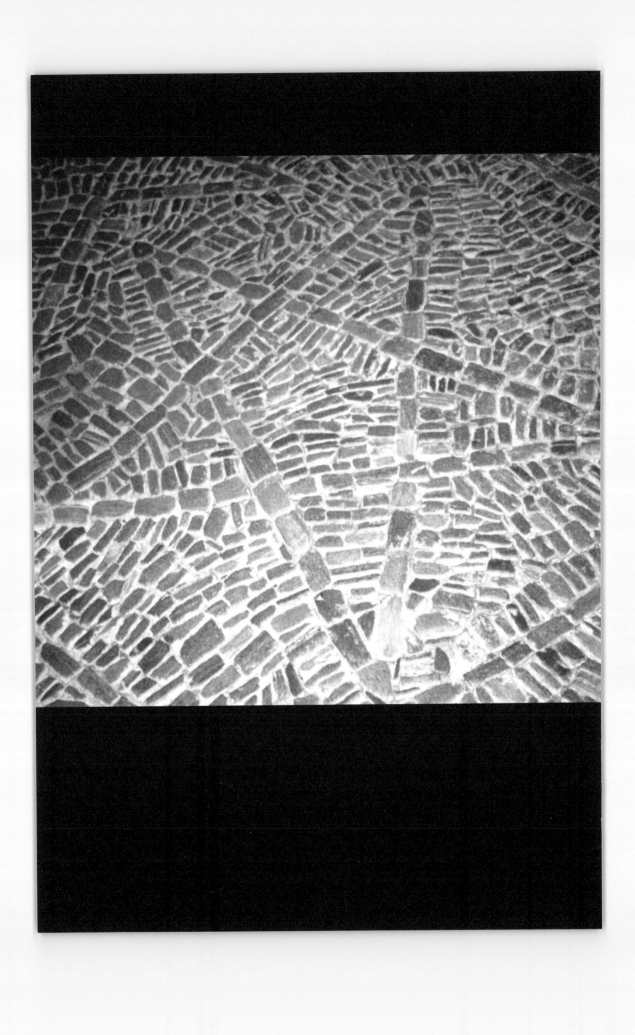

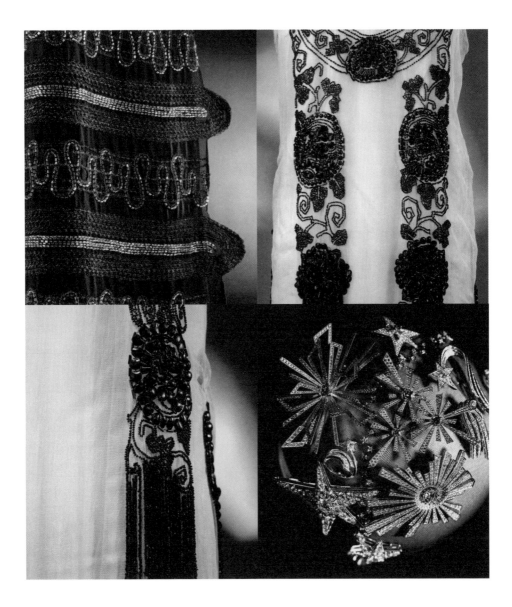

Left: One of the five-point star motifs featured in the mosaic floor of a corridor in Aubazine Abbey.
Above: The intricately patterned paved corridors are reflected in many of Chanel's designs. Here their
influence is suggested in the stitching and beading of Chanel's evening dresses, and her diamond jewellery,
in which the star motif is ever present. Bottom right photograph by Jérôme Schlomoff.

feel, within these immovable confines, knowing that outside her father was always travelling, always beyond her reach? On Sundays, the orphan girls walked to the Calvaire, a cross on the hill beyond Aubazine. They came out through the gate that separated them from the village – a gate kept locked and bolted at all other times – and walked up the path behind the abbey, following the mountain stream that provided water for the followers of St Etienne. The path is steep, through chestnut woods and pine forests; and it is still quiet here, footsteps muffled by fallen leaves and damp earth, the silence broken only by the occasional cry of a bird. In a clearing, you can look down the gorge to the monastery, and it seems smaller when seen from this perspective, yet monolithic nevertheless, as much a part of the landscape as the forested hillsides.

This was where Gabrielle walked; though the contours of the landscape were still taking shape in Chanel's imagination decades afterwards, when she looked back to Aubazine from the sumptuous salon of Rue Cambon. She told her friend Claude Delay about the woods into which she escaped from the house of her aunts; fleeing there early in the morning, sometimes on foot, sometimes on horseback, hoping that the gypsies would steal her away. The horses were wild in her legend, unshod and reared for the cavalry officers who came to see her aunts once a year. The aunts never dreamt that she could ride; nor did they know that she was accompanied by a red-headed farmer's boy. She spun a story of romance, telling Delay of the time she was given a present of rose-scented soap by one of her boy cousins. The fragrance was intoxicating for both of them: 'My cousin kissed me passionately, I let him. The frenzy of the provinces … I didn't see him again for three months. That's the sort of thing that makes a woman of one.'

Did Gabrielle truly become a woman at Aubazine? She lived in the convent until she was 18, as did her sisters. One of them, Julia, fell pregnant here in mysterious circumstances; a nominal father was found to give the baby boy a name – on his birth certificate he was registered as André Palasse – but when Julia died in 1910, the boy was left an orphan. Chanel seldom referred to her elder sister; on the occasions she did, her remarks were contradictory. 'She only loved the convent,' she told Delay, yet also claimed that Julia had loved her husband, that she killed herself by slitting her wrists when she discovered that he had a mistress.

Whatever the true circumstances of André's birth and his mother's death, Chanel took on her 6-year-old nephew and brought him up as her own – indeed her lover, Boy Capel, became his godfather – yet she chose not to keep him in Paris with her, but sent him to be educated at an English boarding school. People used to speculate about André's origins, as they still do. Even now, if you talk to the elderly lady who lives in a house across the road from the abbey, where she was born, just as her mother and grandmother were before her, you might hear another story, that the baby was Gabrielle's, not Julia's. 'That's what I heard,' says the old lady, 'but who knows if it is true?' What she does know for certain is that Mademoiselle Chanel returned to Aubazine from time to time, long after she had become rich and famous. 'She arrived here in a big black car, we used to see her, but she was always very discreet, very private. Mademoiselle Chanel would visit one nun in particular, who still lived in the convent, and I wondered if she came to visit her whenever she was broken-hearted? She used to give money to the nuns, and she would stay and talk to them for a while, but she never stayed the night here. No, she never again slept within the walls of the abbey …'

Mademoiselle Chanel did not mention Aubazine to her friends; nor even utter its name to her great-niece Gabrielle Labrunie, the daughter of André Palasse, to whom she was very close. 'I wouldn't have dreamt of asking her about the past,' says Madame Labrunie, when I question her about Aubazine. 'And if I had asked, she would have told me it was none of my business. She always said she was interested in what was ahead of her, not what had already finished.'

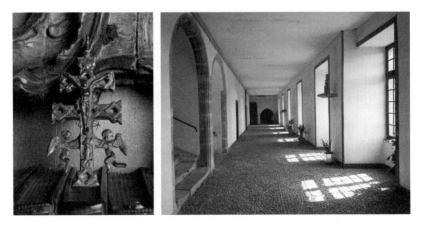

Left: The double-barred, gilt bronze cross Chanel kept in her apartment.
Right: The mosaic-paved corridor on the first floor of the monastery, patterned with loops and crosses, stars and moons.

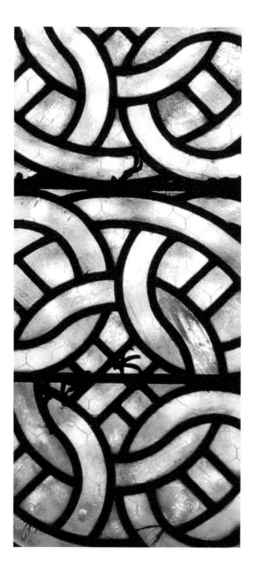

There is no figurative stained glass in the Cistercian
abbey of Aubazine, but the panes create geometric
patterns. Their knots and loops form the
antecedents of the double C of Chanel's logo.
Opposite photograph by Frédérick Astier.

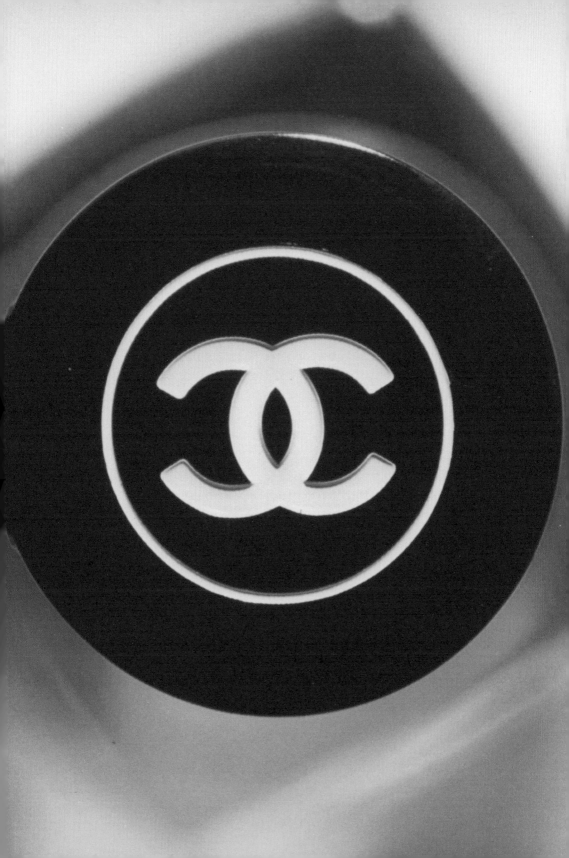

But Chanel did allow some stories to slip out. To Claude Delay, she spoke of being taught to sew by the aunts, hemming and seaming her trousseau; and of how she wore a white shift in which to bathe herself, because it was a sin to look at one's body. She said that she sewed cross-stitches on her nightgowns, to make them look Russian. Sometimes she used to rub her nose to make it bleed at night; the blood dripped on her white nightdress, and when she cried out for someone to come to her bedside, a nun would emerge. Slashes of red appeared elsewhere in her narratives: two cherries that she stole to eat before her First Communion, before she panicked and sought absolution from the priest for her wickedness; the bloodstains on her nightdress when she reached puberty, not understanding what had happened to her but believing she had hurt herself; and her reddened skin, when the aunts beat her. 'I remember that they used to take my knickers down to spank me. First there was the humiliation. Then it was very unpleasant, your bottom was as red as blood.'

She talked in vivid detail about the dresses and linen she remembered from childhood, elaborate stories that may have contained a kernel of truth, though perhaps they came from the serialised romances that she read as an adolescent ('I found them in the attic of my aunts'). Her aunts had huge cupboards filled with shelves of freshly laundered white linen that smelled of verbena and rosewood. When they went to mass, the aunts wore jade crosses and veils over their faces, their throats edged in white material, in contrast to their black dresses. When Gabrielle saw a school of black-clad orphans go past, she said, she hid away to weep for them; she felt sorry for them in their black aprons.

But Gabrielle insisted that she was not an orphan; nor was she to be pitied like them. Her father sent her a white dress from America for her First Communion. It was all ruffles and lace, she told Delay, with layers of billowing organdie petticoats and a long veil, two rosaries, a string of pearls, and a pair of silk stockings to wear underneath. Gabrielle loved the dress as a child, but in later life she declared that it must have been chosen by her father's girlfriend, a 'tart' with dubious taste. She gave a slightly different version of the story to Paul Morand: 'Shortly before he left for America, my father bought me a first communion dress, in white chiffon, with a crown of roses. So as to punish me for being proud, my aunts said to me: "You're not going to wear your crown of roses, you'll wear a hat." What agony it was, on top of so many other things, such as the shame of having to confess to the priest that I had stolen two cherries! To be deprived of the crown!'

Yet another version of the story (to Marcel Haedrich) did not involve a white dress from America, nor her father. Instead, in this telling of the tale of the First Communion, her aunts wanted her to wear a cap like a peasant girl's, but Gabrielle insisted on something different, and in the end she got her way, and wore a white paper crown of thorns with artificial roses.

Such victories were rare, however. Gabrielle was more often thwarted by the aunts, as she explained to Haedrich, with all the minutiae that you might expect from a woman whose early career was as seamstress and milliner. Unlike the orphan girls at the convent, who wore black uniforms, she claimed to have had a little tailored black alpaca suit; her aunts gave her a new one every year in the springtime. 'I should have liked a pink dress or a sky-blue one,' she said wistfully. 'I was in mourning all the time, while the peasant girls wore blue and pink. I envied them.' In the summer, the aunts gave her 'a horrible leghorn hat', the details of which still haunted her, with its 'little piece of velvet and a rose above the brim'. In the winter, she was made to wear a cloche, 'very hard, with a kind of feather on it. I was told it was an eagle's feather, but I knew it was a turkey's, stiffened with paste. There was a little rubber band in the back that went under one's hair, to hold the hat in place when it was windy. I thought the whole business was very ugly.'

At last, at the age of 15, Gabrielle was allowed to order a dress of her own, without intervention from the aunts, and she chose 'a clinging mauve material', but her body was still that of a child, 'with nothing for it to cling to. The dressmaker had put a bit of taffeta at the bottom, with a flounce. Parma violet underneath!' She'd come up with the idea for the flounced dress from a novel – and perhaps this is the closest to the truth that Gabrielle could admit, in her account of a loveless teenage girl who lost herself in fiction. 'I thought that Parma violet was ravishing. My heroine wore it on her hat. The dressmaker didn't have any more, so she put a twig of wisteria on mine.' But when the long-awaited morning came for Gabrielle to wear the dress for the first time, to Sunday mass, her aunts told her to take it off, and they sent it back to the dressmaker, along with the twig-trimmed hat.

Had Gabrielle ever even seen herself in the violet dress, summoned up from the paper pages of a romance? In the house of her aunts, there were no mirrors. She could not glimpse her reflection anywhere; she was nowhere to be seen. If she made up stories from then on, you can understand why; for out of these loose threads, Gabrielle created an image of herself.

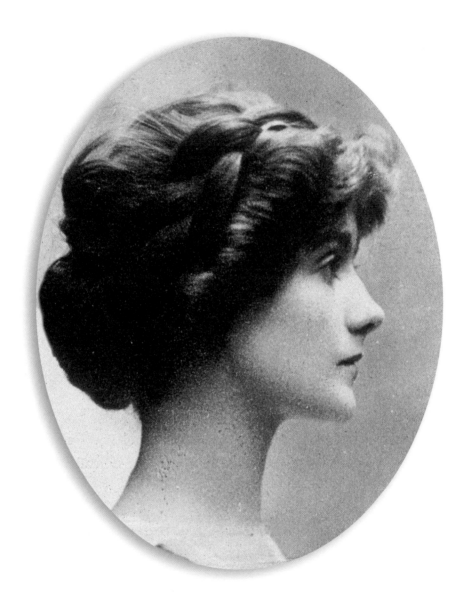

An early photograph of Chanel, 1909.

COCO

When Gabrielle turned 18, she finally left the nuns at Aubazine, who kept on only those girls with a religious vocation to join the order's novitiate. She was not completely abandoned, however; nor was she without family, despite her father's continuing absence. He had been one of 19 children, and his parents were still very much alive; indeed, their youngest daughter, Adrienne, was only a year older than Gabrielle. Although her father's family seem not to have figured in her early life, or when he abandoned the children after their mother's death, several relatives did appear thereafter. That they included two aunts (neither of them nuns, nor at all like the 'aunts' Chanel described in her subsequent stories of childhood) has added further confusion to the task of her biographers. But at some point during Gabrielle's later years at Aubazine, she began to spend an occasional holiday with her paternal grandparents and Adrienne, to whom she became as close as if they were sisters, and also with another of their daughters, her aunt Louise, who had married a railway employee, Paul Costier. Louise and Paul had no children of their own, and invited Adrienne and Gabrielle to visit them in Varennes-sur-Allier, a station on the Vichy to Moulins line, where Paul was employed as stationmaster. And it was to Moulins that Gabrielle was sent at 18 to the Notre Dame school, a religious institution run by canonesses where her aunt Adrienne was already being educated.

It is not entirely clear whether Gabrielle's sisters, Julia and Antoinette, accompanied her to Moulins; according to one of the stories that Chanel told Claude Delay, Julia had left an orphanage at 16 and was married. But she also spoke to Delay of a holiday spent with her sister at a convent in Corrèze. The food there was awful, she said, and the nuns were foolish little country girls who played shuttlecock, not at all like the fierce aunts in whose house Gabrielle had been raised. In this strange and unlikely sounding convent, Gabrielle played the organ and sang, impressing the nuns, who were amazed at her talent; just as they had been astounded by Julia's piano playing: 'When my sister had been playing the piano they used to look at her fingers to see what she had on the ends of them. Little peasants!'

But no one was impressed by Gabrielle in the Notre Dame school in Moulins, for she was one of the charity pupils who were provided with a free place, and therefore treated differently to those whose family could afford to pay for their education. Here it was Gabrielle who was dismissed as a little peasant – the kind of girl who might be made to feel inferior to those who had piano lessons; a girl who wore a plain pauper's uniform with second-hand shoes rather than the more expensive outfits of the fee-paying students. It was here, too, that she was given further instruction in how to sew, which had already formed a substantial part of her education at Aubazine. If she was not to be a nun, then she must earn her living like other orphans, and there was always work available for a seamstress. More sewing took place during Gabrielle's holidays with her aunt Louise, from whom she learned how to trim and embellish hats, to add to the practical needlework skills she had acquired from the nuns. Adrienne also visited, and as well as darning, the girls fashioned new collars and cuffs out of remnants of white linen to trim their sober black convent uniforms. In the evenings they read the romances that Louise had cut out and saved from magazines and periodicals, hand-sewn together, and carefully stored in the attic.

'You don't know the damage country attics can do to the imagination,' Chanel told Delay, recalling the stories that she had absorbed as a girl. Her favourites had been by Pierre Decourcelle, a prolific author of romances who also wrote for *Le Matin* and *Le Journal*. Chanel described him to Delay as 'a sentimental ninny', yet also acknowledged his influence on her as her 'one teacher'. But to Marcel Haedrich, she admitted that her 'aunts' had educated her to recognise the 'solid substance' of orderliness, 'for having things done right, for chests filled with linens that smell good, and gleaming floors'.

While the nuns taught her the value of cleanliness, Pierre Decourcelle gave her a taste for the forbidden. As Chanel remarked to Haedrich, she lost herself in his stories, 'melodramas in which everything happened in a wild-eyed romanticism', and longed to live in their world, instead of in her aunts' house:

'I thought all that was awful because in my novels there was nothing but silk pillows and white-lacquered furniture. I'd have liked to do everything in white lacquer. Sleeping in an alcove made me miserable, it humiliated me. I broke off bits of wood wherever I could, thinking, *what old trash this is*. I did it out of sheer wickedness, for the sake of destruction. When one considers all the things that go on in a child's head … I wanted to kill myself.'

It was not the only time that Chanel talked about her desire to kill herself as a child – as if her longing to escape, and her craving for glamorous romance, could be fulfilled in suicide. 'At the time, I often used to think about dying,' she told Paul Morand. 'The idea of causing a great fuss, of upsetting my aunts, of letting everyone know how wicked they were, fascinated me. I dreamt about setting fire to the barn.'

If her suggestion was that in being wicked she would reveal the wickedness of others, then perhaps she believed that by dying she might find her rightful place in life. Gabrielle grew up to discover that suicide was not her way out; yet in a sense (however nonsensical it might appear to others), she did need to kill something of herself in order to make her escape. She felt unloved – by the 'aunts', by the family who had abandoned her to the care of nuns, by her absent father – although the stories she read had taught her that love conquered all; that desire and passion set men and women alight. An element of her conflict emerges in the tales she told of love (and the lack of it); of the sacred and the profane. Given her aversion to providing any detail about her family – other than the fictional aunts who stand in for the nuns at Aubazine (and possibly those at the convent school in Moulins) – the occasional mentions are significant. To Claude Delay, she referred to her uncle Paul Costier, the stationmaster, sending her a first-class railway ticket ('because I wouldn't go second-class – it was a bore'). In other versions, Chanel described her abortive attempt to escape to Paris with Adrienne from her uncle and aunt's house in Varennes. They had only enough money for second-class tickets, but Gabrielle insisted on sitting in the first-class carriage, for which they were fined by the conductor; without any funds to sustain them in the capital, the runaway girls were forced to return home. Except that Gabrielle did not feel herself to be at home anywhere – not at Aubazine, nor at school in Moulins, nor in the Costiers' house. When she arrived to stay with Paul and Louise, she told Delay, her uncle was warmly affectionate, but her aunt was detached and cold. At night, Paul came into her bedroom to kiss her goodnight, and said, 'You'll stay a nice long time, won't you?' But Gabrielle sensed that her aunt didn't approve of her, and so she left the next day. According to Claude Delay, more than half a century later, Chanel 'still felt the chill' of rejection, expressing it as if she had been left entirely alone.

She was also without God, or at least that was what she told Delay. Gabrielle's loss of faith had occurred in Aubazine, at her First Communion, after her father had supposedly sent her the dress from America. It is unclear from her account whether she was actually wearing this unsuitable dress in church – instead, she spoke of her fascination at the sight of the barefoot mendicant monk who conducted a three-day retreat with the children before their First Communion, a man in a long home-spun robe with a girdle (a description reminiscent of St Etienne himself). 'When I got there – the monk and his bare feet and his oration – that was the life I'd been waiting for. Inside the church it was like a mirage. It got dark at five, the candles were lit, I could hear the breathing of the boys and girls around me, in the half-light, almost asleep. I said at confession afterwards it had inspired profane feelings in me.'

When the priest instructed her to meditate upon the Stations of the Cross in front of the other girls as a penance, Gabrielle refused, saying that she would do so in bed later that night. 'The Catholic religion crumbled for me,' she told Delay. 'I realized I was a person, outside all the secrecy of confession.' And yet, despite the confessions she made to Delay – a young woman at the time, but who was to come to understand the confessional aspect of her career as a psychoanalyst – Chanel could never quite admit to what followed next.

To Paul Morand, she spoke of horses. Her aunts bred horses, she said, and sold them to the army. Gabrielle was wild – 'untameable' – and ran wherever she pleased. 'I mounted our horses bare-back (at sixteen, I had never seen a saddle), I caught hold of our best animals (or occasionally other people's, as I fancied) by their manes or their tails. I stole all the carrots in the house to feed them.' (This was not the only time Chanel recalled stealing food as a child; she described hiding away from the aunts and cutting herself huge slices of bread that she took to eat in the lavatory. But the cook saw her, and said, 'You'll cut yourself in half.')

With the horses came the soldiers, arriving at her 'aunts' house' to buy their mounts: 'Fine hussars or chasseurs, with sky-blue dolmans and black frogging, and their pelisses on their shoulders. They came every year in their beautifully harnessed phaetons; they looked in the horses' mouths to see how old they were, stroked their fetlocks to check that they weren't inflamed, and slapped their flanks; it was a great party; a party that for me was fraught with a degree of anxiety; supposing they were going to take my favourite horses away from me?' One wonders if Chanel knew what she was doing as she told this story to Morand when she was in her sixties; whether it was a story that she was telling herself, or if she was teasing him.

Whatever her motive – unconscious or not – her tale takes on a darker, almost sadistic tone. The officers could not choose her favourite horses; Gabrielle said she had made sure of that by galloping them unshod on flinty ground so that their

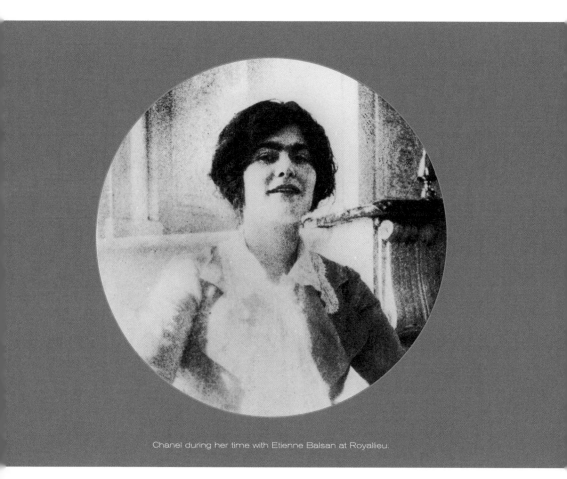

Chanel during her time with Etienne Balsan at Royallieu.

hooves were ruined. But one of the soldiers caught on: '"These horses have hooves like cattle, their soles have gone and their frogs are rotten!" he said, referring to our best-looking creatures. I no longer dared to look the officer in the eye, but he had seen through me; as soon as my aunts had turned away, he whispered in a low voice: "So you've been galloping without shoes, eh, you little rascal?"'

It seems highly unlikely that Chanel encountered any army officers while she was under the care of nuns in the orphanage at Aubazine; but she undoubtedly came across them in Moulins, after she had left the Notre Dame boarding school. The town was dominated by the military, for several regiments were garrisoned there, including the Tenth Light Horse, the 10ème Chasseurs, who wore scarlet breeches and rakish peaked caps. The Mother Superior at Notre

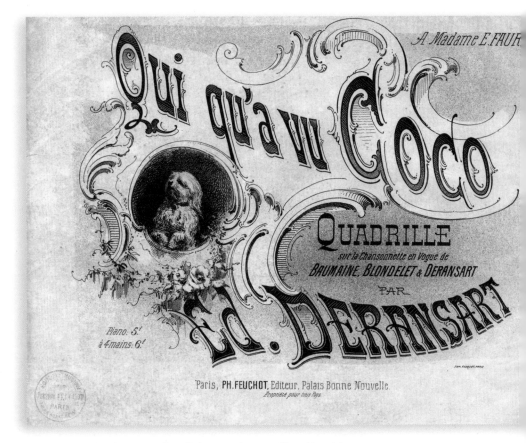

The score cover for 'Qui qu'a vu Coco?', the song that gave Chanel her nickname.

Dame had found employment for Adrienne and Gabrielle as shop assistants and seamstresses in a draper's store on the Rue de l'Horloge, which sold trousseaux and mourning clothes to the local gentry, as well as layettes for newborn babies. The girls shared an attic bedroom above the shop, and also worked at the weekends for a nearby tailor, altering breeches for cavalry officers. It was there that Gabrielle and Adrienne were spotted by half-a-dozen men, who started taking them out at night to La Rotonde, a pavilion in a small park in Moulins, where concerts were held for audiences from the local barracks. They were rowdy affairs – a combination of music hall and soldiers' saloon – but Gabrielle was determined to start singing on stage, and eventually found a regular evening slot, accompanied first by Adrienne, and then as a solo performer. She had only two songs in her repertoire: 'Ko Ko Ri Ko' (its refrain was the French version of 'cock-a-doodle-doo') and 'Qui qu'a vu Coco?', a ditty about a girl who had lost her dog. Soon the audience greeted her with barnyard cockerel calls, and christened her with the name of the lost dog. Thus Gabrielle became Coco, a metamorphosis that might have been humiliating rather than liberating, but nevertheless led to the birth of a legend.

Chanel never talked to her friends about this episode of her life, even in the most guarded of terms; other than to deny it to Paul Morand, dismissing it as foolish legend, along with the other stories in circulation: 'that I have come up from goodness knows where; from the music hall, the opera or the brothel; I'm sorry, for that would have been more amusing.' She did, however, mention the name of the cavalry officer who was to become her lover, Etienne Balsan, and referred to his horses as providing the means of her escape. To Morand, she declared, 'horses have influenced the course of my life,' and told a story of being sent by the aunts to the Auvergne spa town of Vichy, to spend the summer with her grandfather, who was taking the waters there. 'I was so glad to have escaped … from the gloomy house, from needlework, from my trousseau; embroidering initials on the towels for my future household, and sewing crosses in Russian stitching on my nightdresses, for a hypothetical wedding night, made me feel ill; in a fury, I spat on my trousseau.' In this version, she knocked five years off her age, and had herself sewing (and loathing) her own trousseau, rather than those of wealthier women in the shop where she laboured in Moulins. But her desire to be freed from the aunts and their legacy was manifest. 'I was sixteen. I was becoming pretty. I had a face that was as plump as a fist, hidden in a vast swathe of black hair that reached the ground.' And Vichy, with its casino and cafés and Belle Epoque opera house, its boulevards and gardens landscaped for Napoleon III, was to be the backdrop that she chose for her adventure: 'Vichy was a fairyland. A ghastly fairyland in reality, but wonderful to fresh eyes … Vichy was my first journey. Vichy would teach me about life.'

It was in Vichy, she said, that she went to a tea party and 'made the acquaintance of a young man, MB [Monsieur Balsan]; he owned a racing stable.' They arranged to meet the following day, in fields where horses grazed beside the river. There, she heard the roar of a fantastical torrent of water, whereupon Balsan asked her to go with him to his house in Compiègne. She said yes, and ran away with him: 'My grandfather believed I had returned home; my aunts thought I was at my grandfather's house.'

Chanel told a similar story to Bettina Ballard, a young *Vogue* editor in Paris whom she befriended in the Thirties; although in this version she was even younger. 'She escaped the aunts before she was sixteen,' recounted Ballard. 'She went to visit her grandfather at Vichy and was so afraid that she would be sent back to the aunts that she stopped a handsome young officer in the park and asked him to take her away with him. He did just that, but he took her home to his father's chateau. It was Etienne Balsan.'

Claude Delay heard a more embellished tale of Chanel encountering Etienne Balsan at a Vichy tea party: she had been taken there by her aunt Adrienne, who was by then involved with the Baron de Nexon (a relationship that was in fact a real one, and although the Baron's parents were fiercely opposed to the affair between their son and a seamstress, the two eventually married, many years afterwards, in a romance worthy of those that Adrienne and Gabrielle had read as teenagers). In this gothic account, Chanel told Balsan that she had been beset by bad luck ever since the death of her mother and her father's departure to America, and announced to him that she was going to kill herself: 'All through my childhood I wanted to be loved. Every day I thought about how to kill myself. The viaduct, perhaps …' Despite this somewhat unorthodox introduction, Balsan was sufficiently intrigued to provide a different way out by inviting her to see his stables and house, a former abbey named Royallieu.

And so Coco went with him there, to an abbey that had become a house of pleasure, leaving Gabrielle behind her, locked away in a shadowy place where no one might find her, nor the torn remnants of her past.

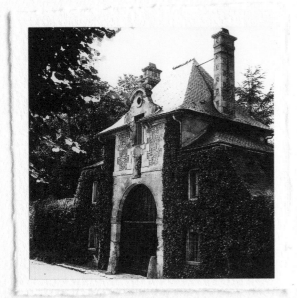

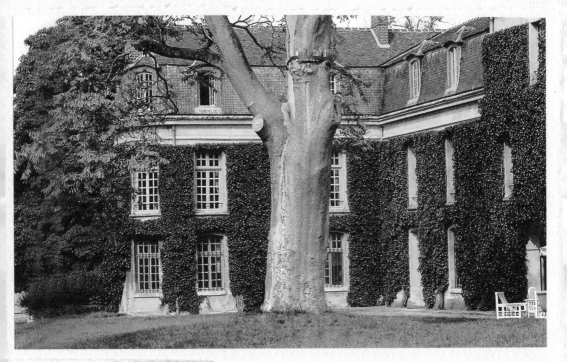

The château de Royallieu and its gatehouse (top).

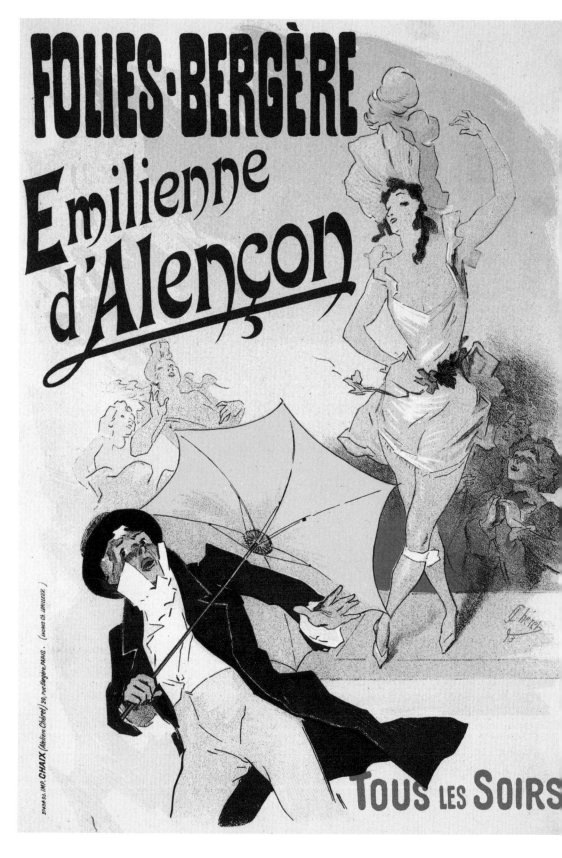

COURTESANS
AND CAMELLIAS

'Since I am not yet of an age to invent, I must make do
with telling a tale. I therefore invite the reader to believe
that this story is true.'
Alexandre Dumas, *La Dame aux camélias*

There are many mysteries in the myth of Coco Chanel,
but few more perplexing than her years with Etienne
Balsan at Royallieu; perhaps because Balsan never gave
away her secrets, however often he was questioned in
later life, when Chanel was far more famous than him.
In the drama of Chanel's life – a drama in part of her own
making, as well as of others – Balsan has been cast as
a rich playboy, the roué who introduced the little
orphaned seamstress into the decadent world of the
Belle Epoque, deflowering her in an unsentimental
education. While there may be some truth in this portrait,
Chanel also used Balsan as a stepping stone from
Moulins to Paris, gaining poise in place of an innocence
already lost. The two of them continued to be friends
until his death in 1953, and if their initial sexual
relationship had been characterised by his infidelities,
Balsan nevertheless displayed a lifelong loyalty to
Chanel. He remained unmarried, apparently unrepentant
and unfailingly discreet.

Balsan's father had died when he was 18, his mother
a few years later, leaving Etienne and his two older

brothers heirs to a solid fortune made in textiles. The family business, based in Châteauroux, a traditional wool town in central France, had been well established for a century, supplying the French army with uniforms and the British military during the Boer War. As a boy, Balsan was sent to boarding school in England, where he showed more interest in horses than anything else: he arrived with his dog, bought himself two hunters, and rode to hounds more often than he attended classes.

After his parents' death, he made it clear to his more industrious brothers, Jacques and Robert, that he had no intention of following them into the family business. (Both of them continued to run it with the same success as their forebears; Jacques also went on to distinguish himself as a fighter pilot during the First World War, and in 1921 married Consuelo Vanderbilt, after her divorce from the Duke of Marlborough.) Instead, Etienne enlisted in the army and was posted to Algiers with a light cavalry regiment, the Chasseurs d'Afrique. As his nephew François Balsan later reported in a privately printed family history, Etienne fell asleep on sentry duty one afternoon, and having been discovered in this compromising position by the governor of Algiers himself, was thereafter confined to the guardhouse. During his period of punishment, the regiment's horses were afflicted with a mysterious skin ailment. Balsan sent a message to his commanding officer proposing a deal: if he were to come up with a cure for

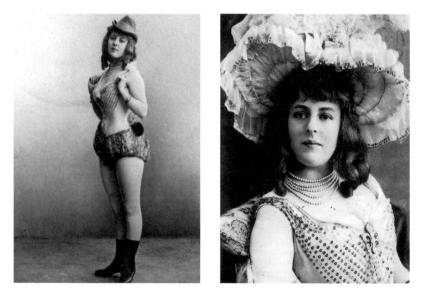

Emilienne d'Alençon, a famous actress and courtesan who spent time at Royallieu.

the disease, he would be released. The young officer duly applied a successful remedy (the recipe for which he had learned in England), and, much to his relief, was subsequently transferred from Algeria to Moulins.

By the end of 1904, when he was 24 (and Chanel was 21), Balsan had completed his military service as a cavalry officer and elected to pursue more sporting equestrian activities. He found a suitable estate to purchase in Compiègne, in Picardy, about 45 miles north-east of Paris. The region was formerly a vast forest where the kings of France hunted in the Middle Ages, and while large expanses of woodland remained, the area had become established as a leading centre for racehorse trainers and thoroughbred stables. As such, it was a perfect location for Balsan's new property. Royallieu had originally been built in 1303 as a monastery, was later remodelled as a royal hunting lodge, and then converted into a convent for Benedictine nuns in the seventeenth century. The nuns were driven out by the Revolution, but the portrait of its first abbess, Gabrielle de Laubespine, was still hanging on the staircase when Balsan moved in. And there she remained, a silent witness to his reign, during which Royallieu was devoted to the worship of horses and the pursuit of amusement and pretty women.

At some point in 1905 Chanel followed him there, in circumstances that remain quite unclear. They had met at Moulins, and that they became lovers is certain. But Balsan already had a mistress in residence at Royallieu, Emilienne d'Alençon, a famous courtesan-turned-actress. She was 14 years older than Coco, and although past the first bloom of youth, still widely regarded as one of the leading beauties of the day. Decades later, however, when Chanel described Emilienne to Marcel Haedrich, it was as if the two women had been separated by great age, as well as by experience. 'Etienne Balsan liked old women,' she said, with some terseness. 'He adored Emilienne d'Alençon. Beauty and youth didn't concern him. He adored *cocottes* and lived with that one to the scandal of his family.'

But it wasn't as simple as that. Emilienne came and went from Royallieu as she pleased, and at one point took a new lover, Alec Carter, a famous English jockey. Balsan was similarly diverted by other girls, some of whom would come to stay at Royallieu. No one knows how this curious arrangement was reached and maintained, or where Chanel fitted into the hierarchy. Several French writers, including Marcel Haedrich, have related gossip that Coco had to eat her meals with the servants in her early days at Royallieu, particularly when Balsan had his upper-class friends or family to stay. But Chanel herself gave little away, even to Claude Delay, beyond portraying Emilienne as having worn 'heavy gowns and spotted veils', like an ancient Miss Havisham. She described herself, in contrast, as free and unencumbered, dressing 'neither as a great lady nor as a scullery maid': a young tomboy, spending her days galloping on horseback through the forests. 'I didn't know any people; I knew the horses,' she said, as if to protect herself from the memory of the isolation she suffered at the time, not understanding her position in the household (neither servant nor châtelaine). And yet, as always, she sought to define herself by her idiosyncratic choice of clothes. Unlike Emilienne, Coco wore simple riding breeches and equestrian jackets from a local tailor, thus distinguishing herself as somehow unique; if not yet the one and only Coco Chanel, then at least not just another *cocotte* in Balsan's stable of women.

But whatever she chose to wear, she was also kept in her place. And for all the freedoms of Royallieu – a house where social conventions seemed not to apply; where courtesans and aristocrats drank champagne together, and men were free to enjoy more than one girl at a time – it was also a form of imprisonment. To Morand, Chanel described herself as having been a minor, below the age of consent; too young to be away from home, and desperately homesick. 'I was constantly weeping,' she said to Morand, and then gave him a curious blend of truth and falsehood about the lies that she had previously invented for Balsan. 'I had told him lies about my miserable childhood. I had to disabuse him. I wept for an entire year. The only happy times were those I spent on horseback, in the forest. I learned to ride, for up until then I hadn't the first idea about riding horses. I was never a horsewoman, but at that time I couldn't even ride side-saddle.

'The fairy tale was over. I was nothing but a lost child. I didn't dare to write to anyone. MB was frightened of the police. His friends told him: "Coco is too young, send her back home." MB would have been delighted to see me go, but I had no home any more.'

Thus she cast herself and Balsan as caught in a trap of their own making; but as she elaborated on her story to Morand, emphasising Balsan's fear of the authorities, Chanel remade herself into a helpless girl with no control over her destiny (which may well be how she felt at the time), while also acknowledging the damage done by her lies (even as she told lies about her lying). 'MB was afraid of the police, and I was afraid of the servants. I had lied to MB. I had kept my age a secret, telling him that I was nearly twenty: in actual fact I was sixteen.' In actual fact, she was over 21 when she arrived at Royallieu, and she continued to live there well into her twenties.

But the biggest secret of all was whether or not Coco became pregnant during the course of her relationship with Etienne Balsan. Several of her friends believed that she did: some speculated that she had an abortion that left her infertile, others that she had the baby boy who she claimed was her nephew rather than her son. Balsan ended up in later life as a neighbour to Chanel's nephew, André, and to André's daughters, Gabrielle and Hélène, and was certainly close to the family. Beyond that, it is impossible to establish the truth of the rumours. Chanel told Delay that her sister Julia had married at 16, given birth to a son, and then killed herself because of her husband's infidelity. But even if this were a veiled clue to a possible pregnancy of her own, the date would be as blurred as the rest of the dates that she shifted and erased. Julia was born in September 1882, and would therefore have been 22 when her son André was born in 1904; a year older than Gabrielle, who was by then already involved with Balsan. Nevertheless, the idea of being a frightened 16-year-old seems to have been in some sense real to Chanel, however unreliable her stories appear in retrospect. Hence her description to Morand of herself at 16, venturing out to the races at Compiègne while she was still living with Balsan (a man supposedly so scared of the authorities that he had to hide her away, like a timid Bluebeard, to keep her out of view of the police). 'I wore a straw boater, set very low on the head, and a little country suit, and I followed events from the end of my lorgnette. I was convinced that no one was taking any notice of me, which shows how little I knew about life in the provinces. In reality, this ridiculous, badly dressed, shy little creature, with her three big plaits and a ribbon in her hair, intrigued everybody.'

Perhaps this was the consoling story that Coco told herself when it appeared that no one cared (not the police, nor her family, nor anyone else, for that matter): that she was intriguing, even when it seemed that she was never the centre of attention. At least Emilienne d'Alençon took a certain interest in Coco, while apparently unperturbed by her presence, if Chanel's description of her to Claude Delay is to be believed. 'Emilienne d'Alençon used to ask me, "Well, are you happy?" I answered, "I'm neither happy nor unhappy – I'm hiding. It's like home here, only better."'

But she was sufficiently unhappy to write to her aunt Adrienne – who was still the mistress of the Baron de Nexon, though not yet married to him – to ask her to send the money for a train fare. In telling this story to Delay, Chanel did not specify where the train might take her; but in any event, she claimed that Adrienne wrote back to say that Coco should not leave Royallieu: 'Whatever you do keep out of the way or they'll put you in a reformatory.' Who were 'they', that could lock up a woman for bad behaviour? Except, of course, as Chanel reiterated to Delay, she was still a little girl; so young that she used to fall asleep at the table and weep, because she was up past her bedtime, and at her aunts' house she would have been asleep long before. But in this version Bluebeard was transformed into a perfect gentleman: '"I'll take you home," said Balsan. "I'll tell them that I'm bringing you back just as I found you and you're still only a little girl."'

The idea of herself as a little girl was to permeate the rest of Chanel's life, and yet, as is evident in Truman Capote's description of her in 1959, it was also suggestive of a particular blend of innocence and experience that was so profitably displayed in her own appearance, and upon which she went on to make her fortune in couture. Capote observed: 'Chanel, a spare spruce sparrow voluble and vital as a woodpecker, once, mid-flight in one of her unstoppable monologues, said, referring to the very costly *pauvre* orphan appearance she has lo these last decades modelled: "Cut off my head, and I'm thirteen." But her head has always remained attached, definitely she had it perfectly placed way back yonder when she *was* thirteen, or scarcely more, and a moneyed "kind gentleman", the first of several grateful and well-wishing patrons, asked petite "Coco", daughter of a Basque blacksmith who had taught her to help him shoe horses, which she preferred, black pearls or white?'

Capote's portrait of Chanel was written just a year after *Breakfast at Tiffany's*, his glittering depiction of the balancing act undertaken by a beautiful girl dependent on the patronage of rich men; and he was alert to the imaginative possibilities of modern fairy tales. But it would be unkind not to recognise the real pain that Chanel suffered, even as she distanced herself from the past in storytelling (for telling stories is, amongst other things, a way in which to imagine a happy-ever-after, and for the misunderstood to come to an understanding of their tribulations).

So there she was; poor little Coco ('Qui qu'a vu Coco?'), imprisoned in another abbey, surrounded by the forest of Compiègne. The nuns' regime had vanished, and in pride of place was a courtesan – the famous Emilienne, a former mistress of the king of Belgium, among others; a *cocotte* so highly prized that Leopold II had in turn introduced her to King Edward VII, to whom she allegedly declared that French aristocrats were the only men who knew how to make love to a woman. Emilienne had been heaped with diamonds and endearments; men had lost their hearts and their fortunes to her; although some had come up with a more practical arrangement, such as the eight members of the Jockey Club who had pooled their resources in order to procure her attention on a regular basis.

Coco was still the outsider looking in, the girl with no money and no father, just as she had been at school, with all the unease and uncertainty that such a position entailed. Even so, if her years in Aubazine had taught Gabrielle everything she knew about needlework, then her time in Royallieu gave her an equally thorough education in how to stitch the empty hours together, to make something of herself. She spent six years there – a period of apparent idleness, punctuated by fancy dress parties and horseriding; of lengthy boredom and occasional debauchery; of setting herself apart from the courtesans who came and went from Royallieu. But for all her efforts at distancing herself, she was intrigued by the beauties who entertained the men; along with Emilienne, there was another *cocotte*-turned-actress, Gabrielle Dorziat, a charming young singer named Marthe Davelli, and Suzanne Orlandi, the mistress of Balsan's friend Baron Foy. Coco watched and waited; she saw the manner in which Emilienne ceased to be Balsan's lover but remained his friend. And Coco listened to Emilienne's stories, as well as telling her own, taking heed of the woman who had come from nothing – the daughter of a Parisian concierge in Montmartre, who had made a teenage debut scantily clad in a circus act – and ended up with something more precious than her ample wealth. 'The only serious person I met in those days was Emilienne d'Alençon,' Chanel remarked to Haedrich; for Emilienne not only wrote the poetry to prove it but was turned into prose by Marcel Proust. (She was said to have inspired the writer's portrait of Rachel in *A la recherche du temps perdu*, a demimondaine who ensnares the heart and jewels of the young aristocrat, Robert de Saint-Loup).

After a time, Coco realised that she preferred the courtesans to the sneering society women. At least Emilienne was clean, she said; unlike the supposedly respectable wives and mothers, who smelled dirty to Coco. 'I thought the *cocottes* were ravishing with their hats that were too big and their heavy make-up,' she observed to Haedrich. 'They were so appetising!' Not that she wanted to dress like them – all her efforts went into creating herself as a gamine,

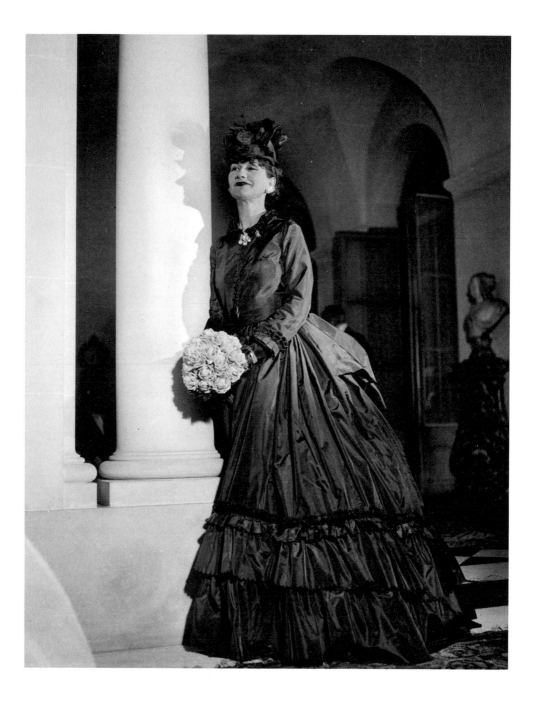

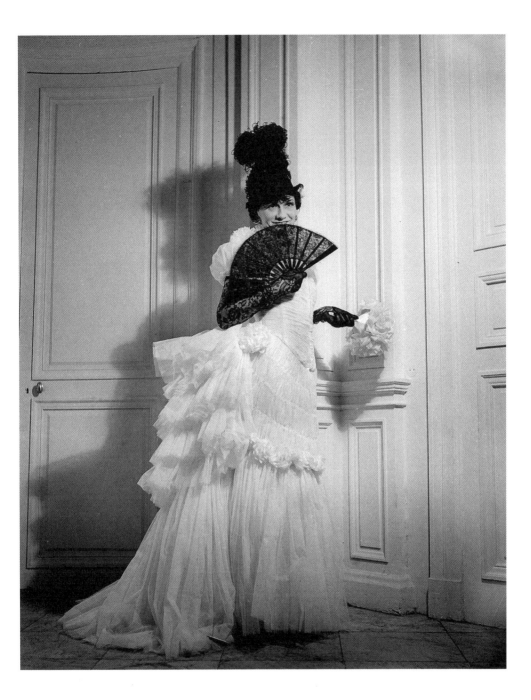

choosing sober androgyny over their crinolines and whalebone corsets, their feathers and lace and chinchilla. She wore softly knotted schoolboy ties, and simple white shirts with Peter Pan collars; and little straw boaters, as plain as a convent uniform.

But her taste for romance did not leave her, and neither did her sense of loss. Perhaps this is why she responded with such heightened emotion to Alexandre Dumas's novel *La Dame aux camélias*, and its stage version starring Sarah Bernhardt as Marguerite Gautier, a courtesan who nevertheless remained the embodiment of purity, a tragic lover who dies of consumption, having stayed untainted by the vice all around. '*La Dame aux camélias* was my life, all the trashy novels I'd fed on,' she said to Delay, who recognised the link between Marguerite and Chanel's story of her mother's deathbed – the drops of red blood coughed onto white sheets and a snowy handkerchief. But in this particular narrative, Chanel placed herself centre-stage, as a provincial 13-year-old on a trip to the theatre in Paris with her aunts. She sobbed her way through the entire performance of *La Dame aux camélias*, she told Delay; and her grief was so noisy that the rest of the audience complained. Nevertheless, she was dressed for the part that she had assigned herself: 'I was in black. It looked nice, with my white collar. In the provinces, you wear your mourning until it falls off you in pieces! People told my aunts I ought to have another dress. "But she's an orphan," they said. "When she's 16 we'll see."'

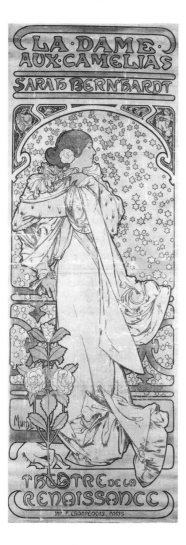

The poster for Sarah Bernhardt's *La Dame aux camélias* at the Théâtre de la Renaissance, Paris.

On other occasions, however, Chanel said that she was already living at Royallieu when she went to see *La Dame aux camélias*, accompanying her aunt Adrienne and the Baron de Nexon; and her account veered between disdain and distress: either she wept so loudly that the rest of the audience hissed at her, or she declared her disgust for Bernhardt as grotesque, like 'an old clown'. Something of that abhorrence and fascination remained: when Sarah Bernhardt died in 1923, Chanel joined the lines of other sightseers, then found herself troubled by the difference between the staged beauty of Marguerite's death in *La Dame aux camélias* and the grim reality of the cadaver before her. 'It was terrible,' she told Delay, 'they were queuing up. Sarah was dead and all I saw was a poor little lifeless ruin with a scrap of tulle … I was pale as death. The sordidness of it all …'

In Delay's sympathetic interpretation, the inconsistencies of Chanel's response to *La Dame aux camélias* suggested ambivalence, rather than an aversion to the truth; not least because of her proximity to her mother's deathbed, and the unavoidable sight of the pale corpse lying beside the children as they waited for their father to return. But if Chanel was haunted by the memory, she was also aware of its potency, an archetypal scene for others as well as herself.

Later, many years later, when Chanel had slipped away from her life as a kept girl, replacing its shadowy uncertainties with what looked like the security of a self-made woman, the white camellia would appear in her work: in fabric prints, or shaped into diamonds and pearls; embossed on buttons, preserved in corsages. And in her salon, they glittered as crystals from her chandelier, and were carved into her Coromandel screens. These replications were in some sense true to life, in that they had no scent – for the camellia is without fragrance, and therefore does not decompose from sweet-smelling purity to the odour of decay. It is, perhaps, the perfect symbol of death as portrayed on stage in its least brutal way; the death of a courtesan or an abandoned woman, tragic yet compelling for an audience; stripped of the horror of visceral pain and fear and animal smell.

After her mother died, Chanel told Delay, she had been instructed to kiss her dead body, to kiss the corpse on the lips. For ever afterwards, she was possessed of a very developed sense of smell, and was revolted by anything redolent of dirt. The courtesans smelled good, she said, but the society women were filthy. And Coco always kept herself clean.

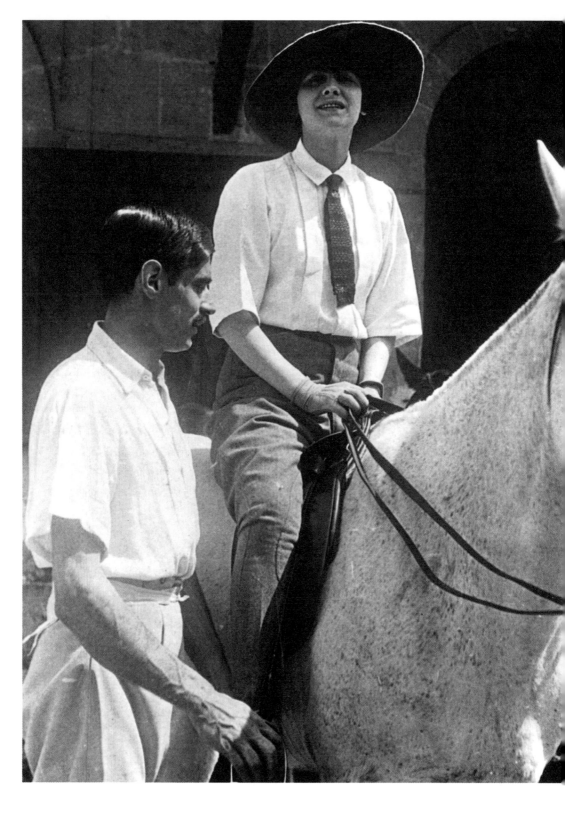

THE DOUBLE C

His name was Arthur Capel, but his friends called him Boy, in an Edwardian era when English gentlemen were still able to celebrate their continuing freedoms long after they had turned from boys to men. Boy's origins were swathed in romance, and he came to Paris amidst murmured speculation that he was connected in some mysterious way to the British aristocracy through the Capell family, who were descended from the Earls of Essex; or that he was the illegitimate son of a rich French father, possibly a Jewish financier. But there has never been any conclusive proof of either tale, and the more prosaic version is that he was exactly who he said he was: the son of Arthur and Bertha Capel, raised with two sisters in comfortable circumstances in a prosperous Catholic family whose money came from coalmines in the north of England. Born in 1881, educated at Beaumont (under the instruction of Jesuit priests) and Downside (a Catholic boarding school attached to a Benedictine abbey and monastery in Somerset), Capel subsequently went into the family business, expanding his father's holdings with energetic determination.

But for all his Catholic education and hard-headed work ethic, Capel was also an accomplished playboy and polo player, sharing an enthusiasm for fast horses and pretty women with his friend Etienne Balsan. It was at Royallieu that Coco came across Capel, and there that a curious triangular relationship developed between Boy and Balsan and the girl who was mistress to no

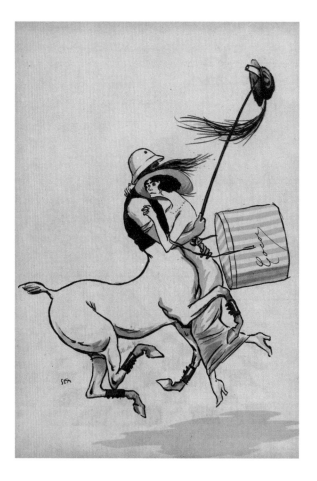

Chanel and the polo-
player Arthur 'Boy'
Capel, as caricatured
by Sem. 1913.

one. Nevertheless, what was in reality a lengthy and convoluted process became, in Chanel's retelling of it, an instant and dramatic incident that began on a trip away from Royallieu. 'MB took me to Pau,' she told Paul Morand, and conjured up for him a vivid scene set against the blue sky and snow-capped Pyrenees: 'the babbling mountain streams that flow down to the plains; the fields that are green in every season ... the red coats in the rain, and the best fox-hunting land in Europe ...'

In this verdant landscape – the fertile territory of Chanel's half-imaginary past – there was a fairy-tale castle with six towers, and galloping horses, and the sound of their hooves on cobblestones. And there, too, centre-stage in this glorious place, was Boy Capel. 'In Pau I met an Englishman,' she said to Morand. 'We made each other's acquaintance when we were out horse-trekking one day; we all lived on horseback.' They drank wine together; it was 'young, intoxicating and quite unusual', and so was the Englishman. 'The young man was handsome, very tanned and attractive. More than handsome, he was magnificent. I admired his nonchalance, and his green eyes. He rode bold and very powerful horses. I fell in love with him. I had never loved MB.' Yet at first, she and Capel did not speak. 'Not a word was exchanged between this Englishman and me. One day I heard he was leaving Pau.' She asked him to tell her the time he was travelling to Paris; no other conversation was necessary. 'The following day, I was at the station. I climbed onto the train.'

It was 1909, and Chanel was 26 by then, just under two years younger than Capel; though she told Claude Delay that Boy called her 'my dear child' when she declared that she was leaving Balsan for him. She held out the letter she had written to Balsan to explain her decision – 'My dear Etienne, I shall never be able to repay the kindness and comfort you've given me while I've been with you.' Boy wouldn't listen to her, wouldn't allow her to leave, in this retelling of a story that Chanel often told (always a variation on a theme); but she followed him, and dashed onto the train with her suitcase. Three days later, Balsan arrived in Paris, having pursued her there from Pau; jealousy had made him realise that he loved her after all.

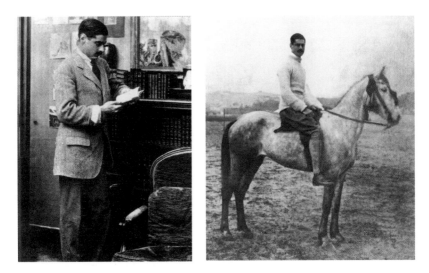

Left: Boy Capel in the apartment in Boulevard Malesherbes.
Right: On horseback in Morocco.

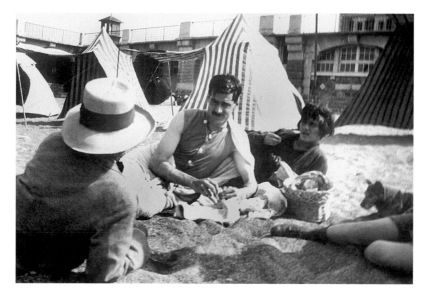

Chanel and Boy Capel on the beach in Saint-Jean-de-Luz, 1917.

This version of the love affair with Capel – Coco's most romantic love story and a defining episode of her life – cast her as a girl who was not yet a woman. Indeed, she suggested that she was a virgin, and needed to consult a doctor in Paris before the love between a girl and Boy could be consummated. By then, she told Delay, Balsan had taken himself off to Argentina to mend his broken heart, and Capel had asked a doctor in Paris to take care of her. At this point, her narrative becomes unusually physical in its details, as if flesh and blood had overtaken whimsical romance. Boy was a man with a string of women, as well as polo ponies, and his mistresses would ask him when he was going to leave little Coco, but his reply was certain: 'I'd rather cut my leg off.'

Instead, Coco was dispatched to the doctor, who performed a mysterious gynaecological procedure with a snip of his scissors. 'The seat of pleasure is a question of structure,' she told Delay, with her odd blend of the graphic and the cryptic. 'As far as I'm concerned, if it hadn't been for that little snip of the scissors … After that, it didn't hurt any more.'

It was at about this time, she continued, that she ordered a tightly fitted dress from Chéruit, a fashionable Parisian couturier, in blue and white grosgrain: 'I looked like the Virgin Mary.' But it was so constrictive around the waist that when she wore the dress out to dine at the Café de Paris with Boy, she had to ask him to undo it for her. Afterwards, she couldn't close its fastenings – Coco was undone in public – and didn't have an evening coat to cover herself up. At that moment, she vowed never to wear corsets again.

There are echoes of a similarly uneasy shifting between freedom and subjugation, liberty and compulsion, in Chanel's description to Morand of her relationship with Boy. They lived together in Paris, and he meant everything to her – 'he was my father, my brother, my entire family' – and there he instructed her as if she were his child. 'Our house was full of flowers, but beneath the luxurious surroundings Boy Capel maintained a strict outlook, in keeping with his moral character, which was that of the well-brought-up Englishman. In educating me, he did not spare me; he commented on my conduct: "You behaved badly ... you lied ... you were wrong." He had that gently authoritative manner of men who know women well, and who love them implicitly.'

But his implicit love manifested itself in explicit abandonment and infidelities; although Chanel seemed to accept that this 'lion of London society' had every right to be unfaithful to her. She maintained to Morand that Capel adored her as much as she adored him; that he was a perfect gentleman. 'His manners were refined, his social success was dazzling,' and yet he was 'only happy in the company of the little brute from the provinces, the unruly child who had followed him. We never went out together (at that time Paris still had principles). We would delay the delights of advertising our love until later, when we were married.' At the same time, Boy continued to enjoy the diversions of other women. Coco said she didn't care – or at least, that is what she claimed to Morand – and yet her description of Capel's behaviour hints at an anxious imbalance between anger and acceptance; and then there is that phrase of his again (or was it hers?) about chopping off his leg. 'Boy Capel's beautiful girlfriends would say to him angrily: "Drop that woman." Not being in the least jealous, I pushed him into their arms; this baffled them and they kept on repeating: "Drop that woman." He replied in that utterly natural way he had ... "No. You might as well ask me to chop off a leg." He needed me.'

But she also needed him – financially, as well as in every other way – and she was aware that he had the capacity to run away from her whenever he chose to; just as her father had run from her mother, and from her, too. Perhaps there were times when Coco felt angry enough to want to chop her lover's legs off. Instead, she turned her scissors on his clothes. These she stole and cut up, so that he could no longer wear them out again. Yet in doing so, she transformed

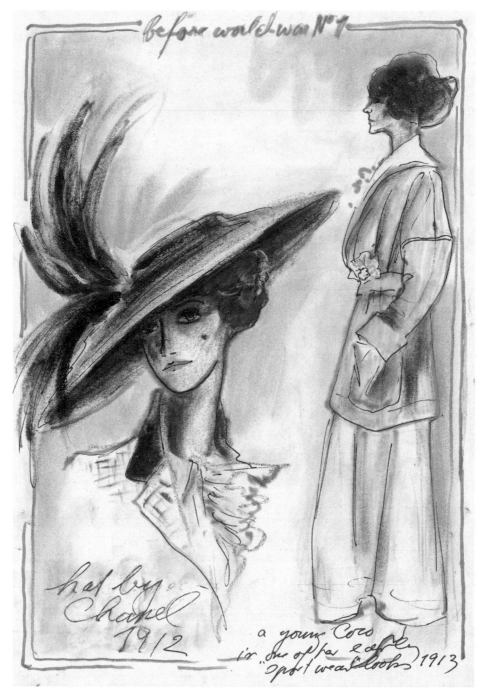

before world war N°1

hat by Chanel 1912

a young Coco in one of her early "sport wear" looks 1913

Chanel, by Karl Lagerfeld.

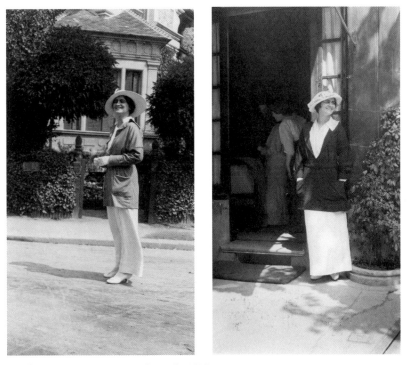

Left: Chanel in her own designs, Deauville, 1913.
Right: In front of her boutique in Deauville, 1913.

them into something new and uniquely her own, eventually building an empire upon the desire of other women to possess her creations; women who sought her, Coco Chanel, rather than Boy Capel.

That came later, however. First, she had come up with a plan to sell hats, although the question remained as to who, precisely, was to back her business, and where she was to live, and whether Balsan had been abandoned altogether. Many years later, confiding in Marcel Haedrich, Chanel said that she went on seeing Etienne Balsan after she left Royallieu, and he continued to declare his love for her. 'We lunched and dined together – Etienne, Boy and I. Occasionally Etienne talked about killing himself, and I wept. I wept so! "You aren't going to let Etienne kill himself," I said to myself. "You'll set them both free. Go throw yourself into the Seine!"'

Other, less torrid versions give more emphasis to Etienne and Boy's financial discussions about who should pay what to keep Chanel. To Morand, Chanel claimed that Balsan returned from Argentina with a bag of lemons, which had gone rotten, as a gift for her. It remains unclear whether or not he intended this to be symbolic, in some unspecified way, or if Chanel herself had conjured up the rolling lemons as a mystifying metaphor, or was simply for once telling the truth. All that emerges with any certainty from her account to Morand was that matters between the three of them were confused: 'there were tears and quarrels. Boy was English, he didn't understand; everything became muddled. He was very moral.'

But to Haedrich, Chanel presented herself as the muddled one of the threesome, a little girl who didn't understand the machinations of two older men. 'I was just a kid,' she said, insisting that she had celebrated her eighteenth birthday with Capel when she came with him to Paris. 'I had no money. I lived at the Ritz and everything was paid for me. It was an incredible situation. Parisian society talked about it. I didn't know Parisian society ... It was very complicated. The *cocottes* were paid. I knew that, I'd been taught that. I said to myself, "Are you going to become like them? A kept woman? But this is appalling!" I didn't want it.'

What she did want was to earn her own living. Eventually, after protracted negotiations, Balsan and Capel agreed to share the cost of setting her up in business to sell the hats that she was already making for herself, and for her friends (and their girlfriends). Among her first clients were Emilienne d'Alençon, Suzanne Orlandi and Gabrielle Dorziat, the *cocottes*-turned-actresses who began to wear Chanel's designs on stage and in magazines. Capel covered the running costs; Balsan provided the Paris premises at his bachelor apartment in

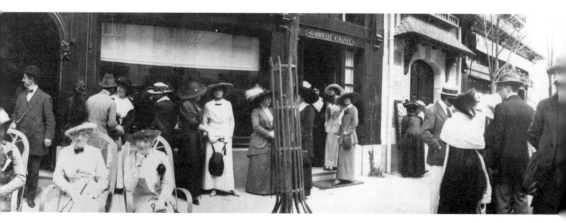

Chanel, amongst passers-by, in front of the Chanel boutique in Deauville, 1913.

Boulevard Malesherbes. 'They had decided to give me a place where I could make my hats,' she said to Haedrich, 'the way they would have given me a toy, thinking, "Let's let her amuse herself, and later we'll see." They didn't understand how important this was to me. They were very rich men, polo players. They didn't understand anything about the little girl who came into their lives to play. A little girl who understood nothing of what was happening to her.'

It seems highly likely that Coco did understand something of her circumstances, or at least the practical arrangements that had been put in place; but her constant emphasis on her youth and innocence, when she was already in her late twenties, is perhaps more indicative of real confusion on her part, rather than her simply being disingenuous. After all, her status was ambiguous with these men who said that they loved her but treated her like a plaything. And troubling questions still remained. What were their real feelings for her, and how long would they be sustained? How would she survive without them and which of them would be left heartbroken?

The one certainty was her decisive approach to fashion. Just as at Royallieu, Coco dressed like a young convent girl or a schoolboy, and made hats that were stripped of embellishments, of the frills and furbelows that she dismissed as weighing a woman down, and being too cumbersome to let her think straight. They weren't entirely original – at first, she bought simple straw boaters from the Galeries Lafayette department store, and then trimmed them with ribbon herself – but they were chic. 'Nothing makes a woman look older than obvious expensiveness, ornateness, complication,' she said to Claude Delay in old age,

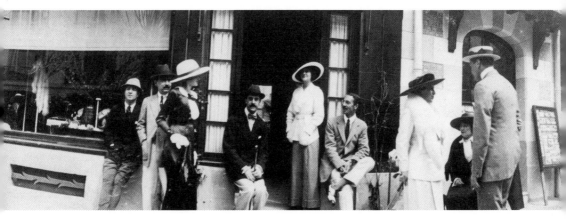

Chanel (centre), with two men, believed to be Boy Capel (centre left) and Etienne Balsan (centre right), at the entrance to the boutique.

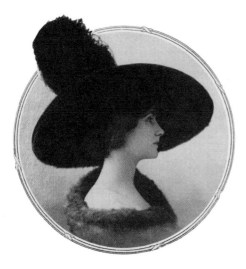

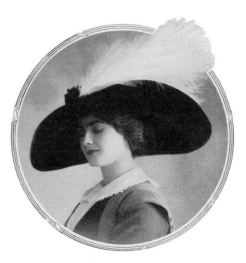

The first known portraits of Chanel wearing her own hats, published in the theatre magazine *Comoedia illustré*, October 1910.

still wearing the little straw hats of her youth. 'I still dress as I always did, like a schoolgirl.'

And in doing so, Coco began to edge her way to the centre of attention, elbowing past her rivals and competitors, whether the society ladies or the *cocottes* or couturiers. (Paul Poiret, whose fame at the time was such that he dubbed himself the 'King of Fashion', said of Chanel's early days as a milliner, 'We ought to have been on guard against that boyish head. It was going to give us every kind of shock, and produce, out of its little conjuror's hat, gowns and coiffures and jewels and boutiques.') Thus the day came, she told Morand, when she felt able to insist that Boy should dine with her at the casino in Deauville, rather than attend a gala there without her: 'All eyes were on us: my timid entrance, my awkwardness, which contrasted with a wonderfully simple white dress, attracted people's attention. The beauties of the period, with that intuition women have for threats unknown, were alarmed.'

Whether they were prompted by alarm or jealousy or simple curiosity, the beauties flocked to buy hats from Chanel at her milliner's establishment. Soon, her business had grown too successful for Balsan's apartment, and backed by Capel – whose own fortunes were prospering further – she opened new premises on 1st January 1910 at 21 Rue Cambon. 'I still have it,' she told Paul Morand. 'On the door, it read: "*Chanel, modes*".' She summoned her sister, Antoinette, and her aunt Adrienne to Paris to help – both of them beautiful, as well as skilled seamstresses; Adrienne still the consort of Baron de Nexon – and Chanel worked alongside them, but also went out and about, as her own best model. 'In the grandstands, people began talking about my amazing, unusual hats,' she said to Morand, 'so neat and austere … Customers came, initially prompted by curiosity. One day I had a visit from one such woman, who admitted quite openly: "I came to have a look at you." I was the curious creature, the little woman whose straw boater fitted her head, and whose head fitted her shoulders.'

But still, she sensed danger all around. Eventually, she told Haedrich, she ventured out to Maxim's for the first time, accompanied by three escorts ('one of them was an Englishman who was determined not to be impressed by anything'). It was in 1913, and respectable women did not eat dinner at the restaurant, but Coco was happy to be there with Capel and his friends. 'I'd been told that the *cocottes* went to Maxim's,' she remarked. 'I liked the *cocottes*: they were clean.' But as in the convent at Aubazine, even amidst cleanliness, there was blood.

A couple sat down at the next table, and immediately, another woman appeared, and asked the man to come outside. Coco watched as the man shook his head, a gesture met with a volcanic eruption of violent rage. 'She broke a glass and began to slash at his face with the base of it. There was blood all over. I fled at once, I went up the stairs, the little spiral stairway. I ran into a room and crawled under a table covered by a cloth. I didn't want to see any more of that quarrel and that blood. How horrible! I was weeping because the three men I was with had done nothing. All that mattered to them was that they shouldn't be spattered by the blood.'

Thus Boy, her supposed protector, nevertheless left her vulnerable; and all she could do was to hide beneath a cloth. She had lost her heart to Capel, and he proved himself capable of being heartless, at least in the ease with which he conducted his infidelities. 'He really understood me,' she told Haedrich, 60 years later. 'He handled me like a child. He said to me, "Coco, if only you'd stop lying! Can't you talk like everyone else? Where do you dig up the things you imagine?"' But she was not imagining his affairs with other women, even though she pretended not to care (and in doing so, was perhaps false to herself). 'I couldn't have cared less whether he was unfaithful,' she said to Haedrich. 'I

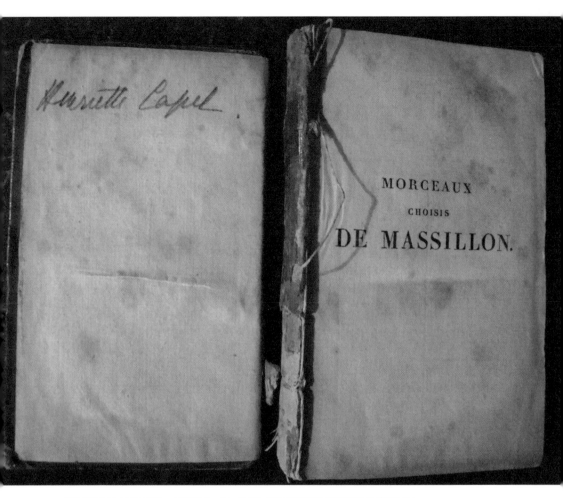

Frontispiece of *Morceaux choisis ou recueil*, by Jean-Baptiste Massillon, in Chanel's apartment, with the signature of Boy Capel's sister, Henriette Capel.

found it rather dirty, but it didn't count between us.' And to Morand, she claimed to have had so much fun with Capel that nothing else mattered. '"Tell me who you're sleeping with, it would amuse me greatly," I would say to him.' Boy Capel laughed, she said, but in other accounts she did not seem to be as amused as he was, nor quite as nonchalant as she had claimed to be.

True, to the outside world, they were a glamorous and successful couple. Chanel's business was growing, and she began to sell clothes, as well as hats. As always, she based her designs on what suited her – boyish jersey pieces, many of them inspired by Capel's own English sportswear – and he backed her taste with his capital. But it was as if she had put away her dreams of romance – of the mauve dress she longed for as a young girl – and seemed to accept that bridal lace would never be hers. 'The age of extravagant dresses, those dresses worn by heroines that I had dreamt about, was past,' she said to Morand. 'I had never even had those convent uniforms, with capes, adorned with pale blue Holy Ghost, or Children of Mary, ribbons, which are a child's pride and joy; I no longer thought about lace; I knew that extravagant things didn't suit me. All I kept were my goat-skin coat and my simple outfits.

'"Since you are so attached to them," Capel said to me, "I'm going to get you to have the clothes you have always worn remade *elegantly*, by an English tailor." Everything to do with Rue Cambon stemmed from there.'

But for all the outward success of her designs – and the impeccable surface that she presented to the outside world – inside, something was troubling her. 'I often fainted,' she told Haedrich, recalling a day at the racetrack when she had collapsed three times. 'I had too much emotion, too much excitement, I lived too intensely. My nerves couldn't stand it. And all at once … I was standing beside a gentleman who had a horse running. Suddenly I had the feeling he was slipping away from me, fast. What a terrible feeling. I fell to the ground, thinking, this is it, it's all over.'

She did not name the gentleman slipping away from her; but if she did fear the loss of Boy Capel (her lover who was also 'my brother, my father, my whole family'), it may have contributed to her sense of overwhelming emotion. 'Several times I'd been brought home unconscious,' she said to Haedrich. 'These weren't any hysterical woman's swoons. I fell down, my eyes turned black … I was taken for dead.' Chanel returned to these episodes again and again in her conversations with Haedrich. 'They talk to me about attacks of nerves,' she said (without specifying who 'they' might be). 'For two years I couldn't cross a street or go into a church. So I stopped going to Mass …' Yet whatever the true cause of her dread and anxiety, she believed that Capel had a miraculous ability to heal her: 'Boy Capel cured me, with exceptional patience, simply by repeating: "Faint if you want to." He took me wherever there were people, and said: "I'm here. Nothing can happen to you. Faint while I'm here."'

But he wasn't always there; he came and went; he appeared and disappeared. When she worked, she said, her health recovered; and although she never admitted it, the House of Chanel seemed to give her more stability –

a sense of where she stood in the world – than she gained from Boy Capel. Hence the story she often told of her distress at discovering that Capel had deposited bank securities as a guarantee for her business and overdrafts, and that the money she believed she was making had not yet repaid her debt. On the evening he told her this, they had been on their way to dinner in Saint-Germain; she immediately insisted that they return to the apartment they now shared in Paris. 'I felt sick,' she told Morand. 'Impossible to eat … We went up to our flat in the Avenue Gabriel. I glanced at the pretty things I had bought with what I thought were my profits. So all that had been paid for by him! I was living off him … I began to hate this well-brought-up man who was paying for me. I threw my handbag straight at his face and I fled.'

She rushed outside, running through a downpour of rain as stormy as her outburst, not knowing where she was going. But Capel ran after her, caught up with her on the corner of Rue Cambon, and took her home to the apartment that he paid for.

The following morning, she told Morand, she went back to Rue Cambon at dawn. '"Angèle," I said to my head seamstress, "I am not here to have fun, or to spend money like water. I am here to make a fortune."' A year later, Chanel was earning sufficient money to have no more need of Capel's financial support, and she rejoiced in her independence. Her clothes looked simple – sleek and fluid, designed to be worn without corsets and with insouciance – and she sometimes gave the impression that her success as a designer had come as easily as slipping on a cardigan. It may be that her aesthetic subverted the cliché that appearances can be deceptive (whatever the subterfuges Chanel practised in reshaping her life, the twist she gave to modern fashion was that the line of beauty need not necessarily be misleading). 'Fashion, like landscape, is a state of mind, by which I mean my own,' she declared to Morand; but her territory of effortless chic took far more planning and hard-headedness than she let on. The rewards, however, were considerable, for her work, like her clothes, liberated Chanel from other constrictions. 'I was my own master, and I depended on myself alone,' she told Morand. 'Boy Capel was well aware that he didn't control me: "I thought I'd given you a plaything, I gave you freedom," he once said to me in a melancholy voice.'

Even so, the House of Chanel still linked them together; for in some unspoken way they had set it up as partners. There was no business contract to bind them together, just as there was no marriage certificate, but it

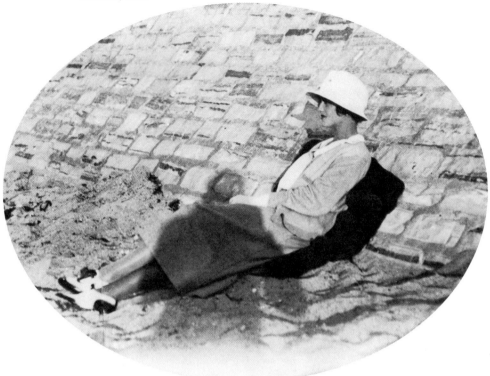

Chanel on the beach
in Biarritz, 1920.

nevertheless joined them, as the double C logo seems to suggest; Chanel and Capel; overlapping, but also facing away from each other.

Something of this capacity for closeness, combined with an ability to turn their back on one another (and others, too), is apparent in the role that both played in the upbringing of André Palasse. Chanel had some support from Capel when she assumed responsibility for her nephew; and although she revealed little about the circumstances of his childhood, she did tell Delay that Capel had called André his son, and that every time the little boy saw a coal barge on the Seine, he would say, 'Look, that's ours.' (Capel had already expanded into coal transportation, as well as mining.) 'It's not ours, it's Boy's,' Coco would tell him; and she smiled as she told Delay the answer that André gave her: 'But he told me you're going to marry him.'

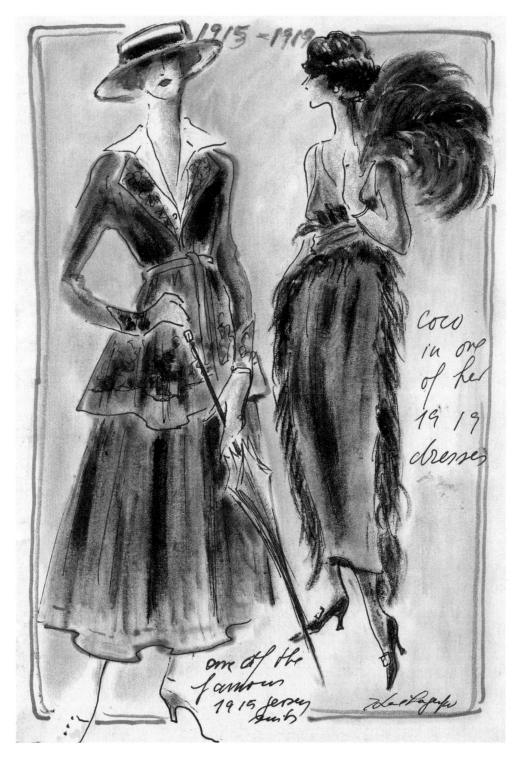

1915 - 1919

coco
in one
of her
19 19
dresses

one of the
famous
1915 jersey
suits

Some of Chanel's creations from the period 1915–19, by Karl Lagerfeld.

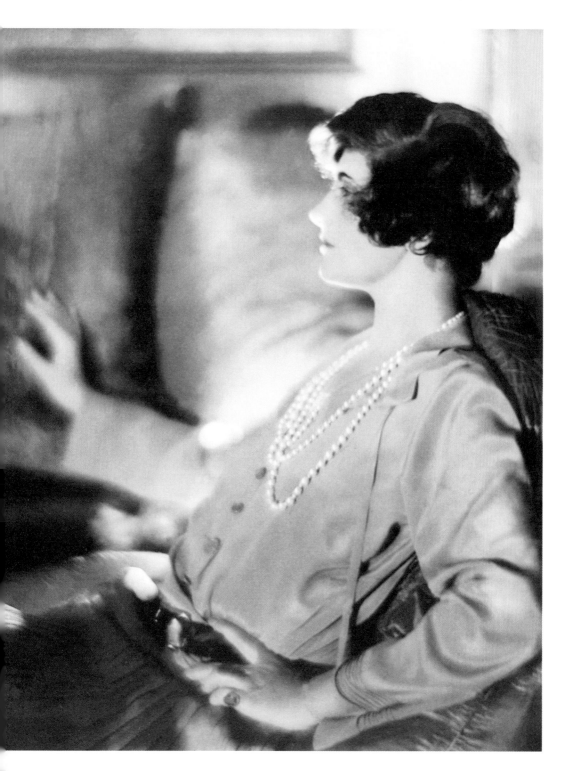

Chanel with bobbed hair, white pearls and a satin blouse, circa 1920.

No marriage transpired, and Coco sent André to boarding school in England, to Beaumont, where Boy had been educated. Here the little boy was taught to speak perfect English, and to behave with British reserve, remaining at a distance from his aunt, who may have been his mother, and from her lover, who called him his son. André's daughter, also named Gabrielle, was born in 1926, and recalls her childhood with absolute clarity, but learned quickly never to question her father or her great aunt (whom she still refers to as 'Auntie Coco') about anything relating to the family history. Gabrielle accepts with apparent equanimity the circumstances of her father's childhood, and the possibility that Coco might have been her grandmother rather than her great aunt. 'Several people who were close to her were sure that this was true,' she says, but also acknowledges that she will never know the truth. 'There were so many things she invented – she invented a fairy tale that had nothing to do with reality – even though she lived her own fairy tale, by making her way from the orphanage in Aubazine to Rue Cambon. But the truth hurt her too much – she preserved herself by hiding the truth – and she found a way of putting aside the things that hurt her.'

While André was cared for in England, Chanel's business flourished, even in the shadow of the First World War. She had opened her first shop in Deauville in 1913; the following summer, after the outbreak of hostilities, Capel (by then a captain in a British army division in France) suggested that she withdraw from Paris to the safety of the seaside resort. There, according to the story she told Paul Morand, Boy 'rented a villa for his ponies'. Along with the polo ponies, there were legions of fashionable women who had retreated to Deauville that year, all of whom needed new clothes. Chanel had brought several milliners with her, rather than dressmakers, but soon adapted to the wartime restrictions, and set her employees to work. 'There was a shortage of material,' she explained to Morand. 'I cut jerseys for them from the sweaters the stable lads wore and from the knitted training garments that I wore myself. By the end of the first summer of the war, I had earned two hundred thousand gold francs!'

A less romantic version of the story is that jersey was the only fabric she was able to buy in sufficient quantity from textile manufacturers; but in any case, Chanel rose to the occasion, even as France seemed to fall around her. Royallieu had been taken by the German forces, reclaimed by the French and then turned into a front-line hospital; Antoinette and Adrienne left Paris, along with thousands of other women, and came to join Coco in Deauville. Meanwhile, a letter arrived from her brother, Alphonse, saying that both he and their younger brother, Lucien, had joined up – Lucien in the infantry, and Alphonse as a mechanic repairing army tanks. Coco wrote back to Alphonse, sending money and encouragement, in a letter that appears to suggest that he had been injured or sick: 'I am happy to hear that you have a month of convalescence to get better. Rest and take good care of yourself. I am busy with lots of things and have practically no time for myself. I will write to your wife – don't be too anxious – perhaps everything will finish sooner than we think ...'

Despite the horrors of the Front Line, her sales continued to increase in Paris and Deauville, and a new boutique, which she had established in Biarritz in 1915. For Chanel's simple jersey jackets, straight skirts and unadorned sailor blouses looked more and more like the only appropriate fashion to be seen in amid the sombre anxieties of war. They were chic, but not showy; monochrome, in keeping with the mood of the times; clothes that could be worn to drive an ambulance or an army car, as relevant to women's wartime work as to a seaside promenade. 'Fashion should express the place, the moment,' Chanel would later observe to Paul Morand, and even if her words were spoken with the benefit of hindsight, she had seized her moment just as old certainties seemed to be giving way. 'I was witnessing the death of luxury, the passing of the nineteenth century, the end of an era.'

She watched its demise without sympathy, knowing that her time was coming, that the grandeur she had witnessed would soon crumble, choking on its own excess. Chanel had come of age in a period of magnificence, but also of decadence; in her words, 'the last reflections of a baroque style in which the ornate had killed off the figure, in which over-embellishment had stifled the body's architecture, just as parasites smother trees in tropical forests. Woman was no more than a pretext for riches, for sable, for chinchilla, for materials that were too precious. Complicated patterns, an excess of lace, of embroidery, of gauze, of flounces and over-layers had transformed what women wore into a monument of belated and flamboyant art. The trains of dresses swept up the dust, all the pastel shades reflected every colour in the rainbow in a thousand tints with a subtlety that faded into insipidness.'

But Coco was going to change all that; Chanel was going to impose black.

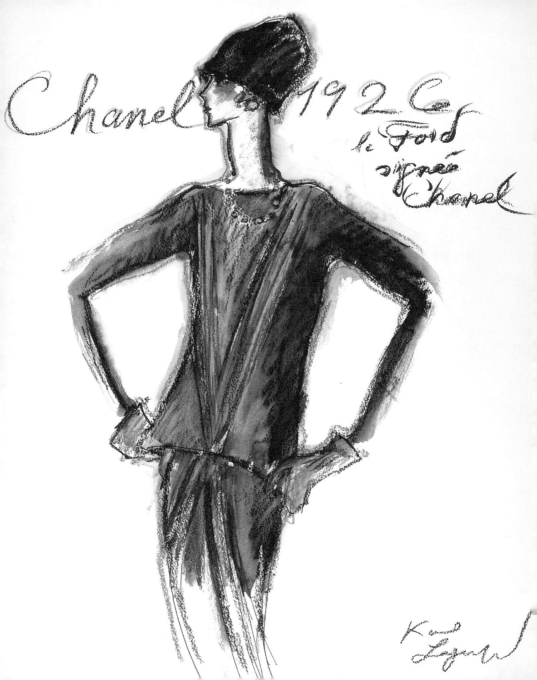

Chanel 1926
le Ford
signée
Chanel

Karl
Lagerfeld

THE LITTLE BLACK DRESS

In July 1918, an aristocratic beauty named Diana Wyndham wrote a letter to her friend Duff Cooper, from Beaufort Castle in Scotland, where she was visiting her sister Laura and enjoying balmy days in 'a sea of bluebells, gorse and broom'. The youngest daughter of the fourth Lord Ribblesdale (a former government chief whip in the House of Lords), Diana Wyndham was possessed of connections that placed her at the heart of upper class society. Her father's portrait by John Singer Sargent reveals why King Edward VII admired him for his courtly stateliness (the king referred to Ribblesdale as 'The Ancestor', because of the impression he gave of having stepped out of an oil painting). Diana was 25, ten years younger than Coco Chanel, but she had already been married, in 1913, and widowed the following year. Her first husband, often described as one of the handsomest men in London, was Percy Wyndham, half-brother to the Duke of Westminster. An officer in the Coldstream Guards at the time of their wedding, he was killed in action in France on 14th September 1914; his death was followed less than a year later by that of Diana's brother.

'Dearest Duff,' she wrote to a man as well connected as herself, who had joined the Foreign Office after Eton and Oxford, and was currently serving in the Grenadier Guards, 'Lots of things have happened since I saw you – I've been ill, we've nearly lost the war, and I think I'm going to marry Capel after all – so next time

I see you, you'll be staying with me in my luxurious apartment in the Avenue du Bois.'

Diana had had a brief flirtation with Duff Cooper three months previously, and so had no need to explain the family references that followed in her letter – to her sister Laura, who had married Simon Fraser, the 14th Lord Lovat, or to her aunt Margot Asquith, the wife of the former prime minister. But it appears she did want to justify her actions to Cooper, following the disapproving responses she had received from Margot Asquith and another of her aunts to her decision to marry Boy Capel. Diana had met the handsome captain while she was driving an ambulance for the Red Cross in France, close to the front line; and their relationship may have been more passionate than Coco Chanel preferred to admit. If Diana was not yet pregnant with Capel's child when she wrote to Duff Cooper, she would have been soon afterwards, given the birth of her first baby the following April.

Not that an unplanned pregnancy was the cause of her aunts' condemnation: they already had other grounds on which to object to Capel, which emerge in Diana's letter to Cooper: 'I wrote, the other day, to Lucy and Margot, breaking [to] them the news and have today received masterpieces from them – Lucy's letter worse than a farewell dinner, saying her heart has never ceased aching since she received mine, that Paris did not lead to high ideals or morality, that it was selfish of me to marry and leave father, that he [Capel] was half French and not fond of country life, and Margot [wrote] much on the same lines, giving some well-aimed hits at the Versailles Council, since he [Capel] has become political secretary on the Council.'

Yet as Duff Cooper knew, Boy was very much on the up. He had made a fortune out of coal during the war, expanded into shipping, and in between balancing the demands of various mistresses had somehow found the time to write a well-received book, *Reflections on Victory*, which proposed a formula for international peace. Captain Capel was also a highly regarded liaison officer between France and Britain, being a trusted friend of both Georges Clemenceau, the elder statesman of French politics and prime minister from 1917, and Lloyd George, munitions minister in Asquith's cabinet and his successor as prime minister. (Hence Capel's appointment as political secretary to the Allies' War Council, based in Versailles.)

'I suppose you will take much the same line,' continued Diana in her letter, reflecting on her aunts' disapproval, 'knowing your feelings on the subject – and

I look for nothing but abuse from the world, but I prefer this sort of marriage to the humdrum "*mariage de convenance*" and feel quite certain that this one is fraught with great possibilities and charm. My one regret is that I'm not marrying you, Duffie dear, but I don't think you ever asked me, or did you? It might anyway have been more popular with the "aunties" but we could never have afforded a flat in Paris, not even a "bed-sitter". Do write to me and say you're pleased about it, and that you like my "darkie". I adore him!'

As it turned out, the next time Duff and Diana met, in October 1918, she had already married Boy Capel (a late summer wedding at Beaufort Castle in Lord Lovat's private chapel), and Cooper was less than impressed. His diary for 8th October records a rather busy day in Paris – cocktails at the Crillon, lunch at the Ritz with Diana, tea at Les Ambassadeurs, a visit to her flat at 88 Avenue du Bois, dinner at Maxim's, followed by a revue, and finally a trip to a brothel. Somewhere within this packed itinerary, Cooper took against Capel, 'whom I don't like the look of'. Two days later, he liked him even less. 'I had arranged to go down to Versailles with Diana and lunch there. I hired a motor from the Ritz and went to her about midday. She met me with the news that Capel forbade our lunching at Versailles on account of the number of officers who would see her lunching there. It seemed silly ...' He and Diana duly ate elsewhere, and then went for a walk around Versailles; walking having not yet been forbidden by Capel. 'She is a delightful companion. How beautiful was Versailles with its native melancholy enhanced by the yellowing branches and fallen leaves.'

In later life, Chanel did not discuss her lover's marriage to Diana; in fact, she barely acknowledged that it had taken place. Perhaps this is how she dealt with it at the time. She already knew that he had other women, other mistresses, and it seemed evident that nothing would come of his earlier promises that she would be his wife. Capel was ambitious, and an aristocratic wife would consolidate his social standing and possibly dispel the speculation about his origins in a way that Coco Chanel could not. (Whether or not he was illegitimate, Diana's reference to him as 'half French' might suggest that the circumstances of his birth were still a talking point.) Of course, Chanel was also ambitious – as was evident in her ascent through Parisian society. She had gone from milliner to dressmaker to couturière, and was now admired by baronesses and princesses; she had climbed from the half-light of the demimondaine to the spotlight of worldly acclaim.

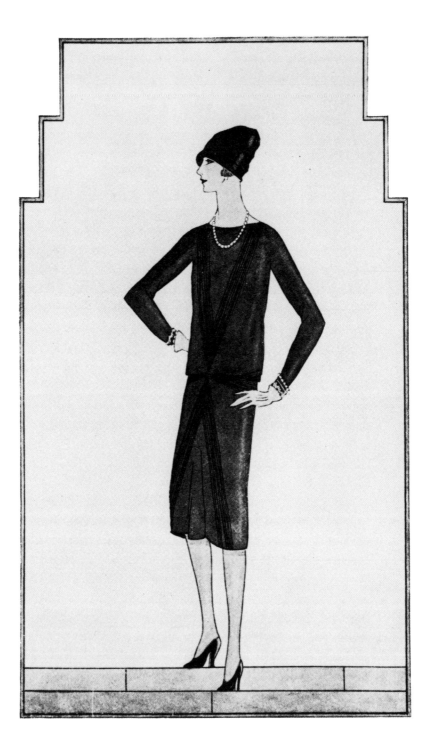

Drawing of the 'Ford' dress by Chanel, published in American *Vogue*, October 1926.

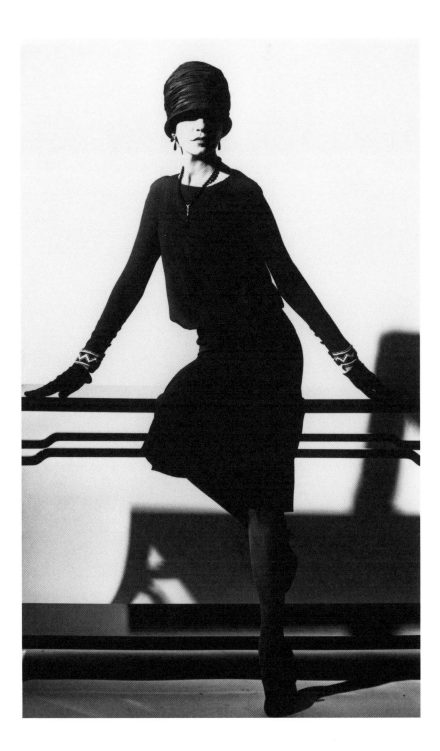

Reconstruction of the 'Ford' dress, photographed by Karl Lagerfeld.

But for all her commercial and social success, Chanel did not yet understand the unwritten code of the British upper classes, nor Boy's adherence to its conventions and etiquette, despite his apparently carefree enjoyment of Paris. Many years later, Chanel told Bettina Ballard that during her affair with Boy she had yearned for the romance of the 'sticky French sentimental' novels she read, but he thought it demonstrably absurd; making this clear by subverting the rituals of an adoring love affair. After she complained that he never gave her jewellery, he bought her a tiara from Cartier, but she didn't understand what it was or how to wear it. 'He knew so much more than I did. I jumped at him furiously, pounding my fists on his chest and crying, "What is it, why do you tease me, why do you make me feel ridiculous?"' She gave a similar account to Paul Morand, and of the consequences of asking Boy to send her flowers. 'Half-an-hour later, I received a bouquet. I was delighted. Half-an-hour later, a second bouquet. I was pleased. Half-an-hour later, another bouquet. This was becoming monotonous. Every half-hour the bouquets kept arriving in this way for two days. Boy Capel wanted to train me. I understood the lesson. He trained me for happiness.'

And yet she was not happy. When Chanel sought advice from a friend about the tiara, she discovered that it should be worn to the opera, but this was not possible, as Capel rarely took her out with him in public. 'Thus did our happy days pass at Avenue Gabriel,' she told Morand. 'I hardly ever went out. I dressed in the evening to please Capel, knowing full well that there would shortly be a moment when he would say: "why go out, after all, we're very comfortable here."' So there they stayed, surrounded by the Coromandel screens he had introduced her to and which she came to adore, in part because, like medieval tapestries, they allowed her to re-create her home wherever she might move to. 'He liked me among my surroundings, and there's a girl-from-the-harem side of me which suited this seclusion very well.'

But the girl from the harem is unlikely to wear a white wedding dress, or a bridal veil over her long hair. And while Arthur Capel was searching for a suitably aristocratic wife, Coco Chanel made herself look like a boy: breastless and hipless and shorn of the conventions of womanhood. 'In 1917 I slashed my thick hair,' she said to Morand; 'to begin with I trimmed it bit by bit. Finally, I wore it short.' When people asked her why she had cut it short, she answered, 'Because it annoys me.' 'And everyone went into raptures, saying that I looked like "a young boy, a little shepherd". (That was beginning to become a compliment, for a woman.)'

Chanel gave a different, and more detailed version of that radical haircut to Claude Delay, which suggested a number of intriguing associations: between shortening skirts and bobbing her hair; the power of wearing black instead of the conventions of white; between cleanliness and coquetry. Her story started with a trip to the opera with several friends. She was dressing for the evening at the apartment in the Avenue Gabriel (no mention of Boy Capel, who was often away, not only in the arms of other women, but also as an army officer undertaking clandestine missions for his friends in government). 'I'd never been to the Opera before. I had a white dress made by my own *modistes*. My hair, which came down below my waist, was done up round my head in three braids – all that mass set straight upon that thin body.' She had so much hair, she said, that it was 'crushing me to death'; but fate intervened, and gave her freedom. 'There was a gas burner in the bathroom. I turned on the hot tap to wash my hands again, the water wasn't hot, so I fiddled with the pilot-light and the whole thing exploded. My white dress was covered in soot, my hair – the less said, the better. I only had to wash my face again – I didn't use make-up. In those days only the *cocottes* used make-up and were elegant. The women of the bourgeoisie weren't groomed – and they wore hats that flopped all over the place, with birds' nests and butterflies.'

But nothing was going to stop her from going out that night, not even her burnt hair. 'I took a pair of scissors and cut one braid off. The hair sprang out at once all round my face. In those days I had hair like sable.' Undaunted, she cut off the second braid, and then told her maid to cut off the third; the girl began to cry, but Chanel didn't care – or at least, she said she didn't care about the loss of her hair, or of the soot-stained white dress. 'I slipped on a black dress I had, crossed over in front – what a marvellous thing, youth – and caught in at the waist, with a sort of minaret on top.'

With bobbed hair and little black dress Chanel was neither slave girl nor wife, but something of her own making. Everyone at the opera was looking at her, she told Delay; they were all so impressed that 'the darling of the English became the beauty of Paris.' Afterwards, however, the flat in Avenue Gabriel contained something macabre within it. 'When I got back that evening the maid had washed my hair and my braids were waiting for me in the bathroom like three dead bodies.' Thereafter, whenever designing a new fashion collection, she cut off her own hair: 'I've always plied the scissors.'

There was no such clear schedule for the cut-off point in her relationship with Boy Capel, despite his marriage and the birth of his first child in April 1919 (a daughter named Ann). Chanel's affair with him continued, partly conducted in a villa she had rented in Saint Cloud, just outside Paris. And by October 1919, Diana Capel was involved in a romance with Duff Cooper (who had himself married Lady Diana Manners, a famous society beauty and actress, less than four months previously). Duff Cooper's diary offers some insight into the ensuing intrigue and entanglements. On 29th October, he wrote that he had met that evening with both Dianas at the Ritz in London, along with some other friends. Diana Capel 'was looking most lovely. She has had her hair cut short but is letting it grow again. Dinner was not very successful. The two Dianas never harmonize – I don't know why it is.' Afterwards, it was raining, and he started walking Diana Capel home. 'In Piccadilly we got a taxi and I drove with her to Curzon Street. I made love to her and kissed her and promised to meet her next day. I felt rather guilty when I got home.' Despite his guilt, two days later he arranged a secret lunch with Diana Capel: 'I had to lie terribly [to his wife].' Even so, the lunch was 'very agreeable. She was looking charming. Intrigue of this sort has a fatal fascination. I don't care for her one thousandth part as much as I care for my own Diana, and when I got back to the latter and found her very low with a headache having been alone all day and wretched that I hadn't lunched with her but believing all my lies, I felt a monster of wickedness and cruelty.'

Cooper's affair with Mrs Capel continued through November and December 1919, as did Captain Capel's with Coco Chanel (the convergence of interlinked Cs once more forming a curious reflection of Chanel's own logo). On 5th November, Cooper took his wife to the opera in London, 'wheeled her into the Royal Box and then went off and dined with the other Diana … We had a pleasant evening, sitting by the fire and making love. She doesn't care at all for me and I not really very much for her but it amuses us.' On 11th November, Armistice Day, Cooper and his wife went to a Victory Ball, where he discovered Diana Capel 'looking very well in gold trousers'. On 17th December he bought Diana Capel a Christmas present of jewellery from Boucheron.

What happened next was the event that Chanel defined as marking her forever – the deepest cut to her heart; the wound that would not heal. Although she never revealed the precise details of the tragedy, and they have tended to be misreported, an outline of the truth can be pieced together through diaries, letters, newspaper reports and Chanel's own testimony. On 22nd December 1919, Captain Arthur Capel was killed in an accident while driving from Paris to Cannes. According to *The Times* and Reuters, he was travelling with his mechanic, a man named Mansfield, when one of the tyres burst on his car; the mechanic was seriously injured. Capel himself was to be buried on Christmas Eve in Fréjus, just inland from St Raphael on the Côte d'Azur.

Diana Capel was in London at the time – Duff Cooper's diary records that she had gone back to Paris after their encounters the previous month, but returned to England on 22nd December. She telephoned Cooper on the morning of the 23rd, still unaware of the death of her husband. 'I had no idea she was in London and was delighted to hear her,' wrote Cooper in his diary that night. 'She had come over from Paris the day before. Capel had meanwhile started for the South of France where she was to join him in a fortnight.' (Other sources say that the Capels had planned to spend Christmas together in Cannes.) Diana Capel already had a lunch date that day – with Lady Rosslyn – but invited Cooper to join them; afterwards, he accompanied Diana to a bookshop, and thence to Asprey's, where she had arranged to meet Lady Rosslyn again. The taxi journey from the bookshop to Asprey's was 'a long and very pleasant drive, long because of the blocks in the traffic, pleasant because I kissed her'. She jumped out of the taxi, forgetting the book she had just bought; when Cooper noticed this, he returned, to find her standing on the pavement in front of Asprey's. 'I put the book into Diana's hands and at the same time noticed an expression of horror on the face of Lady Rosslyn who was standing behind her. But I thought no more of it and drove away.' It was not until the following morning, Christmas Eve, when Cooper opened the papers, that he was shocked to discover the news of Captain Capel's death in France.

When word of Boy's death reached Paris, one of Chanel's friends from her days at Royallieu, Léon de Laborde, volunteered to break the news to her. It was late at night by the time he arrived at her villa in Saint Cloud, and it took some time for her butler to come to the front door; Mademoiselle was sleeping, he said, but Laborde insisted that she be woken. When Chanel came down the stairs, he later recalled, she was wearing white pyjamas, and her short hair was tousled: 'the silhouette of an adolescent, a youth in satin'. He told her that Boy was dead, and her face crumpled in agony, but there were no tears. 'The worst of it,' said Laborde, 'was this woman crying with dry eyes.' Then she packed a bag, and he drove her through the dawn to the south of France, until they reached the Riviera, where Capel's sister Bertha was staying in a suite of rooms in a palace hotel. (Like her brother, she had married well – indeed, he had seen to it – thereby acquiring a large income and the title of Lady Michelham.) Bertha offered Chanel a bed to sleep in, but she said no, still dry-eyed, and sat up all night on a chaise longue. Boy's body was burnt beyond recognition, and had already been sealed in a coffin before Chanel's arrival. She did not want to go to the funeral; instead, she asked Lady Michelham's chauffeur to drive her to the scene of the accident. According to the driver, Chanel stood beside the wrecked car, which had not yet been moved from where it had crashed at the side of the road, and touched it with her hands, as if it were a living creature. Then she sat down and wept, and this time the tears overflowed.

'In losing Capel, I lost everything,' she told Paul Morand, a quarter of a century later. But she did not lose the House of Chanel that Boy had helped her to establish. And despite his betrayals, Capel did not stop providing for her after his death, along with the rest of his female dependants. When his will was published, by far the largest portion of his estate of £700,000 went to his wife and child (and future legal proceedings ensured that part of his fortune was passed to his second daughter, June, born in the summer of 1920, whose conception he had been unaware of at the time of his death). The will also included a bequest of £40,000 to Mademoiselle Chanel; an equal sum was left to an Italian countess, a young widow whose husband had been killed in the war. Chanel's share was sufficient to invest further in her business (she expanded her premises in Rue Cambon), and to buy a villa of her own, Bel Respiro, in Garches, on the western outskirts of Paris.

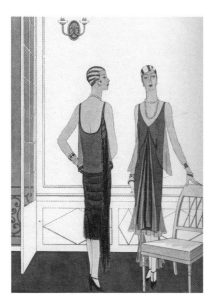

Variations of Chanel's little black dress, published in French *Vogue*, April 1926.

Diana Capel was to marry for a third and final time in 1923 – to the 14th Earl of Westmorland – and became a longstanding client of Chanel. But in circumstances that remain a tantalising mystery, Diana and Coco had somehow established an acquaintance in the aftermath of Boy Capel's death. For it was from Bel Respiro that Diana Capel wrote an undated letter to Duff Cooper, presumably soon after Chanel had moved into her newly redecorated villa in March 1920. 'My dear Duff,' wrote Diana, from the house of Chanel, 'I haven't written before to thank you for the letters because I have been, and still am, and I suppose shall go on being so terribly, desperately unhappy, but I like to feel your sympathy surrounds me and that you are thinking of me.'

What, one wonders, did Coco and Diana think of each other? Both had suffered the loss of Boy Capel, and both had been made to suffer by him. Duff Cooper recorded in his diary in January 1920 that at the time of Capel's death, Diana's relationship with her husband had become 'impossible'; 'he had entirely ceased to live with her and hardly ever spoke to her … he confessed she had got on his nerves and he could hardly bear her presence.' No record survives of what passed between Coco and the pregnant Diana. Indeed, no one appears to have known of their time spent together then; and notwithstanding the curious bond they shared, one can only speculate about the origins and nature of their relationship. Julian Fane, Diana's son from her third marriage, observed her enduring reticence on the subject of Capel and Chanel. 'I can recall my mother referring to Boy Capel only twice,' wrote Fane in a memoir about his mother, 'to say he was very witty and amusing on occasions and if he wanted to be, and to complain that Chanel had refused to return furniture he had lent her.' But Fane knew from his mother's friends that Diana had been unhappy from the early days of her marriage; before she gave birth to her first daughter, she had spent Easter alone in Paris, 'minus her husband and crying in front of a fire that was also out.' As for her part, Chanel kept her feelings about Diana private.

Chanel's grief at Capel's death was too profound to remain entirely hidden; she manifested her bereavement by ordering that Bel Respiro be painted beige on the outside, but with its window shutters lacquered in black, so that when the shutters were fastened, it was as if the eyes of the house were closed. In her previous house in Saint Cloud, where Capel had visited her, she had commanded that her bedroom be decorated in black – walls, ceiling, carpet, sheets – all in the colour of mourning in memory of her dead lover. After only one night, however, she changed her mind, giving instructions that the decorator should redo it in pink, and telling her butler, 'Get me out of this tomb.'

One of the surprising things about Boy Capel, the playboy industrialist, was that he was also a theosophist, and taught Coco that there was a life after death, although not of the kind she had been educated to believe in at Aubazine. 'Nothing dies, not even a grain of sand, so nothing is lost,' she later told

Claude Delay, in explanation of Capel's theosophy and its influence on her. 'I like that very much.' Any bitterness she had felt towards Capel appears to have been removed from her public celebration of his memory. To Paul Morand, she spoke of his 'rare spirit' and his 'gentle authority', which she never found in another man. 'Beneath his dandyism, he was very serious, far more cultured than the polo players and big businessmen, with a deep inner life that extended to magical and theosophical levels.' If her belief in his power contained an element of magical thinking, then it was true to his own. Six months after his death, she said to Morand, she received a visit from 'an unknown Hindu gentleman', who gave her complete faith that Capel was watching over her, still offering her his protection. According to this story, the Hindu gentleman said to her: 'I have a message for you, Mademoiselle. A message from someone you know … This person is living in a place of happiness, in a world where nothing can trouble him any longer. Receive this message of which I am the bearer, and whose meaning you will certainly understand.' She did not tell Morand – nor anyone else – the details, but her faith in Capel was restored: 'it was a secret that no one, other than Capel and I, could have known.'

So the wishful link was kept intact, and although it was secret – as mysterious as the mosaic symbols in Aubazine; as cryptic as a medieval Catholic code – it nevertheless survived Capel's death. And whatever the details of Capel's message to Chanel, something of their bond has endured. There is the double C, and there is black; the colour of mourning turned into a celebration of chic. True, the little black dress wasn't formally identified as the shape of the future until 1926, when American *Vogue* published a drawing of a Chanel design, and announced: 'Here is a Ford signed Chanel.' It was an apparently simple yet elegant sheath, in black crêpe de Chine, with long narrow sleeves, worn with a string of white pearls; and *Vogue* proved to be correct in the prediction that it would become a uniform, as widely recognised as a Ford automobile; fast and sleek and discreet.

The black dress, nevertheless, had made its appearance long before that. Chanel herself identified its origins as dating back to 1920, in a conversation with Paul Morand: 'At about that time, I remember contemplating the auditorium at the Opera from the back of a box.' She understood her own mind by then – she did not need anyone to tell her that a tiara should be worn to the opera. And she did not approve of what she saw before her: 'those reds, those greens, those electric blues', brought into fashion by her great rival, Paul Poiret, 'made me feel ill.' And

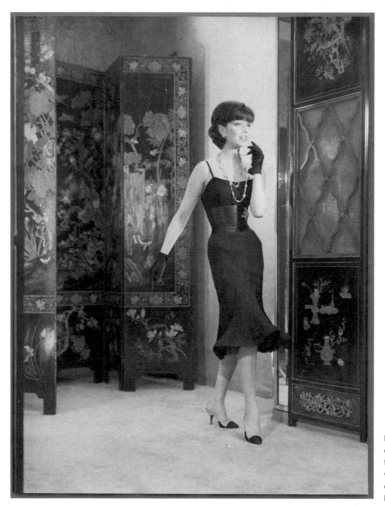

Marie-Hélène Arnaud,
one of Chanel's
favourite models,
wearing a black
chiffon cocktail dress.
Peter Fink, 1959.

so – or so she said to Morand – Coco made a vow to herself: 'These colours are impossible. These women, I'm bloody well going to dress them in black … I imposed black; it's still going strong today, for black wipes out everything else around.'

But Coco Chanel was not wiped out; she was not consumed in the wreckage of the end of her affair with Boy Capel. She moved onwards, propelled into the Jazz Age; even propelling the age forward in her own image; carrying other women with her in her wake, out of the past and into the future, wearing black as a symbol of strength and freedom.

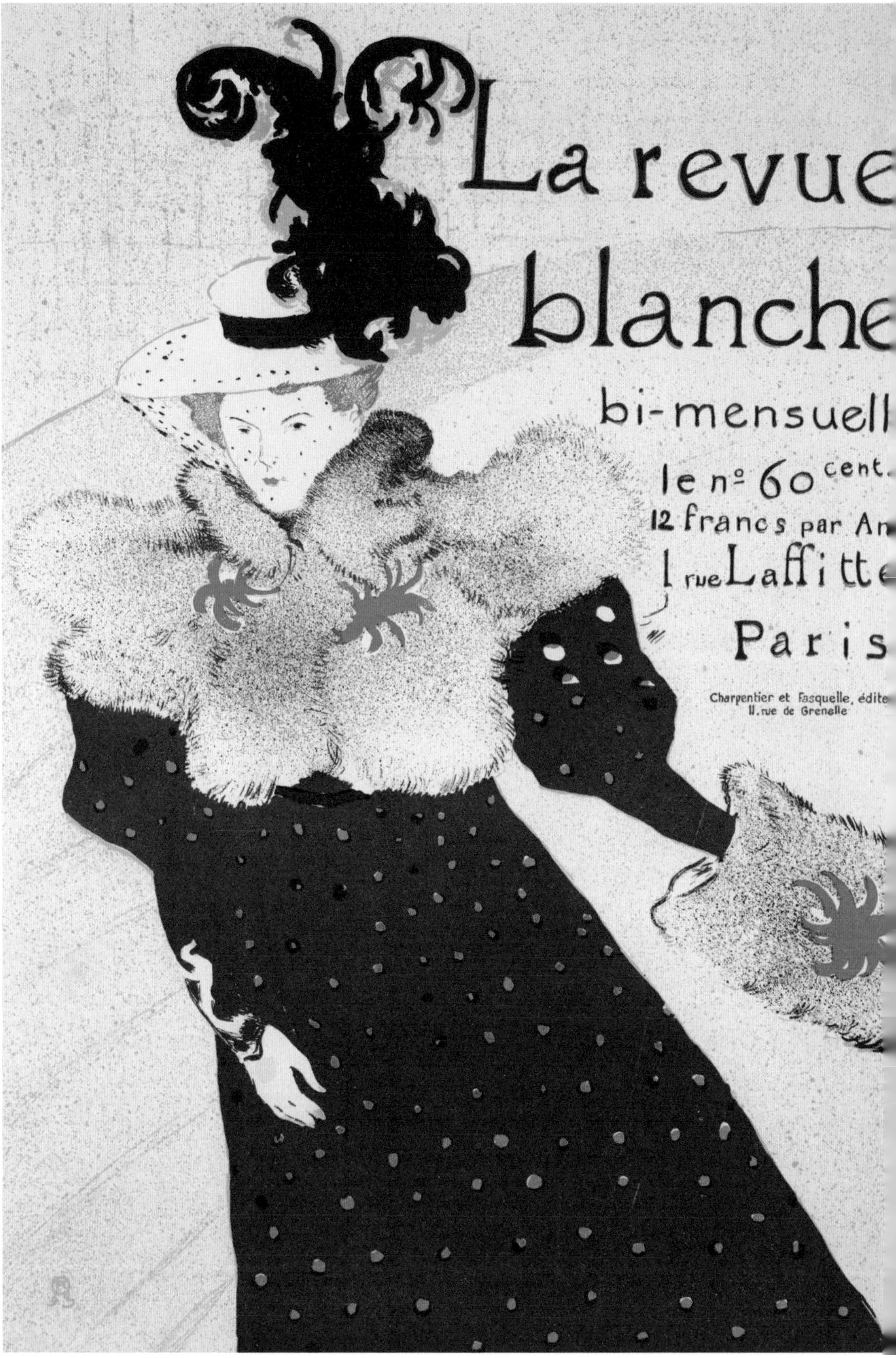
La revue
blanche
bi-mensuell
le nº 60 cent.
12 francs par An
1 rue Laffitte
Paris
Charpentier et Fasquelle, édite
11, rue de Grenelle

MISIA AND THE MUSE

If Boy Capel was the love of Chanel's life, then Misia Sert was her closest friend; not that the two women's relationship was always friendly, for it was too passionate to be contained by friendship, and sometimes spilled over into jealousy, even hatred, occasionally with what seemed like sexual intensity. That their relationship began when Capel was already turning his attentions away from Chanel is not coincidental; and if Misia's own description of the meeting is to be believed, it was love at first sight, at least on her part.

Misia – who was so famous at the time that she was known throughout Paris by her first name – met Chanel in 1917. This was an era when Misia was queen of the city, a muse who had reigned over artists since her youth, capricious and compelling, a law unto herself, with a court who paid heed to all her pronouncements. 'What I admire in Misia is that *joie de vivre* always concealed behind a mask of ill-humour; that perfect poise, even in moments of despair,' observed Paul Morand in his diary in April 1917. 'And then Misia is Misia, someone with no equal and, as Proust says, a monument.' As such, she had been painted by Renoir, Vuillard, Lautrec and Bonnard; inspired the poetry of Mallarmé, the prose of Proust, the music of Debussy and Ravel, and the gossip of Cocteau and Picasso. A gifted pianist herself, Misia had sat on Liszt's knee and performed Beethoven for him as a child. 'Ah, if only I could play like that,' he said, with his customary charm, and predicted a dazzling

Henri de Toulouse-Lautrec's poster for *La Revue blanche* (1895), for which Misia Sert modelled.

CHANEL 95

future for her; thereafter, Misia was taught the piano by Fauré, who regarded her as a prodigy. Her powerful position at the centre of the inner circle of Parisian art was consolidated by virtue of her close friendship with Serge Diaghilev, the director of the most sought-after ballet company in the world at the time, Ballets Russes. Chanel was 11 years younger, and not yet as socially pivotal in Parisian society, but Misia fell for her when they met at a dinner party at the home of Cécile Sorel, a glamorous French actress who was already a client at Rue Cambon.

Sorel was living in an apartment on the Quai Voltaire, where the windows were draped with leopardskin; 'somewhat moth-eaten', recalled Misia in an unpublished chapter from her memoirs, which she dictated in the late Forties. 'At the table my attention was immediately drawn to a very dark-haired young woman. Despite the fact that she did not say a word, she radiated a charm I found irresistible. She made me think of Madame du Barry [an eighteenth-century milliner's-assistant-turned-courtesan; mistress to Louis XV, and guillotined in the French Revolution]. Therefore I arranged to sit next to her after dinner. During the exchange of banalities appropriate to a first meeting in a salon, I learned that she was called Mademoiselle Chanel and had a milliner's shop in the Rue Cambon.

'She seemed to me gifted with infinite grace and when, as we were saying goodnight, I admired her ravishing fur-trimmed red velvet coat, she took it off at once and put it on my shoulders, saying with charming spontaneity that she would be only too happy to give it to me. Obviously I could not accept it. But her gesture had been so pretty that I found her completely bewitching and thought of nothing but her.'

Misia went straight to Rue Cambon the following morning in search of the woman who had so enchanted her. 'In her little boutique one found sweaters, hats, and accessories of all kinds. When I arrived, two women were there talking about her, calling her "Coco". I don't know why the use of this name upset me so, but my heart sank: I had the impression that my idol was being smashed. Why trick out someone so exceptional with so vulgar a name? I was indignant!'

And then Chanel herself appeared, 'the woman I had been thinking about since the night before'. Misia started talking to her, and did not stop; Chanel hardly spoke a word. 'Magically, the hours sped by … The thought of parting from her seemed unbearable.' That night, Misia and José-Maria Sert, a flamboyant Spanish painter who was to become her third husband, went to dinner at Chanel's apartment. 'There, in the midst of countless Coromandel screens, we found Boy Capel, who represented important British interests in Paris.'

But Misia had eyes only for Chanel; to such an extent that her lover (who, like Capel, had his own '*petites amies*') was somewhat discomfited. 'Sert was really scandalized by the astonishing infatuation I felt for my new friend. I was not in the habit of being carried away like this ...'

In fact, Misia was frequently carried away by passion: for artists, musicians, husbands, ballets; for melodrama and tragedy, in which she was often centre-stage. But she also had a talent for amusement; for amusing others, and herself, amidst the tumultuous sagas that she created around her, and those that were not of her own design. Misia was the inspiration for Cocteau's heroine, the Princesse de Bormes, in his novel *Thomas l'imposteur*, and his description of her still has a compelling immediacy, even now, when she has been relegated to a

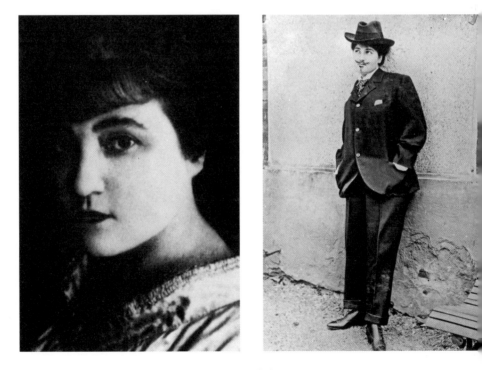

Left: Misia, 1905. Right: Misia dressed as a man, circa 1910.

footnote in the histories of others. 'She played with life the way a virtuoso plays the piano. Like a virtuoso, she was able to create great effects as easily with mediocre as with the most beautiful music. Her duty was pleasure … She had understood, unlike most women in her set, that pleasure is not to be found in things themselves but in the way you take them …' And at well over 40, the Princesse, like Misia, 'had sparkling eyes in the face of a young girl, eyes that boredom could deaden in a second'.

Born in St Petersburg on 30th March 1872, Misia was the daughter of a Polish sculptor, Cyprian Godebski. Her mother, Eugénie Sophie Servais, died giving birth to her, having followed her unfaithful husband to Russia when she was nearly nine months pregnant. Misia's story was even more dramatic than Chanel's: at the time of her birth, her father was having an affair with his mother-in-law's sister, who became pregnant with his child. This muddled state of affairs was not improved by Godebski's lack of interest in Misia, or any of his other children; they were handed on from his mistresses to wives to assorted relatives, while he pursued his successful career as an artist. Yet despite (or perhaps because of) her father's absences and neglect, Misia grew up to fall in love with charismatic men who subsequently abandoned her in the unhappiest of circumstances.

Like Chanel, she was educated by nuns, although the high walls that confined Misia were in the heart of Paris, at the Convent of the Sacred Heart on the Boulevard des Invalides (now the Rodin Museum). She was sent there at the age of 10, after the death of her maternal aunt, who had previously been caring for her; though Misia continued to see her father and stepmother, Matylda Natanson, on at least a monthly basis, at their grand house in the Polish district of Paris, near the Parc Monceau. Her stepmother died when Misia was 15, whereupon her father summoned his daughter from the convent, and ordered her to kiss the corpse. Misia later recalled that she never forgot the terror of that enforced kiss, or the sight of the veiled lady standing beside her father at the bedside, his mistress, Catherine, the Marquise de Ganville.

Misia's life continued in this theatrical manner, like the gothic romances she was fond of reading as a girl; yet despite her tendency to lop years off her life with a similar alacrity to Chanel (both women altered the birth dates in their passports, erasing a decade with a stroke of their pens), she had no need to invent the details of her extraordinary escapades. That some of her adventures sound implausible makes them no less real. But they were often marked by a curious

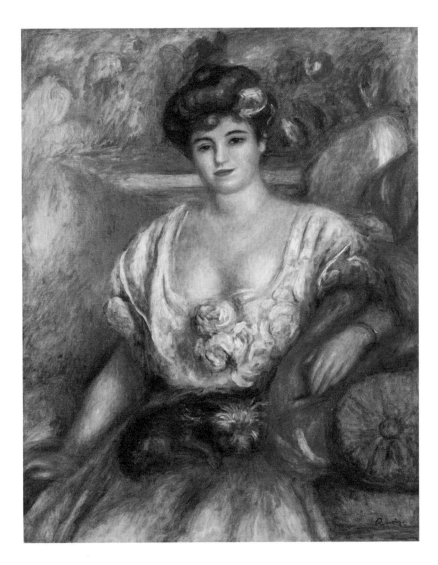

blurring of the boundaries of her familial and emotional ties; a reflection, perhaps, of her father's somewhat incestuous relationship with his wife's aunt. Misia's first husband, for example, was her first stepmother's nephew; and if that seems confusing, then what followed was even more complicated. Married at 21 to Thadée Natanson, the editor of *La Revue blanche*, an influential avant-garde arts magazine, Misia was subsequently pushed into the arms of Alfred Edwards, a

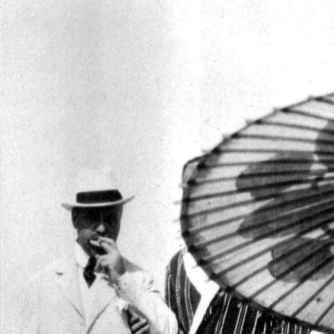

newspaper magnate with an immense fortune and vast property holdings, including the Théâtre de Paris and its adjoining casino. In a drama that enthralled Paris, it was Natanson himself who did the pushing, after he resolved to hand over his wife in return for financial rescue by Edwards. The latter had fallen for Misia as soon as he first saw her (and what Edwards wanted, Edwards got, even if he had to pay dearly for it). Misia was 28 at the time, and the ensuing triangular relationship was not yet resolved five years later, when she married Edwards in 1905; for whatever else the consequences of the wedding, resolution was nigh on impossible with a man of such violent and peculiar passions. Edwards' chief sexual perversion was coprophilia, but his jealousy could be equally disturbing; he was so possessive that when he took Misia to Madrid in 1903, he confined her to their hotel room, aside from the occasional shopping expedition. 'Edwards went out alone, after carefully locking the door of my room,' she recalled in her memoir. 'I spent whole days locked up. He was as jealous as a wild animal, and I should not have been surprised to hear him roaring outside my door.'

Eventually, his obsession with Misia burnt itself out, and he fell in love with another woman, a bisexual demimondaine-turned-actress named Geneviève Lantelme, who had embarked upon her career in her mother's brothel at the age of 14. Edwards and Misia were divorced in February 1909, four years after their wedding; he promptly married his quarrelsome, cocaine-snorting mistress, who drowned in the Rhine in 1911 after falling overboard (some say she was pushed) from Edwards' yacht. He died of influenza in 1914, by which time Misia was already involved with José-Maria Sert, another larger-than-life figure, whose ambitions were evident in the gigantic, elephantine frescos and Rococo murals that he made for the ballroom of the Waldorf-Astoria hotel in New York, and subsequently for the Rockefeller Center.

This, then, was the couple that Coco met in 1917, and after Capel's death, she was swept further into their tempestuous emotional life. 'Misia has been my only woman friend,' recalled Chanel to Paul Morand 30 years later, in an occasionally sour reminiscence that seems to suggest something other than friendship. Thus she ascribed the catalyst for their relationship – or rather, for Misia's intensifying attachment to her – as being the death of Boy Capel: 'I have seen her appear at the moment of my greatest grieving; other people's grief lures her, just as certain fragrances lure the bee.'

Chanel professed herself to be unimpressed by Misia. To others, she was the Divine Misia, but apparently not to Chanel. 'We only like people because of

...anel (left), Misia (centre) and Madame Philippe Berthelot (right) on the beach the Venice Lido, circa 1930.

CHANEL 101

their failings,' she said to Morand. 'Misia gave me ample and countless reasons for liking her.' Chanel then proceeded to eviscerate her friend, at some length and with apparent relish. 'Misia is to Paris what the goddess Kali is to the Hindu pantheon. She is simultaneously the goddess of destruction and of creation. She kills and scatters her germs, without realising … She is like the St Bernard who brings you back to shore with your head under water.' Clearly, Misia got under Chanel's skin, although Chanel preferred to see herself as tough enough to resist penetration, and Misia as a parasite that could not gain entry. 'She was never able to find the chink in the armour, which nevertheless exists. For a quarter-of-a-century, the worm has made its way around the fruit without ever being able to get inside it.'

But before the rivalry, there was sympathy and affection. As Chanel (somewhat grudgingly) admitted to Morand, she turned to Misia and Sert (nicknamed Jojo by Misia) after Capel's death, for they 'were moved to see a young woman weeping her heart out in grief … So began a close relationship which would last until Sert's death, with all the ripples that a clash of characters as entrenched as ours can stir up.' Such was the intensity that after the Serts' wedding in August 1920, they took Chanel with them on their honeymoon to Italy; if not a sexual ménage-à-trois, it nevertheless seemed to enthral all of them.

In her subsequent description of the episode to Paul Morand, some of this mutual bewitchment emerges, as well as the strangeness (and occasional estrangement). Both women were captivated by Sert; indeed, Misia had fallen in love with him on a previous trip to Italy, where by day he had brought alive for her the paintings of Caravaggio and Tintoretto, and by night had seduced her with more conversation, as well as by other means. When Sert talked to Misia, as she later recalled in her memoir, his words were 'punctuated by hands so eloquent that I was hypnotised by his thumbs, which turned into the air like question marks – thumbs that were animated, rough, ferocious, inquisitorial, caressing and domineering: the thumbs of an artist and, at the same time, a conqueror.'

Chanel gave an equally visceral description of Sert to Paul Morand, but her fascination was tinged with disgust: 'This huge, hairy monkey, with his tinted beard, his humped back … loved everything colossal. He slept in black pyjamas, never washed, and, even naked, looked as though he was wearing a fur coat, so hirsute was he … He had hair everywhere, except on his head.' Nevertheless, something of his extraordinary physicality appealed to her, as did his erudition; Sert, she said, 'guided me through museums like a faun through a familiar forest'. He was 'the ideal travelling companion', she continued, 'always good humoured', leading Misia and Chanel on rambling expeditions across Italy 'in search of some osteria where you could eat birds rolled in vine leaves'. When they got lost, he bought a pig and roasted it by the side of the road; and although both Misia and Chanel ate very little, 'Sert, who was lavish by nature, ordered rare wines, and meals that made our table look like a painting by Veronese or Parmigiano.' If Chanel told him not to order any more food, as she could not – would not – eat it, he replied, 'I shall order another three zabagliones with maraschino cherries! Whether you want it or not!'

And yet for all his life-loving bonhomie, Chanel was aware of something macabre about Sert; which may have been part of what enchanted her, as it did Misia. Both women told different versions of a story about Sert and a stork: Misia declared that he had seen a stork die of hunger in front of a mound of food because its beak had been sawn off; Chanel passed on Cocteau's gossip that it was Sert himself who had cut off the stork's beak. Neither of them appear to have made the association with the stork as mythic emblem of fertility, the white bird that brings a newborn baby to earth; or as a Christian symbol of the Annunciation, the revelation to Mary that she would conceive a child who would be born the Son of God. But the mutilated stork – which occasionally turned into a swan in Chanel's memory – seemed to be in some sense present in the minds of these two childless women. Not that they alluded to their childlessness on the honeymoon with Sert. Instead, they listened to him talk about the beauty of the dead, and the glamour of decay. When they first arrived in Rome, at night, weary from the journey, Sert coaxed Chanel and Misia out on a tour of the city by moonlight. At the Coliseum, he conjured up for them the parties that might still take place there amidst the ruins, with balloons painted gold, floating light in the darkness. A quarter of a century later, Chanel told Morand that she would never forget 'the wonderful things' he said to her in his beguiling Spanish accent, turning French into a language all his own: 'Architecture is the skeleton of the city. Everything is in the skeleton, Madmachelle; a face without bones doesn't last: you, for example, Madmachelle, you would make a very beautiful corpse.'

But Chanel also recognised his capacity for cruelty, and his art left her confused and alienated: 'those swollen muscles, those demented contortions of figures'. In retrospect, Sert seemed to her as grotesque as his paintings, yet still compelling: 'an enormous gnome who, inside his hump, like a magic sack, carried gold as well as rubbish, extremely poor taste and exquisite judgement,

the priceless and the disgusting, diamonds and crap, kindness and sadism …'
And it was Sert – the man who cut off a stork's beak – along with Misia, 'a
parasite of the heart', who were to rescue Chanel from her consuming grief over
Boy Capel. On that strange honeymoon trip to Italy – the Serts' nuptial
celebrations, when Chanel was still in funereal mourning for Capel – she found
herself in a church. 'One day I went to ask St Anthony of Padua to help me to
stop mourning,' she told Paul Morand.

'I can still see myself in the church, before the statue of the saint, to the left,
among the fine sarcophagi of Venetian admirals. A man in front of me was
resting his forehead against the stone slab; he had such a sad and beautiful
face, there was so much rigidity and pain in him, and his exhausted head
touched the ground with such weariness that a miracle took place within me. I'm
a wretch, I told myself; how shameful! How could I dare compare my sorrow of
a lost child, for whom life has scarcely begun, with someone in this distress? An
energy immediately flowed through me. I took new heart and decided to live.'

Her allusive reference to a lost child might seem to have no place in the
triangle of Misia and Sert and Chanel; although she often referred to herself as
a child in her narrative to Morand – a naive girl with Etienne Balsan and Boy
Capel, too young to know what she was doing. She still had an air of
youthfulness, as the embodiment of the chic *garçonne* look that was the
prevailing fashion of the time. *Vogue* acclaimed Chanel as possessing 'the secret
of eternal youth'; yet in 1920, on her journey to Italy, she turned 37; a birthday
that she may or may not have acknowledged, for she had already obscured the
year of her birth. Capel was dead, and her nephew, who had almost – but not
quite – come to represent their son, was far away, being educated at boarding
school as an English gentleman. (As for Capel's own daughters: Diana Capel
had returned to England with their little girl, Ann, before giving birth to his second
and posthumous baby, in June 1920, just a few weeks before Chanel went on
honeymoon with Misia.) But if Chanel had claimed the role as lost child, she
nevertheless behaved with adult guile.

By then, Chanel was already becoming entangled in a power struggle with
Misia – not for Misia's husband, but to supplant her in some other, less clear-cut
way. It was in the course of that summer in Italy that Chanel became a silent
witness to Misia's intense friendship with Diaghilev; and in Venice that she
listened to their discussions about how he was to raise enough money to revive
Le Sacre du printemps, the ballet that had caused uproar in Paris when it was

first performed in 1913. Money, or the lack of it, was always an issue for Diaghilev, and therefore for his creation, the Ballets Russes, which he loved as dearly, and ferociously, as if it were his only child (although if it were, then his impulses were also incestuous, given his passionate relationships with a sequence of the ballet's leading men, from Nijinsky to Serge Lifar). Perhaps Chanel felt excluded at first; certainly, there is a hint of jealousy in her description to Paul Morand of Misia's relationship with Diaghilev: 'Misia never left Diaghilev's side; between them it was one of those whispered, doting relationships, spiteful, affectionate, riddled with snares ...'

The snares were evident to Chanel, possibly because she had set at least one of them. After she returned to Paris from Italy, she made an unannounced visit to Diaghilev and told him that she was prepared to help him finance a revival of Le Sacre du printemps, on the condition that he did not mention this to anyone. Given the closeness of his relationship with Misia, one might assume that Chanel could not have expected Diaghilev to remain silent; and yet, in asking him to keep this secret in return for the 300,000 francs he desperately needed from her, she was creating a bond between them. Her motives may have been purely artistic; certainly she told Paul Morand that while bankrolling Diaghilev, she preferred not to take any credit in return. 'I did not prevent Diaghilev's ballets from collapsing, as people have said,' she remarked to Morand. 'I had never seen Le Sacre du printemps before 1914. Serge spoke about it as if it had caused a scandal and been a great historical moment. I wanted to hear it and to offer to subsidise it. I don't regret the 300,000 francs that it cost me.'

One wonders what it cost Misia to discover that her protégée had pre-empted her; the younger woman going behind her back, straight to the great Diaghilev, and thereby becoming a patron, if not quite a muse. An even clearer signal of Chanel's arrival in the world of avant-garde art came in 1922, when Jean Cocteau asked her to design the costumes for his stage adaptation of Antigone. The production opened in Paris at the fashionably experimental Théâtre de l'Atelier in December 1922, with sets by Picasso (a vast blue seaside sky and white Greek columns); music composed by Arthur Honegger; and costumes by Chanel, 'because she is the greatest couturière of our age,' according to Cocteau, 'and it is impossible to imagine the daughters of Oedipus poorly dressed.' Vogue agreed: the February 1923 issue of the American and French editions of the magazine ran extensive coverage of her designs under the headline 'Chanel Goes Greek While Remaining French', and praised her sensitive approach. Antigone's 'heavy white wool robe … is exactly the robe we see on Delphic vases; it is a beautiful recreation of something archaic that has bcen intelligently illuminated.'

Chanel's position as a participant in art, rather than simply a patron, was further consolidated when she designed the costumes for the Ballets Russes production of *Le Train bleu* in 1924, working alongside Picasso, who created the stage curtain and programme. It was at this crucial point that Misia, whether motivated by real concern or mounting envy, declared that she must protect Chanel from Picasso – as if his magnetism needed her intervention – which caused Chanel such irritation that she was still complaining about it over 20 years later to Paul Morand. 'I had no need of being protected from anyone except from Misia. For where Misia has once loved, the grass doesn't grow any more.'

Thus Chanel's relationship with Misia grew murkier, overshadowed by her suspicion that Misia was always scheming; or as she said to Morand, 'sniffing some dark intrigue'. (It was to Morand, too, that she quoted the musician Erik Satie's observation about Misia: 'Here comes the cat, let's hide our birds …')

Into this potent, unsettling liaison came a poet: Pierre Reverdy, a man as charismatic as Diaghilev, as close to the heart of the avant-garde as Picasso; and even more passionately committed to the art of Modernism than Misia or Chanel. Later, he wrote, 'I pity those who, having lived through that marvellous period, failed to participate in it, sharing its often disheartening and painful trials, its incomparably powerful emotions, its spiritual felicity. I doubt that there has ever been so much blue sky or sun in the entire history of art, or so much responsibility heroically assumed.' Six years younger than Chanel, Reverdy was an ardent advocate of the idea of the artist as mythic hero; he was sensitive, mystic, troubled, impoverished, and married, to a seamstress named Henriette with whom he shared a garret in Montmartre. Misia discovered him first, just as she had discovered so many talented artists, buying his self-published books of poetry (the binding hand-sewn by his devoted wife) when no one else was interested; then helping to finance his short-lived yet influential journal, *Nord-Sud*, which Reverdy had founded in 1917 alongside his fellow writers Max Jacob and Guillaume Apollinaire. It was named after the Métro line that ran between Montmartre and Montparnasse, the two centres of bohemian Paris where Reverdy's friends and peers were at the forefront of Surrealism, Cubism and Dadaism; and with Reverdy as editor, *Nord-Sud* led the way in publishing the early works of Louis Aragon and André Breton, with illustrations by Fernand Léger, Georges Braque, Juan Gris and André Derain.

Reverdy's companions also included Picasso, who illustrated a book of his poems and drew a portrait of him in 1921, hair cut short, tie neatly knotted; the apparent antithesis of bohemian Paris, yet a fellow inhabitant of the Montmartre tenement where Picasso, Gris and Modigliani lived and painted, 'with no support other than their own keenness and daring', according to Reverdy. In fact, Misia did all she could to sustain them, and was swift to introduce the young poet into

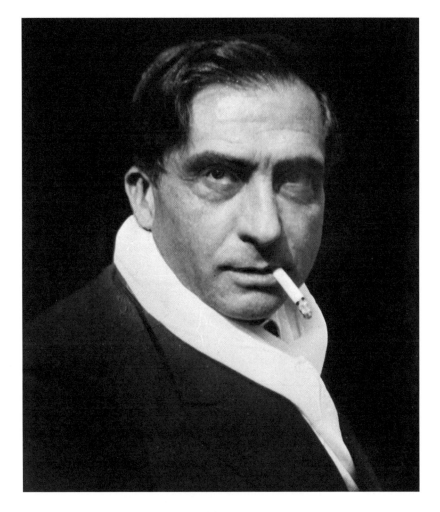

Pierre Reverdy, the French poet and lover of Chanel. Albert Harlingue.

her salon, where he watched the rich and great at play. Lobster was served on silver platters by a white-suited Polish butler, while Misia's blue macaw shrieked amidst the barbed chatter of the guests. 'Life in society is one huge adventure in piracy and cannot be successful without a great deal of conniving,' observed Reverdy, the son of a Languedoc wine-grower and grandson of a woodcarver and stonemason; a man who saw himself as separate to Misia's world of chic Parisian society, and yet found himself drawn into it. He was, he said, 'the one who only came to see, not to be seen', but Misia liked what she saw in him: his dark hair and darker eyes, and something else, beneath his skin, which she described as 'the radiant beauty that never dies'.

Reverdy responded to Misia with more than simply gratitude for her patronage: he respected her as a literary judge of his work, and was also sympathetic to her sorrows, as well as her passions. When she wrote to him praising his poetry, he replied, 'I am happy that it moved you and that the life from which it springs and the sincerity which – in the absence of talent – has given it birth should have found an echo in the life and in the sincerity which are yours … From your letter I see that your life, however blessed with pockets of light, is not without its dark colours and layers of bitterness.'

It was Misia who introduced Reverdy to Chanel after the death of Boy Capel; possibly as a diversionary tactic of some kind, although as was often the case, her precise motives remained unfathomable. But Reverdy seemed to have already fallen for Misia, his wife notwithstanding. 'I love you so much, I think of you with so much tenderness,' he declared in an undated letter to Misia, written while he was on a retreat from Paris, in the Benedictine abbey of Solesmes in Normandy. 'You cannot imagine how much or in what way. Sometimes one of your phrases, a word you have spoken to me, strikes my heart, and then this sweetness is mixed with the bitterness of not being able to embrace you, to put my hand on yours, of not being able to see you.'

Despite this declaration of love, and Misia's undoubted affection and admiration for Reverdy, the two did not embark upon an affair. Instead, the poet's passion was transferred to Chanel, and Misia appeared to offer her tacit approval, urging her friend to spend time alone with him, and to read his poetry, in much the same way that Sert had encouraged Chanel to discover the glories within the museums and art galleries of Italy. Whatever else Misia's intentions, perhaps she recognised in Reverdy the contrasts that were in some ways reflected in Chanel; these two outsiders drawn to Paris, both of them compelled by its sophisticated society, yet also suspicious of it. Reverdy had arrived in Paris in 1910, not long after Chanel established herself there, and although he was prone to silence, as she was (at least at the beginning of her career), he also had tumultuous outbursts. 'I was born to be a boxer, a bullfighter,' he said to Picasso. 'But thank God poetry, like painting, is a man's work and tough, a violent combat that is decided in one single round.'

As contradictory and contrary a character as Chanel, Reverdy also declared that, to be a poet, one must be ascetic. His dictum – both for himself, and for the Surrealists influenced by him – was 'to work on an empty stomach and in a cold state'; the opposite approach to that advocated by Rimbaud ('the systemic disorder of all the senses'). In order to create, said Reverdy, an artist must retain lucidity, 'to seize the object on the wing'; and there is a faint echo of his words in Chanel's subsequent maxim: 'Fashion is not simply a matter of clothes; fashion is in the air, borne upon the wind ...' She did not see herself as an artist like him – she repeatedly described herself as an artisan who 'works with her hand' – and yet her precision and commitment to her craft was reminiscent of Reverdy. Like him, she seized what she saw 'on the wing', making the elusive into something material. But unlike him, she became rich in doing so; and while material gain eluded Reverdy, he also eluded Chanel. She had left the abbey of Aubazine far behind her, even though its shadows and purity were incorporated into her work; but she could not keep her poet beside her. Reverdy, a committed Catholic convert, fled from Paris to the abbey of Solesmes in 1925, needing its silence and austerity in order to write; his wife joined the adjacent nunnery, where she remained for the rest of her life. He spent two years at Solesmes without seeing anyone outside the monastic community; then returned to Paris for a short time in 1927, before disappearing once again to the abbey, where he lived as a recluse until his death in 1960.

At some point, before his withdrawal from Paris to the abbey, Reverdy and Chanel fell in love, with Misia as an observer, almost a third party to their secret relationship, like Reverdy's silent wife. He gave Chanel his books, inscribing his name, and hers, in the frontispieces of slim volumes that she treasured alongside her famous collection of diamonds and pearls; and he continued to present her with his first editions, sometimes his manuscripts, with handwritten dedications, from 1921 to his death in 1960. (On the 1926 manuscript of *La Peau de l'homme*, he wrote to her, 'You do not know, dear Coco, that light is best set off by shadow.')

She gave him her own words, too, a selection of aphorisms that she paid him to polish to perfection. Reverdy was dependent on her financial support, and she may have offered him this task as a tactful way of providing him with some vital income; and yet he also remained independent from her, in an unspoken balancing act, which pivoted upon Chanel's respect for him. Long after their affair ended, she continued to express her admiration for Reverdy, celebrating his writing as consummate artistry, and expressing her dismay that others had eclipsed him in fame and worldly success. When he advised her to read François de La Rochefoucauld's seventeenth-century *Maximes*, she did so, and strived to emulate his concision in epigrams of her own, refined and reworked by Reverdy:

'If you were born without wings, do nothing to prevent their growing.'

'Luxury is a necessity that begins where necessity ends.'

'True generosity means accepting ingratitude.'

'To disguise oneself is charming: to have oneself disguised is sad.'

'For a woman, to deceive makes only one kind of sense: that of the senses.'

In doing so, Chanel was not his muse, nor simply his patron, but they did participate together in a form of artistic enterprise, beyond the usual conception and formations of a love affair. She used Reverdy to hone herself, in her ongoing act of self-creation, so that she dazzled alongside the Divine Misia (perhaps gathering strength from the knowledge that her polished sheen would be offset by the simplicity of her trademark little black dress). The oddness of this collaboration did not detract from its power – the self-made woman drawing upon a man who sought to lose himself in faith; a couturière for whom fashion was a religion, falling in love with a poet for whom mysticism and materialism combined in the striking imagery of his work. 'Jewels are caught in the lyre/ Black butterflies of delirium', he wrote in 'Le Coeur tournant', a poem first published in 1931, although possibly written before then (*'Les bijoux sont pris dans la lyre/ Les papillons noirs du délire …'*). And while 'Toujours l'amour' – a poem that appeared at the beginning of 1927, at the same time as Reverdy resurfaced in Paris – is generally interpreted as an otherworldly exploration of the love of God, it contains within it the gleam of the worldly, a proliferation of light, in a luminous vision of diamonds and pearls. (*'Sous les lueurs des plantes rares/ les joues roses des cerisiers/ les diamants de la distance/ Et les perles dont elle se pare.'*)

Reverdy wrote in the shadow of the abbey of Solesmes, his faith in God sometimes shaken by doubt; Chanel worked beneath the dazzle of her crystal chandeliers, her faith in herself occasionally receding into the darkness at the corner of the room. The contemporary writer Paul Auster has observed, 'Reverdy's strange landscapes, which combine an intense inwardness with a proliferation of sensual data, bear in them the signs of a continual search for an impossible totality. Almost mystical in their effect, his poems are nevertheless anchored in the minutiae of the everyday world; in their quiet, at times monotone music, the poet seems to evaporate, to vanish into the haunted country he has created. The result is at once beautiful and disquieting, as if Reverdy had emptied the space of the poem in order to let the reader inhabit it.'

Open one of the faded leather-bound volumes of Reverdy's poetry that still stand on a bookshelf in Chanel's private apartment, and she seems close at hand, hovering in that mysterious white space between the poet's enigmatic lines, shimmering for an instant. Then she vanishes, as you leaf through the pages; but perhaps once upon a time she found herself there, a perfect composition of darkness and light, just as a reader or writer would have wished her to be.

Handwritten dedication from Pierre Reverdy to Chanel in the frontispiece of *Pierre Reverdy* by Jean Rousselot and Michel Manoll:
Chère Coco
Le temps qui passe
Le temps qu'il fait
Le temps qui fuit
De mon obscure vie
j'avais perdu la trace
La voilà retrouvée plus
sombre que la nuit
Mais ce qui reste clair
c'est que de tout
mon cœur je vous
embrasse
Et qu'importe tout ce
qui suit
P.

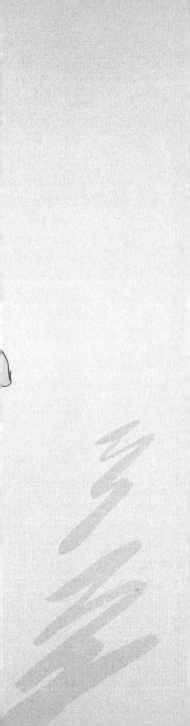

NUMBER FIVE

'Paul Valéry used to say: "A woman who doesn't wear perfume has no future." Well, he was quite right.'
Coco Chanel, interviewed in 1968.

'Spray yourself wherever you might be kissed. A woman who overdoes it with perfume has no future, for she will only offend her friends and admirers.'
Chanel, quoted by Pierre Galante in *Les Années Chanel*

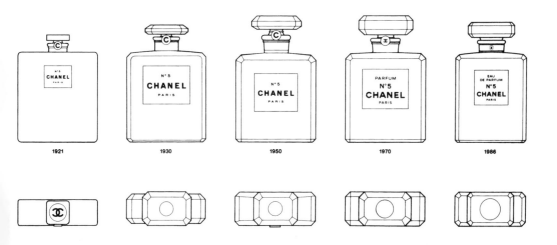

Coco was always contrary, which is the first thing to remember when telling the story of Chanel N°5; a story that is a fairy tale, yet also the solid foundation of her empire. N°5 was multiplied a million times over – and more, far more – in a dizzying proliferation that made Coco Chanel rich and recognised around the world, so that her name became a brand, and her face as famous as her logo. But in the beginning, before the beginning … Where do you begin with once upon a time?

You could start in the summer of 1920, when Coco Chanel met Ernest Beaux, an expert perfumer who had established a laboratory in Grasse in the south of France. She had been introduced to him by her Russian lover at the time, the Grand Duke Dmitri Pavlovich, who knew Beaux as the perfumer to the tsars. If anyone had scent in his blood, it was Beaux: he was born in Moscow in 1881 to a French father and German mother, and his elder brother Edward was the administrator of Rallet, the leading perfume and soap manufacturers in Russia, and suppliers to the Imperial Court, with factories employing hundreds of workers. At 17, Ernest began his career as a laboratory assistant at Rallet, rising to become the company's technical director by 1907, a position that he held until the revolution in 1917 forced him to leave. He had already achieved great success in Russia with the launch of his 'Bouquet of Napoleon' in 1912, created to mark the centenary of the Battle of Borodino. If this seems a curious inspiration for a perfumer, given that it marked a blood-drenched and short-lived victory for the Napoleonic troops in their invasion of Russia, Beaux nevertheless received widespread acclaim for his work.

And Beaux himself was a soldier, as well as a chemist, a combination that might explain his scented celebration of Napoleon; or perhaps his Bouquet was suggestive of his French ancestors, or the alliance between Russia and France, renewed in 1893. At any rate, he served in France during the First World War, from 1914 to 1917, and was awarded the prestigious *Croix de Guerre* and *Légion d'Honneur* for his bravery by the French authorities. After the Revolution, when Rallet was seized by the Bolsheviks, Beaux was commissioned by the British to join the White Russian army as a counter-intelligence officer, and travelled to the far north, to Arkhangelsk (a stronghold of the anti-Bolshevik White Army, supported by Allied Entente forces). Yet again, his courage was honoured: this time with the British Military Cross.

In 1919, he finally arrived in the south of France, to be reunited with a number of former colleagues from Rallet who had set up a new operation in La Bocca,

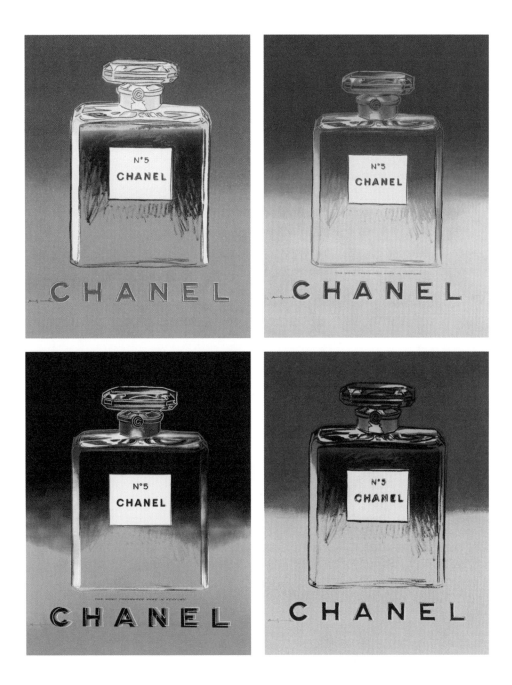

Previous page left: A stylised portrait of a flapper of the Roaring Twenties, and a tribute to the Chanel N°5 perfume, by French artist and caricaturist Sem, 1921. Previous page right: The evolution of the Chanel N°5 bottle, from 1921 to 1986. This page: Silk screens of the Chanel N°5 bottle by pop artist Andy Warhol, 1985.

near Cannes. When Beaux started work in the laboratory, he was determined to re-create a note of perfume that he had encountered during his military service; and in order to do so, experimented with aldehydes, the new chemical compounds that were to become an essential ingredient of Chanel N°5. According to a speech that Beaux gave in 1946, he remembered the precise circumstances of the origin of the scent, as well as the specific note that had inspired it:

'I've been asked some questions about the subject of the creation of N°5. When did I create it? In 1920 exactly, upon my return from the war. I had been part of the campaign in a northern region of Europe, above the Arctic Circle, during the midnight sun, where the lakes and rivers exuded a perfume of extreme freshness. I retained this note and recreated it, not without difficulty, for the first aldehydes I was able to find were unstable and unreliable. Why this name? Mademoiselle Chanel, who had a very fashionable couture house, asked me for some perfumes

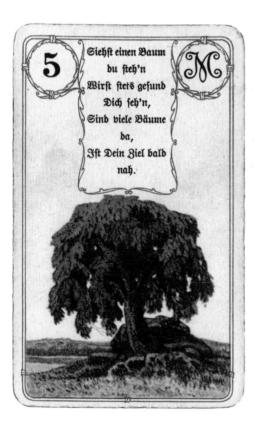

Chanel's number 5 Tarot card: 'Should you see a rooted tree / You will always look upon yourself as being healthy, / And should there be many trees, / Your goal shall soon be near.'

for it. I came to present my creations, two series: N°1–5 and 20–24. She chose a few, one of which was N°5. "What should it be called?" I asked. Mademoiselle Chanel replied, "I'm presenting my dress collection on the 5th of May, the fifth month of the year; let's leave the name N°5." This number would bring her luck.'

That's the story, anyway; and it gave rise to the fable that Chanel N°5 was also launched on 5th May – a pleasing tale, for which there is an unfortunate lack of evidence. Nor is there any proof of the equally pervasive legend that the design for the geometric bottle-top was inspired by the outlines of Place Vendôme, upon which view Mademoiselle had gazed with Dmitri from her suite at the Ritz. All that is known for certain is that the scent went on sale in 1921. But further speculation has run along these lines: that having been taught the precepts of theosophy by Boy Capel, Chanel would have known the numerological significance of the number five, as representative of the fifth element – the legendary *quinta essentia* of the alchemists; the Classical quintessence of which the cosmos is made. No matter whether or not these precepts can be directly linked to the five-sided stars in the paved mosaic in the corridor of Aubazine, or to her astrological birth sign of Leo, the fifth sign of the zodiac, the number was said to be etched in Chanel's psyche, embedded in her subconscious like the stones of the abbey at Aubazine. Together, these supposedly occult components formed a myth as enduring as it is alluring (and after all, myth is as important an ingredient in Chanel N°5 as aldehydes).

But if Gabrielle Chanel believed in magic, it was more likely to be of her own making. Towards the end of her life, when she talked to her friend Claude Delay, Chanel often mentioned her invention of N°5 – as *her* creation, no one else's. In Delay's retelling of the story, Chanel had gone to the south of France to escape from her grief over Capel's death. 'She took refuge on the Côte d'Azur where, breathing in essences and the fields of May roses, she invented the perfume – N°5 – which was to obsess the world. The name was a chance, not premeditated. She called it that because it was the fifth bottle and five is a pretty number.' Even so, while five may have had no particular meaning to Chanel, at least not in this particular account, the perfume that came to represent the future also had links to her past. Chanel spoke to Delay about the potent scent of her childhood memories: of the smell of lye soap at her aunts' house, of their linen cupboard fragrant with herbs; of the polished floors and furniture, in a place where everything was clean. There might not have been enough love to go round, but there was something good in her aunts' scrubbed purity; and later, when she met Emilienne d'Alençon and other courtesans, Chanel was reminded of what was also good in them. 'I liked Emilienne d'Alençon a lot. She smelled clean.'

Thus cleanliness went hand in hand with goodness (if not godliness), and also bestowed a curious kind of status on women, as well as summoning up the past for Chanel. She told Claude Delay that 'the sense of smell is the only one that is still instinctive. It lives on nostalgia, the subconscious.' And yet nostalgia was not sufficient reason to continue to wear a particular scent; it was important to choose one's own, rather than have it chosen; it was a statement of individuality and of independence. 'Women wear the perfumes they're given as presents,' she said to Delay. 'You ought to wear your own, the one you like. If I leave a jacket behind somewhere, they know it's mine. When I was young, the first thing I'd have done if I had any money was buy some perfume. I'd been given Floris's Sweet Peas – I thought it was lovely, country girl that I was. Then I realised it didn't suit me.'

Many years later, in Ernest Beaux's laboratory, Chanel sniffed out what did suit her, and declared it to be 'a perfume such as has never before been made – a woman's perfume with a woman's scent'. N°5 was, in some ways, revolutionary, in its blend of the natural and synthetic, thanks to Beaux's discovery of the importance of aldehydes in enhancing and stabilising ingredients such as jasmine, a key component in Chanel N°5, along with ylang-ylang, neroli, May rose, sandalwood and Bourbon vetiver. Perfumes had traditionally consisted of a single yet heavy floral note, but Beaux came up with the scent that Chanel sought, in her quest to define herself as a designer committed to modernity; a formula that she described a 'a bouquet of abstract flowers'. And she also added another element to Beaux's expert chemistry: an understanding of the alchemy of desire. The evening after she had chosen the sample of N°5 in Beaux's laboratory, Chanel took a vial of the scent to the most fashionable restaurant in Cannes. As she dined with Beaux and a few friends, she surreptitiously sprayed the women who passed their table with the new perfume. 'You've got to be able to lead them by the nose,' she told Delay, many years later, having done so with her original customers for N°5, spraying it in her boutiques in Deauville, Biarritz and Paris, and proffering little samples before production was underway, underplaying her commercial ambitions, but nevertheless suggesting to her best clients that they were in on the secret long before anyone else.

By the mid-Thirties, when Chanel befriended Bettina Ballard (then a young American editor working in the Paris office of *Vogue*), she related the tale of

La Marquise de la Flaconnerie, a caricature of Chanel in a bottle of Chanel N°5. Sem, 1923.

N°5 without mentioning Ernest Beaux, despite the fact that he had become technical director of Les Parfums Chanel in 1924. 'She concocted Chanel N°5 when she was trying to recover in the south of France in the Twenties from the accidental death of Boy Capel,' wrote Ballard.

'A maker of flower essences at Grasse let her make her own mixture to divert her. When she tested her fifth attempt, she picked up the plain bottle in which she had mixed it, wrote a number 5 in her own hand, and said, "Now I will sell this," and she did, all over the world. It was the perfume that started what the couturiers call their "insurance"; that is, money that they make from lending their famous couture names to a perfume that they don't have to change every season the way they do their clothes.'

In fact, Chanel was not the first couturière to sell scent (her old rival, Paul Poiret, had launched Les Parfums de Rosine a decade before her, naming it after his daughter), but she was the first to lay claim to it. And her claims were legendary: that she could smell the hands that picked the flowers she was given; that she could recognise the unique scent of the forest of Compiègne from a single branch of pine, years after she had ridden there with Etienne Balsan. And she could smell dirt, she said, even in the most glamorous of salons, and was repelled by it. 'I was appalled,' she told Morand, recalling her first visit to Misia's apartment, filled with spun glass and sequins. 'It smelt of filth downstairs; there was no surface upon which you could use a duster or apply any polish …'

But Misia had a different version of events, in which she was a catalyst for Chanel's first perfume, if not quite a muse (and dirt had nothing to do with its germination). According to an unpublished chapter in Misia's memoir, 'Coco always had a genius for discovering the essence of something gigantic in the most minuscule idea suggested to her. If the grain of sand you offered her had some interesting quality, she could turn it into gold. I should like to give an example that is almost miraculous.'

Misia's story – a fairy tale within a fairy tale – began with her claim to have met Lucien Daudet, secretary to the Empress Eugénie, wife of Napoleon III. Daudet was wearing the empress's scent, Violettes Imperiales, and seemed like a man possessed. 'He had been diligently going through the papers of the beautiful Eugénie, to whom he was devoted, body and soul. He seemed literally embalmed in the perfume of the woman whose grace illuminated the Second Empire. "Just imagine, Misia," he said, "I discovered an astonishing beauty formula among the letters of our dear great empress. The faith she had in it is my best guarantee of its effectiveness. But you'd better read this document and tell me as a friend, since we're alone, if it wouldn't be possible to sell this lost formula to some cosmetics house – without revealing the name of the illustrious person who used it to keep her beauty alive." With these words he handed me a sheet of paper …'

The narrative was a Misia classic – somewhat vague in its logic and chronology, yet dramatic, with herself playing a central role. The sheet of paper had apparently remained within her possession and she quoted it at length in her memoir, under the title *The Secret of the Medicis*. 'Shortly before the war, excavations performed in the underground passages of a famous royal chateau on the banks of the Loire brought to light several manuscripts by René the Florentine, Perfume-Maker to Queen Catherine de' Medici. Among those manuscripts there appeared *The Secret of the Medicis*, the famous eau de toilette which made it possible for Queen Catherine, for Diane de Poitiers, and later for Queen Marie de' Medici to brave the years, yet to keep, even in old age, a ravishing skin and the complexion of a young girl.'

Misia's first reaction – or so she claimed – was amusement, but this was immediately followed by inspiration. '"You want six thousand francs for this formula," I said to him; "You shall have it." I had just thought of Coco. Since everything she touched succeeded, why not launch a Chanel eau de toilette based on this formula?' Misia's story was hazy on detail (what was the formula and who re-created it, and when?), yet she told it with aplomb. 'Painstakingly, we experimented with a very severe bottle, ultra-simple, almost pharmaceutical, but in the Chanel style and with the elegant touch she gave to everything. A few weeks later, L'Eau Chanel made its appearance. It succeeded far beyond our wildest hopes. It was unbelievable, almost as if we had won first prize in a lottery! "Why don't you really go in for perfumes?" I said to Coco. "It seems to me, after the success of L'Eau Chanel, that René the Florentine is the goose that laid the golden egg."

'At that moment Mademoiselle Chanel, who at first considered the eau de toilette a plaything, had the genius to see the future possibilities of this new idea. And from the start her perfumes were so successful that Chanel N°5, N°22 and Bois des Iles [the scents created by Beaux in swift succession, along with Cuir de Russie and Gardénia] were soon in demand on all five continents. And that is how the sorceress, with a flick of her wrist, started with the minuscule

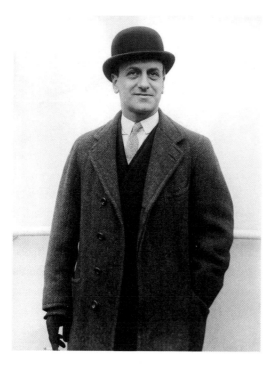

Pierre Wertheimer, who founded Les Parfums Chanel in 1924 with Chanel.

idea *The Secret of the Medicis* had given me and created an industry of such importance that, one by one, all the fashion houses followed in her path. Thanks to her, they managed to balance their budgets during the years when they were threatened with bankruptcy!'

Chanel, continued Misia, in her characteristic blend of self-effacement and egotism (the two qualities that made her such a potent muse), was to play a central role in the transformation of women; but it took Misia to see her potential. 'I felt it so strongly that, from our first meeting, I could hardly wait to make others aware of it. One could say that it is easy to help a beautiful diamond to shine. Still, it was my privilege to help it emerge from its rough state, and – in my heart – to be the first person to be dazzled by it.'

Needless to say, when Misia showed Chanel the chapter in which she featured in her memoir, Chanel demanded that it be withdrawn from the book. It is unclear what, precisely, she most objected to: the story about *The Secret of the Medicis*, or the role that Misia assigned herself in the legend of Chanel. But whatever the provenance of René the Florentine's miraculous formula, the man behind the throne of Chanel N°5 was someone else entirely: Pierre

Wertheimer, the owner (with his brother Paul) of Bourjois, one of the largest cosmetics companies in France.

Chanel was introduced to Wertheimer by Théophile Bader, proprietor of Galeries Lafayette, after she had asked Bader to stock her perfume in his department store (which also happened to be the place where Chanel had originally bought her straw boaters, simple pieces that she trimmed with ribbons for herself, and for her first millinery clients). Bader was quick to see the commercial potential of Chanel N°5, at the same time as pointing out to her that if it were to be sold in Galeries Lafayette, as well as in her boutiques, the scent would need to be produced in far greater quantities than Ernest Beaux could supply from his laboratory. But the Bourjois factories might be able to do so; hence the meeting between Pierre Wertheimer and Coco Chanel at the Deauville racetrack, where one of Wertheimer's large stable of horses was running.

The Wertheimers were a Jewish family, as rich and successful as the Rothschilds, but apparently even more intent on privacy. Their roots could be traced back to medieval Germany, although they had been thoroughly French for generations: knowledgeable art collectors as well as expert businessmen, who had transformed Bourjois from a nineteenth-century theatrical make-up company into a thriving cosmetics and perfume manufacturer. Pierre Wertheimer's decision to back Chanel was to add a new dimension to his family's business empire; their association was to last a lifetime, and still continues today, for the Wertheimers have kept Chanel in private ownership, while other couturiers and beauty brands have become absorbed into global conglomerates. The current owners, Pierre's grandsons Alain and Gerard, remain as discreet as their predecessors, but a carefully preserved archive can be found in the former Bourjois factory in Pantin on the northern outskirts of Paris. Production of Chanel perfume and beauty products began here in 1924 (and Bourjois products even earlier, since the factory was opened in 1891), and there is a faint scent of rose oil that still lingers, as if embedded in the brickwork after over a century of manufacturing. Fifty years ago, the factory employed 800 people, making everything from lipstick to the polished glass stoppers for Chanel N°5. But perhaps the most precious artefact within the factory is the past; or more precisely, the heritage that is contained in the neatly filed records of Bourjois and Chanel.

On one of the upper floors, overlooking the train tracks that were used to export crates of scent bottles and make-up from here to all over Europe, is an archive of Chanel beauty products. In immaculate glass display cases are the earliest examples of Chanel N°5, the double C logo still pristine in black against the unblemished white packaging; white as the walls of the room that contains them (a perfect white box of a room, where nothing intrudes from the outside world). Beside the perfumes is a photograph of Coco and Dmitri Pavlovich, taken soon after their romance began, and another of Ernest Beaux; the pictures and the bottles of scent are preserved in the same glass case, like relics in a shrine to a long dead saint.

In another vitrine, on the other side of the white room, is a carefully arranged display of the first Chanel lipsticks and face powders: the earliest a red lipstick from 1924, in a tiny ivory case marked with a single C, followed by a more substantial black tube in 1929, and a bullet-shaped metal cartridge design from 1934. Nowhere is there any visible sign of the Wertheimers, but the archives contain the relevant numbers: when Les Parfums Chanel was established in April 1924, Mademoiselle owned 10 per cent of the company, the Wertheimers had 70 per cent, with the remaining 20 per cent going to Théophile Bader (who was subsequently bought out by the Wertheimers).

To categorise Pierre Wertheimer's long-standing relationship with Coco Chanel as a business arrangement based on straightforward arithmetic would, however, be too simple for a union as complicated and intense as the most enduring marriage. Wertheimer was far more loyal to Chanel than any of her lovers; and although each tormented the other at different points in their lives, with such antagonism that Pierre had to employ a full-time lawyer simply to deal with her, as they pressed their opposing sides in a combat reminiscent of a bitterly fought divorce, they nonetheless retained a mutual respect.

Wertheimer's initial majority investment in the perfume company was a mark of his confidence in Chanel, but the return was so profitable that Coco was to regret having retained only 10 per cent of the business that bore her name. Thus her battle over numbers flared up periodically: she wanted a larger share of the profits, but Pierre Wertheimer resisted her attempts to wrest a greater percentage from him. Their legal disputes and manoeuvres included acrimonious feuds, worthy of the most elaborate Medici drama; but eventually, a kind of harmony prevailed. The two of them somehow added up to N°5; more than the sum of their parts, and never less than committed to the mathematics of their union. If five was Chanel's lucky number, then it took Wertheimer to make her luck into solid profit. And in doing so, he gave her the freedom and independence to live her life without relying on a husband; though she could never be rid of Wertheimer, or he of her, in a mysterious alchemy that turned perfume into gold.

When you walk through the empty corridors of the factory at Pantin, down the staircase to the silent basement vaults that contain the most precious records of Chanel, the scent of roses becomes fainter, and finally disappears. But on the other side of the locked doors into the depths of the building – the innermost sanctum – is a drawer that contains a small, original bottle of N°5. The golden liquid inside the glass is almost entirely gone now – evaporated or diminished by time – but pick up the bottle, using protective white gloves, and you come close enough to sniff the glass top. It smells nothing like the Chanel N°5 that I am wearing – rare perfume, unlike fine wine, does not improve with age. But even so, it carries with it a strange potency; the precious scent of a vanished woman, the last traces of an invisible ghost.

You can follow the trail of this perfume elsewhere in the Chanel empire: to Rue Cambon, of course, where a young assistant would spray N°5 in the entrance to the building a moment before Mademoiselle Chanel walked in every day, having been warned of her imminent arrival by the doorman who had ushered her out of the Ritz. The scent still lingers around the mirrored staircase, and in her private apartment, where she scattered N°5 on the hot coals of the fireplace. And it also pervades the gleaming modern building at Neuilly on the outer edge of Paris where the current creator of Parfums Chanel, Jacques Polge, oversees the continuation of tradition, as well as the formulation of new fragrances, all of them inspired by Coco Chanel (not simply in name, but also as a means to capture the essence of her allure). He is only the second director of perfume at Chanel since Ernest Beaux's retirement in 1954, arriving at the company as its 'nose' in 1978, and is as adept at quoting Proust as he is at identifying several thousand different olfactory bases. Proust, he notes, wrote that perfume is 'that last and best reserve of the past, the one which when all our tears have run dry, can make us cry again'. If Chanel N°5 was in its way revolutionary – both in its chemistry and in the modernist design of its bottle, and its logo and label that needed no translation into different languages – then it has also come to represent constancy, an unbroken connection with the woman who made it her own. N°5, like all the best scents, seems in one sense to be entirely abstract – a complete thing in itself, rather than a conceptual philosophy – but it is also a catalyst to the imagination; a clue to unravel the mystery of Coco Chanel, as immaterial yet unyielding as the designer herself.

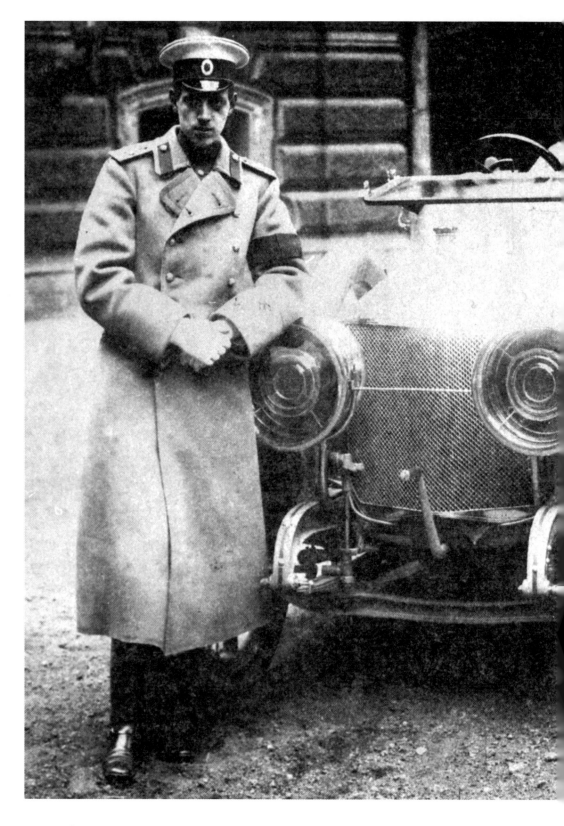

THE RUSSIANS

On 10th April 1917, Paul Morand, by then a diplomat as well as a writer, went to visit Misia, as he often did. 'She is in bed,' he reported in his diary, 'buried in pink pillows and lace, sick with a stalactitic cold; even her colds are rococo … She speaks enthusiastically about the Russian Revolution, which she sees as an enormous ballet.' Tsar Nicholas II had abdicated just a few weeks previously, Lenin had not yet seized power from the provisional Russian government, and the Ballets Russes had found themselves in something of a diplomatic muddle on the eve of a gala performance in Rome. In normal circumstances, the performance would have begun with the national anthem, but now no one felt it appropriate to sing 'God Save the Tsar', so Diaghilev persuaded Igor Stravinsky to provide a last-minute orchestration of a Russian folk song instead. All this Morand had discovered from Misia — at the centre of everything, as usual, despite having taken to her bed — and although she expressed some sympathy for the plight of the tsar, she was easily diverted. 'She says the Tsar has been robbed … deprived of everything … that the Revolution is the triumph of Rasputin, who always said, "If I disappear, you will disappear …" In the middle of her speech Sert arrives … He has bought all the balloons from a vendor in the Tuileries. Overjoyed, Misia forgets her cold and stands in her bed, plays with the multicoloured bunch of balloons, ties her griffon to the string to see if he'll float in the air. But the dog is too heavy.'

Thus did the Russian Revolution touch Misia's Paris – a dark cloud passing, casting a shadow over the balloons and lapdogs; but entertaining, in its own way – and Coco Chanel seemed to take much the same view. Like Misia, she saw an overlap between the Ballets Russes and the political revolutionaries; or so she said to Paul Morand, recalling the October Revolution in 1917, when the Bolsheviks took over from the provisional government. Diaghilev, she recalled, had talked to her about the weeks leading up to the Revolution when he was working with the Ballets Russes in Switzerland, while Lenin and Trotsky were preparing their own dramatic entrance. 'He [Diaghilev] was rehearsing in Lausanne, in a hangar; Stravinsky was working … next door; Lenin and Trotsky were waiting on the shores of Lake Leman for the moment when they were to return to Russia, in a sealed carriage.' In retrospect, Chanel concluded that these parallel events amounted to 'one and the same thing'. History did not prove her right, but her personal life was shaped by the consequences of revolution (and for Chanel, the personal tended to take precedence over the political). 'The Ballets Russes had jolted the world of dance; October 1917 had jolted the whole of Russia, and Paris became filled with émigrés.'

Chanel's path soon crossed with a number of those émigrés – including the Grand Duke Dmitri Pavlovich and Ernest Beaux. Having embarked upon a profitable relationship with the latter and a passionate affair with the former, she declared that 'every Westerner should have succumbed to "Slavic charm" to know what it is. I was captivated.' But she was also captivating – chic and rich and independent; more than a match for a Grand Duke who had found himself penniless after the Revolution. If legend is to be believed, they were introduced in Biarritz in July 1920 by Dmitri's then lover, and Coco's friend from her past life at Royallieu, Marthe Davelli, who had become a famous soprano. 'If you're interested you can have him,' Davelli is supposed to have remarked to Chanel. 'He really is a little expensive for me.'

Towards the end of her life, when Chanel was talking to Claude Delay (long after Dmitri had married an American heiress), she described the Grand Duke, and others like him, as diminished, almost emasculated by their poverty in exile: 'Those Grand Dukes were all the same – they looked marvellous but there was nothing behind. Green eyes, fine hands and shoulders, peace-loving, timorous. They drank so as not to be afraid. They were tall and handsome and splendid, but behind it all – nothing: just vodka and the void.'

Even so, when she encountered Dmitri in 1920, he was undeniably glamorous, and surrounded by scandal and mystery that gave some edge to his reputation as a penniless playboy. A first cousin of Tsar Nicholas II, he had been involved in the plot to murder Rasputin in 1916, and his escape from Russia thereafter was to save his life, unlike those of the majority of his family (including his father), who were subsequently executed by the Bolsheviks. According to Chanel, in her conversations with Paul Morand, she had already met Dmitri in 1914, but had not seen him since then, until they chanced upon one another six years later.

'We dined together,' Chanel remarked to Morand. 'I saw him the following day. In a very friendly way, I say to him: "I have just bought a little blue Rolls, let's go to Monte Carlo."

"I have no money, all I've got is fifteen thousand francs …"

"I'll put in the same amount," I replied to the Grand-Duke. "With thirty thousand, we'll have enough to enjoy ourselves for a week."'

(As it happened, she later observed to Claude Delay, the manager of the hotel in Monte Carlo didn't want to give the Grand Duke a bill: '"Oh yes, you must," I told him. "Just a little one."')

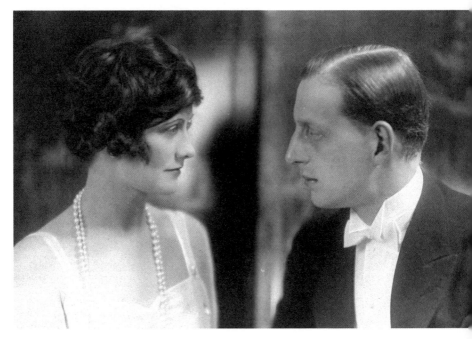

Chanel and Grand Duke Dmitri, 1920.

Igor Stravinsky, José Maria Sert, Chanel and Misia Sert at the Paris Fair, 1920 (clockwise from top left).

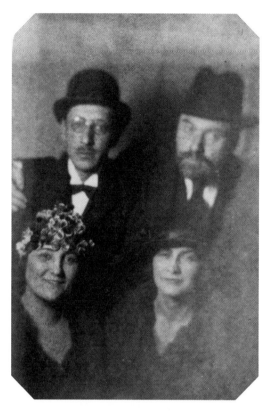

But he wasn't the only Russian that she was supporting, nor the only one who sought her attentions, or whose attention she had bought. Chanel's relationship with Diaghilev had been founded on her financial donation to the Ballets Russes to support the revival of *Le Sacre du printemps*; a gesture that also made her central to the life of its composer, Igor Stravinsky. In his autobiography, written in 1935, Stravinsky referred to Chanel's patronage: 'As Diaghilev's affairs were at this time in very low water financially, the reproduction of the *Sacre* had been made possible only by the backing of his friends. I should like especially to mention Mlle Gabrielle Chanel, who not only generously came to the assistance of the venture, but took an active part in the production by arranging to have the costumes made in her world-famous dressmaking establishment.'

What Stravinsky did not disclose was that Chanel had also provided a home for himself and his family, offering them her villa at Garches, Bel Respiro, when the composer was utterly impoverished. A brief postcard he wrote to a friend, dated 22nd September 1920, bears the Bel Respiro address, and refers to his 'nerves' as being 'in poor condition'. His autobiography provides even less detail, but dates his stay at Garches as taking place in 'the winter of 1920–1921 … Diaghilev was just then giving a new production of *Le Sacre du printemps* at the Théâtre des Champs-Elysées.' Whether or not the composer's memory was correct, the date on the postcard would suggest that Stravinsky moved into the villa swiftly after the Grand Duke moved out, for Dmitri had been staying there with Chanel towards the end of the summer of 1920.

Despite his nervous anxiety, Stravinsky's work appeared to flourish in Garches. During his time at Bel Respiro, he completed his *Symphonies pour instruments à vent* (originally commissioned as a memorial to Claude Debussy, who had died in 1918, and later regarded by admirers as a masterpiece of Twenties Modernism); and also composed a series based around the number five. If the *Symphonies* would become recognised as a significant piece of

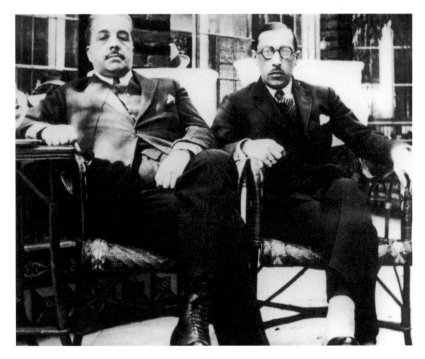

Sergei Diaghilev (left) and Igor Stravinsky (right) during their
Ballets Russes collaboration, 1921.

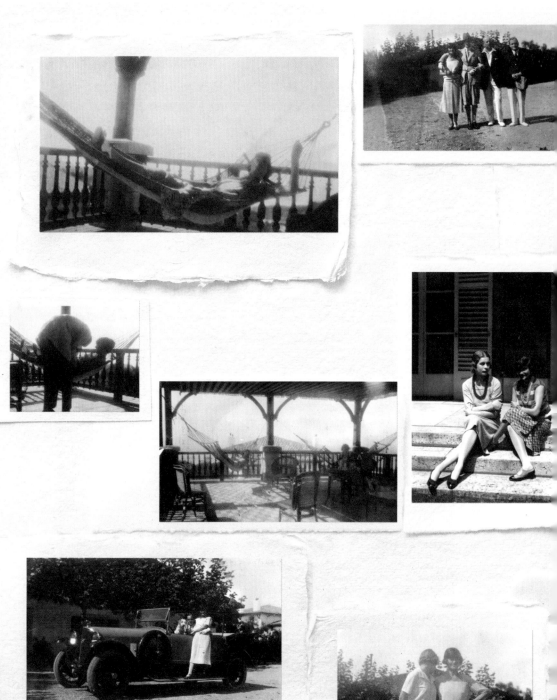

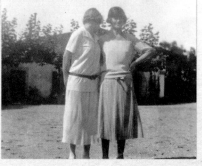

Top left, centre left and centre: Chanel and Dmitri at Villa Maitena in
Guéthary, 1924. Top right: Chanel, Dmitri, and two friends at the Villa
Ama Ttikia in Biarritz, 1924. Centre right: Chanel and Lady Abdy on
the steps of Chanel's home, 29 Faubourg Saint-Honoré, Paris, 1929.
Lower left: Chanel and Dmitri at Villa Ama Ttikia. Lower right: Chanel
and Zina Rachewskia at Villa Ama Ttikia.

musical radicalism, notwithstanding its roots in a traditional Russian past, his simpler compositions for the piano, *Les cinq doigts*, were equally intriguing to those who suspected that Stravinsky was in love with the woman behind Chanel N°5. His memoir gives no clue as to whether there was a direct link. But it nevertheless offers some insight into the composer's understanding of the appeal of simplicity, in ways that might have found a parallel with Chanel's own manner of working, whereby her hands sought to form pleasingly unfussy designs. Stravinsky himself identified the unembellished quality that characterised *Les cinq doigts*: 'In these eight pieces, which are very easy, the five fingers of the right hand, once on the keys, remain in the same place sometimes even for the whole length of the piece, while the left hand, which is destined to accompany the melody, executes a pattern, either harmonic or contrapuntal, of the utmost simplicity.'

It would be too glib to suggest that their fingers were doing the talking; but nevertheless, gossip began to spread that Chanel and Stravinsky were having an affair, while his wife Catherine was ailing with consumption in an upstairs bedroom in Bel Respiro. There is no evidence that their flirtation was consummated at Garches, but whatever the circumstances, they were venturing onto territory as volcanic as *Le Sacre du printemps*, a scandal sufficiently enthralling to occupy popular imagination. The ballet's explosive premiere in May 1913 had changed the musical landscape, not only because of Stravinsky's revolutionary dissonant score and Nijinsky's overtly sexual choreography, but also because of the audience's response. Brawls had broken out in the aisles of the Paris theatre, while Diaghilev switched the lights on and off in a vain attempt to quieten the clamour, and Nijinsky stood in the wings, shouting out the beats to the dancers as the music was drowned out by catcalls and cheers. Debussy had witnessed the original performance, and described *Le Sacre* as 'an extraordinary, ferocious thing', and its composer as 'a young savage who wears tumultuous ties and kisses ladies' hands while treading on their feet. When he's old, he'll be unbearable.'

Seven years later, when Chanel met Stravinsky, she appeared equally dismissive; or at least she was in her recollection of him to Paul Morand. 'He was still not very cosmopolitan, and he was very Russian in his ways, with the look of a clerk in a Chekhov short story. A small moustache beneath a large rat-like nose. He was young and shy; he found me attractive.' Stravinsky maintained his silence on the subject (although his second wife was to dismiss the idea that he and Chanel had had an affair); while Chanel claimed that she refused to respond to Stravinsky's advances when he embarked upon a pursuit of her. Not that this prevented an ensuing drama, at least according to Chanel in her account of the story to Morand: '"You're married, Igor," I told him, "when Catherine, your wife, gets to know …"

'And he, very Russian: "She knows I love you. To whom else, if not to her, could I confide something so important?"

'Without being jealous, Misia began to spread gossip. She had sensed that something was happening without her knowing: "What are you doing? Where are you going? People tell me that Igor walks your dog, explain yourself!"'

Chanel provided no further explanation of the dog-walking episode to Morand, nor to anyone else for that matter; and somewhat disappointingly Misia's own memoir casts no more light on the affair, although she did refer to Chanel penetrating 'the famous, carefully guarded game preserve' that constituted smart Parisian society at the time (thanks to Misia's introductions, of course). 'Coco came to know Diaghilev at my house, as well as the whole group of artists that gravitated around the Ballets Russes. And they found in her a faithful, very generous friend. Stravinsky in particular fell desperately in love with her! Afterward she was to give him a house in Garches and, frequently, financial help too.'

In fact, the house was never Stravinsky's to keep, although it provided a refuge for him and his wife and children; just as it had done a few months previously in 1920 for the pregnant Diana Capel and her young daughter, not long after the death of her husband, Chanel's lover, Boy Capel. In hindsight, a curious pattern seems to emerge, whereby Chanel created, and re-created, complex triangular relationships; far more intricate than her double C logo, even trickier than the choreographed steps of the Ballets Russes, but endlessly repeated, albeit with different components and shifting characters. In this particular version, as described to Morand, Chanel saw herself as betrayed by Misia, rather than being the betrayed lover, or the cause of a husband's betrayal of his wife. The plot was labyrinthine, and shifted suddenly from dog-walking to divorce. 'Misia feared catastrophe,' Chanel told Morand, on the uncertain grounds 'that Stravinsky might divorce in order to marry me'. At this point, she said, José-Maria Sert became involved, allegedly taking Stravinsky to one side and telling him that Boy Capel had entrusted Chanel to his care (an unlikely scenario, given that Capel had no reason to suspect that he would die young).

The intrigue, according to Chanel, continued thus: while Sert was warning off Stravinsky, Misia acted as chorus and messenger: 'Misia came back to me, stirring up the drama: "Stravinsky is in the room next door. He wants to know whether or not you will marry him. He is wringing his hands."'

After the hand-wringing and the room-hopping came the music; or so Chanel claimed to Morand. 'Stravinsky came back,' she said, although it was not clear where he was coming back from (the edge of despair, perhaps?). 'He came back every day and taught me about music; the little I know about it, I owe to him. He talked to me about Wagner, about Beethoven, his bugbear, about Russia.' Eventually, he talked to her about going to a different place. '"The Ballets [Russes] are leaving for Spain," Stravinsky said to me. "Come with us."' Chanel's reply was worthy of a romantic novel: 'I will go and find you.'

Instead, she promptly went to Monte Carlo instead, with Dmitri by her side, in her new Rolls-Royce. 'We set off,' she told Morand. 'Misia was watching. She immediately sent a telegram to Stravinsky, in Spain: "Coco is a little seamstress who prefers grand-dukes to artists." Stravinsky almost exploded. Diaghilev sent me a telegram: "Don't come, Stravinsky wants to kill you."'

Chanel was furious with Misia, who denied any involvement in the affair. 'I fell out with Misia for weeks, following this treacherous telegram. She swore to me that she had sent no such thing. Once again, I forgave her. In any case, Misia turned the wheel of fate, she also turned its page; she intervened, and from that day forth Stravinsky and I never saw each other again.'

Yet she continued to support him, and Misia acted as a go-between in this matter, as in so many others. Whatever the truth of Chanel's version of events, by February 1921 Stravinsky had fallen in love with a ballet dancer who was to become his second wife, Vera de Bosset. The composer subsequently divided his time between Vera and his wife, Catherine – whose tuberculosis was worsening – until Catherine's death in 1939 (a year after their eldest daughter had also died of TB). Notwithstanding the complications of this unhappy triangle – the dying wife, the guilty husband, the other woman – Chanel's involvement remained essential, for her money was required to keep the show going. If she was late in a payment, the uneasy structure came close to cracking; hence Stravinsky's anxious letter to Misia, written on 6th February 1933:

'I'm dreadfully sorry always to be asking you for something or bothering you with my petty affairs, but you know Chanel has not sent us anything since the 1st and so we are without a radish to live on this month; therefore I ask you to be kind enough to mention it to her … I thank you in advance for all your kindness, which is so great that one easily gets into the habit of counting on it, and I embrace you thousands and thousands of times, very warmly …'

Such was the intensity of the intrigue – and the convolutions of the plot – that work might have seemed impossible or irrelevant; but Chanel's career continued, unabated, and by doing so, kept a great many others afloat. Indeed, her complex web of relationships with the various Russians – Stravinsky,

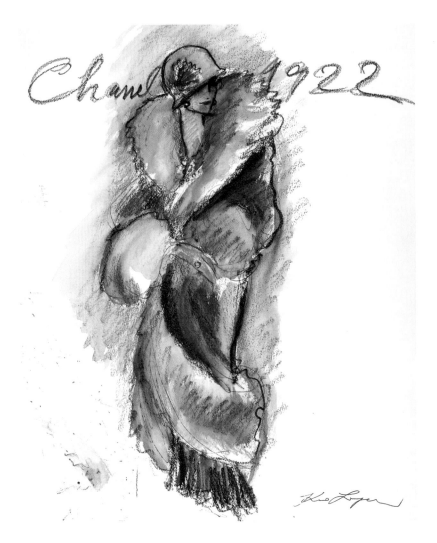

One of Chanel's 1922 Russian-inspired designs, as drawn by Karl Lagerfeld.

Diaghilev, Dmitri – found a profitable means of expression in her burgeoning business. Having successfully bottled the essence of her romance with the Grand Duke in Cuir de Russie, the perfume she produced with Ernest Beaux in 1927, Chanel employed exiled Russian aristocrats as sales assistants and models at Rue Cambon; not necessarily as an act of charity, but as the living embodiment of the fashion and scent she was selling to her customers, who had followed her lead in embracing Slavic charm.

For if Diaghilev had taught her anything, it was that there was an eager market for the romance of Russia, in which the lines between art and fashion and ballet and entertainment had been redrawn. Chanel looked, and Chanel saw: the designs by Picasso and Cocteau for the Ballets Russes, the leaps of imagination as great as those made on stage by Nijinksy. She had experienced the emotional potency of the Ballets Russes – hence her declaration to Claude Delay: 'It was when I saw the Diaghilev ballet that I decided I was going to live in what I loved' – but she also sensed its commercial potential. For whatever her impetuous feelings for Stravinsky or Dmitri, Chanel recognised something of her own pragmatism in Diaghilev's work ethic. 'From the day I first met him, until the day I closed his eyelids, I have never seen Serge take a rest,' she said to Morand. And while the Parisian *beau monde* applauded the Ballets ('all were in raptures about the essential colours and about harmonies of tones'), Chanel watched Diaghilev's machinations behind the scenes. 'He got straight down to business ... he invented a Russia for abroad, and, naturally, abroad was taken in ... Since everything in the theatre was only trompe l'oeil, false perspectives were necessary: the Russia of the Ballets Russes succeeded in the theatre precisely because it was built on fictional material.'

Chanel grasped this, and then turned it into her own material; literally, by commissioning Dmitri's older sister, Grand Duchess Maria Pavlovna, to make embroidered fabric. Although they had been brought up under very different circumstances, they shared something in common. Both women had learned needlework from nuns in their childhood; both had lost their mothers (Maria's had died just after giving birth to Dmitri); and Maria was raised by her aunt, Grand Duchess Elizabeth Feodorovna, a woman who combined day-to-day practicality with a certain emotional distance, in the manner of Chanel's 'aunts', the nuns. (After the assassination of her husband, Elizabeth sold her jewels and luxurious possessions and became a nun, founding a convent in Moscow; she herself was murdered by the Bolsheviks in 1918 – a grotesque killing, whereby she was thrown down a mineshaft, then stoned and set on fire – and subsequently canonised by the Russian Orthodox Church).

Maria – or Marie, as she referred to herself – had first met Chanel in the autumn of 1921 in Paris, where she was living in impoverished exile with her second husband, Prince Sergei Putiatin. Marie's memoir, published in 1932, draws an unusually clear-sighted portrait of Chanel, cutting through the sulphurous clouds of gossip and scandal to see the woman at work. 'At the time I met her she was not much older than I was,' wrote Marie (at 31, she was seven years younger than Chanel), 'but somehow, you did not think of her age, nor did you particularly notice her looks. It was the firmness of her jaw, the determined carriage of her neck that struck you. You were swept off your feet by the fierce vitality she exhaled, the quality of which was inspiring and infectious. Mlle Chanel was an innovator and a revolutionary in her particular line. Until her time Parisian dressmaking was an art exercised by very few initiates and jealously guarded by them. They studied and dealt with the tastes of a comparatively small group of fastidious and smart women; the fashions would therefore take a long time to reach the multitude and, when they reached it, would be disfigured beyond recognition. There would be no such thing as a season for one article or a vogue for another. The mode was created by what was designed for the lovely Countess

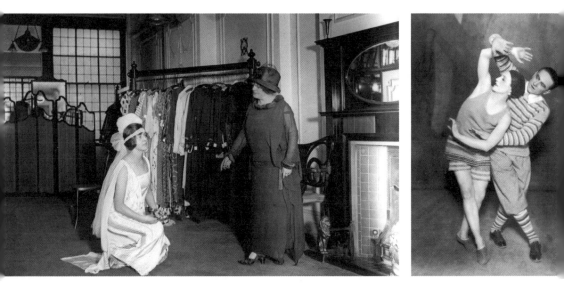

Left: Marie Pavlovna, Grand Duchess of Russia (seated) with the Dowager Empress Marie Fyodorovna, 1923. Right: Lydia Sokolova and Leon Wolzilkowsky dancing in Diaghilev's Ballets Russes production of *Le Train bleu*, in costumes designed by Chanel, 1924.

of So-and-So or the Princess of This-and-That and what was becoming to them. Individualism reigned supreme, to the detriment of business. Mlle Chanel was the first to cater to the public in its broader sense and to produce a standard which appealed to every taste, the first to democratise the art of dress-making for purely economic reasons. The post-war trend was for simplicity and informality. Chanel adapted it to clothes and she struck the right note.'

The Grand Duchess – like her brother – needed Chanel, but unlike Dmitri, she wanted to earn her own living, and pay her own way. Her first husband was the second son of the Swedish king; she had seen the splendour of pre-revolutionary Tsarist Russia, and lived amidst the riches and royalty of European courts. But Marie also witnessed the changes that had overtaken them, and the speed with which the rules had shifted; and she knew, through bitter experience, that no one was insulated from the masses; that the Revolution was here to stay. 'We had been torn out of our brilliant setting,' she wrote of herself and her extended family, 'we had been driven off the stage still dressed in our fantastic costumes. We had to take them off now, make ourselves others, more everyday clothes, and above all learn how to wear them.' As Marie gave up her past – selling her jewels to support her husband and brother – she also recognised the future, and the woman who would be central to its fashions. 'Chanel personified her

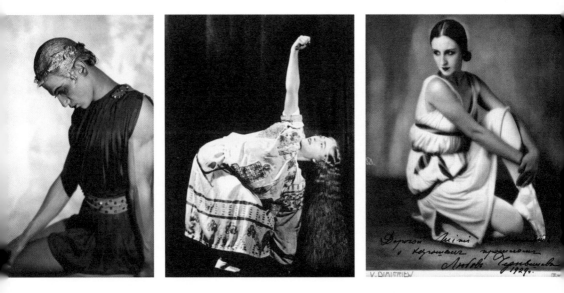

Left: Serge Lifar in *Apollon musagète* by Stravinsky, 1928. Centre: Lydia Sokolova in Stravinsky's Ballets Russes production of *Le Sacre du printemps*, 1920. Right: Lubov Chernicheva in a costume designed by Chanel in 1929 for *Apollo*.

time and, although affecting an attitude of sublime contempt for public taste, she catered to it assiduously.'

While her brother continued his affair with Chanel, Marie came often to visit her studio in Rue Cambon, sitting quietly in a corner, and seeing how the designer was both a copyist, and much copied. The Grand Duchess also observed Chanel's ability to combine creativity with hard-headed business sense (unlike her former rival, Paul Poiret, who made and lost his fortunes); and to do so on a daily basis. In the autumn of 1921, for example, 'She had just then imported some multi-coloured Faro Island sweaters and had conceived the idea of using their design for embroidery on silk blouses. One day as I came in I found Mlle Chanel engrossed in an argument with Mme Bataille, the woman who did the embroidery for the house. They were both examining the finished pieces of a crimson crêpe de Chine blouse. Chanel was beating down the price and she was speaking so quickly and volubly and had so many arguments at her disposal that Mme Bataille was staggered.'

The Grand Duchess listened as the haggling continued; not that Chanel was prepared to barter or give an inch. 'The end of this very one-sided conversation I remember as follows: "I am telling you, Mme Bataille, that I cannot pay six hundred francs for this work!" said Mlle Chanel.

'Mme Bataille, a stout person in a tight-fitting black dress, the perspiration standing out on her forehead, endeavoured in vain to interpose a word in the torrent of Mlle Chanel's arguments.

'"Mademoiselle will allow me to call her attention ..." panted Mme Bataille.

'"To what, Mme Bataille?" interrupted Chanel immediately. "I wish you would tell me the reasons for charging me this ridiculous price; as I have told you already I can't see them at all, myself."

'"The blouse is embroidered with real Chinese silk, one kilo of which costs at present ..."

'"I don't care what kind of silk you use – real or artificial," continued Mlle Chanel; "it is none of my business. What I want is to sell the blouse. As it is, it is too expensive; therefore you must charge less for it. That's all."'

Chanel had, as Marie observed, made a judgement on costs 'in one shrewd glance', and would brook no further argument, while Bataille stammered and reddened in her formidable presence. Finally, the interview was drawn to a close: '"My chère," Chanel again interrupted firmly, "it is, it seems to me, quite as much in your own interests as in mine to produce these blouses in larger quantities;

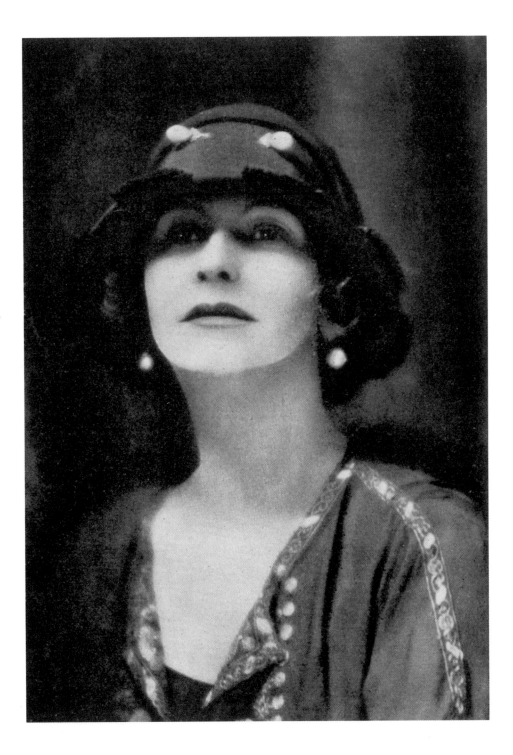

Chanel in a Russian-inspired blouse of her own design. Rehbinder, 1923.

you must understand this and be reasonable. Come down in your price. You're not the only one to make embroidery in Paris, and anybody would be only too delighted to do the work for me. You can take it or leave it as you please."'

Chanel waved her hand, indicating that the interview was at an end, and Mme Bataille disappeared through the door, whereupon Marie stepped forward, offering to do the embroidery for 450 francs per blouse. Chanel looked dubious, but said she could try; thus the Grand Duchess came to be a seamstress. She bought herself a sewing machine, and spent a month on a factory floor in one of the poorest districts of Paris, learning how to operate it; for Chanel needed machine embroidery in relatively large quantities to meet her burgeoning orders. 'It took me about a month to master the intricacies of an embroidery machine,' wrote the Grand Duchess in her memoir, 'to acquire a certain amount of technical ability and speed. And then I had the machine sent to my apartment. When it arrived, I placed it right in the middle of the drawing room and, seating myself on the sofa, I looked at it from a distance. It stood there on the carpet between two armchairs and a table littered with knick-knacks and photographs – hard, sturdy, and aloof, with the light gleaming coldly on the polish of its steel parts … Just once or twice in my life, my past with all its antecedents has appeared to me not in separate scenes but as one whole, a map with all the incidents fitting into one vast picture, but seen from a new angle, like the impression one gets in looking at a familiar landscape from an aeroplane. This was such a moment, and it made me feel small and helpless. I was now going to walk out of that landscape and create an absolutely fresh pattern for myself.'

In some ways, Marie did create something new for herself: on 5th February 1922, it was her embroidery that was, for the first time, the centrepiece of the Chanel spring collection. The Grand Duchess christened her business Kitmir (naming it after the Pekinese dog owned by the former Russian ambassador to Washington, who had retired to Paris after the Revolution; he was a traditionalist, she remarked in her memoir, who 'refused to compromise with a new world, his loyalty to what had been before amounting to a religion'). After opening a workshop, Marie employed several Russian girls, and as the business expanded, the number of her employees grew to 50 or so.

Nevertheless, something of a previous world remained, at least in the sense that Chanel's designs were inspired by long-established Russian influences. She reinterpreted the *roubachka* (a traditional embroidered blouse), the *pelisse* (a military style coat with frogging) and the sailor's jacket (its lines borrowed from the Russian military uniform), as well as using swathes of fur; working in an atmosphere imbued with the scent of Cuir de Russie.

And Marie herself could not forget what had gone before, as she browsed through warehouses in search of reels of embroidery silk for her work for Chanel, on expeditions that took her into 'a world still full of its own peculiar poetry'. Here she found the materials of her past, ready to be reassembled again into something new. 'I came across a pale yellowish twist like the one used in the convents in Moscow where I learned from the nuns the ancient art of embroidering faces of saints with one colour of silk, shading the emaciated cheeks by changing the direction of the stitches. There was also the real gold and silver thread which never tarnished and with which were embroidered the crowns and halos ...'

And she also discovered French silks from Lyon, some of them made to patterns that were centuries old; patterns that she 'recognised as old friends; I had seen them on the brocaded curtains and furniture coverings in the palaces at Tsarskoie-Selo and Peterhof. Piece after piece of brocade and silk both plain and fancy was unrolled for me to admire, a wealth of taste, artistic wisdom, and experience accumulated for generations ...'

Marie found comfort in the familiar patterns, and drew on them in her embroidery for Chanel. And as the elements of fashion reassembled themselves – old materials transformed into apparently new designs – the collaboration between an exiled Grand Duchess and a peasant-girl-turned-autocrat served, amongst other things, as a reminder both of transformation and of tradition; of survival, amidst the seismic shifts and aftershocks of revolutions great and small.

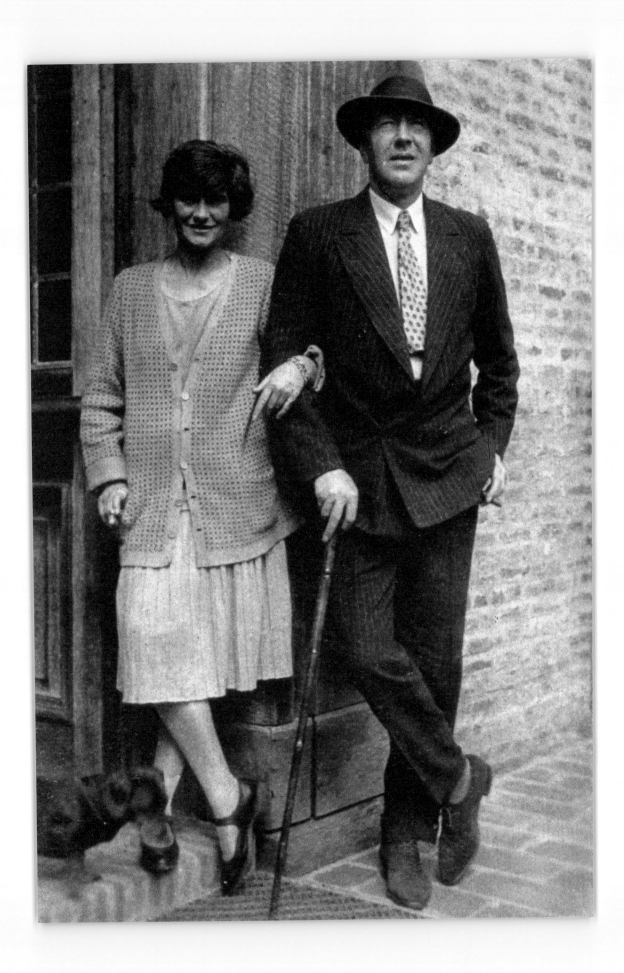

THE DUKE OF WESTMINSTER

On the wild western edge of Scotland, not far from Cape Wrath, a river runs through heather-covered hillsides, towards the dark waters of Loch Stack. It is as remote a place as any in Europe – there are no crofts, no crops – and golden eagles still fly above the high mountains, and deer inhabit the glens. But this landscape is a cherished wilderness, its severe grandeur protected from encroachments, and has been so for more than a century. Comprising over 100,000 acres, the Reay Forest estate was leased by the 1st Duke of Westminster in 1866 from his father-in-law, the Duke of Sutherland, and bought outright in 1920 by his heir, the 2nd Duke of Westminster (known to his family and friends as Bendor, after his grandfather's Derby-winning stallion).

On a summer's afternoon, the pale-grey sky reflected in the quiet pools of the River Laxford, it seems unassailably distant from Paris; a Highland sanctuary, hidden by ramparts of cliffs and sheer granite crags, beyond the reach of fashionable chatter or couture collections. But in the beautifully preserved fishing records of the Reay estate office, there are leather-bound volumes containing pages that mark the visits of Mademoiselle Chanel to the river, and her considerable success as a fisherwoman. The first date her name appears is 27th May 1925; according to the records, she caught a 9lb salmon in the Duke's pool. A few days later, on 1st June, Mademoiselle Chanel had landed a bigger fish – over 12lb, and half a pound heavier than the

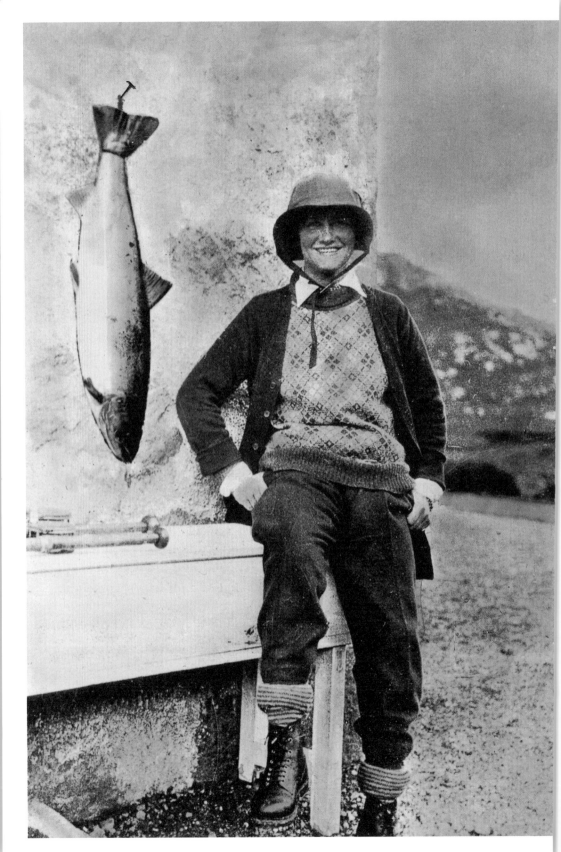

salmon caught that day by her host, the Duke of Westminster. As the summer progressed, so did Mademoiselle's fishing skills; she was on the River Laxford and Loch Stack throughout June, July and August, reeling in salmon and sea trout. On 30th September 1925, she caught her biggest one yet, a 17lb salmon, and landed another of the same size the following day.

Two years later, in 1927, after Chanel had enjoyed a third summer of fishing with the Duke of Westminster on the Laxford, Winston Churchill joined them for a week at the end of September. Churchill's friendship with Bendor (whom he affectionately dubbed Bennie) was long-standing, and they had remained close throughout the Duke's two marriages (to Shelagh Cornwallis-West, from whom he had separated in 1913, and then to Violet Nelson, his wife from 1920 to 1924). Indeed, Churchill and the Duke were related through marriage, for after the death of Winston's father, Lord Randolph Churchill, his mother had married Bendor's brother-in-law, George Cornwallis-West, in 1900. Thus Churchill had been a frequent visitor to Bendor's houses on the Sutherland estate – Stack Lodge, beside the River Laxford, and Lochmore, a turreted granite Victorian mansion overlooking the loch – and it was from Stack that he wrote to his wife, Clemmie, in early October 1927:

'Coco is here in place of Violet. She fishes from morn till night, & in 2 months has killed 50 salmon. She is vy agreeable – really a gt & strong being fit to rule a man or an Empire. Bennie vy well & I think extremely happy to be mated with an equal – her ability balancing his power. We are only 3 on the river & have all the plums.'

In the evenings, the three of them played the card game bezique in the sitting room of the wood-panelled fishing lodge, where stag antlers still hang on either side of the fireplace. Stack Lodge remains much as it was when Chanel stayed here in the Twenties – the upstairs bedrooms snug beneath the eaves; cottage rooms, unlike the ducal splendour of Lochmore – and there is still no other building in sight, its mountain views and isolation maintained by the narrow stone bridge that is the sole way across the river to the lodge. The mansion at Lochmore is equally quiet – empty now, its echoing rooms inhabited only by the sightless heads of stags, their glass eyes gone or clouded, and a cabinet of stuffed birds, kestrel and curlew, jacksnipe and grouse – and its windows overgrown with roses gone wild.

It was here that Bendor died, in July 1953, after returning from a fishing expedition; and the diarist Chips Channon captured something of the grandeur of his life, as well as a way of life that died with him: '… magnificent, courteous, a mixture of Henry the Eighth and Lorenzo il Magnifico, he lived for pleasure – and women – for seventy-four years. His wealth was incalculable; his charm overwhelming; but he was restless, spoilt, irritable, and rather splendid in a very English way.'

The Duke's reputation as a playboy had already been established three decades previously, when Coco Chanel first met him in Monte Carlo at the end of 1923. Over six foot tall, heavily set, and weather-beaten from sailing and shooting, but still handsome at 44, Bendor was hugely attractive to women, without being particularly sophisticated. 'He is a kindly, good-humoured fellow, like a great Newfoundland puppy,' wrote one of his friends, Wilfrid Blunt, 'much given to riotous amusements and sports, with horses, motors, and ladies. The fast life clearly suits him, for he looks a model of health and strength.' Easily bored and constantly on the move, as if he could not bear his own thoughts to catch up with him, Westminster surrounded himself with people; though Chanel later described him to Paul Morand as 'simplicity made man, the shyest person I've ever met. He has the shyness of kings, of people who are isolated through their circumstances and through their wealth.'

The richest man in Britain, with an income reputed to be a guinea a minute, and an immense property portfolio that included most of Mayfair and Belgravia, Bendor had inherited the Grosvenor family fortune outright from his grandfather, the 1st Duke of Westminster, after his death on 22nd December 1899. Bendor was just 20 at the time; he had lost his father as a child (Earl Grosvenor, who suffered from epilepsy, died in 1884, when Bendor was four years old). His mother, Lady Sibell, subsequently married a romantic 24-year-old, George Wyndham, who was only 16 years older than Bendor and treated him more like a younger brother than a son. Bendor was thereafter raised in an atmosphere of great affection, but little in the way of Victorian discipline. His mother and stepfather were leading lights in the aristocratic group known as the Souls, a coterie of rich and beautiful people who professed an adoration of literature, art, nature, and each other. Wyndham was a charming and loving companion to his three stepchildren – Bendor had two older sisters, Constance (always known as Cuckoo) and Lettice – and to his son, Percy, who was born when Bendor was eight. But Bendor's upbringing was a curious mixture of parental absence and indulgence. He always declared he had no memory of his father, Earl Grosvenor, aside from receiving a spanking from him, and his mother and stepfather had busy social lives that often took them away from home; yet Wyndham also bestowed a sense of fun upon his stepson's childhood. Six months after marrying Sibell, Wyndham wrote to his mother about the festivities of his twenty-fifth birthday. 'Everyone was in the best of spirits at breakfast; Sibell complained that her egg had got a little cold, and I said mine had got a little cough. In the morning we had athletic sports, high jump, long jump, and the jump hand-in-hand over hedges, then swinging till luncheon. In the afternoon, cricket … Then races, handicaps until dinner, after dinner we let off all the fireworks … After the fireworks the children went to swing again until half past ten o'clock.'

At Eton, Bendor was a natural athlete, a golden-haired boy who was popular with his contemporaries. Never more than academically average, he joined the Royal House Guards ('The Blues') in 1899 and was posted to South Africa as aide-de-camp to Sir Alfred Milner, the Governor General. When the Boer War was declared later that year, on 11th October, Bendor became ADC to Field Marshal Lord Roberts, Commander-in-Chief of the South African Forces, and thrived on the danger and camaraderie of battle. It was there that he met Winston Churchill, their friendship deepened by the shared experience of a mounted Afrikaaner ambush while they were travelling by train from Pretoria; and subsequently sealed by a day spent fox-hunting together near Cape Town. Two months after his return to England, Bendor was engaged to be married to his childhood sweetheart Shelagh Cornwallis-West; their wedding took place seven weeks later, on 16th February 1901, and Churchill, by then an MP, was amongst the guests. The young couple moved into the London mansion that Bendor had inherited from his grandfather, Grosvenor House on Park Lane, which contained a priceless art collection (including Gainsborough's *The Blue Boy*, Sir Joshua Reynolds' portrait of *Mrs Siddons as the Tragic Muse*, five Rembrandts and a Rubens room); and Eaton Hall, the Duke of Westminster's vast Gothic country house in Cheshire.

The imposing interior of Eaton remained much as it had done in the 1st Duke's lifetime – *The Adoration of the Magi* by Rubens hung at the top of the staircase, the steps of which were flanked by medieval suits of armour; the panelled dining room, large enough to seat 60 people, was lined with family portraits by Gainsborough and Reynolds – but Bendor introduced new amusements to the estate. Aside from the traditional diversions of hunting and shooting, there was cricket, croquet, tennis, boating, a nine-hole golf course, and a regular polo tournament, where 10 teams and 92 ponies would be put up

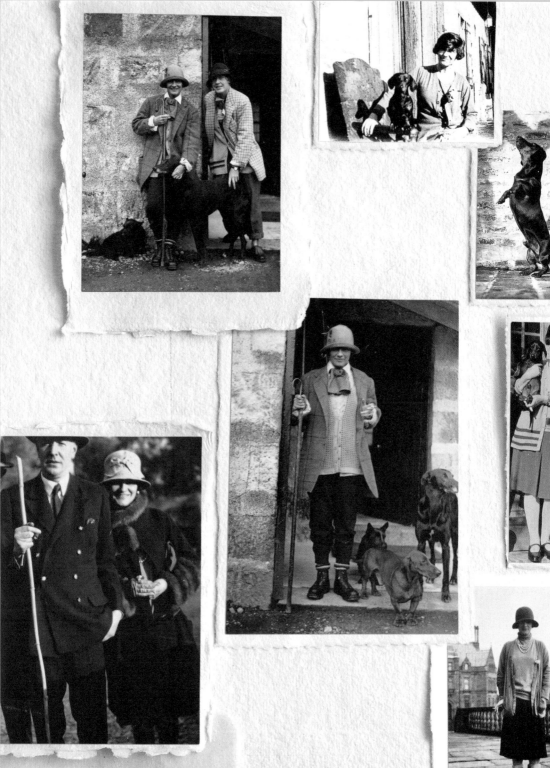

Previously unseen pictures from a private album. Top left:
Chanel with Vera Bate at Lochmore. Top right: Chanel at
Mimizan, the Duke of Westminster's hunting lodge in France.
Centre: Chanel in Scotland. Centre right: Chanel at Eaton Hall.
Bottom left: Chanel with the Duke of Westminster at Eaton Hall.
Bottom right: Chanel on the terrace at Eaton Hall.

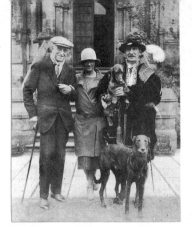

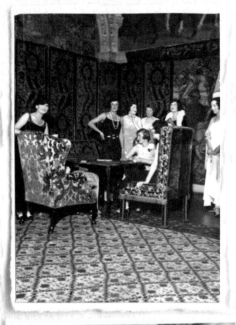

Top left: Chanel at Eaton Hall. Centre left: Chanel at Mimizan.
Centre right: Chanel (left) in the drawing room at Eaton Hall,
photographed by the Duchess of Marlborough.
Lower centre right: Chanel (in sapphire) entertaining the Duke
of Westminster's house party in the drawing room at Eaton
Hall. Bottom: The grounds of Eaton Hall.

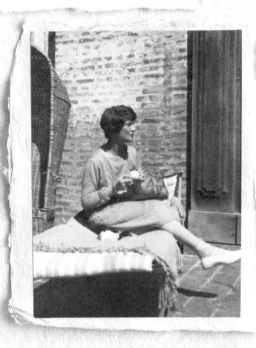

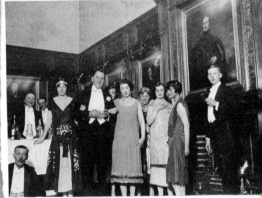

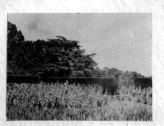

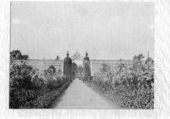

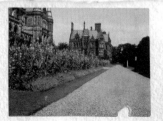

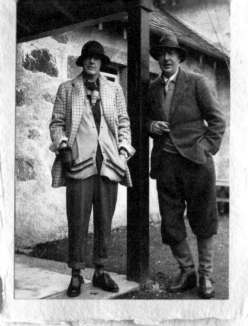

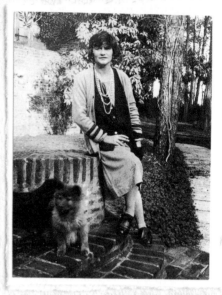

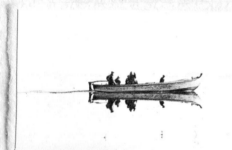

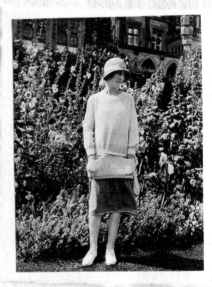

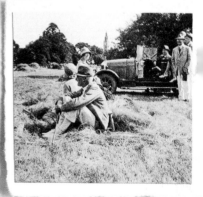

Top left: Vera Bate and the Duke of Westminster in Scotland.
Top right: Chanel at Mimizan. Centre right: Chanel in the garden at
Eaton Hall. Bottom left: The Duke of Westminster's estate in Scotland.
Bottom right: The grounds of Eaton Hall.

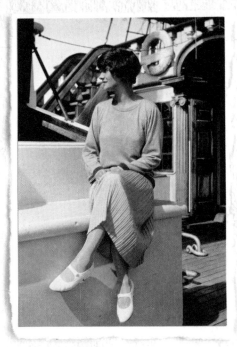

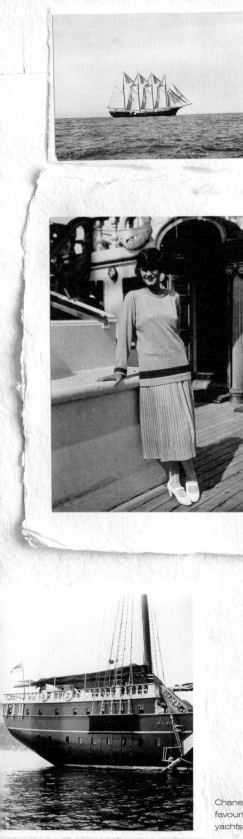

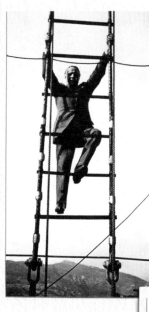

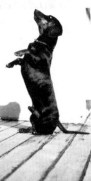

Chanel, the Duke of Westminster and his favourite dachshund aboard one of his yachts, the *Flying Cloud*.

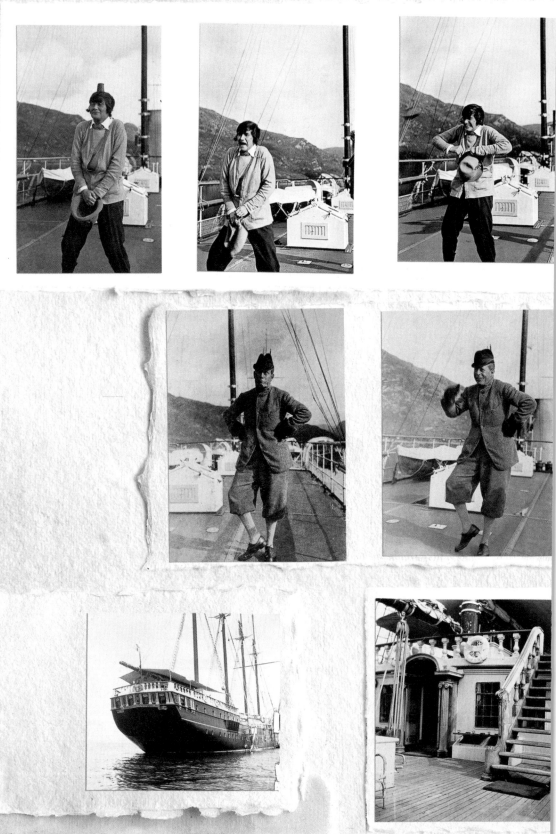

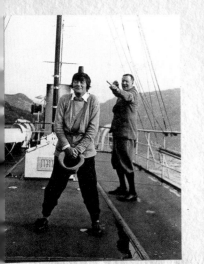
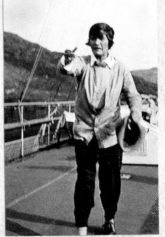
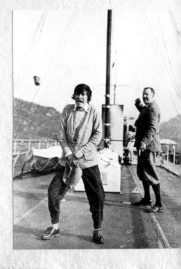

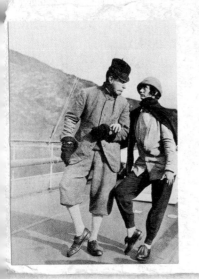
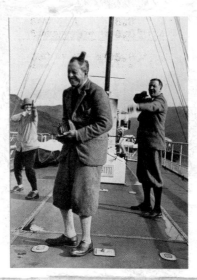

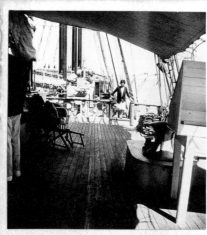
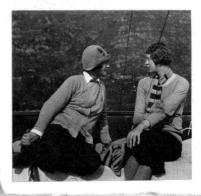

Chanel with friends and the Duke of Westminster aboard
the *Flying Cloud*.

for a week. George Wyndham, by then a Conservative MP and Chief Secretary for Ireland, observed approvingly: 'I welcome keenness at his age in anything and he is delightfully keen. The whole place has been turned into the embodiment of a boy's holidays … He has constructed a steeple-chase course and a mile-and-a-half of high tarred rails … The old Deer-house is now the home of badgers whose lives have been spared after digging out to assist fox-hunting. The stables are crammed with hunters, chase-horses, polo ponies, Basutos, carriage horses, American Trotters and two motor cars. He enjoys it all from morning to night … But it's all very boyish and delightful: no luxury.'

And in some sense, Bendor did seem to have brought a youthful informality to Eaton; a not inconsiderable feat, given the grand scale of the house, after his grandfather had commissioned Alfred Waterhouse, the architect of the Natural History Museum in London, to remodel it into a Victorian palace which sceptics compared to St Pancras station. The Gothic style was 'perfectly suited to modern needs', Waterhouse had declared, in defence of his redesign of Eaton in the 1870s (a process that took 12 years, at a cost of over £600,000); but the sheer size of Eaton was daunting, for as one visitor commented, it was 'a huge pile, like a small town'. By the time the house was completed, the 1st Duke had already begun to have grave doubts about it. 'Now that I have built a Palace,' he wrote to his daughter-in-law Lady Sibell, 'I wish I lived in a cottage.'

Yet Bendor seemed happy at Eaton in the early years of his marriage, occupying a private wing with Shelagh, along with his large pack of dachshunds, who accompanied him everywhere but proved so impossible to house-train that several maids had to follow in their trail, mopping up behind them. The birth, in 1902, of the Westminsters' first child, a baby girl named Ursula, did not supplant Bendor's beloved dogs from his affections; and life went on much as before, with regular house parties at Eaton of up to 60 guests, and an army of liveried staff to cater to them. Even more lavish entertaining took place at Grosvenor House; such was the splendour of the parties that Marie, Crown Princess of Romania (herself a granddaughter of Queen Victoria), described a ball there in July 1902 as 'the finished perfection' of a season of 'peace and plenty'. In her memoirs she noted the beauty of the young Duchess of Westminster, 'a tall, brilliantly effective woman, covered with jewels', and of Shelagh's sister, Daisy, by then the Princess of Pless, 'gold-clad, with a high diamond tiara on her honey-coloured hair'. There was dancing in the ballroom and an 'exquisite supper-hall': 'This enormous blue-and-silver flower-filled room was a feast for the eye … Perfectly liveried footmen with that stately deportment peculiar to English servants, every one of them picked out for their fine figures and good looks, prodigious flowers, exquisite china, glass and silver, clever lighting, flattering to the complexion; in the distance soft music. I sat there drinking in all this beauty rendered possible only by generations of civilisation and wealth. This was perfection: no doubt it had meant much thought, effort also, but the effort was not felt, there was neither hustle, haste nor confusion; it was all as though it could not be otherwise, and therein lay that exquisite feeling of peace and content.'

Yet for all the polished surfaces, the gleam of serenity and the security of wealth, the Duke and his wife were not quite at peace together. In March 1903, after one of the many house parties at Eaton – the guests this time included the Prince and Princess of Wales – Daisy was sufficiently concerned about her sister to record in her diary, 'Poor little girl, she cried yesterday; but I told her every woman gets more and more disappointed as she gets older, and no husband turns out to be as one expected.' The following year, in November 1904, Shelagh gave birth to a baby son, Edward George Hugh Grosvenor; but despite Bendor's delight at gaining an heir, the couple began to spend more time apart. They still entertained on a lavish scale, but often travelled abroad separately, each in their own yacht, and with their own retinues of servants. Rumour had it that Shelagh was involved in a romance with the Duke of Alba, one of the most dashing of the so-called 'Eaton set' who socialised with the Westminsters; and Bendor enjoyed his own liaisons, or what he described as 'nocturnal adventures', which were amongst the many diversions on offer at house parties, as long as a façade of decorum was observed. (The most important thing to remember on a surreptitious night-time excursion, according to Bendor, was to walk on the side of the staircase, as it creaked less.)

The marriage remained intact, however, until a tragedy exposed the painful cracks and splinters. In February 1909, the Westminsters' 4-year-old son died of appendicitis at Eaton, following an operation that had been delayed for several days after the boy had first fallen ill. Bendor blamed Shelagh, accusing her of neglect and carelessness; Shelagh, as consumed with grief as her husband, did not attend Edward's funeral. 'Oh! what a big blank he has left in my life,' she wrote to Daisy a fortnight later. 'I feel as if the world had grown suddenly dark, and I am groping to see and touch a little light.'

A few days afterwards, Bendor and Shelagh sailed for Monte Carlo with their daughter, Ursula, to stay with Princess Daisy and her husband, but the darkness still lay upon them. 'The weather has been awful, snow storms, rain and thunder,' reported Daisy in her diary on 7th March, '… the sea was dreadful, enormous waves breaking on the shore and a swell on, just as if a great tidal wave was running over us … We walked afterwards to the stone pier (not very high) – really a sort of breakwater – in Cannes. A lot of children were playing about and as we turned to go home they shouted that a child had fallen in and was drowned. We ran back, but there was nothing to be done. Shelagh turned and said: "Bendor will go in, for God's Sake, stop him …" and

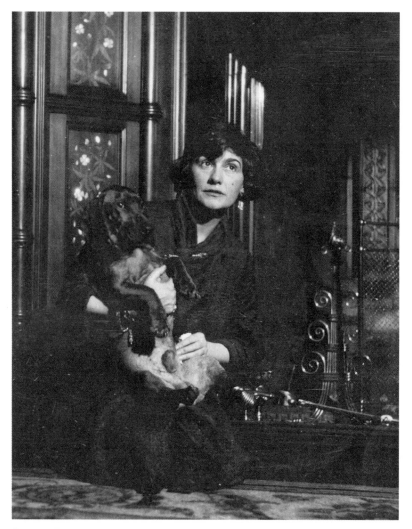

Chanel at Eaton Hall.

as I climbed down to the rocks to hold him, I heard him groan. He would have gone in, in a moment, if there had been the slightest chance, but the waves were enormous and there was nothing to be seen.'

Bendor was only 29 at the time of his son's death – his thirtieth birthday was on 19th March, soon after that sombre day in Cannes – and most people assumed that he would father another heir, and that the young couple's life would resume as before. Certainly, Daisy's diary entry for 14th November 1909 suggested that there was reason to be hopeful. 'My happy surprise is – that little Shelagh writes she is almost certain she is getting a baby – and oh, I am so glad, please God it will be a boy ... I only hope that she will grasp at the little rays of sun in her life and be thankful for every bright day.' In fact, Shelagh's grief had not abated; she still thought she could hear her dead son's footsteps along the long, shadowy corridors of Eaton, and her nights in London were solitary ones. As soon as her pregnancy had been confirmed, Bendor ceased to sleep in the same house as her, nor did he dine with her; or indeed have any contact with her at all, except when they were entertaining guests.

Perhaps the marriage might have recovered if the third child had been a boy, but on 27th June 1910, Shelagh gave birth to a baby girl, christened Mary. Shelagh's mother Patsy Cornwallis-West wrote to Daisy: 'Shelagh's little baby ... is, alas, a little girl! ... she has only seen it once in the dark, and Bendor not at all ... God help them both.'

God did not come much into the unravelling of their marriage, although Bendor, who was unexpectedly capable of exhibiting devout faith, did attend Holy Communion with one of his lovers, Gertie Millar, the most popular musical comedy star of the day. The daughter of a Bradford millworker, Gertie was already famously alluring when she met Bendor, and their affair lasted for several years, until she discovered that he was involved with the ballerina Anna Pavlova. There were also rumours that the Duke was in love with Pamela Lytton, the woman who had devastated Churchill when she rejected his proposal, marrying instead the 2nd Earl of Lytton, with whom she had two sons.

In January 1913, Bendor wrote to his wife from his remote hunting lodge in France (a relatively new acquisition, where he established a pack of a hundred Cheshire hounds and 40 horses, along with numerous servants in Grosvenor livery, all of them in constant readiness should His Grace wish to hunt boar in the surrounding forests of Mimizan). His letter was firm and to the point. 'I think you will agree with me that our present mode of living is impossible, and cannot go on any longer … As I cannot for a moment imagine that living at my two houses alone in London and the country can be a source of satisfaction to you, I have requested my solicitor to make you such an allowance as would enable you to live as you should, in the utmost comfort.'

His offer of £13,000 a year was turned down by Shelagh's solicitors, and she wrote to her husband, asking him to reconsider his decision. 'I write to make one more appeal to you for the children's sake, if not for your own and mine. I beg you to return to me. If you do so, I am willing to allow all bygones to be bygones, and do what I can to make you happy.'

The Duke refused, and the legal wranglings continued; although there was some happier family news the following month, when Bendor's much-loved half brother, Percy Wyndham, announced his engagement to Lord Ribblesdale's daughter, Diana Lister. On 16th April 1913, the day before their wedding, Bendor hosted a celebratory dinner for both families at Grosvenor House. Afterwards, the groom's father, George Wyndham – by then an eminent politician, though at 49 a far more disillusioned figure than he had been at the time of his own marriage – wrote to Wilfrid Blunt about his son's forthcoming wedding: 'It is just possible that they have "hit off" an alliance of Heroic Love combined with matrimony. If this should prove to be so, they are lucky. In any case they are happy and exuberant for the moment. As a rule people do not know how to love; as an exception they love now here, now there; as a rarity almighty lovers find each other after both are married. It is extravagant to suppose that Percy and Diana are going to be lovers and, also, husband and wife. But it is pleasant to contemplate the hypothesis.'

Less than two months afterwards, George Wyndham died in Paris, while on holiday there with Bendor. His death, at first thought to be caused by heart failure, then by a blood clot, was unexpected, and a bitter blow to Bendor, to whom Wyndham had been a constant and loving friend, if not quite a surrogate father, for over a quarter of a century. A fortnight later, Bendor and Shelagh's solicitors finally agreed on the terms of a legal separation, and a kind of calm was restored as the rituals of the Season continued, the balls and polo parties, grouse shoots and tennis tournaments. But with the British declaration of war against Germany in August 1914, those familiar routines were utterly disrupted. Bendor rejoined his regiment, and paid a visit to Winston Churchill, by then First Lord of the Admiralty, just before reporting for duty. At the French front he saw much of his half-brother, but for a tragically short time, as Percy Wyndham was killed in the early weeks of the war, on 14th September. 'He went in good company with several of his friends in a way most befitting to him, with a heap of Germans slain around him,' wrote Bendor to his sister Cuckoo. Wyndham's death left his wife, Diana, a young widow (thus setting in motion the odd sequence of coincidences that introduced Diana into the lives of Boy Capel and Coco Chanel; for it was Capel who was to become Diana's second husband). But this, and other deaths in battle of the Grosvenor family, did nothing to stop Bendor's vigorous commitment to the war; indeed, he seemed energised in a manner that he had not displayed since he last served as an officer, in South Africa. This time, his enthusiasm for motoring found expression in his instigation and financing of a squadron of armoured vehicles, which saw action in France and then in Egypt, where Bendor deployed them to rescue 91 British prisoners-of-war. Bendor was recommended for a Victoria Cross for his bravery, and Sir John Maxwell, who led the British forces in Egypt, wrote of him: 'A less determined or resourceful commander might well have shirked the responsibility of taking cars on the first occasion 30 miles, and on the second 115 miles, into unknown desert with the uncertainty of the cars being able to negotiate the country and the amount of resistance that was likely to be encountered. I venture to think these actions constitute a record in the History of War.'

In the event, Bendor received the DSO, and after protracted bouts of tropical fever, he left North Africa and went to work for Churchill at the Ministry of Munitions, accompanying him to meetings with Clemenceau in Paris (where it is entirely possible the Duke might have encountered Boy Capel). Churchill, recalling these war years in later life, gave some indication of the admiration he felt for one of his oldest friends. 'If he had not been a Duke he would have got the VC in the First War. He is incapable of expressing himself, but he is always thinking a hundred years ahead.'

This observation might also apply to the Duke's relationships with women, at least in his determination to have a son to inherit his title and estates, and ensure his influence on future generations of the Grosvenor family. The woman that he chose to be his second wife was Violet Nelson, the youngest daughter of a wealthy self-made man, Sir William Nelson. She had been married once, to George Rowley, an Old Etonian and officer in the Coldstream Guards, with whom she had a son, born in 1915. Violet was an excellent horsewoman as well as an attractive member of smart London society; and at 29, there seemed no reason why she should not give Bendor the heir he so desperately desired. After her divorce, Violet married Bendor on 26th November 1920 at a registry office on Buckingham Palace Road. (The bride wore a blue and green plaid dress, a fur stole and a black hat with a brown veil; the groom was in a dark overcoat and bowler hat.)

The union produced a new yacht, but no baby; perhaps in consequence, Bendor lavished much money and attention on his boat, which he christened the *Flying Cloud*. One of the largest private yachts in the world, it had a crew of 40 and white sails flying over a white wooden deck, pristine as a virginal wedding dress or a newborn's christening gown, rising above the piratical black hull. 'This is a most attractive yacht,' wrote Winston Churchill to his wife while aboard in August 1923. 'Imagine a large four-masted cargo boat, fitted up in carved oak like a little country house, with front doors, staircases & lovely pictures. She can sail 12 knots and motor 8, & accommodate 16 guests. Benny very charming & Violet too …'

Four months later, when Chanel met Bendor in Monte Carlo, he immediately asked her to dine aboard the *Flying Cloud*, which was anchored close by. They had been introduced by Vera Bate (*née* Arkwright), a friend of Bendor's and others in the small world of the British aristocracy, who was working for Chanel, less as a model (though she was a handsome, statuesque figure in her Chanel outfits) than as a facilitator whose social connections were invaluable. Chanel described it thus to Paul Morand: 'I have employed society people, not to indulge my vanity or to humiliate them (I would take other forms of revenge, supposing I were seeking them), but … because they were useful to me and because they got around Paris, working on my behalf.'

As it happened, Vera's origins were gossiped about in Paris in a not dissimilar way to Boy Capel's; though in her case the facts are more readily excavated from the ash of ancient scandals. Her mother, Rosa, was a younger daughter of Captain William Baring of the Coldstream Guards, himself the grandson of the merchant banker Sir Francis Baring. In 1878, at the age of 24, Rosa married Captain Frank Arkwright, also a Coldstreamer. Their first child was a son, Esme, and their second (at least for official purposes), born in 1885, was Sarah Gertrude (thereafter known to all as Vera). In fact, Rosa and her first husband were already estranged at the time of Vera's birth, and divorced that same year. There was some speculation that Vera was fathered by the first Marquess of Cambridge, Prince Adolphus of Teck, but it seems equally likely that her actual father was Colonel George Fitzgeorge, whom Rosa married on 25th November

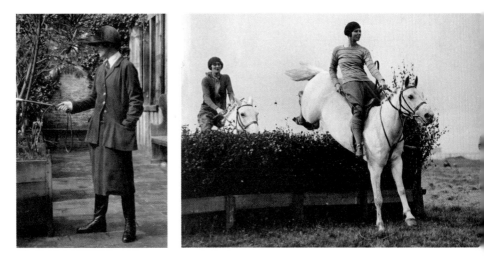

Chanel in riding habit, and right, horse-jumping (far left).

1885, just a couple of months after Vera's birth. Fitzgeorge was a man whose own origins were somewhat complicated, for he was the illegitimate grandson of King George III. But whether or not he was her father or stepfather, Fitzgeorge was also bankrupt, leaving Vera with no option but to earn her own living.

In 1916, she married an American, Fred Bate, an officer in the US army, who was subsequently employed by the American broadcaster NBC in London. The Bates had a daughter, Bridget (who was to become a model, for Man Ray amongst others, and then an artist in her own right); but Vera spent a great deal of time away from her husband and daughter, as she was when she encountered Bendor during the Christmas season in Monte Carlo. Westminster joined Vera and Chanel at their table, and promptly issued the invitation to his yacht; Chanel accepted, later telling a convoluted version of the story to Paul Morand. In this account, she changed Vera's name to Pamela (perhaps because, by the time of her conversations with Morand, she had fallen out with Vera), and declared that the entire transaction was down to money: according to Chanel, Vera/Pamela said to her, 'Do me a favour. It won't cost you anything. If you do it for me, I shall be given a present ... Westminster has just arrived. His yacht is lying at anchor off Monaco. He wants to meet you. I have promised, in exchange for a reward, to take you to dine there.' Chanel was amused by such plain speaking, she said, although not surprised. 'I was accustomed to Pamela, accustomed to seeing women purely as monsters.'

If Chanel saw women as money-grabbing monsters, then she may also have had mixed feelings about her lover at the time, the Grand Duke Dmitri, who was dependent on her financial support, as were a variety of others (Diaghilev, Stravinsky, et al.). But as was clear from her very first dinner with Westminster, her substantial wealth was entirely eclipsed by his. For here was a man, like Boy Capel before him, who could provide her with absolute financial security, even if she chose not to accept it, yet whose fidelity could never be guaranteed. Chanel's hesitation, for several months, before embarking upon an affair with the Duke is suggestive, amongst other things, of her uncertainty when faced with this complex equation of loss and gain, or the unanswerable question of whether love, like money, could be counted upon. In the end, she told Claude Delay, she favoured Westminster over Dmitri – 'I chose the one who protected me best' – but she could never fully trust either. There were good reasons not to do so – both men were incorrigible womanisers – and yet perhaps there was something in their lack of commitment that was familiar to her. After all, despite the determination with which she had obscured her origins, Chanel remained her father's daughter, bearing the name and legacy of a man who had vanished from her life; a man who had broken his promise and her belief that he would return having made his fortune.

It was as impossible for Chanel as it was for anyone to ignore Westminster's wealth and power, however resolved she may have been to remain independent. 'Westminster is the richest man in England, perhaps in Europe,' she said to Morand, before adding a caveat in parenthesis: '(No one knows this, not even him, especially not him.)' In fact, everyone knew it, including Bendor, for his inheritance was an essential part of his identity, emblematic of his sense of himself. Having made this odd disclaimer, Chanel continued, 'I mention this firstly because at such a level wealth is no longer vulgar, it is located well beyond envy and it assumes catastrophic proportions; but I mention it above all because it makes Westminster the last offspring of a vanished civilisation, a palaeontological curiosity …'

As she described Westminster to Morand in 1946, her ambivalence about him (and about Englishmen, or possibly all men) was threaded through with genuine affection, of the kind that Chanel rarely expressed at that point in her life, when her unhappiness had solidified into bitterness, even malice. 'Ten years of my life have been spent with Westminster,' she said, eliding the many years thereafter, and with them his third marriage (in 1930, to Loelia Ponsonby, the decorous daughter of a royal courtier) and the Second World War. 'Beneath his clumsy exterior, he's a skilful hunter. You'd have to be skilful to hang on to me for ten years. These ten years were spent living very lovingly and very amicably with him. We have remained friends. I loved him, or I thought I loved him, which amounts to the same thing. He is courtesy itself, kindness personified. He still belongs to a generation of well-brought-up men. All Englishmen, for that matter, are well brought up, until they reach Calais at least.'

Of course, she knew the stories about his two wives and multiple mistresses; and although Bendor was beguiling, she had already lost her heart to an Englishman, who then broke it twice over. 'I am sure it was Boy who sent Westminster to me,' she told Claude Delay, as if the English still stuck together, even in the afterlife. But to Paul Morand, she declared, 'Westminster liked me because I was French. English women are possessive and cold. Men get bored with them.'

Was she thinking of one Englishwoman in particular: of Diana Capel? In a curious quirk of coincidence – or as she saw it, fate, orchestrated by Boy Capel from beyond the grave – she had found herself being pursued by Diana's first husband's half-brother. This might have had no significance, were it not for the fact that Diana had represented a way into the British aristocracy for Boy Capel; but the entrée offered to Coco by Bendor was infinitely grander. Even as she tried to remain aloof, he wooed her with the fruits of his land and his riches; at times quite literally, sending baskets of exotic produce that he had picked himself from his hothouses at Eaton, and camellias, gardenias and orchids from his gardens. Once, during the Duke's ardent courtship of Chanel, a crate of fresh vegetables was delivered to her in Paris. When the butler unpacked its contents, he discovered a large uncut emerald hidden in a jewel case at the bottom. On another occasion, Chanel's manservant answered the door to find a vast bouquet of flowers hiding the face of the deliveryman, and was just about to tip him when he recognised him as Bendor. A few days later, the Duke called on Coco at Rue Cambon with the Prince of Wales at his side, as if to prove that he was a royal equal, even as he paid court to her; soon afterwards, she finally succumbed to his charms.

By the spring of 1924, Coco and Bendor were an item: he was seen at rehearsals for *Le Train bleu*, the Ballets Russes production for which she had designed the costumes; and she joined him for cruises aboard the *Flying Cloud*. A yacht, she later remarked to Claude Delay, was by far the best place to begin a love affair. 'The first time you're clumsy, the second you quarrel a bit, and if it doesn't go well, the third time you can stop at a port.'

But it did go well, and doors opened for her everywhere. At Eaton, she slipped into the role of châtelaine with the same ease as she wore her silk fringed evening gowns, in sapphire blue or black, designed so as not to crease when they were packed for travelling. She rode and hunted at Eaton and accompanied Bendor to the races; and after he bought another Scottish mansion, Rosehall, in 1926, she decorated it with her characteristic style, introducing what was said to be the first bidet in the Highlands in an en-suite bathroom, with hand-blocked French wallpaper on the bedroom walls, and beige-painted drawing rooms downstairs. 'This is a vy agreeable house,' wrote

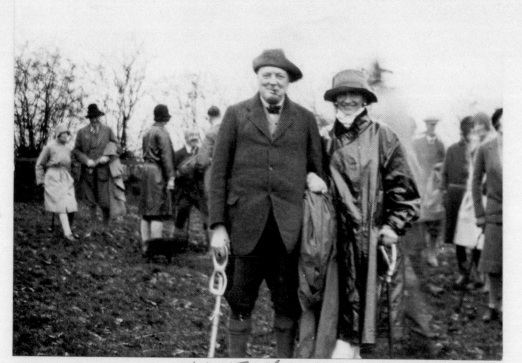

Above: Chanel with Winston Churchill at Eaton, 1929.
Right: Fishing records from Lochmore, 1927.

Date	Name	Place	Salmon	Weight	Grilse
	Brought forward.		237	3559½	39
1st.	Rt. Hon. W. Churchill.	Top Pool.	1	20	
"	Rt. Hon. W. Churchill.	Lower Top Pool.	1	12	
"	Mlle. Chanel.	Duchess Pool.	1	24	1
"	Mlle. Chanel.	Duchess Pool.	1	16	
"	Mlle. Chanel.	Upper Duchess Pool.	1	19	
"	Mlle. Chanel.	Duchess Pool.	1	15	
"	Mlle. Chanel.	Island Pool.	1	16	
"	Mlle. Chanel.	Fern Pool.	1	17	
"	Mlle. Chanel.	Fern Pool.	1	15	
3rd.	Mlle. Chanel.	Top Pool.	1	18	
"	Mlle. Chanel.	Duchess Pool.	1	17	
"	Mlle. Chanel.	Duchess Pool.	1	12	
"	Mlle. Chanel.	Meadow Pool.	1	14	
"	Duke of Westminster.	Ridge Pool.	1	18½	
"	Rt. Hon. W. Churchill.	Meadow Pool.	1	14	1
"	Sergt. Thomson.	Home Pool.	1	14½	
th.	Mlle. Chanel.	Lower Top Pool.			1
"	Mlle. Chanel.	Duchess Pool.			1
"	Rt. Hon. W. Churchill.	Lord Belgraves Pool.			1
5th.	Rt. Hon. W. Churchill.	Meadow Pool.	1	14½	1
	Carried forward.		254.	3836.	45.

Winston Churchill to his wife, whilst on a fishing trip to Rosehall in May 1928. 'Only Benny, Coco & one of his ADC's, Ernest Ball. The air is most exhilarating, keen and yet caressing … Coco got three fish yesterday. This place is 45 miles from Loch More but both rivers are available. This morning it is raining wh[ich] is good for fishing.'

Churchill had already observed Chanel approvingly on a boar-hunting expedition to Mimizan, and thereafter in Paris, where he visited her at her workrooms in Rue Cambon. On 27th January 1927, Churchill wrote in a letter to his wife: 'The famous Coco turned up & I took a gt fancy to her – A most capable and agreeable woman – much the strongest personality Benny has yet been up against. She hunted vigorously all day, motored to Paris after dinner, & is today engaged in passing & improving dresses on endless streams of mannequins. Altogether 200 models [outfits] have to be settled in almost 3 weeks. Some have to be altered ten times. She does it with her own fingers, pinning, cutting, looping, etc. With her – Vera Bate née Arkwright. "Yr Chief of Staff?" Non – "One of yr lieutenants?" Non. "Elle est là. Voilà tout."'

It was in Mimizan that Chanel had a riding accident, when one of the hunting party let a tree-branch spring back at her, which split open her upper lip. Her face was covered in blood, staining her white riding stock; Bendor shouted out, 'Who was the idiot who did that?' and stopped the hunt immediately. Years later, the story was still fresh in her mind as she recounted it to Claude Delay: the Duke had sent for a doctor, but when the man arrived, he turned out to be a vet, who sewed her up with pig's bristle: 'His thread was too thick – provincial.' Chanel took the train back to Paris to see her own doctor, accompanied by a monkey and a parrot that she had bought as pets the previous day, screeching at each other in an unintelligible language ('Brazilian, I think') all through the night journey. She told Delay that she had wept while the monkey clung to her skirt, that it was her 'first breakdown'; which was perhaps an allusion to her realisation that the Duke's protection of her was not complete; or maybe at that moment, badly stitched up and as frightened as the monkey beside her, she really did feel close to the edge.

It was a constant juggling act, of course, for Chanel to maintain her business, and be at Bendor's side. 'He was simplicity itself, simple as a tramp,' she said to Delay; but his demands were nevertheless considerable, and often at odds with her commitment to her business. There was an episode when he shipped over her seamstresses to Eaton, so that she could work on a collection at the same time as being with him; and while he joined her in Paris for her biannual shows – generally held on 5th February and 5th August – he could never hide his restlessness at being with her in Rue Cambon. 'The tiger paced up and down,' she told Delay, even when Bendor knew that she would leave with him in the evening. For more often than not, she organised her schedule in order to travel with him, to places and in the manner of his choosing. 'Westminster has houses everywhere,' she said to Paul Morand. 'On every new trip, I discovered them ... in Ireland, in Dalmatia, or in the Carpathians, there is a house belonging to Westminster, a house where everything is set up, where you can dine and go to bed on your arrival, with polished silverware, motor cars (I can still see the seventeen ancient Rolls in the garage at Eaton Hall!) with their batteries charged, small tankers in the harbour, fully laden with petrol, servants in livery ... On the moors of Scotland, the grouse are ready to be shot, or the salmon to be fished; at the same moment, in the forest of Villers-Cotterets or in the Landes, the stalkers who track the wild boar or stags have only to saddle their horses to prepare the way and pick up the right scents; you have to wonder whether they sleep in their red clothes, or whether the captains of the yachts, which are always under sail ... are not in reality painted onto their poop-decks, and, in short, whether this absurd fairyland (which isn't even intentional, but which exists because that's the way it has been, for generations) is not a bad dream, a tramp's dream.'

It might have been her father's dream – the peddler tramp, who criss-crossed a country but never found what he was looking for – or her childhood fantasy that she would be rescued from the nuns, and live happily ever after as a fairy-tale princess. In reality – if such a thing could be felt, and relied upon, in the dizzying whirlwind of life with Bendor – Chanel was a 40-year-old woman, and as the years passed with him, it became clear that she was not going to become pregnant, despite the doctors she consulted. She entertained his friends – Churchill, the Duke of Marlborough, Lord Lonsdale – and hunted three times a week at Eaton during the season; but her life in Paris had less appeal for him. Aside from Vera Bate, a frequent guest at Eaton and Lochmore (where her name sometimes appears alongside Chanel's in the fishing records), Bendor had little in common with those she was closest to. 'My friends bored him,' she said to Morand. 'He couldn't understand Misia at all, and she couldn't understand England at all. He was appalled by Sert, who sawed off swans' beaks so that they would die of hunger, and who pushed dogs into the Grand Canal in Venice.'

But still, her relationship with Bendor's country strengthened, and whatever her ambivalence towards Englishwomen, she dressed them, and impressed them. In the early June 1927 issue of British *Vogue*, a headline announced the biggest fashion news of the summer: 'Chanel Opens Her London House'. The illustrations showed four models in Chanel pieces, all of them designed for outings in British high society: two white taffeta gowns, 'simple and unadorned', for debutantes to wear to court; and two afternoon frocks for Ascot, one a little black dress in lace, the other in blue silk polka dots.

'Chanel, one of the most popular of great French couturiers, has come to London,' reported *Vogue*. 'In a beautiful Queen Anne house, with panelled walls and parquet floors, mannequins graceful and slender as lilies show us Chanel's latest collection …' The house was close to Westminster's own Georgian residence in Mayfair, Bourdon House on Davies Street (he had sold the lease of Grosvenor House at the end of 1924, during his divorce from Violet), but no mention was made of the Duke in the *Vogue* piece, despite previous items that had appeared in the gossip columns of British newspapers speculating on the possibility that he might marry a famous French couturière.

Nevertheless, the article was an indication of what everyone in smart London society already knew: that Chanel's love affair with Bendor was reflected in her new collection, not least in its implicit understanding of the clothes that were required for the Season; that her status was assured in the British upper classes, even if she had not married the Duke; and that the new House of Chanel in London was also the house that Westminster had given her.

According to *Vogue*, 'We have seen in her collection a number of frocks designed for Ascot and those private functions for which in England one is always more formally dressed than for similar functions in France. We see also in this designer's conception of a Court dress a new idea, strikingly successful in the way it reconciles a charming modernism with a traditional formula. We love tradition as we love beautiful old houses, but we love also that element of youth which makes itself felt wherever it might be; like a blossom, ingenuous and frail, which has just opened in the heart of an old garden, the debutante presented at Court appears, flower-like and youthful, made more charming by the striking contrast she presents with the ancient walls of the Royal palace.

'The Chanel workrooms in London employ only English workgirls under the direction of French *premières*. Only English mannequins show the models. Here in an essentially practical sense, useful to both countries – to Great Britain and to France – is an *entente cordiale*, French chic adapted to English tastes and traditions.'

As it happened, Chanel was also incorporating something of Scotland into her new designs. At Lochmore, she borrowed Bendor's clothes, making his tweeds her own, and wearing them with a panache not usually associated with traditional sporting garb. Having adopted the Duke's wardrobe, she then started sourcing fabrics from a Scottish tweed mill, and turning them into her characteristically soft little jackets and suits. Something of the same process occurred during her stays in Eaton, where she was inspired by the striped waistcoats of Bendor's liveried footmen and butlers, transforming them into what became known to readers of *Vogue* and *Harper's Bazaar* as 'Chanel's English Look', which also included the loose woollen cardigans that she herself wore with the yards of real pearls that the Duke gave to her, a new rope for every birthday, and many others besides.

But for all the gifts of jewels, there was to be no wedding ring. No proof exists that he ever proposed to her, despite the much-repeated story of Chanel refusing to marry Bendor with her famous declaration, 'There have been many Duchesses of Westminster, but only one Coco Chanel.' In fact, this is a myth, as apocryphal as the legend about her childhood with the aunts; and in old age, when asked about the anecdote, she denied having anything to do with its origin, declaring it to be far too vulgar for her to have uttered such nonsense to Bendor: 'He would have laughed in my face if I had ever said it.' A more likely starting point came from a conversation she had at lunch with a diplomat, Sir Charles Mendl, at the British Embassy in Paris. When he asked why she had turned down Westminster's proposal, she replied that there were 'so many duchesses already', to which he added, chivalrously, 'and there's only one Coco Chanel.'

Although their relationship did not produce a child, the heir that Bendor desperately sought and which would have almost certainly resulted in their marriage, it did create something of significance, of which ghostly traces still remain. The graceful Chanel interiors at Rosehall are crumbling now, ceilings collapsing as dry rot takes hold of the timbers, shards of broken glass on the subsiding floors, the French wallpaper fading and the beige paint peeling away; but white azaleas continue to flower in the garden, as they did when Mademoiselle strolled there. And if you walk along certain streets of Mayfair, you can still see a number of double Cs embossed upon the old lampposts; a final emblem of the Duke's gesture towards Coco Chanel, a silent mark of their union, and of the melding of British tradition with French couture, in a style all of its own.

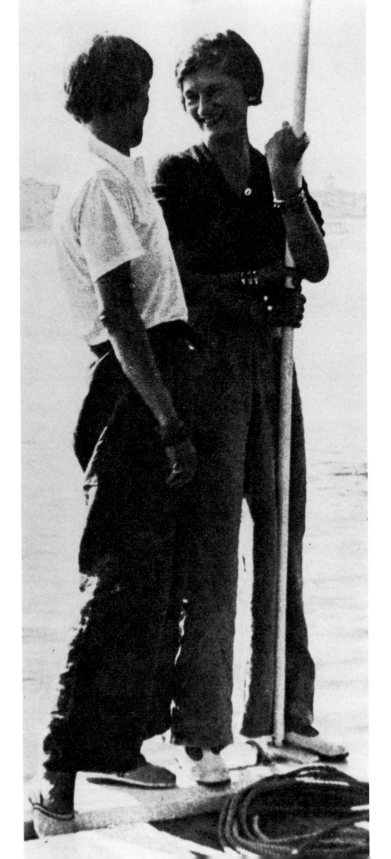

RIVIERA CHIC

If the Duke of Westminster reigned over Eaton and Lochmore, and set the course of journeys aboard his yachts, there was one place that Chanel could call her own, where he would be her guest. La Pausa was entirely her creation, a graceful villa on the French Riviera at Roquebrune, high above the wooded promontory of Cap Martin, with a commanding view of the Mediterranean. It took its name from the legend that Mary Magdalene had rested beneath the olive trees there on her flight from Jerusalem after the Crucifixion, and a chapel dedicated to Our Lady of la Pausa lay close by. In February 1929, Coco Chanel signed the deed of sale for the five acres of land upon which La Pausa was to be built. The general assumption has tended to be that Bendor bought the plot of land and financed the construction of La Pausa, but it was Chanel's name on the deed, and the 1.8 million francs in payment came from her bank account, rather than the Duke's.

Chanel's financial independence was already well established by the time she bought La Pausa; she had a boutique in nearby Cannes, which had opened in 1923, along with a substantial and expanding share of Rue Cambon in Paris. (After buying number 31 Rue Cambon in February 1918, she had added number 29 in April 1923, number 25 in April 1926, and 27 and 23 in October 1927.) Even so, the house that Chanel built in Roquebrune was not simply a splendid outpost to her

n board the Duke of Westminster's yacht with opera singer Marthe Davelli, 1930.
verpage: Models seated on the back of George Baher's yacht. Left to right: June Cox; E. Vogt, earing a dark wool sweater and white flannel skirt by Chanel; Lee Miller, with a scarf by Chanel; d Hanna-Lee Sherman. Edward Steichen, 1928.

CHANEL 173

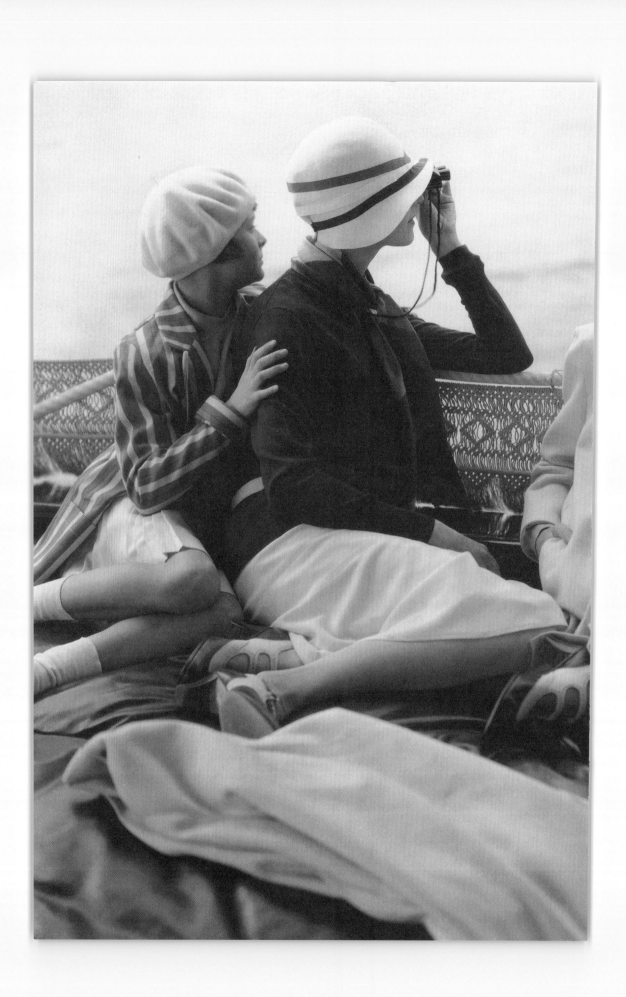

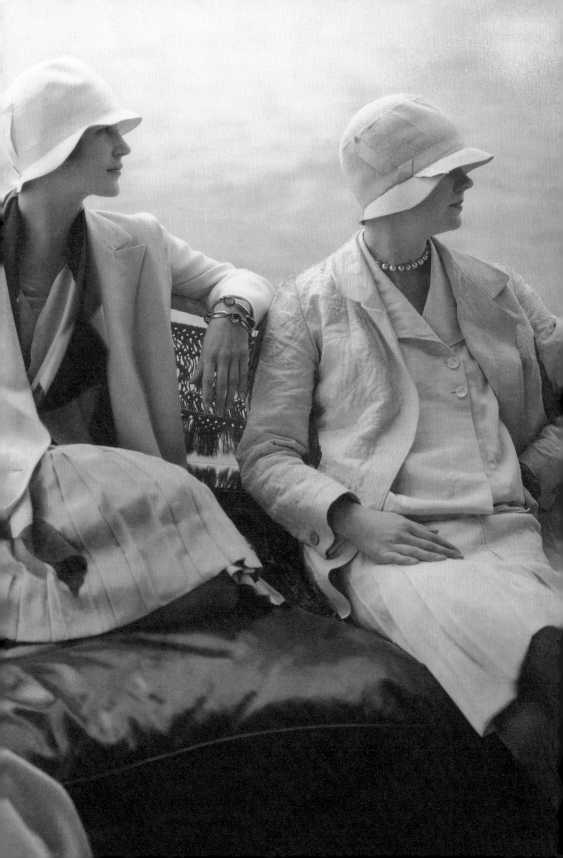

Paris empire, but was itself central to the high society that flourished on the Côte d'Azur.

Chanel was by no means the first to arrive in the Riviera colony of bohemian Americans and Europeans, nor did she invent its associated fashions. But as was often the case in her career as a designer, she was quick to distil its essence, absorbing it into her own style, and selling it to customers eager for her clothes.

She had already proved her understanding of Riviera chic in her costume designs for Diaghilev's *Le Train bleu* in 1924, a ballet that had a scenario by Cocteau and which took its name from the luxury overnight express train from Paris to the south of France. The Ballets Russes production also reflected an existing creative connection between Paris and the Riviera; notably in Picasso's stage curtain, which was based on his famous painting of two women running along a beach, their white tunics falling away to reveal bare breasts, the sky blue behind their ecstatic, monumental figures. In turn, Chanel's costumes were inspired by the sports clothes that she had popularised in the resorts of Cannes, Deauville and Biarritz: striped tricots and bathing suits, beach sandals and golf shoes, tennis dresses and shorts; and perhaps by the crews' uniforms on the Duke's yachts ('navy and white are the only possible colours,' she remarked, after her first trip aboard the *Flying Cloud*. 'The Navy's colours.')

Nevertheless, Chanel's deft designs were not without precedents on the Riviera. By 1923, a wealthy young American couple, Gerald and Sara Murphy, were in situ, having previously been introduced to the pleasures of Antibes by their friend, the composer Cole Porter. They drew their fashionable friends from Paris to stay with them during the summer months, thus transforming the traditional Riviera season, which had previously been at its height over Christmas. The Murphys were fans of jazz and art and sunbathing and parties, and their seaside house, Villa America, was the backdrop to all these, as a coterie of socialites, musicians, writers and artists spilled in and out of its doors. Picasso visited, along with Stravinsky, Fernand Léger, Man Ray, Dorothy Parker, Ernest Hemingway, F. Scott Fitzgerald and his wife Zelda; all of them united by their sense of being in a vanguard, yet often disunited by quarrels and sexual jealousies and too many cocktails. Several of these dramas were portrayed by Fitzgerald in his novel *Tender Is the Night*, where parties become the set-pieces for the narrative. 'I want to give a really *bad* party,' announces the hero, Dick Diver, at one point, as his wife surveys the calm view of the Mediterranean sea, several hundred feet below their villa. 'I mean it. I want to give a party where there's a brawl and seductions and people going home with their feelings hurt and women passed out in the cabinet de toilette. You wait and see.' Other fragments emerged in the letters that Zelda wrote to Scott after her mental breakdown, when she remembered the wildness of summers past, from her locked room in a Swiss sanatorium. ('I would like to be walking alone in a Sirocco at Cannes at night passing under the dim lamps and imagining myself mysterious and unafraid like last summer …')

Thus the landscape of the glamorous Riviera – or at least that semi-imaginary place where the Lost Generation danced and wept and drank its way through the Jazz Age – existed before Chanel built her palace there. And some of what came to be seen as her trademark Riviera style was already in evidence on the beaches where the Murphys swam and laughed with their friends, and in Villa America itself, with its interiors of white walls and black satin. Striped sailor tops had been seen on Picasso and Gerald Murphy (himself an artist, whose career had begun when he assisted on sets for the Ballets Russes soon after his arrival in Paris in 1921); and Sara Murphy was famous for wearing her pearls to the beach because, she explained, they wanted sunning. Hence the scene in *Tender is the Night* where the beautiful heroine – Nicole Diver, an evocative portrait inspired by Sara and Zelda; the ultimate incarnation of the Beautiful and the Damned – reclines on a dazzling beach: 'Her bathing suit was pulled off her shoulders and her back, a ruddy, orange brown, set off by a string of creamy pearls, shone in the sun. Her face was hard and lovely and pitiful.'

In Fitzgerald's Riviera, Chanel played only a minor role, providing the scent for Nicole Diver towards the conclusion of the novel, which also suggests the end of an era: 'She put on the first ankle-length day dress that she had owned for many years and crossed herself reverently with Chanel Sixteen.' In fact, Chanel was on her way to becoming far more central to the seductive image of the Côte d'Azur than as the mere purveyor of perfume; and Fitzgerald's failure to pay much attention to her was perhaps as much a symptom of his alcoholic malaise as it was a reflection of her precise status in the shifting sands of what constituted smart society. 'One could get away with more on the summer Riviera, and whatever happened seemed to have something to do with art,' he wrote in *Echoes of the Jazz Age*; an observation that could equally well have been applied to Chanel's life at La Pausa; indeed, to the villa itself.

For if Villa America represented the Murphys' motto – 'Living well is the best revenge' – then La Pausa was similarly beguiling, the epitome of a particular style of life which later became known as a lifestyle. It was fashionable, but also

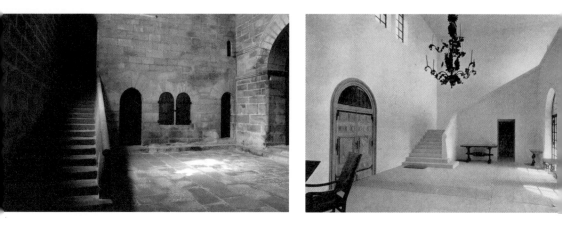

The twelfth-century staircase and archways of Aubazine (left) that Chanel sent her architect to view when he was designing her Riviera house of La Pausa (right).

encompassed French tradition, in a manner as attractive to the British upper classes as it was to Parisian bohemians. Most important of all, La Pausa was built on Chanel's own past, as well as marking out her territory for the future.

Hence the fact that the villa was bought in her name, rather than Westminster's. And while the Duke's influence and presence were evident in La Pausa – inevitably, given the regularity of his yachting trips along the Riviera – Chanel made all the important decisions about how the villa was to take shape. Her original meeting with La Pausa's architect, Robert Streitz, was held aboard the *Flying Cloud*, moored offshore from Cannes; thereafter, she would take the Blue Train from Paris to Monaco on her lightning visits to the site. Streitz was only 28 at the time, and the building was his first substantial commission, but his ambition to build 'the ideal Mediterranean villa' was readily accepted by Chanel. Four decades later, in conversation with the French journalist Pierre Galante, Streitz recalled that the Duke's sole instruction was simple: 'I want everything to be built with the best materials and under the best working conditions.'

Chanel's first request to the architect was significantly more personal: she told Streitz that she wanted him to re-create a large stone staircase in the villa's entrance hall from the original that she remembered from her childhood at Aubazine. So as to be sure that the details were exact, she dispatched him to visit the abbey; an extraordinary request, given Chanel's obliteration of the orphanage from her previous accounts of her past. In Aubazine, Streitz found the staircase just as she had described it – its steps worn from centuries of footfalls, rising out of the darkness of the abbey to the first floor, where generations of monks had walked, followed by the orphans behind them. He was sufficiently discreet never to repeat the exact details of his conversation with the Mother Superior of the convent, who still recalled Gabrielle Chanel from her days in the orphanage. But having studied and photographed the staircase in the abbey, he designed a precise replica for La Pausa, which became the centrepiece of the house.

Streitz remembered Chanel as remarkably generous in her dealings with him – after his car broke down, and he was forced to travel by bus to La Pausa, she gave him one of her cars, and insisted that he keep it. But she could also be ferociously intimidating. 'She was certainly intelligent,' Streitz told Galante. 'In discussions one always had a feeling of one's own inferiority.' And he quickly learned to avoid lingering after their conversations, having discovered to his cost that he might overhear her calling him a complete idiot. The project's chief building contractor, Edgar Maggiore, felt a similar mixture of respect and anxiety when dealing with his demanding client. 'Mademoiselle knew what she wanted,' he told Galante, remembering her orders that the pristine villa should have the patina of age, with handmade roof-tiles – over 20,000 of them – and that the brand-new shutters should be made to look weathered. She visited the site at least once a month during its construction, sometimes returning to Paris on the same day; but on one occasion, when she was too busy to leave Rue Cambon, Maggiore sent one of his workers to Paris, so that she could choose the exact colour of the plaster to be used on the façade.

Despite her exactitude, Maggiore also remembered Chanel's forbearance, and her laughter when she sank to her knees in mud while inspecting the villa's massive foundations. 'She was always very cheerful when she visited Roquebrune,' he said; and perhaps as a consequence the villa rose from the ground with remarkable speed, taking less than a year to complete. When it was finished, La Pausa consisted of three wings, each facing inward towards a spacious courtyard, with cloisters reminiscent of Aubazine. Its grace and beauty launched Streitz's distinguished career, and in later life he remembered La Pausa as his 'good luck building'. The construction costs had been immense – 6 million francs – and Chanel's expenditure on the interiors was equally lavish. Yet in the end, La Pausa gave the impression of serenity and simplicity.

To Chanel's great-niece Gabrielle Labrunie, it was a magical landscape; remaining vivid in her earliest memories as the place where she visited 'Auntie Coco' and her godfather, Bennie. In the same way that Boy Capel had assumed

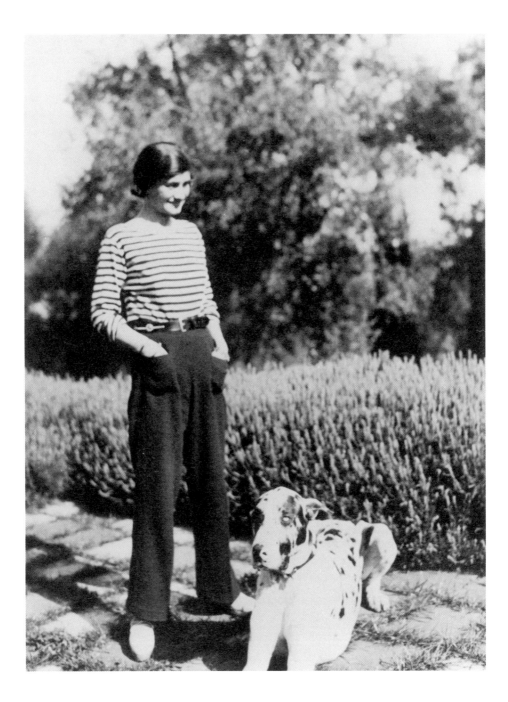

Chanel in her sailor's matelot at La Pausa with her dog Gigot, 1930.

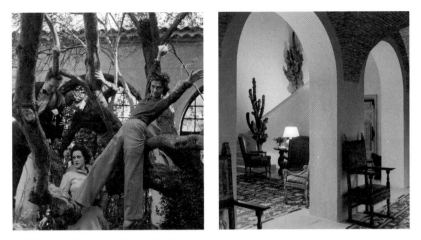

Left: In the garden of La Pausa with friends. Roger Schall, 1938.
Right: Interior of the villa. Roger Schall, 1938.

some parental responsibility for her father, André Palasse, so Westminster became Gabrielle's godfather soon after her birth in 1926. Gabrielle was fluent in English, having spent much of her early childhood living with her parents and younger sister in Mayfair, where her father was employed to oversee Chanel's London business, and in Huddersfield, where a British Chanel factory had been established. She remembered the soot in their garden in Huddersfield (the green leaves coated in powdery black), and her visits to the Duke's London residence, Bourdon House, where she was invited to children's tea parties and birthday celebrations. But it was La Pausa that seemed to her to be enchanted: 'I was certain that there were fairies in the garden in Roquebrune. They were in the trees, and there were stars entwined in Auntie Coco's bed …'

The surviving pictures of Chanel's bedroom at La Pausa still show the stars that her great-niece remembers so well. They were carved in wrought iron to Coco's design, surrounding the bed in which the Duke was her guest; the emblem of her own domain (and perhaps also a subtle reminder of the stars she walked upon as a child, decorating the mosaic floor at Aubazine).

That La Pausa was entirely hers was made clear in the description of it that appeared in the March 1930 issue of American *Vogue*, under the headline 'Mlle Chanel's House'. 'There is no doubt that Mademoiselle Gabrielle Chanel is a person with very rare taste,' declared *Vogue*, 'and it is therefore not in the least surprising that she has built for herself one of the most enchanting villas that ever materialised on the shores of the Mediterranean … To begin with, she chose the site very carefully … On the left is all the lovely sweep of the Italian coastline, and, on the right, the Rock of Monaco and the town of Monte Carlo form one of the most breathtaking views in the whole Riviera while in one huge semicircle in front of the house stretches the blue of the Mediterranean.'

The garden was planted according to Mademoiselle's wishes – 'groves of orange trees, great slopes of lavender, masses of purple iris, and huge clusters of climbing roses'. Not content with the existing olive grove at La Pausa, she had also instructed Maggiore to transplant 20 ancient olive trees from Antibes, one of which grew in the centre of the courtyard (another echo, perhaps, of Aubazine). The villa's monastic quality was apparent in its cloisters, as well as in the central staircase and the cleanliness of its interiors; but for all this, it was a place in which to luxuriate. 'The house itself is long and Provençal,' reported *Vogue*, 'the grey of its walls melting into the soft tint of the wood of the olive trees.' The cloisters were built along three sides of the patio, providing shade 'where one may coolly doze away the hottest hours of the summer afternoons'. Inside, the villa was decorated in a manner completely dissimilar to Chanel's Baroque apartment at Rue Cambon or the Victorian Gothic of Eaton Hall. 'The motif seems to be an entire absence of knickknacks or unnecessary items. Everything one needs is there – and the most perfect of its kind – but there is nothing superfluous.'

There were white taffeta curtains to match the white walls of the dining room, and beige silk curtains in the living room and bedrooms, all of it the perfect backdrop for its owner. Bettina Ballard set the scene in a subsequent piece for *Vogue* describing a house party at La Pausa. 'About one o'clock everyone appears in the great hall – mornings don't exist in the South, and you see no one before lunch. Mademoiselle Chanel is generally the last, and her appearance on the high white balcony above the hall starts the day's animation … She wears navy jersey slacks with a slip-on sweater and a bright red quilted bolero … Her red canvas espadrilles have thick cork soles – excellent for walking.' Chanel rarely left the property, according to Ballard, except for her long afternoon rambles over narrow rocky paths. Meanwhile, the villa was run with immaculate efficiency by her Italian majordomo, Ugo. 'The comfort of the house is phenomenal … Each bathroom, for example, has a servants' entrance, so that your bath can be drawn, your shoes and clothes taken away to be pressed or cleaned, without your being disturbed. You press a button and breakfast appears in two minutes – your coffee and milk in thermos pitchers to keep hot all morning.'

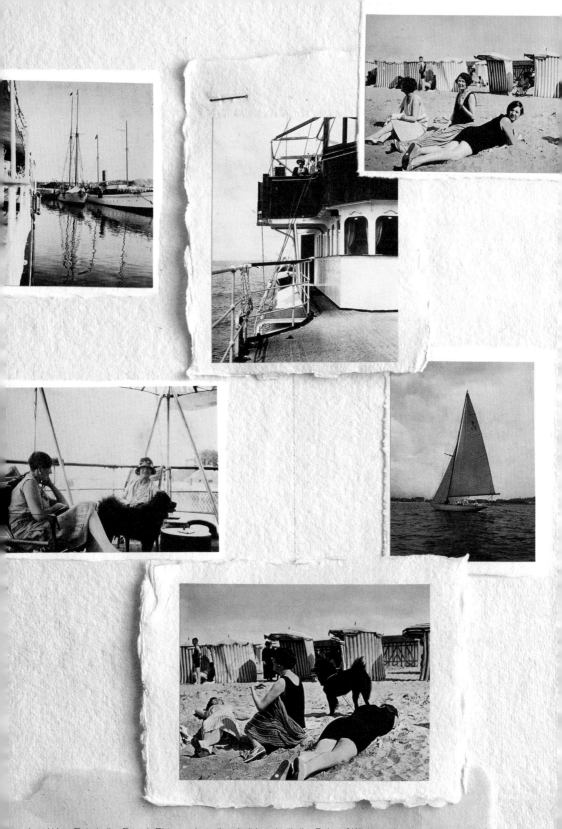

Chanel and Vera Bate in the French Riviera, where they holidayed with the Duke of Westminster.

Meal times were informal buffets, where people could sit where they pleased, and eat what they wanted, in whatever order they chose (the very opposite of dining at Eaton, where footmen hovered throughout numerous courses). Ballard observed her fellow guest, Misia Sert, eating 'one dish of salad after another', while the men piled 'chops and steak and chicken all on the same plate'. The dress code was equally relaxed: 'You dress or not as you choose for dinner. Chanel herself wears black velvet slacks with the pink satin pyjamas showing about two inches round the ankles. With them she clings to her fine woollen slip-on sweaters brightened by strings of emeralds and pearls.' Thus she held court, generally without sitting down at the table: 'Mademoiselle Chanel, who eats very little anyway, is the prize entertainment, standing in front of the huge fireplace, making superb conversation ...' Later, writing in her memoir, Ballard also recalled Chanel's stories about her childhood tribulations; of how she was shut up indoors after her mother's death by her two old aunts in the Auvergne: 'The aunts' stone house had small windows that were always kept closed, and they sat primly in their rusty black dresses in the dark parlour sewing or reading, their eyes on the small dark girl who was supposed to be studying or sewing but who kept looking out of the windows.' Over lunch at La Pausa, Chanel told Ballard that years after escaping from the aunts, she had terrible nightmares that they would find her: 'She still had recurrent dreams that a door would open and there they would be, the two tight-lipped, black-clad women, come to take her away.'

The aunts never came, despite Chanel's mysterious hints that they knew where to find her; and she was safe in her realm, 'designed to give her the maximum of privacy and her guests the maximum of liberty'. Yet for all its freedoms and desirability – and that of its hostess – La Pausa did not keep the Duke from straying. The *Flying Cloud* continued to carry its master on his ceaseless travels; its presence so ubiquitous that it even appeared in the opening scene of Noël Coward's *Private Lives*, when Amanda and Elyot stand on a hotel balcony in a fashionable French resort, looking out to sea:

Amanda: Whose yacht is that?

Elyot: The Duke of Westminster's I expect. It always is.

Amanda: I wish I were on it.

Elyot: I wish you were too.

But the restless Duke still alighted at La Pausa in the summer of 1929, in between outings to the Monte Carlo casino, as did Winston Churchill (a regular guest at Lord Rothermere's nearby villa at Cap Martin, along with the Prince of

Wales). Salvador Dalí and his wife were frequent visitors; indeed, Dalí was inspired to paint there, including a still life entitled *L'Instant sublime*, which depicted a snail, a telephone receiver, and a drop of water about to fall on a frying egg. Bendor was also seized by the desire to capture La Pausa on canvas, albeit in rather more conventional watercolours; as was Churchill, although he holidayed at the villa more often after its sale to Emery Reeves, his literary agent, in 1953.

Serge Lifar – Chanel's favourite among Diaghilev's ballet dancers, and a star of *Le Train bleu* – stayed at La Pausa, and the rest of the company was in residence nearby at Monte Carlo for annual seasons there. Jean Cocteau recuperated at the villa during his periodic attempts to give up opium. And Vera Bate – by now remarried to an Italian officer, Colonel Alberto Lombardi – was ensconced in a small house at the bottom of the garden, lent to her by the munificent Chanel. Gabrielle Labrunie remembers playing with Vera's daughter, Bridget Bate, at La Pausa, and also the song that Coco used to sing to her in the open-top car that swung along the coastal road, then up into the hills of Roquebrune. She can still hum the tune, and the refrain, which she sings as she shows me the picture of herself as a child in the garden of La Pausa, holding a bunch of white flowers. 'It goes something like this,' she says: '"I laughed at love, thought it all wrong, but now I sing a new song …"' That's what Auntie Coco sang.'

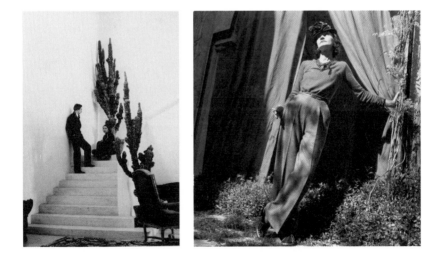

Left: Salvador Dalí and his wife Gala, La Pausa. Numa Blanc Fils, 1938.
Right: Chanel in the gardens of her Mediterranean home. Roger Schall, 1938.

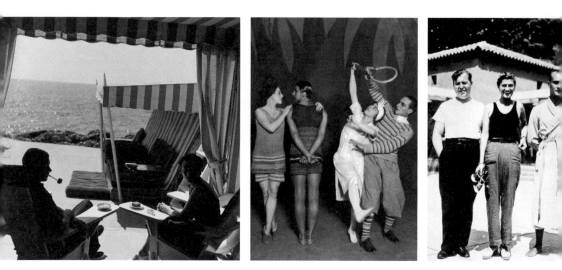

From left: The Duke and Duchess of Windsor sitting in the shade of their cabana in the south of France. Roger Schall, 1938. Left to right: Lydia Sokolova, Anton Dolin, Bronislava Nijinska and Leon Woizikowsky in Diaghilev's Ballets Russes production of *Le Train bleu*. Chanel in Monte Carlo with Christian Bérard and Boris Kochno, 1932.

But the angry sound of arguments between the Duke and Chanel began to disturb the peace of La Pausa, waking up the other guests in the night; and when she joined him on the *Flying Cloud* the rows continued, always about his infidelities and her humiliation. Once, when Bendor tried to make amends for an affair that Chanel had discovered by giving her a large emerald, she accepted it from him, and then, without a word, let it slip from her hands overboard into the sea. On another occasion, when they had been cruising along the Riviera for several days, the Duke gave her a pearl necklace as a peace offering for having flirted with a younger woman. Again, Chanel simply threw it into the waves.

By the end of 1929, it was clear that Bendor was determined to find a new wife who could bear him a son. At 46, Chanel still looked remarkably youthful – and it is likely that the Duke believed her to be younger than she was – and their affair was not yet over (Chanel came to stay with him at Eaton in mid-December 1929, for example, and was photographed at his house party and shoot). But Bendor took little time in proposing to a young Englishwoman, Loelia Ponsonby, less than a month after meeting her in a London nightclub. They were engaged just before Christmas (a day or two after Chanel's visit to Eaton), and married in February 1930; not that this got in the way of his seasonal visit to the Riviera. Loelia's subsequent memoir, *Grace and Favour*, described how he set off for

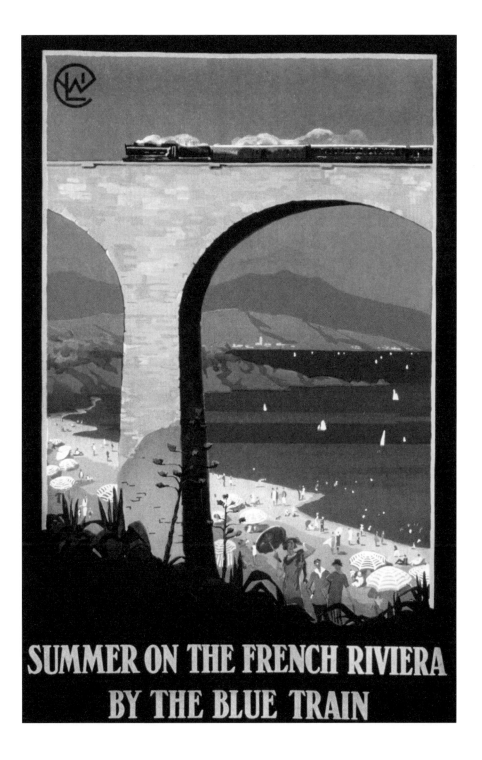

SUMMER ON THE FRENCH RIVIERA
BY THE BLUE TRAIN

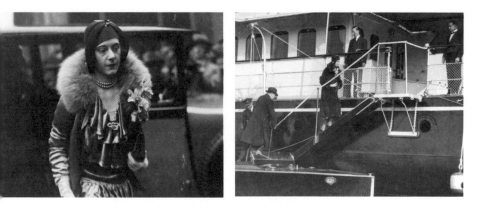

Left: The Duchess of Westminster, Loelia, third wife of the Duke of Westminster, on her wedding day, 20th February 1930. Right: The Duke and Duchess of Westminster boarding his yacht, the *Cutty Sark*, as they make their way to their honeymoon on the French Riviera, February 1930.

France the morning after their engagement, to spend Christmas in Monte Carlo: 'I had a dreadful suspicion that a particularly elegant French lady would be meeting him there.' The following month, Loelia was given no choice but to be presented by the Duke to Chanel in Paris, as if by way of inspection. On their way to her apartment, Bendor stopped to buy a present at Van Cleef et Arpels: 'when he came out he patted his pocket and said, "Not for you." Maybe he was joking. Maybe not. I never knew for certain.'

Loelia had been brought up at St James's Palace, the daughter of a quintessential courtier. Her father had been an assistant private secretary to Queen Victoria, then to Edward VII, and later Keeper of the Privy Purse under George V. But nothing in her childhood training in etiquette and protocol had prepared her for the frosty encounter with her fiancé's celebrated mistress. 'At that time Mademoiselle Chanel was at the height of her fame, her quiet, neat, uncomplicated clothes being considered the epitome of all that was most chic. Small, dark and simian, Coco Chanel was the personification of her own fashions. She was wearing a dark blue suit and a white blouse with very light stockings (light stockings were one of her credos). Described in this way she sounds as if she looked like a high-school girl, but actually the effect was of extreme sophistication.'

Over 30 years after this alarming introduction, Loelia still recalled the dazzle of Chanel's jewels, many of which had been given to her by the Duke (for not all had been thrown overboard the *Flying Cloud*). 'When I saw her she was hung with every kind of necklace and bracelet, which rattled as she moved. Her sitting-room was luxurious and lavish and she sat in a large armchair, a pair of tall Coromandel screens … making an effective backcloth. I perched, rather at a disadvantage, on a stool at her feet feeling that I was being looked over to see whether I was a suitable bride for her old admirer – and I very much doubted whether I, or my tweed suit, passed the test … Frantically searching around for something to say, I mentioned that Mrs George Keppel had given me a Chanel necklace as a Christmas present. At once I was made to describe it. No, said Mademoiselle Chanel. It had certainly not come from her. She would never dream of having anything like *that* on sale. And the conversation dropped with a bang.'

Poor Loelia, whose marriage was doomed from the start, and whose honeymoon on the *Flying Cloud* was as miserable as her meeting with Chanel. The yacht had been fitted out with the solidity of an English country house – the cabins reached through an ornamental doorway and furnished with Queen Anne furniture, including a four-poster bed for Loelia – but it was nonetheless a boat that rolled with the swell. 'I think I can claim to be the worst sailor in the world,' confessed Loelia, 'and it really was the irony of fate that I should become part owner of two enormous yachts, capable of sailing on any ocean and not to be able to spend a happy moment on either.'

As for Chanel, she kept as hard and lovely a look on her face as a Scott Fitzgerald heroine, displaying a brittle fortitude while she lost her beloved Bendor to another woman. But two days after the Duke's wedding to Loelia, he came to see Coco in Paris, and then, at last, she cried.

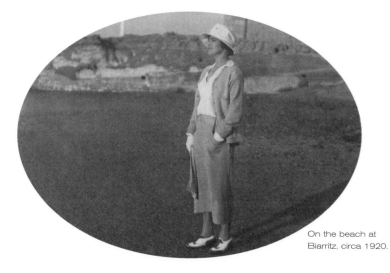

On the beach at Biarritz, circa 1920.

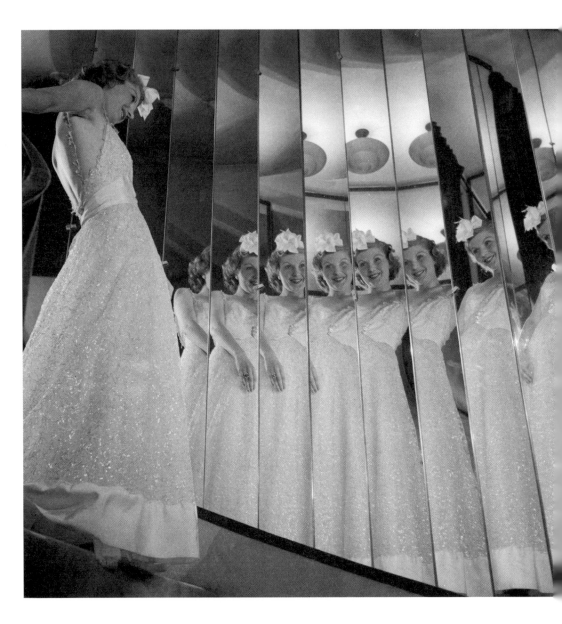

THE WOMAN IN WHITE

Coco Chanel was never the bride, but she understood the potency of a white dress, even before the craze for white satin that swept Paris fashions in the wake of the Wall Street Crash. Women had worn white long before Chanel, of course, and before the Crash, but she took credit for a new vogue for white, and in some sense, this was her due. The little black dress did not entirely disappear with the Roaring Twenties; nor were the lengthening hems of gossamer white gowns a direct consequence of the catastrophic collapse of stock values in October 1929. Nevertheless, in one of those curious shifts of fashion that are in part emblematic, and yet also apparently perverse, the black days of the Crash were followed by a style that Chanel characterised as 'candid innocence and white satin', which prevailed in the dark shadow of the Depression.

Later, in her long conversations with Paul Morand in the winter of 1946, exiled from Paris to the snows of St Moritz, Chanel repeated her credo, almost as if she needed to reassure herself that she (and she alone) had the clarity of vision to embrace both black and white. 'Women think of every colour, except the absence of colours,' she declared. 'I have said that black had everything. White too. They have an absolute beauty. It is perfect harmony. Dress women in white or black at a ball: they are the only ones you see.'

Certainly, when Chanel dressed in white, she was there to be seen, as is evident if you flick through the

del, with a camellia in her hair, on the mirrored staircase of
House of Chanel. François Kollar, 1937.

CHANEL 191

society pages of fashionable magazines from 1929 onwards. Chanel is omnipresent: in early 1931, for example, she is wearing white beach pyjamas and jewelled bracelets on the Venice Lido, alongside her fellow couturier, Lucien Lelong; soon afterwards, she is in immaculate sporting whites, shoes and hat, on her tennis court at La Pausa, escorted by the glamorous Baron Hubert von Pantz. The following year she appears aboard Lieutenant Commander Montague Graham White's steam yacht in Poole Harbour, looking crisp in a white dress and jacket (despite the dreary weather and the unprepossessing presence of her host's shaggy dog). There are numerous pictures, too, of Chanel poised in white satin and glistening pearls at parties and balls in Paris and Monte Carlo; and many more of white evening gowns worn by her clients to glittering social occasions. Janet Flanner, the Paris correspondent for *The New Yorker*, reporting on the frenetic round of June balls in 1930, noted the booming trade that Chanel was doing in the summer after the Wall Street Crash, when Parisian parties were 'unusually frequent, fantastic, and … remarkable for representing the true spirit of their time'. Most beautiful of all was the White Ball, given by a 'niece of the late Pope Leo XIII', where Jean Cocteau concocted white-plaster masks and wigs. Mademoiselle Chanel's white gowns were much in evidence there, and elsewhere, in a season that seemed to reflect a dazzling defiance to the encroaching economic gloom.

Sadly, there is no photograph of the magnificent white evening dress that Chanel wore to the ball given by the Duke of Westminster in June 1928 to mark his youngest daughter Mary's eighteenth birthday and debut into London society. By this point, the Duke's relationship with Mary's mother, his first wife, Shelagh, was sufficiently amicable for them to co-operate on the preparations for the party. Moreover, Mary had personally invited Mademoiselle Chanel to the ball. Chanel, who at that time was still very much Bendor's mistress, not only accepted the invitation, but gave a dinner party for Mary before the ball, attended by the Duke, Shelagh and her second husband, and Mary's older sister Ursula and her husband. When the dinner was over and the moment came to leave for the ball, which was taking place across the road from Bendor's house in Mayfair, Chanel said that her guests should go on ahead, as she wanted to change out of her white dress into another one. They duly departed, but when Chanel had still not arrived half an hour later, Bendor sent an aide to fetch her. He returned, with the message that Mademoiselle was unwell. The Duke was sufficiently concerned to leave the party and visit Chanel himself; whereupon he found her

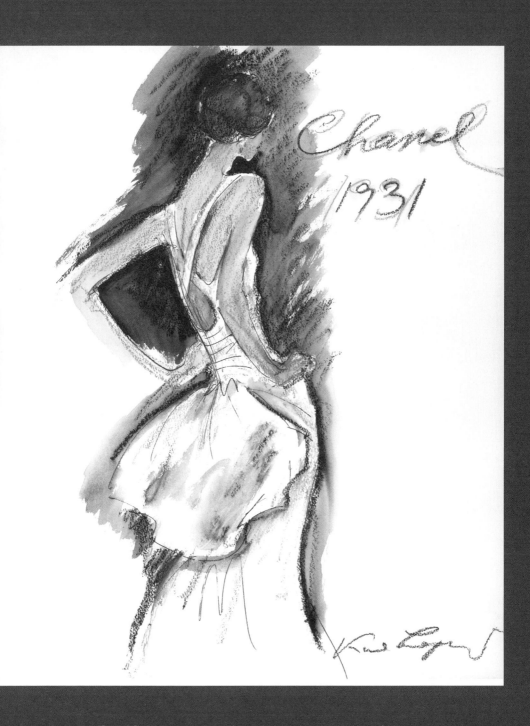

Chanel
1931

One of Chanel's white dresses from 1931, as drawn by Karl Lagerfeld.

in bed, her face as white as the gown she had just taken off. Re-telling the story to Claude Delay, Chanel said that Bendor had wanted to call a doctor, but she simply put her arms around him, and gently rubbed her face against his shoulder. When he saw the traces of white talcum power and face cream on his black jacket, he understood that her illness was faked, in order to avoid any potential embarrassment at the ball. 'You see,' she said to the Duke, 'in the first place I don't like doing things that bore me. And in the second you wouldn't really have liked it either.'

In relating this tale to Delay, Chanel said that she had known that her invitation to the ball had been gossiped about for weeks previously, with mounting speculation as to whether the Duke's mistress would arrive alongside his first wife and take her place amidst members of the Royal family and eminent politicians. In the event, her absence caused as much conversation at the ball

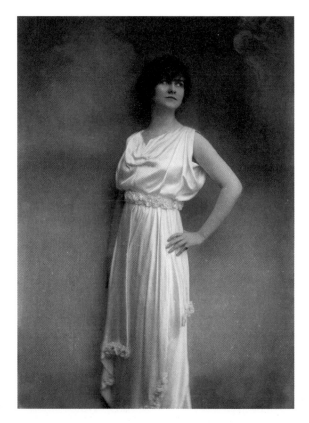

Chanel dressed in white.

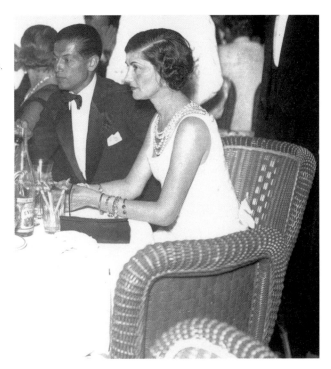

as her presence would have done; but the Duke was apparently amused, and
when Shelagh sent a message offering to visit the invalid in her sickbed, Chanel
replied that this would not be necessary, and dispatched a large bouquet of
flowers to the Duchess the following day.

Thus Chanel, as a mistress, would not appear in bridal white at the coming-
out ball for her lover's daughter, but she nevertheless used white in her designs
to create the same sense of purity as was evident in the nuns' wimples and
collars at Aubazine. Those closest to her at the end of her life – Claude Delay
and Gabrielle Labrunie – recall that her sheets were always of plain white cotton
('as simple and unadorned as the white cuffs of her convent uniform,' says
Delay). In old age, Chanel reminisced about the white sheets and petticoats
that were washed by maids at the house of her aunts; everything boiled clean,
in the blue steam-filled air. But it was in the same laundry-room that Chanel
learned about the facts of life; in her account to Delay, she said that one of the
laundry-maids hid her growing pregnancy under a white apron, but eventually
explained it to young Gabrielle, as she folded the pristine linen.

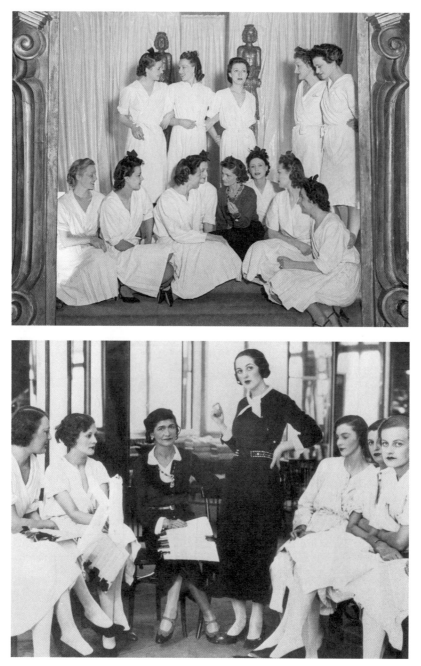

Top: Chanel (dressed in black) surrounded by models in white, at the House of Chanel in Rue Cambon. Roger Schall. Bottom: Surrounded by models at a fitting session in London, 1932.

If white was the colour of innocence and purity, it was also used by Chanel for seductive evening dresses, albeit with an ethereal quality. Her friend Colette – a writer with an even more scandalous past than Chanel's own – described the couturière at work on a white dress, in a portrait of Chanel published in *Prison et paradis* in 1932. She saw Chanel as 'a little black bull … in her butting energy, in her way of facing up to things'; and her description also suggests the conflicting impulses between the earthy and the unearthly in the creation of a delicate white dress. 'Mademoiselle Chanel is engaged in sculpting an angel six feet tall. A golden-blond angel, impersonal, seraphically beautiful, providing one disregards the rudimentary carving, the paucity of flesh, and the cheerlessness – one of those angels who brought the devil to earth.

'The angel – still incomplete – totters occasionally under the two creative, severe, kneading arms that press against it. Chanel works with ten fingers, nails, the edge of the hand, the palms, with pins and scissors right on the garment, which is a white vapour with long pleats, splashed with crushed crystal. Sometimes she falls to her knees before her work and grasps it, not to worship but to punish it again, to tighten over the angel's long legs – to constrain – some expansion of tulle … With her loins taut and her legs under her thighs, Chanel is like a prostrated laundress beating her linens … [her movements] like the quick genuflections of nuns …'

Clearly, Chanel had a sense for the visual impact of white, enjoying the contrast it provided with the bronzed skin that she had made so fashionable since her earlier holidays on the Riviera. 'A very white earring on the lobe of a well-tanned ear delights me,' she remarked to Paul Morand, and then described to him how she had watched a group of American girls swimming in the sea at the Venice Lido. 'How much more beautiful these young women would be … if they had dipped their pearls into the waves, into the sea from which they first came; and how brightly their jewellery would glitter if worn on a skin bronzed by the sun …' In her hands, white was never pallid, and she used it with absolute precision ('It mustn't look like whipped cream,' she told Claude Delay). Reporting on Chanel's innovative all-white spring collection in 1933, French *Vogue* was suitably dazzled: 'A new way of presenting dresses adds to this powerful and palpable springtime feeling that reigns at Rue Cambon. Chanel, for the first time, showed all her white dresses in one sitting. It was as if the place had suddenly been transformed into an orchard in Normandy.'

Yet after her years in Aubazine, Chanel could not fail to be equally aware of the spiritual symbolism of white, which may be why she had used it to such powerful effect in the winter funeral of a young friend, the poet Raymond Radiguet, who had died of typhoid fever in December 1923. Chanel had taken charge of all the arrangements, directing that his body be placed in a white coffin, then carried by a white hearse pulled by white horses, to a church filled with white flowers.

And in the procession of white dresses that Chanel created for herself and others, perhaps the most significant were those associated with grief or mourning; as if honouring the medieval tradition of French queens and European royalty, for whom the fitting colour for deepest mourning was deemed to be white rather than black. Hence the famous portrayal of Mary Queen of Scots by François Clouet in 1559 as a young widow dressed '*en deuil blanc*'; the same costume of white mourning that she wore for her doomed second marriage to Lord Darnley.

Chanel seldom designed wedding gowns – just a handful during the Thirties – and she always scorned the custom whereby they were shown as the finale of a Paris collection, declaring that she wanted no such 'circus' in her own shows. One of the very few that she did make was for her younger sister, Antoinette, who had worked for Chanel since the start (hers is the first name listed on the opening page of the employee records, as a *vendeuse* at 21 Rue Cambon, beginning on 1st January 1910). On 11th November 1919, the first anniversary of the Armistice, Antoinette married a Canadian airman whom she had met the previous year. The bride wore white, and the witnesses to the wedding were Boy Capel – by then a husband himself – and Maurice de Nexon (her aunt Adrienne's long-standing 'fiancé', who was not able to marry Adrienne until his disapproving father died). Antoinette departed for Canada with 17 trunks of luggage, and never saw her sister again. Having run away from her husband after a few months of marriage, the errant bride ended up in Buenos Aires, where she died of alcohol poisoning, not long after the death of Boy Capel.

Chanel never discussed the death of her younger sister; nor did she give anything away about her feelings on the day of Adrienne's wedding, on 29th April 1930, when she finally became the wife of Baron de Nexon, having waited for over 20 years. Chanel was there as Adrienne's witness, as Adrienne had been witness to Chanel; all the way back to their early days as seamstresses bent over the white wedding trousseaux of wealthier women, and their obscure nights as demimondaines in a garrison town.

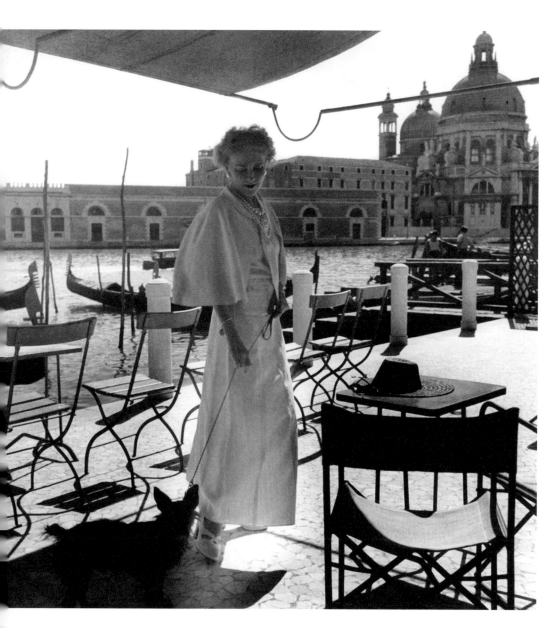

...sia Sert in Venice. Horst, 1947.

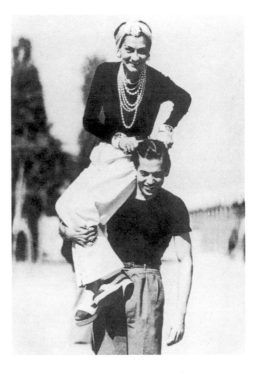

Chanel on Serge Lifar's shoulder.
Jean Moral.

Her past remained shrouded, and when it emerged, it was often in the form of Gothic myth. As a girl, she had read romances where women in white were runaway brides or abandoned lovers; in later years, she told her confidante Claude Delay that *Wuthering Heights* was her favourite novel. There had been a time when she had cried over Emily Brontë's story of passion and loss, as if Cathy – a heroine finally driven mad by love, approaching death in a white dress – echoed her own lament. 'But I've wept so much,' she said to Delay. 'Now I don't cry any more. When you don't cry it's because you no longer believe in happiness.'

Even so, Chanel still revisited the scenes of her past, remaking them while she was replaying them. And the white dress that she most often alluded to was the one that her father sent for her to wear to her First Communion; the hallowed dress of billowing organdie petticoats, and a long white veil. 'It was the first dress, the most important dress, the dress that made her a couturière,' says Claude Delay, when I ask her what might have made it so meaningful; yet its symbolic purity as a dress for the Bride of Christ was also tainted by Chanel's subsequent belief that it had been chosen for her by her father's 'tart'.

If the First Communion dress loomed large in Chanel's memory, then another of her white dresses was to be forever associated with the last rites. In August 1929, she accompanied Bendor on a Mediterranean cruise aboard the *Flying Cloud*. Misia Sert came with them, in mourning for the end of her marriage. (José-Maria Sert had left Misia for a beautiful young Russian girl, Roussy Mdivani, for whom Chanel designed a trousseau. Soon after the wedding the previous summer, in one of the more bizarre convolutions of Misia's love-life, she joined her ex-husband and his new wife on their honeymoon cruise, sharing the marital suite with the bride, while Sert slept in another cabin.)

Midway through the cruise, a radiogram was received aboard the *Flying Cloud*, which the ship's wireless operator handed to Misia. The message came from Diaghilev in Venice: 'Am sick; come quickly. Serge.' The yacht was immediately diverted to Venice, and as soon as it docked, on 17th August, Misia and Chanel rushed to see Diaghilev at the Grand Hotel des Bains on the Lido. They found him in a small bedroom, watched over by his secretary and collaborator, Boris Kochno, and the dancer Serge Lifar (both of whom had been rivals for his affection); he lay racked with pain and in the final stages of diabetes. In the heat of the Venice summer, he was wearing his dinner jacket in bed, drenched in sweat, yet shivering. But as soon as he saw Misia and Coco,

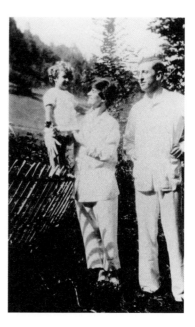

With playwright Henry Bernstein and his young daughter, 1918.

Diaghilev's eyes lit up. 'Oh, how happy I am to see you,' he whispered to the two women. 'I love you in white. Promise me you will always wear white.'

He died at dawn on 19th August, Chanel's forty-sixth birthday. Chanel had returned to the *Flying Cloud* the previous night, but was seized by a strong premonition of Diaghilev's death and asked Bendor to turn back to Venice. She arrived that morning to find Misia trying to pawn her diamond necklace in order to meet Diaghilev's debts, for the great maestro had died penniless. Chanel took over and paid all the outstanding bills, as she so often did; then she organised his funeral. 'The next day,' she told Paul Morand, 'a long procession of gondolas leaves the Orthodox *dei Grecchi* church and makes its way towards the San Michele cemetery, where the cypresses rise above the pink walls bordered in white.'

Morand, who was himself a friend of Diaghilev's, reached Venice several days after his death, too late to attend the funeral. Chanel and Misia both described to him what had happened: they sat with his body in the hotel bedroom, waiting for the coffin to arrive under the cover of darkness, so as not to disturb the other guests. At dawn the following morning, a black gondola had taken Diaghilev in his coffin from the Lido to the Greek Orthodox Church, and from there across the lagoon to the cemetery. Afterwards, Morand wrote his own account of the funeral, published in his book *Venices*: '… the ceremonial floating bier that is used for funeral processions in Venice ferried the magician's mortal remains to the funeral island of San Michele … Whenever I see a funeral procession on its way to San Michele, with the priest in charge of the ceremony standing behind the gondolier at the stern, the funeral director at the prow, and with the silver lion of St Mark concealing its affliction beneath folded wings, I think of Diaghilev, that indefatigable man, lying at rest.'

Diaghilev's grave lies in the Orthodox section of the cemetery on the Venetian isle of the dead, close to the headstone for Stravinsky, who was buried there over 40 years later. The cypresses still rise above the white-bordered walls, just as Chanel described them, and if you close your eyes while the seagulls scream, you can imagine her there, side by side with Misia. Both women wore white dresses to the funeral, bridesmaids to the body in the black coffin; honouring the wish of the great impresario, whose instinct for choreography was with him until the end.

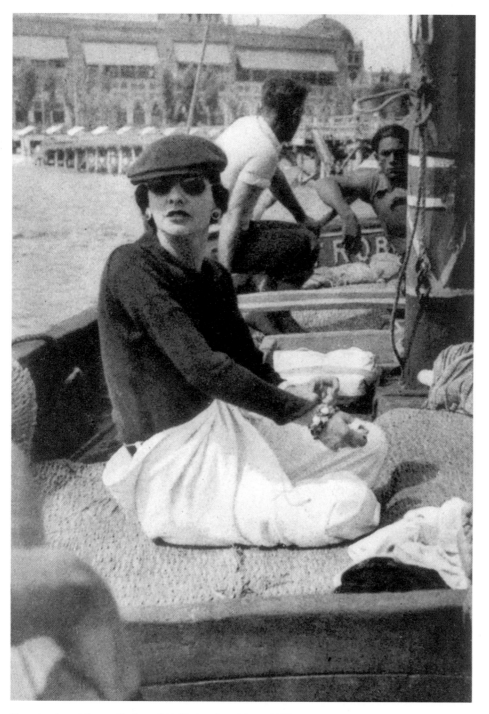

Chanel on board Roussy Sert's yacht in Venice. Grandpierre, 1936.

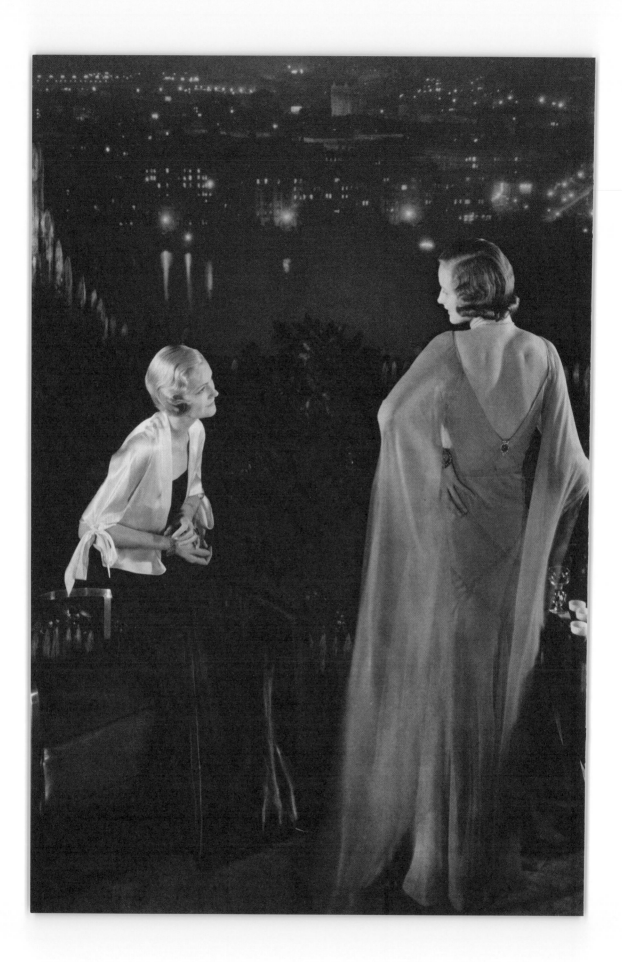

THE PROMISED LAND

On 19th January 1931, the film producer Samuel Goldwyn announced in Paris that Coco Chanel was going to Hollywood, but only after Hollywood had begged her to do so. In a statement reported in *The New York Times*, he declared, 'After more than three years of constant effort, I have at last persuaded Madame [sic] Gabrielle Chanel, fashion dictator, to go to Hollywood to co-operate with me on the vexing question of film fashions.'

Goldwyn's plan was a bold one. As the Great Depression tightened its grip on America and unemployment spread to a quarter of the workforce, he believed that millions of people would want Hollywood entertainment at its most escapist and alluring. Hence Goldwyn's determination to sign up Chanel and ensure that his film stars were dressed in cutting-edge Paris fashion, both on screen and off. It was not the first time that her designs had been seen on a Hollywood actress – Ina Claire wore a striking Chanel black suit trimmed with red fox fur in *The Royal Family of Broadway*, released by Paramount in 1930 – but the deal with Goldwyn represented a far more significant role for Chanel. According to *The New York Times*, 'She will reorganize the dressmaking department of United Artists studios and anticipate fashions six months ahead, solving thereby the eternal problem of keeping gowns up to date … Thus, Madame Chanel may reveal the secret of all impending changes and the American women will be

ft to right: Jacket and evening dress by Lanvin; chiffon dress by Chanel; the terrace of 1200 Fifth Avenue, New York. Edward Steichen, 1931.

enabled to see the latest Paris fashions, perhaps, at times, before Paris itself knows them.'

It was an ambitious, costly and time-consuming project. Goldwyn had been wooing Chanel ever since meeting her with the Grand Duke Dmitri in 1929. Dmitri had married an American heiress, Audrey Emery, three years previously, but remained on good terms with Chanel (as tended to be the case with all her former lovers; she had a talent for friendship, in spite of her occasional flashes of malice). According to an American journalist, who had interviewed Goldwyn for *Colliers* magazine in 1931, 'It all started in Monte Carlo. The Grand Duke Dmitri, of the Romanovs, quite casually introduced Samuel Goldwyn, of the movies, to Mlle Gabrielle Chanel of Chanel. Pleasant talk, pleasant compliments, big inspiration, big contract – and the great Chanel had agreed to come to Hollywood to design clothes for the movies. Admittedly, it's an experiment, a gamble, but on a million-dollar scale.'

In fact, the gamble cost far more than that. Goldwyn had finally secured Chanel's agreement to the deal, after some lengthy hesitation on her part, by guaranteeing her a contract of $1 million. But further outlay was necessary, not least for the special costume department that he set up for her at his studios, employing over a hundred workers, with facilities for cutting, fitting and dyeing fabrics. It was a bold declaration of confidence, both on Goldwyn's part, and on Chanel's. 'This is the first time a couturière of such importance, or indeed any, has left the native heath,' observed Janet Flanner in a wry report for *The New Yorker*. 'Considering what universal style-setting means to Paris for the maintenance of its financial and artistic pulse, the departure of Chanel for California must be more important than that of Van Dyck for the English Court of Charles I. But in a hundred years, the results will probably photograph less well.' As it happened, there had already been an ill-starred precedent in 1925, when Goldwyn's rival, Louis B. Mayer, hired Erté (the Russian-born designer and illustrator who worked in Paris for Paul Poiret). Erté hated his time in Hollywood, and declared upon his return to Paris that 'film stars for the most part are illiterate, crotchety, unshapely,' and that American producers lacked 'the slightest conception of elegance, beauty, or taste'.

Chanel was undoubtedly a bigger catch than Erté, and Goldwyn's investment was more substantial than Mayer's had been. But for all Goldwyn's bullish confidence, many of his competitors and contemporaries remained sceptical about his strategy, as was noted by *Colliers*: 'The world of fashion is watching it, and the world of celluloid … the one thing they all seem to agree on: Chanel has picked herself the hardest job she has ever tackled. The world-famous fashion dictator now tells the duchesses and countesses and queens of the talkies what is chic. And it is just possible that in the talkies they'll talk back! In fact, at least 95 per cent of the people who know all about movie stars and their ways with clothes think they will. Their general attitude is an eyebrow raised way up to here, and something gloomy about, "It isn't what Chanel is going to do to Hollywood – it's what Hollywood is going to do to Chanel."'

Nevertheless, whatever the potential pitfalls, Goldwyn had come up with an offer for Chanel that looked too good to refuse. The million-dollar deal was done at a time when the deepening Depression had hit Paris couture. Previously wealthy American clients whose fortunes had been wiped out were making hurried departures, and even Chanel was forced to cut her prices in half as a consequence. As Janet Flanner reported from Paris, 'The Wall Street Crash has had its effect here. In the Rue de la Paix the jewellers are reported to be losing fortunes in sudden cancellations of orders, and at the Ritz bar the pretty ladies are having to pay for their cocktails themselves … In real-estate circles certain advertisements have been illuminating: "For Sale, Cheap, Nice Old Chateau, 1 Hr. frm Paris; Original Boiserie, 6 New Baths; Owner Forced Return New York Wednesday; Must Have IMMEDIATE CASH; Will Sacrifice."'

And so it was that on 25th February 1931, the woman now deemed a fashion dictator – regardless of her past successes in freeing other women from the tyranny of corsets and hobble skirts – set off for the New World aboard the steamship *Europa*. Chanel took Misia as her travelling companion; unfortunately, by the time they arrived in New York on 4th March, both women had contracted flu. They checked into the Hotel Pierre, planning to recover there, but Chanel was immediately overwhelmed by Goldwyn's publicity machine. A reporter from *The New York Times* was one of many who mobbed her hotel suite, where Chanel appeared to be 'rather bewildered at the scores of interviewers and reception committee members'. Despite the crowd and the flu, Chanel held her own, wearing 'a simple red jersey gown with a short skirt of the severe kind which she first made popular in wartime France', and issuing some suitably strict diktats: a chic woman should dress well but not eccentrically; long hair would soon be back in fashion; and men who used scent were disgusting.

Ten days later, Chanel and Misia departed by train from New York to Los Angeles. Goldwyn had arranged everything for maximum effect. The train was

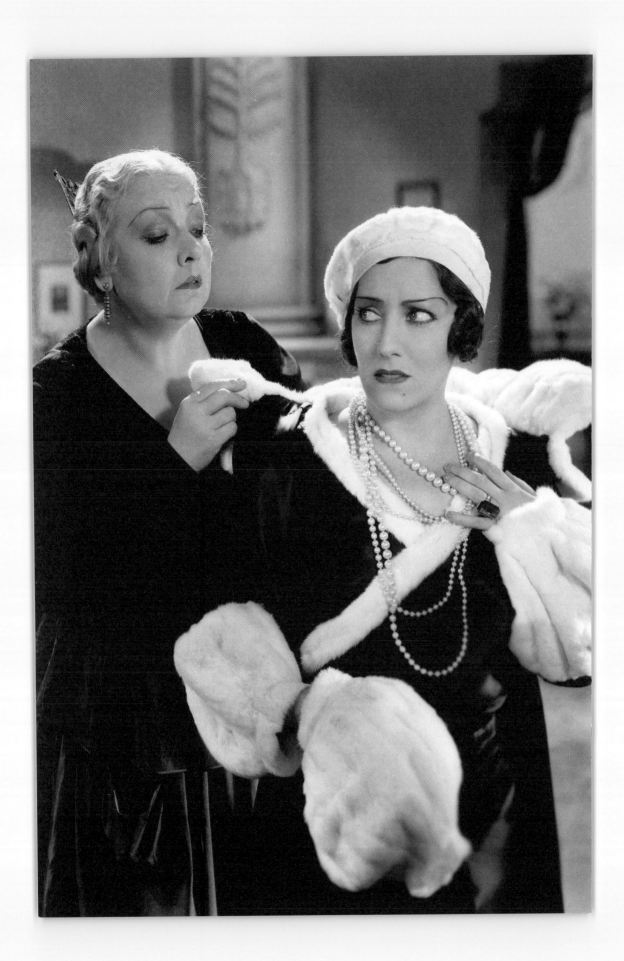

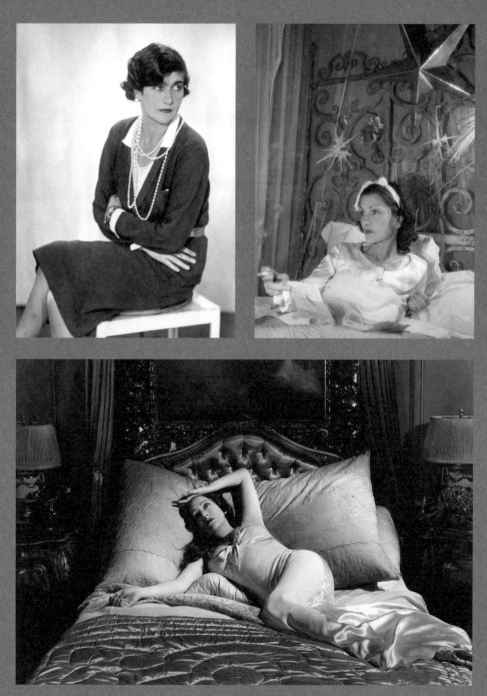

Left: Gloria Swanson, in *Tonight or Never*, costume by Chanel, 1931. Top left: Chanel. Man Ray, 1930. Top right: Chanel in her bedroom at La Pausa. Roger Schall. 1938. Bottom: Gloria Swanson, in Chanel, *Tonight or Never*, 1931.

entirely white, and stocked with large quantities of French champagne, Russian caviar and American journalists, who reported on Chanel's triumphant arrival in Hollywood. Greta Garbo was there to greet Chanel when the white train pulled into the platform – 'TWO QUEENS MEET' trumpeted the headlines – and together with Misia, they were whisked off to a party at Goldwyn's house. There Chanel met more Hollywood royalty: Marlene Dietrich, Claudette Colbert and the directors George Cukor and Erich von Stroheim, who allegedly kissed her hand and asked, 'You are a seamstress, I believe?' Chanel, somewhat uncharacteristically, did not take offence, although she later remarked, 'What a ham, but he really had style.'

Soon afterwards, the seamstress set to work on her first Goldwyn film, a musical called *Palmy Days* starring Eddie Cantor as an assistant to a fraudulent psychic, with dance routines by Busby Berkeley. The film was notable more for its flimsily clad girls than its implausible plot, and Chanel had insufficient time to supervise all the costume design. However, her instinct for fluidity and movement manifested itself in her decision to make four versions of a dress for the ingénue Barbara Weeks; each looked identical but was cut with minute yet precise variations, to be seen at its most flattering in different scenes, whether the actress was standing, sitting or dancing.

Chanel's next job was on *The Greeks Had A Word For Them*, released in February 1932. The title (and some of the storyline) had been changed from the original stage comedy, *The Greeks Had A Word For It*, in order to satisfy the censors; although, as *Time* magazine noted in its review, 'Goldwyn was guided less by a sense of decency than a sense of decoration,' expressly crediting Chanel's involvement. She dressed the three leads – Ina Claire, Joan Blondell and Madge Evans – who were playing glamorous showgirls-turned-gold-diggers. Thirty complete outfits were designed for the actresses, a process that began in Hollywood, although they were completed to Chanel's instructions after she returned to Paris.

Chanel's third and final Goldwyn project was to dress Gloria Swanson as a prima donna opera singer in *Tonight or Never*; and this time, the entire process was undertaken in Paris. The film star, who was herself something of a diva, described her encounter with Chanel in her memoir, *Swanson on Swanson*. After a week of fittings in Paris, there had been a pause in the proceedings, when it dawned upon Swanson that she was unexpectedly pregnant. 'The following day Coco Chanel, tiny and fierce, approaching fifty, wearing a hat, as she always did at work, glared furiously at me when I had trouble squeezing into one of the gowns she had measured for me six weeks earlier. It was black satin to the floor, cut on the bias, a great work of art in the eyes of both of us. I said I would try it with a girdle, but when I stepped before her again, she snorted with contempt and said anyone a block away could see the line where the girdle ended halfway down my thigh.

'"Take off the girdle and lose five pounds," she snapped briskly. "You have no right to fluctuate in the middle of fittings. Come back tomorrow and we'll finish the evening coat with the sable collar. Five pounds!" she cried again, unable to restrain herself. "No less!"'

The following day, Swanson returned to Rue Cambon with a large roll of surgical elastic, and requested that it be made into 'a rubberized undergarment to the knees, or rather, two or three dozen of them'. Chanel was horrified, but Swanson prevailed, citing 'reasons of health'; and eventually, couture corsets were provided, constructed with as much attention to detail as every other garment in the atelier. 'With evident displeasure, the corset maker ran up the panty girdle in muslin first. It worked. Then she made it in snug elastic. It worked even better, although it took three people to get me into it. With the lavish confidence of Harry Houdini hearing twenty padlocks snap shut, I then raised my arms to receive the black satin cut on the bias over my head. It fit like a glove.' By the time Swanson sailed for New York in the summer of 1931, she had 'a whole wardrobe designed for me by Chanel, including a stack of sturdy elastic panties'. And when filming commenced in California, the corsets were sufficiently robust for Swanson to conceal her growing pregnancy. 'I did scrutinize the rushes with thin lips and a nervous eye, but I continued to look all right up there on the screen as the weeks passed. Every one of Coco's seams held.'

Others in Hollywood were less appreciative, however, and *Tonight or Never* proved to be Chanel's last job for Goldwyn. The film – United Artists' big Christmas release – opened to polite reviews (*The New York Times* described it as an 'unusually striking production', partly thanks to Chanel's sartorial creations), but it flopped at the box office. After the fanfare and razzmatazz of Chanel's arrival in Hollywood, she departed, according to *The New Yorker*, 'in a huff', having been told by the movie moguls that 'her dresses weren't sensational enough. She made a lady look like a lady. Hollywood wants a lady to look like two ladies.'

Still, she had made her million dollars – Goldwyn paid up without an argument – and *Vanity Fair*, at least, was sufficiently impressed to nominate Chanel to its

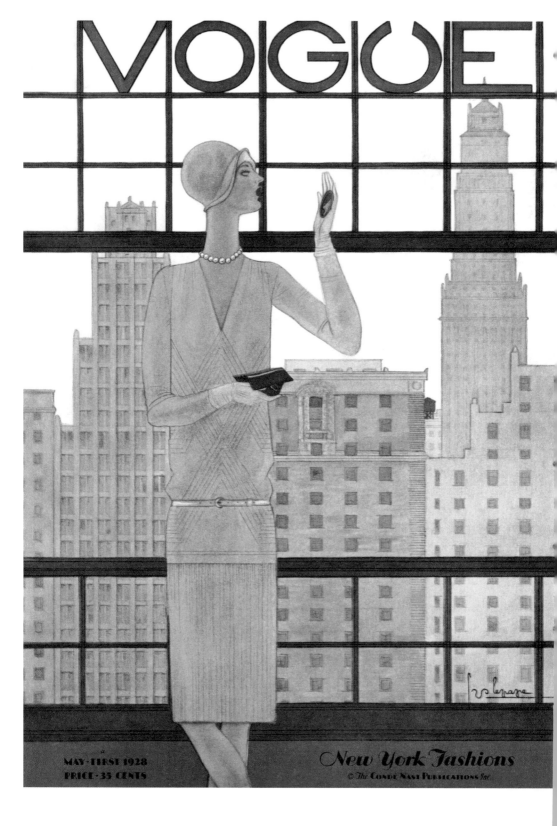

MAY·FIRST·1928
PRICE·35·CENTS

New York Fashions
© The Condé Nast Publications Inc.

1931 Hall of Fame. The magazine declared its reasons for doing so in a brief yet trenchant paragraph: 'Because she was the first to apply the principles of modernism to dressmaking; because she numbers among her friends the most famous men of France; because she combines a shrewd business sense with enormous personal prodigality and a genuine if erratic enthusiasm for the arts; and finally because she came to America to make a laudable attempt to introduce chic to Hollywood.'

If Hollywood did not take to Chanel, then neither was she impressed by the might of the movies. In Paris, she had already collaborated as a costume designer with the most celebrated of modern artists: with Picasso and Cocteau on *Antigone* and *Le Train bleu*; with Cocteau again in 1926 for his play *Orphée* (in which he described the character of Death appearing as 'a very beautiful young woman in a bright pink ball-gown and fur coat'); and the Ballets Russes production of *Apollon musagète* in 1929, composed by Stravinsky and choreographed by George Balanchine. Such triumphs counted for nothing in Hollywood, although Chanel was swift in returning the snub. In later years, when questioned about her trip into the heart of the film business, she was dismissive: 'It was the Mont St Michel of tit and tail.' And to Claude Delay, she emphasised her independence from the monolithic power of the studios: 'The Americans wanted to tie me down, you see, because I out-fashion fashion. But I'm not for sale or hire. In Hollywood the stars are just the producers' servants.' Thus Chanel declared she would not submit to anyone, nor to the dogma that American culture would lead fashion, as well as everything else in the world; and was at pains to make this clear to Paul Morand in 1946, even at a time when she had ceased designing at Rue Cambon. '"Paris will no longer create fashion," I hear people say. New York will invent it, Hollywood will propagate it and Paris will be subjected to it. I don't believe that. Of course, cinema has the same effect on fashion as the atomic bomb; the ratio of the explosion of the moving image throughout cinemas knows no bounds on Earth, but I, who admire American films, am still waiting for studios to impose a figure, a colour, a style of clothing. Hollywood can deal successfully with the face, with the outline, the hairstyle, the hands, the toenails, with portable bars, refrigerators in the drawing-room, clock-radios ... but it doesn't deal any more successfully with the central problem of the body, which it has not managed to dissociate from man's inner drama, and which remains the prerogative of the great designers and ancient civilisations.' And if she had not made herself quite clear with this somewhat complicated theory, Chanel then delivered a more direct parting shot. 'Greta Garbo, the greatest actress the screen has given us, was the worst dressed woman in the world.'

But whatever the disappointments of Chanel's encounter with Hollywood, her journey to America was nonetheless a significant one. For this was the place that she had conjured up for herself in childhood as her father's promised land, the New World where he would make his fortune, having left his daughters behind with the nuns. Claude Delay remembers Chanel's wistful story of finding herself lost in Beverly Hills with Misia one day, searching for an address that they could not find. Eventually, Misia noticed the name Chanel written on one of the gateposts. Still believing in Coco's story of her childhood, Misia cried out in astonishment, 'It's your father. We'll find him and take him back with us. I'll leave Sert.' Chanel's only response was a tart comment that Sert had already left Misia. The rest was left unsaid, although Chanel's ambivalence about America was to crop up again in her conversations with Delay. On the one hand, it was a continent that had made her rich, through the vast sales of her perfumes, for which Americans seemed to have an insatiable appetite. ('They'll buy every luxury,' she said to Delay, 'and the first of all luxuries is perfume.') And yet part of her, austere as a nun, resisted the seductions offered to her by America. Describing her hotel suite in Hollywood to Delay, Chanel listed its comforts with a certain amount of contempt: two bedrooms and four television sets, including one that could be watched in the bathroom. 'All that's for people who have gone soft. The English hide everything, the Americans show everything! America is dying of comfort.'

In her heart, she must have known that her father was not waiting for her in America, although it might have suited her to believe that it had swallowed him up. Many years later, in her solitary white-walled bedroom at the Ritz, Chanel was beset by nightmares, despite the opiates that she used to keep dreams at bay. There was one image that haunted her most, repeating itself over and over again in her restless nights, and which she repeated to Claude Delay. As Delay describes it to me, her eyes fill with tears, this eminent psychoanalyst suddenly overcome with sympathy for her long-dead friend. 'Out of the darkness of sleep, there would appear a white train, with a scented coach full of flowers and COCO CHANEL written on the side. It was carrying a corpse inside – her own body.'

When I ask her if she ever interpreted the dream for Chanel, she shakes her head. 'It was her dream,' she says. 'It was not for me to tell her its meaning. But something tremendously important was contained within that white train. You understand that, don't you?'

I'm not sure that I do entirely understand; for so much of Chanel remains enigmatic – the more you run after her, the more elusive her ghost becomes. Perhaps her spirit is to be found not in the flickering images of her designs for the silver screen, nor in the continuing attempts to portray her on film, but in that fragment of her own dream, in the white train that crossed America, bearing her dead body and carrying her name. Her father was gone, and with him something of her self had died; but all the while Coco Chanel was turning into a myth in her own lifetime, a living legend, gathering speed as she left what she had lost behind.

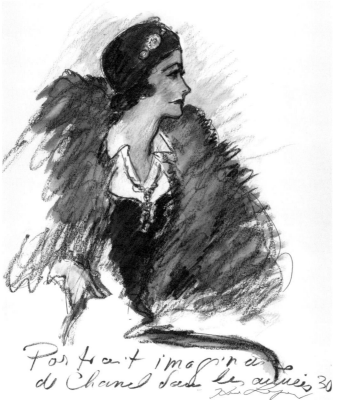

Chanel in diamonds and fur, by Karl Lagerfeld.

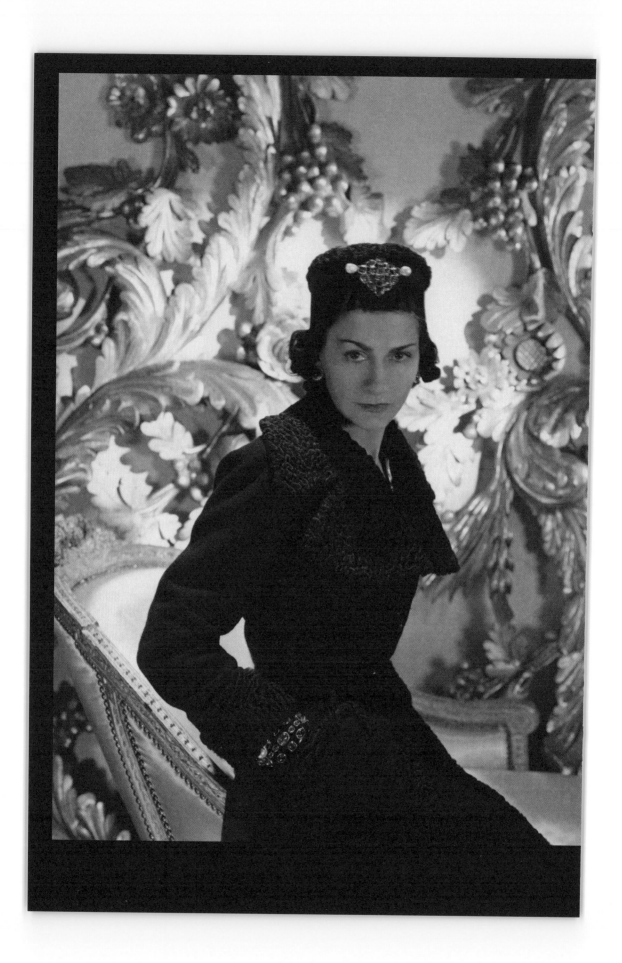

DIAMONDS AS BIG
AS THE RITZ

1st November 1932: All Saints' Day, and a leaden grey sky hung over Paris, a city already in the shadow of the darkening Depression. At this low point in a grim season, Mademoiselle Chanel issued an invitation to an exhibition of diamond jewellery of her own design. The venue was 29 Faubourg Saint-Honoré, a magnificent eighteenth-century Parisian mansion where Chanel was residing at the time. Although she still entertained at her apartment in Rue Cambon (and retreated there, when necessary), Chanel had moved into one of the most prestigious streets in Paris, after a prolonged sojourn at the Ritz Hotel (where she would later return). Her Faubourg Saint-Honoré neighbours included the British Embassy and the Palais de l'Elysée, and her vast ground-floor suite opened out onto even larger formal gardens that stretched as far as Avenue Gabriel. Chanel decorated with suitable splendour: her favourite Coromandel screens and mirrors, a grand piano, and sumptuous carpets and curtains. 'Plush carpet everywhere,' she recalled to Paul Morand, '*colorado claro* in colour, with silky tints, like good cigars, woven to my specifications, and brown velvet curtains with gold braiding that looked like coronets girdled in yellow silk.'

Princesses, duchesses and ambassadors came to the opening party of Chanel's exhibition, and thousands of visitors flocked to see the spectacular jewellery in the subsequent fortnight, paying 20 francs apiece. No

EXPOSITION

DE

BIJOUX DE DIAMANTS

créés par

CHANEL

du 7 au 19 Novembre 1932

chez Mademoiselle CHANEL
29, Faubourg Saint-Honoré, 29

AU BÉNÉFICE DES ŒUVRES

" SOCIÉTÉ DE LA CHARITÉ MATERNELLE DE PARIS "

et

" L'ASSISTANCE PRIVÉE A LA CLASSE MOYENNE "

reconnues d'Utilité Publique

ENTRÉE : **20** FRS

obvious profit was made from the show – the gemstones were on loan from the Union of Diamond Merchants, who had sent a delegation to Chanel a few months previously, asking her to publicise their jewels during the economic slump – and the admission fees were donated to charitable foundations (including La Société de la Charité Maternelle, which happened to have had Marie Antoinette as one of its original patrons). Yet for all its splendour and success, the diamond exhibition also had its puzzling aspects. It wasn't simply the odd juxtaposition of this radiant treasure trove with the gloom of the Crash, although that was notable, in a hardening winter when increasing numbers of unemployed were homeless on the streets of Paris.

Whatever the harsh realities outside the gilt and looking-glass walls of Faubourg Saint-Honoré, inside, Mademoiselle Chanel was giving an unexpected twist to her jewellery designs. She had become famous for her costume jewellery in the Twenties by championing the combination of fake gems with real ones. Indeed, she had made it one of her signature looks, mixing precious stones and glass copies with a supreme confidence not dissimilar to the manner in which she blurred truth and lies. But now here she was, declaring in her introduction to the exhibition catalogue that priceless diamonds were the only way forward 'during a period of financial crisis when an instinctive desire for authenticity is reawakened in every domain'. Which made it all the more mystifying to see her astonishing jewellery designs – a glittering constellation of stars and comets – displayed on eerie wax mannequins, their heads so lifelike that it was difficult to tell whether their eyelashes and hair were real or false. The temptation to reach out and touch them was palpable; but they were enclosed in glass *vitrines*, locked away like waxen Sleeping Beauties, although their eyes were open, unblinking in the dazzle of diamonds reflected against a backdrop of mirrors. And as the lines of visitors made their way past the policemen on guard, none of them knew the secret that Chanel kept close to her heart: that the diamond stars were mirror images of the mosaics on the floor of the orphanage at Aubazine, themselves a reflection of the night sky that the medieval monks had observed when they fashioned their stone corridor.

Something of the mysterious potency of Chanel's alchemical blend was captured by the sharp-eyed Janet Flanner in *The New Yorker*. The reporter had no clue as to the possible provenance of this constellation of diamonds in the salon at Faubourg Saint-Honoré, but she did note the peculiar manner in which Chanel signed her name in the brochure. 'It is not undescriptive that, owing to an odd caesura in her signature, Gabrielle Chanel's name, as she signs it, reads "Gabri elleChanel". In her long, dramatic career as a dressmaker, she has never been more *elleChanel*, or herself, than in this curious exhibition of diamonds just opened in the interests of charity (and diamond merchants) in her sumptuous private *hôtel* in the Faubourg St-Honoré. With that aggravating instinct to strike when everyone else thinks the iron is cold that has, up till now, made her success, she has, at the height of the depression, returned to precious stones "as having the greatest value in the smallest volume"; just as, during the boom, she launched glass gewgaws "because they were devoid of arrogance in an epoch of too easy *luxe*." As a result, what is regarded by underwriters as fifty million francs' worth of borrowed brilliants, and by the pairs of private policemen at every drawing-room door as a terrible responsibility, judging by their miens, has just been put on display among the Coromandel screens and rose-quartz chandeliers which have made Chanel's home notable, if not for its simplicity.'

Flanner, like many other commentators, was struck by the beauty of Chanel's diamond jewellery, and also its ingenuity, whereby 'in the interests of further economy, all of the more elaborate pieces come to pieces: the tiaras turn into bracelets, the ear-drops into brooches; the stars into garters.' This display of versatility had a certain wit to it, but the overall effect was nevertheless one of rich confidence; and if the exhibition was only temporary, it was also suggestive of the permanence of the constellations. As such, it was yet another measure of Chanel's marvellous inventiveness, of her apparently natural instinct for providing fantastical illusion with a gloss of verisimilitude.

News of the incredible Chanel diamonds spread fast – the Paris exhibition was reported in dozens of newspapers across the United States, in what appeared to be a welcome distraction from the worsening economy – and readers from Manhattan to Milwaukee were given a wealth of enthusiastic detail. (*The Philadelphia Record*, for example, deemed the remarkable diamond fringed head-dresses 'startlingly original' and 'singularly unpretentious'.) As was often the case, Janet Flanner gave the most polished first-hand account: 'Mlle Chanel's mountings for the jewels are in design dominantly and delicately astronomical. Magnificent lopsided stars for earrings; as a necklace, a superb comet whose nape-encircling tail is all that attaches it to a lady's throat; bracelets that are flexible rays; crescents for hats and hair; and, as a unique set piece mounted in yellow gold, a splendid sun of yellow diamonds from a unique collection of matched stones unmatched in the world.

'It is perhaps of interest to add that two days after the Chanel Paris diamond show opened, De Beers stock was reported to have jumped some twenty points on the London exchange.'

Thus Chanel's influence was proven to have real power; and the business of fashion, at least in her hands, to be less ephemeral than the financial institutions that had fallen victim to the catastrophic crash in the stock markets. But it was not the first time that Chanel had used jewellery to display her authority, as well as her social supremacy and success. These were made manifest in the manner in which she wore her precious gems – the Duke of Westminster's pearls and emeralds slung over tweeds and plain woollen knits, in an insouciant disregard for tradition – and in her apparently effortless ability to persuade rich women to follow suit. As Cecil Beaton observed in *The Glass of Fashion*, Chanel's genius was to invent 'a mode of brilliant simplicity': 'Ruthlessly women were stripped of their finery, fitted with a tricot and skirt or plain dress; and when they looked like Western Union messenger boys, when they had been reduced to chic poverty, then, and only then, did she drape them with costume jewellery, with great lumps of emeralds, rubies, and cascades of pearls.'

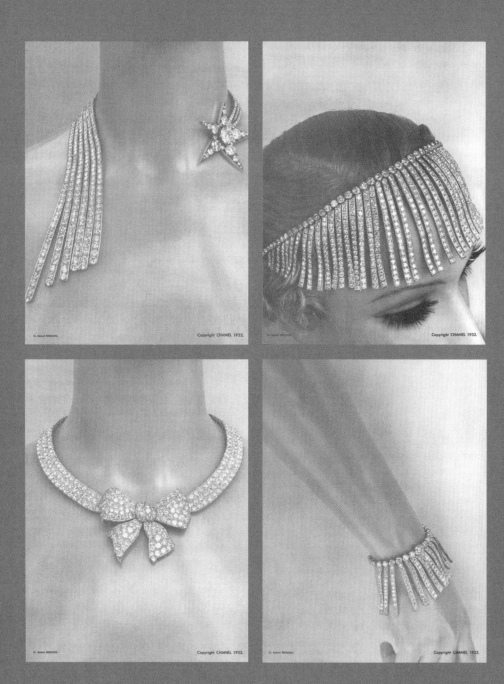

Chanel's 1932 'Bijoux de Diamants' collection, featuring diamonds set in platinum.
Top left: The 'Comète' necklace, a cascade using 649 diamonds. Top right: The 'Franges' necklace, worn as a tiara; diamond fringe mounted on a chain made of 68 diamonds. Bottom left: The 'Nœud' bow necklace. Bottom right: The 'Franges' bracelet. Robert Bresson, 1932.

Proof of Chanel's unrivalled power was also strikingly evident in her employment of aristocrats as artisans to make her jewellery, just as she had previously brought members of the Russian elite into her service. In doing so, the peasant girl from the provinces had leapt over the barriers of class that had encircled Parisian high society; an upturning of the social hierarchy that was made clear in her relationship with Count Etienne de Beaumont. His soirées and costume balls were fabulous affairs, as carefully choreographed as the ballets he patronised; but when Coco Chanel was first befriended by Misia, the dressmaker was not deemed worthy of an invitation to the Count's salon. 'I know perfectly well that in those days "society people" would never dream of inviting "tradespeople",' remarked Misia in her memoir. 'Then again, the latter would never permit themselves to recognize or greet you, except in their own establishments. Consequently Count de Beaumont was probably behaving naturally in not sending Mademoiselle Chanel an invitation; but she was *my* friend, so I felt hurt that an exception had not been made for her.' Misia's comments were as revealing of her relationship with Chanel – loyalty spiked with malice and possessiveness – as they were of Chanel's with Count de Beaumont. But if Misia felt hurt, and Chanel wounded, then an exception was very quickly made for the couturière in her transformation from tradeswoman to trendsetter to leader of the *beau monde*. As Chanel's fame grew, de Beaumont not only welcomed her as an illustrious guest at his parties, but also agreed to work for her as a jewellery designer in the late Twenties. Chanel's subsequent (and somewhat cryptic) account of this episode to Paul Morand indicates that she may not have entirely forgiven de Beaumont for his previous social slights; or perhaps he simply failed to prove his worth to her. 'I know what work is,' she said to Morand. 'I have never hired layabouts. Count Etienne actually slaved away to such an extent that he secretly poached my buyers; he sent them off to his townhouse where he had set up a second workshop, while still retaining … the one he had at my house. I dismissed him, for all who are paid deserve hardship. I don't like dilettantes who take other people's place, be it in literature or couture. It is immoral to play at earning one's living.'

Whatever the unhappy circumstances of the end of Chanel's working relationship with the Count, she continued to see him socially, and still attended his elaborate *Ancien Régime* costume balls. After de Beaumont's departure, she commissioned François Hugo as a jeweller, and another blue-blooded aristocrat, Fulco di Verdura, a Sicilian duke who designed several of Chanel's most famous pieces, including a cuff bracelet crafted around a Maltese cross (in the same shape as the mosaic pattern on the stone floor at Aubazine). Verdura worked for Chanel in Paris for several years, from 1933 onwards, before setting up his own studio in New York as a bespoke jeweller of great renown.

But the man who was to be Chanel's most important collaborator, and also her lover, was Paul Iribe, an exact contemporary of hers with a similarly provincial background. Born Paul Iribarnegaray to Basque parents in 1883 in Angoulême, south-western France, he had shortened his name to Iribe when he came to Paris in 1900. A fiercely ambitious young illustrator, Iribe founded his own satirical journal, *Le Témoin*, at the age of 23, which brought him to the attention of Paul Poiret. The couturier, then at the height of his fame, commissioned Iribe to draw an album of fashion illustrations in 1908. 'He was a most unusual young fellow,' wrote Poiret in his memoirs, 'a Basque, chubby as a capon, with something of both the divinity student and the composing room foreman about him. In the seventeenth century he would have been a court priest; he wore gold rimmed spectacles, a wide-winged detachable collar with a loose sailor-knot tie … He spoke very softly, as though there was always some mystery, and placed a kind of crucial emphasis on certain words, articulating every syllable, as when he said: "That's ad-mi-ra-ble!"'

Iribe's work for Poiret was much praised, and as his fame spread as an illustrator, stylist and designer of fabrics and furniture, so too did his social success. His first wife was an actress, Jeanne Dirys, a celebrated beauty who had contributed to Chanel's early triumph as a milliner when in 1911 she was depicted in a broad-rimmed Chanel hat on the front cover of *Comoedia illustré* in a bold illustration by Iribe himself. A friend and colleague of Cocteau – they launched a new magazine together, *Le Mot*, in 1914, after the demise of *Le Témoin* – Iribe was rapidly absorbed into Misia's inner circle, with all its fashionable absurdities and splendid inconsistencies. During the First World War, for example, when Misia had been given permission to transport wounded soldiers from the front line to Paris, she persuaded several couturiers to donate their delivery vans to be converted to ambulances, and called upon Paul Iribe to be her driver. There are differing reports of Misia's outfit – some say she was dressed in a nurse's outfit especially designed for her by Poiret, others that she wore a business-like tweed suit – but Paul Iribe was dressed like a deep sea diver (for reasons that were never made clear), while Cocteau was in a male nurse's uniform by Poiret, and Sert wore pale grey knickerbockers.

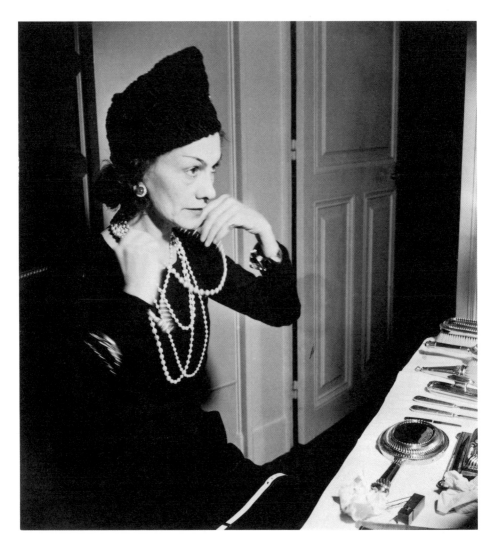

Chanel in pearls. Above: Jean Moral, 1938.
Right: Boris Lipnitzki, 1936.

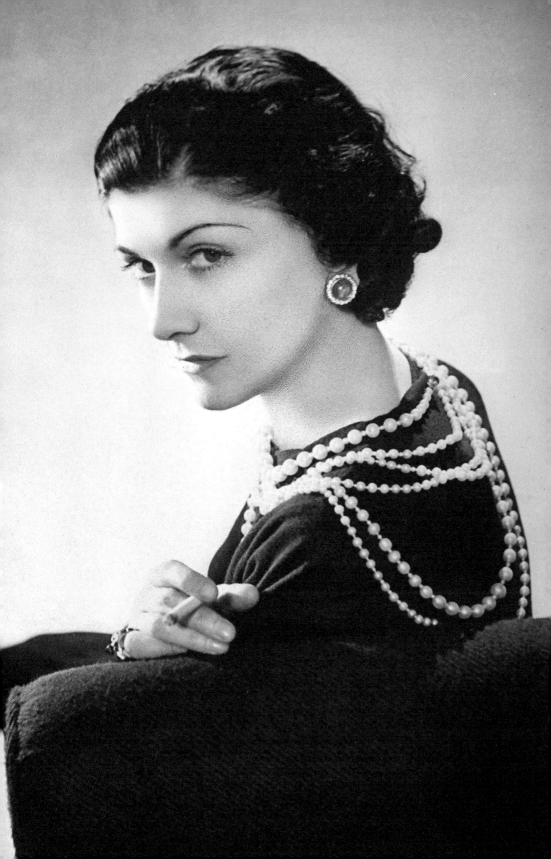

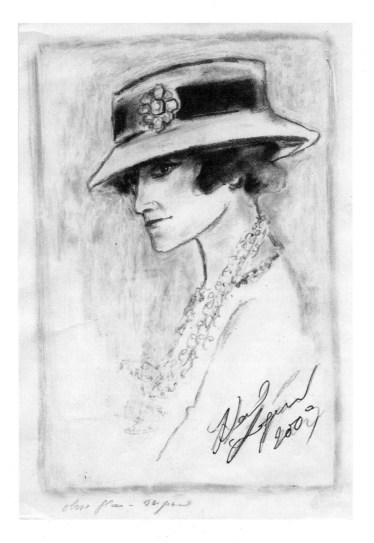

Chanel, by Karl
Lagerfeld.

By 1919, Iribe had made his way to America, where he married an heiress, Maybelle Hogan, and was subsequently employed in 1923 by the Hollywood producer Cecil B. DeMille to design costumes and sets for *The Ten Commandments*. DeMille was sufficiently impressed to allow Iribe to direct a film, *Changing Husbands*, and even after its disastrous reception, the producer entrusted him with the role of art director of another biblical extravaganza, *The King of Kings*. Rumour had it that Iribe was fired when he failed to make practical arrangements for the staging of the Crucifixion. Certainly, he left Hollywood and returned to Paris before the film's release in 1927, whereupon he opened an interior design shop (financed by his rich American wife) on Faubourg Saint-Honoré.

The precise date of the start of his affair with Chanel is unrecorded, but Iribe was definitely involved with her by the time of her diamond exhibition in November 1932; indeed, he was in London on her behalf soon after the opening of the exhibition, attempting to negotiate with the relevant authorities over a demand for customs duty to be paid if the exhibition came to England after Paris. Iribe's efforts were unsuccessful and the planned exhibition at Londonderry House in December was cancelled, despite protestations that the entrance fees were to be donated to a charity of which Queen Mary was patron.

For all his undeniable energy and charm, Iribe was a controversial figure, both for his womanising and for his increasingly nationalistic politics. He had persuaded Chanel to finance a revival of *Le Témoin* in 1933, in which she appeared the following year as the unnamed yet recognisable model for his illustration of Marianne, the incarnation of France, being judged by a sneering panel of foreign leaders (Roosevelt, Ramsay MacDonald, Hitler and Mussolini). *Le Témoin* was right-wing, but party politics were far less important to Iribe than a ferocious, chauvinistic patriotism; he was anti-Semitic, anti-German, anti-fascist, anti-democracy and passionately pro-France. As his rallying cry for the magazine declared: '*Le Témoin* speaks French. Subscribe to it.'

Colette, for one, was hugely suspicious of him, as she made clear in a letter to Maurice Goudeket (her lover and husband-to-be) after encountering Iribe and Chanel together in St Tropez in July 1933. The writer had been a close friend of his first wife, Jeanne Dirys, who had died over a decade previously, having fallen ill soon after he abandoned her; but Colette's antipathy towards Iribe was not simply fuelled by loyalty to a dead woman. Her letter described how she had just run into Misia while shopping in St Tropez; Misia had told her with great excitement that Chanel and Iribe were planning to be married. A few minutes later, Colette felt a pair of hands – 'very fine, cold ones' – covering her eyes. 'It was Coco Chanel ... and a little further along I catch sight of Iribe, throwing me kisses. Then, before I can complete the rite of exorcism, he embraces me, tenderly squeezing my hand between his cheek and shoulder.' Colette did not explain why she felt such dread of Iribe that an exorcism might be necessary, but did quote his response. 'How naughty you are, treating me like a demon!' he declared, to which she replied, 'And even then you don't give up?' Her letter continued, 'But he went on overflowing with joy and affection ... He is slender, lined, and white-haired, and laughs through a set of brand-new teeth. He coos

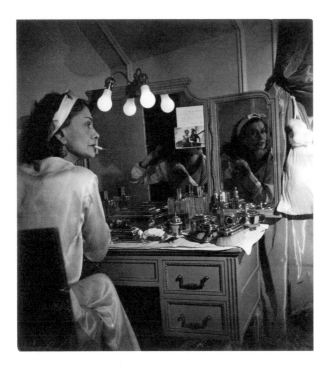

like a dove, which makes it all the more interesting, because you will find in old texts that demons assume the voice and the form of the bird of Venus.'

Chanel herself described Iribe with a certain ambivalence. 'The most complicated man I ever knew was Paul Iribe,' she told Paul Morand. 'He criticised me for not being simple.' Despite his own penchant for high living and his designs for lavish interiors, furniture and jewellery, Iribe started to find fault with Chanel's life at 29 Faubourg Saint-Honoré. Her account to Morand of Iribe's complaints offers far more insight than was usual in her memories of past love affairs. '"I don't understand," he said, "why you need so many rooms … What's the point of all these objects? Your way of life is ruining you. What a waste! Why do you need all these servants? One eats too well in your house. I'd come here more often, I might live close to you, if you knew how I'd be happy with nothing. I loathe pointless gestures, vast expenditure and complicated human beings." … I replied: "So be it. I shall become simple. I shall reduce my standard of living."'

She gave up her lease at Faubourg Saint-Honoré, and rented two rooms in a modest house not far from Rue Cambon, taking with her a Coromandel screen, two heaters, her favourite books and a few rugs. 'When he saw me leaving my house, Iribe was annoyed, jealous, unhappy. "I'm boarding out," I told him. "It's very convenient … and I'm going to start living the famous simple life."' Much to Iribe's irritation, Chanel also suggested to him that he do the same. After some argument, they both moved into the Ritz.

From there, they would have heard the riot that took place on 6th February 1934, when thousands of demonstrators marched from the Place de la Concorde towards the Palais Bourbon. The demonstration has sometimes been referred to as a sinister right-wing assault on democracy, but in fact appears to have been far more confused (and confusing) than that. 'Nobody knows how many people were on the Place de la Concorde the night of February 6;' reported Janet Flanner in *The New Yorker*, 'maybe forty thousand, maybe sixty, with hundreds of thousands more on the Left Bank, behind the Madeleine, down the Rue de Rivoli … struggling to join them.' No matter what conclusions were subsequently drawn from the sectarianism that fuelled the riot, Flanner believed that 'its initial importance lay in its unheralded unity, its passionate, complete popularity. For several years, every class in France has been banditized by state taxes, state politicians, state-protected swindlers; on that one night every class in Paris turned out to protest – from

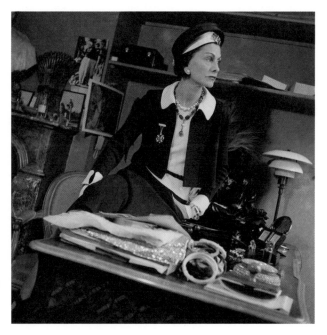

A portrait of Chanel
at her desk.
François Kollar,
1938.

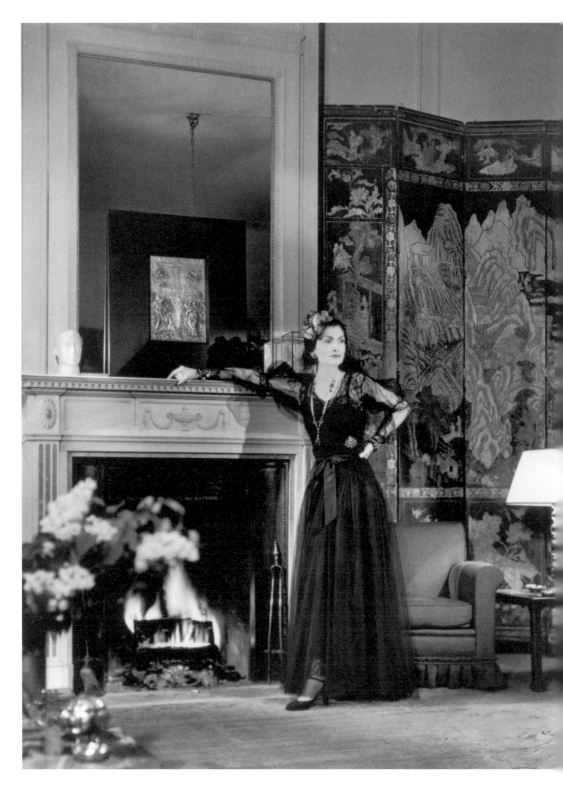

men in Republican derby hats to chaps in Communist caps, from middle-aged, medaled war veterans down to Royalist adolescents who had never battled for anything except, in dreams, for an exiled king. Against horses' hooves, gunshot, and police clubs, this unpartisan mass fought in surprise, struggled with mutual courage, and was struck down without party distinction.'

Other newspapers gave different reports. The Communist *L'Humanité* informed its readers that the fight had been that of the working men of Paris against Fascism, while the right-wing monarchist gazette, *L'Action française*, declared that it had been against Communists, Socialists, Radicals, Republicans, Jews and Freemasons. The Socialist *Le Populaire* accused war veterans and the Right of attempting to overthrow democracy and impose a dictatorship; the Conservative–Nationalist *Le Jour* believed the complete opposite, and announced that the brave war veterans had defeated a dictatorship bid by the Left. Amidst all the frenzy, *Le Matin* came closest to the truth: that the riot on 6th February was 'A Day of Civil War'.

In the aftermath, Janet Flanner counted the cost: 'Official number of dead, twenty, obviously too small; unofficial number, around seventy, also too small except for miracle, considering that over two thousand machine-gun shots were fired into twenty thousand people. French cost of living, compared to French wages, higher by 30 per cent than any other on earth. Taxi strike plus riots coming during spring fashion shows estimated to have cost big houses one million francs each.'

The effect on Chanel was incalculable. Her spring show took place, as usual, on 5th February, narrowly missing the riots, but the atmosphere in Paris was anxiously febrile, and orders may well have been affected. Certainly, she was already well aware of the ongoing effects of the Depression, although her response tended to be one of confidence. She also saw it as her duty to defend the fashion industry against accusations of its irrelevance and frivolity; hence the spirited magazine article that had appeared under her byline in (of all places) *The St. Paul Pioneer Press* the previous year, in February 1933. 'To talk about fashion at a time so full of sadness and hardship seems to be almost a fault of tact,' began the piece, 'but, if you want to think about it, isn't fashion one of the great industries, not only of France but of the whole world?' Chanel then launched into further rhetoric, with a hectoring passion reminiscent of Paul Iribe's political tracts, although her arguments were internationalist, unlike his fervid brand of nationalism. Fashion, she declared, 'allows millions of men and women to earn their living', for it gave work to 'the wool, the cotton and the silk industries, also the industries of feathers and artificial flowers. Also the industry of material weaving and the dye industry. And do you realize what the transportation of those goods means? ... Do you realize what it means for the railroads, the navigation corporations, the customs people, the merchants, the owners of shops, large and small, the salesmen and the saleswomen?'

She then addressed herself directly to her American audience: 'In fighting for fashion, as I do, in keeping it alive, as I do, I have the great pride of knowing that in my way I am helping the wool industry and the great stores of your cities, great or small. I know that I am fighting for work against unemployment, and in that way I may be helping farmers, too, for when there is too much misery in the world your wheat doesn't sell.' But for all her rhetorical self-assurance, Chanel's article ended on a note of uncertainty. 'I want men to be confident of tomorrow, looking at the women dressed in the fashion that I am going to create tomorrow. But although I am a woman, I am not vain enough to pretend to know today what tomorrow is going to be.'

In retrospect, when Chanel considered her past with Iribe, she suggested that it had been doomed from the start. 'My relationship with Iribe was a passionate one,' she told Paul Morand. 'How I loathe passion! What an abomination, what a ghastly disease! The passionate man takes no notice of the outside world or of other people; he sees them merely as instruments; the weather, happiness, the neighbour's rights, these things don't exist for him.' Perhaps Chanel was protesting too much – after all, she had known great passion – but her description of Iribe suggests that she came to feel exhausted by him. Unlike the tender memories she expressed of Boy Capel or the Duke of Westminster, her annoyance with Iribe surfaced in her narrative to Morand, as did her sense that he was jealous of her success. 'I can't help feeling irritated when I think of the atmosphere of passion he built around me,' she said. 'He wore me out, he ruined my health. When Iribe had left for America, I was beginning to be very well known. My emerging celebrity had eclipsed his declining glory.'

Chanel also identified something in Iribe's attitude to her that might have been linked to his own passionate feelings about France, and what it meant to be French. 'For him I represented that Paris he had been unable to possess and control, from which he had departed in a sulk to join Cecil DeMille, down in his

Christian Bérard illustration, featured in American *Vogue*, July 1

Chanel dines at home
in printed pyjamas,
sweater, barbaric jewels.
(Two small Chanels)
Striped linen, flannel jacket.
Checked tussur, chiffon cape-veil.

boring, gloomy studios in California.' Her attempt to analyse Iribe's psyche was not necessarily an accurate representation of his emotions, but it was deeply evocative of what she described as 'those phantoms that we call complexes'. And if her description of him was melodramatic, it nevertheless gave some credence to Colette's view of him as demonic. 'Iribe loved me, but he did so because of all those things that he never admitted to himself, nor admitted to me; he loved me with the secret hope of destroying me. He longed for me to be crushed and humiliated, he wanted me to die. It would have made him deeply happy to see me belong totally to him, impoverished, reduced to helplessness, paralysed and driving a small car.'

Yet Chanel remained uncrushed, apparently indestructible, like her magnificent jewels, with some essential element of herself that remained out of her lover's grasp. Her past 'tortured him'; for he was a Basque, she said to Morand, and displayed the jealousy of 'a real Spaniard'. Thus the domineering French patriot was revealed, at least in Chanel's account, to be an insecure outsider; a foreigner to his own land, and to the elusive landscape of her past, as well. 'Iribe wanted to relive with me, step by step, the whole of that past lived without him and to go back through lost time, while asking me to account for myself. One day, he took me to the heart of the Auvergne, to Mont-Dore, to set out on the trail of my youth. We found the house of my aunts … As I walked beneath this avenue of lime trees, I really felt as if I were beginning my life again. I lingered behind. Iribe walked on alone and, on the pretext of finding somewhere to stay, he asked to see my aunts. They had not changed their attitude towards me, after so many years; he was told if I showed my face, I would not be made welcome. He came back towards me, soothed and satisfied, having found everything just as I had described it to him.'

Of all Chanel's references to her 'aunts', this is possibly the most tantalising, in its hint that Iribe might have come closer to her childhood origins than her previous lovers. He had traced the contours of her recent past – her criss-crossing trail from Faubourg Saint-Honoré to Rue Cambon and to and from the Ritz – but if she did take him to 'the heart of the Auvergne', then who were the aunts that he found there? An imaginary version of the journey might have Paul Iribe finally setting foot in the abbey of Aubazine, walking up the dark stairs and through the door into the corridor paved with stars and crosses. But there were no witnesses to provide evidence of any such visit; nor did Iribe live long enough to tell his own side of the story.

In the late summer of 1935, he left Paris on the night train to join Chanel at La Pausa, a holiday retreat that he had enjoyed many times before, sharing with her all the manifold luxuries of the villa, and her bed with its wrought-iron stars. On 21st September, Iribe joined his lover on the tennis court, overlooking the blue expanse of the Mediterranean; half-way through their match, he collapsed with a heart attack, and died. She never used the tennis court again, but let it grow wild with flowers and long grass, as it remains to this day. Chanel grieved in silence, giving little away to anyone; but many years later, she told Claude Delay that with Iribe gone, even her beloved La Pausa could no longer hold her or console her. And while Chanel now appeared to the outside world as hard as her diamonds, perhaps something far more precious inside her had shrivelled and died.

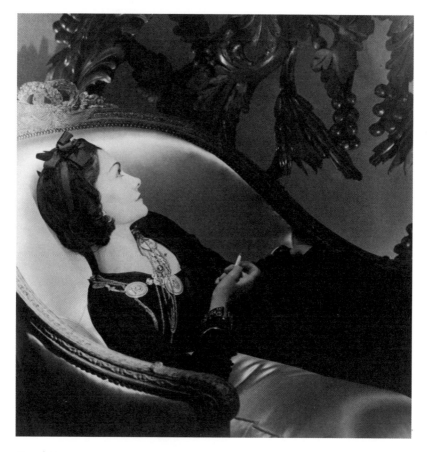

Chanel. Horst, 1937.

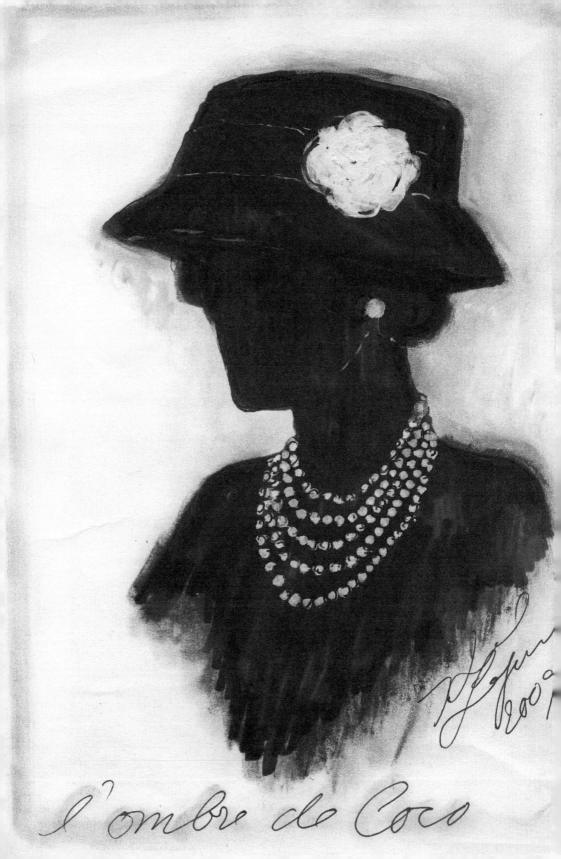

l'ombre de Coco

THROUGH A GLASS, DARKLY

In the tangle of tales told about Coco Chanel – the gossip and speculation and rumours that have spread from newsprint to the internet – one accusation is invariably repeated. Chanel was a Nazi collaborator, whose wartime affair with a German officer leaves her reputation blemished, and the legacy of her visionary fashion designs forever stained.

The truth is less clear-cut than that; the facts not black and white, but merging into a blur of grey. That Chanel's wartime record is imperfect is a reflection both of her own inconsistencies, and the inconsistent recording of them. But her conduct should also be seen in the context of an era of French history marked by a widespread sense of chaos, confusion and uncertainty, as well as terrible tragedy. To acknowledge this is not to act as an apologist for Chanel; and she herself would have been enraged at the very idea, for she declared that she had done nothing wrong in her relationship with the German. Not that he was even German, in her eyes: his mother was English, and he and Chanel spoke English together; an act of solidarity, as if they were setting themselves apart from German-occupied Paris in their own neutral territory, that of Mademoiselle's private apartment at 31 Rue Cambon.

His name was Hans Gunther von Dincklage, and he was 13 years younger than Chanel. She was not blind to the age difference – she was 58 when their affair began

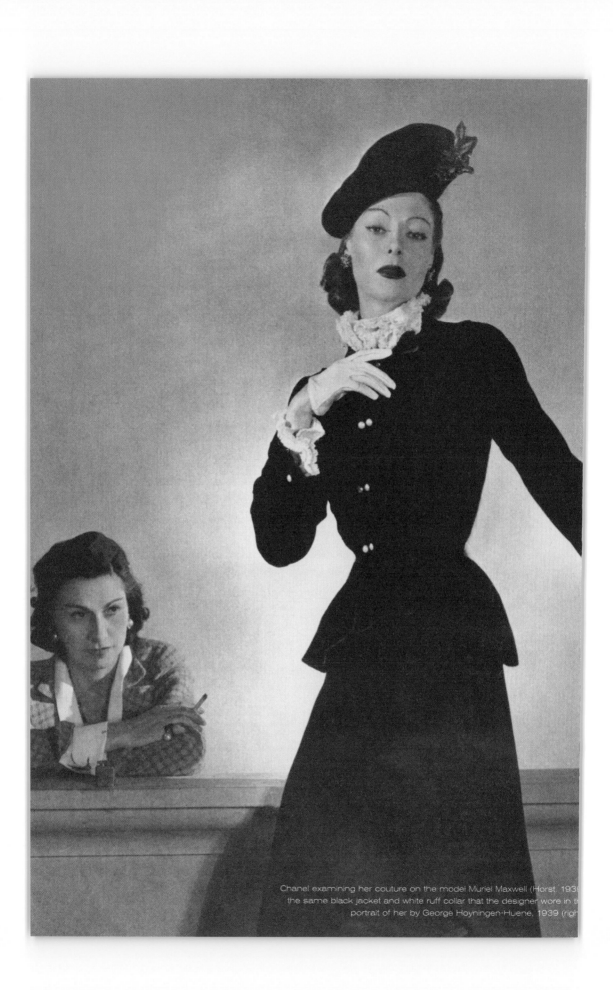

Chanel examining her couture on the model Muriel Maxwell (Horst, 1939)
the same black jacket and white ruff collar that the designer wore in th
portrait of her by George Hoyningen-Huene, 1939 (righ

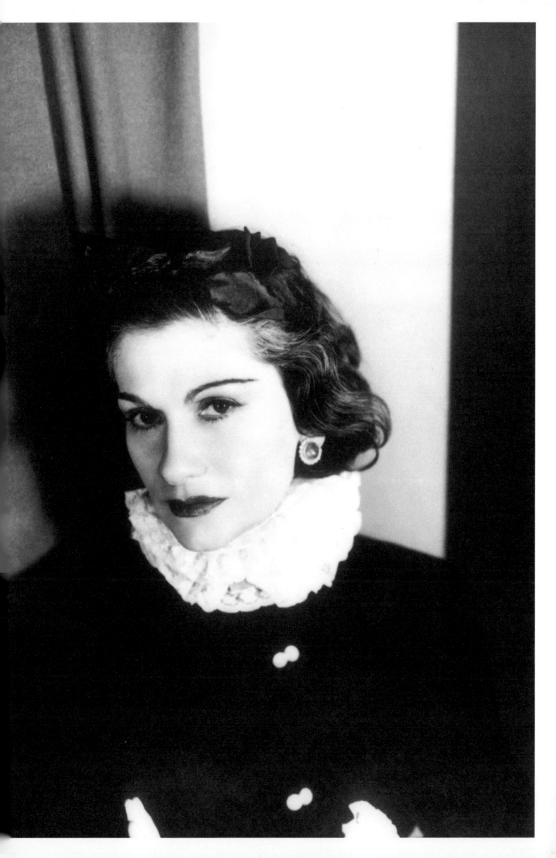

– as was implicit in her famous reply, recorded by Cecil Beaton, to the question of whether she had been involved with a German. 'Really, sir, a woman of my age cannot be expected to look at his passport if she has a chance of a lover.' It may also be that Chanel had reached a point in her life when looking into the mirror was troubling – she could not tear it up with the same disregard that she had ripped the date of birth out of her passport – although she told Paul Morand that she saw herself with harsh clarity: 'The hardness of the mirror reflects my own hardness back to me; it's a struggle between it and me.' But perhaps she was unable to see her German lover without obscuring something of the truth, closing her eyes to his past, as well as his passport; just as she had been apparently blind to previous episodes in her own life.

Von Dincklage was known to his close friends as Spatz, the German for sparrow, a nickname that suggests a swift chirpiness of manner. In fact, he was a tall, blond, distinguished-looking attaché to the German embassy in Paris. Born in Hanover on 15th December 1896, Spatz had arrived in Paris in 1928, where he gained a reputation as a suave playboy. After divorcing his wife in 1935, he had several affairs with smart, rich Parisians, and at some point encountered Mademoiselle Chanel on a social basis, for she claimed to have already known him 'for years' before the start of their affair.

As for his professional activities in Paris: to some observers Spatz was simply an affable, occasionally frivolous, diplomat; to others, a German spy. Certainly, he attracted the attention of French intelligence long before the outbreak of war. According to archives quoted by Edmonde Charles-Roux, one of Chanel's most assiduous biographers, von Dincklage 'was under the orders of the Reich Ministry of Propaganda, using a post as press attaché as cover. His activities in Paris were authorised by a private service contract for one year, effective October 17th, 1933.' Charles-Roux could find no record of any further espionage activities by Spatz. But another of Chanel's biographers, Pierre Galante, himself a French secret agent for the Allies in the Second World War, was certain that von Dincklage had worked in Paris for the Abwehr, the German military intelligence organisation under the command of Wilhelm Canaris from 1935. If this is true, then the murky circumstances in which von Dincklage operated become even more clouded; Canaris had contacts within MI6 after his involvement in several assassination attempts on Hitler, and was executed by the Nazis in April 1945. Galante was sufficiently sure of his sources to claim that 'numerous investigations made by the French counter-espionage services showed that Spatz Dincklage was an important Abwehr agent under the orders of Colonel Waag.' The reference to Waag – a nephew of Canaris – may also have contributed to the unproven rumours that von Dincklage was a double agent, whose loyalties did not lie with Hitler.

If Spatz's record is ambiguous, then Coco Chanel's is even more baffling. The police archives in Paris contain a large dossier on her, dating back to the Twenties, when she first became a target of suspicion. The intelligence on her was often wildly inaccurate – almost comically so, at times – yet also offers the occasional nugget of information. At first, the files contain routine notes of her passport details, in which her date of birth was given as 21st August 1886 (removing three years from her real age, given that she was born on 19th August 1883). In August 1923, the record shows that she successfully applied for a passport to allow her to travel 'to England and other countries'; this followed previous travel visas granted in 1921 (for Spain on 25th July, Germany on 6th October, Holland on 10th October, and Switzerland on 15th October).

At the beginning of 1929, Chanel came under further scrutiny, possibly because of her friendship with Vera Arkwright, who had by then divorced her first husband, Fred Bate, and married Colonel Alberto Lombardi. The Lombardis were under surveillance as suspected spies, and by association Chanel was also the subject of investigation. On 26th January 1929, a report was filed that described her as an '*ancienne demi-mondaine*' who had been welcomed into Parisian society, and was now possessed of excellent contacts in the political and diplomatic world. The police intelligence recorded that she had set up in business in 1910, with the help of one of her 'American' friends (presumably an incorrect interpretation of Boy Capel's nationality); that she had been the mistress of the Grand Duke Dmitri from 1921 until 1924; that she had a Rolls-Royce, and paid 50,000 francs a year for her apartment at 29 Faubourg

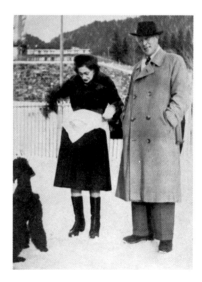

Chanel with 'Spatz', Hans Gunther von Dincklage, at Villars-sur-Ollon, 1949.

Saint-Honoré. There were also several references to the Duke of Westminster, describing his visits to Chanel in Paris, and a slightly prurient suggestion that he was attracted to her seamstresses, or '*petites mains*', and sent them on holiday every year to his chateau in Mimizan. As it happened, Chanel prided herself on the fact that she provided annual holidays in Mimizan for her employees. 'I organised a workers' holiday camp,' she told Paul Morand. 'This experiment cost me millions, which I don't regret. Buildings were constructed to house three or four hundred women. I paid for the travel expenses … with one month's paid holiday, instead of the legally entitled fortnight.'

Whatever the details of the seamstresses' holiday arrangements, the Interior Ministry was sufficiently suspicious of Chanel and the Lombardis to order another police investigation, on 1st October 1930. However, the operation was muddled from the start, given that the instructions were to scrutinise the activities of two married couples: the Lombardis and Monsieur and Madame Chanel. Monsieur Chanel was not identified with a first name, but was allegedly the joint owner of the House of Chanel; and both couples supposedly owned neighbouring properties in Cap Martin on the Riviera. Nothing in the subsequent police report clarified these obvious errors, even though it was hardly a secret that Mademoiselle Chanel was not married. As for the Riviera properties: the most cursory of enquiries would have established that Chanel was the sole owner not only of La Pausa but also of the smaller house in the garden, where the Lombardis often stayed.

Despite these bungling efforts, the police did uncover some intriguing aspects of the Lombardis' lives in Paris and elsewhere. Alberto Lombardi was an Italian cavalry officer, born in August 1893, and therefore eight years younger than his wife, Vera. She had come to France in September 1914 and met Fred Bate during the First World War, while she was working as a volunteer nurse at the American Hospital in Neuilly, and he was an officer in the US army. They were married in 1916, and their daughter Bridget was born in November the following year. The marriage ended in divorce in June 1929, by which point Vera was already involved with Lombardi. Their wedding took place a few months later, on 6th November 1929; Alberto's witness at the ceremony was the military attaché for the Italian embassy in Paris; Vera's was Gabrielle Chanel.

Further reports in the dossier suggest that the French police suspected the Lombardis of spying, possibly for more than one espionage service. They reported that the couple had a German housekeeper, and they made frequent telephone calls abroad – Lombardi rang Munich, Geneva and London on a daily basis, while Vera's international calls occupied her every morning from 6 until 11. They always spoke German or English during these telephone conversations, which were sufficiently lengthy to cost between 1000 and 1200 francs a month; an unusually large expense, although the police report revealed that Vera had a substantial income from Chanel – 30,000 francs a month (at a time when a police superintendent's salary was a tenth of that). She and her husband entertained the Duke of Westminster, amongst other European aristocrats, at their dinner parties; and Vera appeared to have useful connections with several foreign embassies, and an American diplomatic passport. They owned a Chrysler car, which she drove, and travelled frequently to London, Turin and elsewhere. The police investigation also noted that when Lombardi was at home in Paris, he spent his evenings studying and drawing maps of the French capital and its environs.

On 20th January 1931, the Minister of the Interior himself sent a confidential letter to the head of the police service in Paris, ordering a close and discreet surveillance operation into the Lombardis and Chanel. The investigation was to be conducted with extreme vigilance, given 'the nationality of the suspects and the nature of their actions'. But despite their best efforts, the police came up with little in the way of proof of any wrongdoings. They reported that Chanel had financed Paul Iribe's satirical political journal, *Le Témoin*; and then another magazine, *Futur*, regarded (by the police, at any rate) as being left-wing. There was also some vague speculation that Chanel had been the mistress of a writer and financier named Henri de Zogheb (his name does not appear in any other accounts of Chanel, although his wife was a regular couture client at Rue Cambon); and a more accurate reference, in 1934, to her friendship with Winston Churchill.

That long-standing friendship was to be of considerable significance to Chanel in the Second World War, as were Vera's relationships with Churchill and Chanel. Both women were to call on Churchill for help, as well as offering their own help to him, which he was unlikely to have required. Some evidence of their dealings lies in the vaults of the Churchill archive in Cambridge; letters of little consequence when read in the broader context of the global events of the war, yet nevertheless fascinating in their subtle details of past friendships and divided loyalties.

All three of them were linked, in different ways, by their affection for the Duke of Westminster, whose name also crops up often in the meticulously filed correspondence and diaries of the Churchill archives. It was on the Duke's

Scottish estate that they had fished and played card games together; at Mimizan that they had hunted boar; on his yachts that they cruised the Mediterranean; and at Eaton that they enjoyed house parties, horse riding, and pheasant shoots. Thus they possessed shared memories, as well as shared attachments; their pasts were entwined, even when the present looked ever more uncertain, and the future too dark to behold.

Inevitably, there were times when politics overrode friendship; though Churchill was skilled at navigating the hazardous ground that divided the two. In September 1939, for example, when Bendor made a statement opposing the war against Germany, Churchill wrote to him expressing the gravest concern. 'I am sure that pursuance of this line would lead you into measureless odium and vexation.' Churchill did not refer directly to Bendor's membership of The Link (a right-wing, pro-German movement), or to his reputation for anti-Semitism, but he did succeed in bringing him back into line. Thereafter, the Duke's patriotism was to the fore, and he proved himself ready to answer Churchill's call to do 'all that was necessary for winning the war'. Eaton was placed at the disposal of the army, and Bendor's allegiance to his country was never again questioned.

The same could not be said of Vera Bate Lombardi. If Vera and her husband were double agents – as the French security services believed – then it was difficult to be certain which sides they shifted to and from. In June 1936, for example, Vera wrote to Churchill from an address in Rome, urging him to meet Mussolini, 'the Big Man', freshly triumphant after the Italian invasion of Ethiopia. 'My dear Winston,' she began, 'How I wish you were here. I feel that in one hour you would settle everything. Pop out here disguised with a thick black beard and come and see the Big Man! I am afraid none of the English living here see things as they are because they never mix with the Italians and therefore I don't think they quite know what is going on.' The Italians were '100% positive' in their support of Mussolini, she continued, and she strongly advised Churchill to take action. 'This is the moment please believe me to make friends with him. He is ready to do it now and ready if approached by someone who would bring him back …' There is no proof that Vera knew that Mussolini had been given a helping hand at the beginning of his career in politics with a weekly wage of £100 from MI5 (the payments were authorised in 1917 by Sir Samuel Hoare, the Conservative politician who served as an MI5 officer during the First World War, and who had a team of 100 British intelligence officers in Rome at the time). Nor is there any evidence that she was aware that Hoare's appointment as Foreign

Secretary on 7th June 1935 would lead to his negotiations with the French prime minister, Pierre Laval, over territorial concessions to Italy in Ethiopia.

Nevertheless, Vera's own views about Mussolini were set out clearly in her letter to Churchill, despite the giddiness of her tone. 'The important point is he is against Bolchevism [sic] so are we.' It was, she said, in Mussolini's interests 'to be friends – if it is done at once with England.' Vera was conscious of the security issues in writing to Churchill, but she was confident of getting her message to him. 'I wish I could explain this to you but I can't on paper. A friend of mine is taking this to you, don't quote me just send me a postcard to say you got it.'

On 13th June, a letter was dispatched from Churchill to Vera in Rome: 'Thank you so much for your most interesting letter. I hope things will get a little better now.'

Vera continued to work for Chanel in Paris until 1937, when, for reasons that remain uncertain, their working relationship ceased. 'She kicked me out,' Vera later wrote to Churchill. 'It was rather sordid.' Churchill, however, continued to see Chanel when he visited Paris, and their friendship appears to have remained as warm as it had been when she was the mistress of his friend, the Duke of Westminster. Thus it was that Coco witnessed at close hand Winston's dismay during the crisis surrounding the abdication of King Edward VIII. Cocteau recorded in his journal that he dined with Churchill and Chanel at her suite in the Ritz towards the end of 1936. Churchill got drunk, and lamented the king's decision to marry Wallis Simpson. His visits continued even after the outbreak of war on 1st September 1939. Chanel still had her suite overlooking Place Vendôme, and the Ritz archives record that Churchill came on a monthly basis before the German invasion of Paris, and always called on her.

He would have known, therefore, of her decision to close the House of Chanel, as an immediate consequence of the declaration of war. The summer had passed in a whirlwind of parties, including Count Etienne de Beaumont's last great costume ball, to which Chanel came dressed as '*la belle dame sans merci*'. She was also a guest at Lady Mendl's garden party for 750 guests at Versailles, where they were entertained by circus acrobats, clowns and three elephants; in the midst of which mayhem Coco was seen deep in conversation with Wallis Simpson, by then the Duchess of Windsor, and a loyal customer of Chanel. In between the festivities, Chanel was still designing her couture collections – gypsy dresses to dance in, adored by Diana Vreeland at *Harper's Bazaar*, who wore 'the *dégagé* gypsy skirts, the divine brocades, the little boleros, the roses in the hair' – and she was also working on the costumes for a new ballet by her friend

Salvador Dalí, *Bacchanale*. Dalí's production for Les Ballets Russes traced the spiralling delirium of King Ludwig II to music by Wagner, and for all its bizarre Surrealism (a *corps de ballet* on crutches, a set dominated by a vast white swan with a gaping hole in its breast), it seemed in some sense to capture the mood of the moment. Christian Dior characterised Paris as spinning in that 'fatal year of 1939 ... in a burst of follies, which always seem to precede a catastrophe. Paris had rarely seemed more scintillating. We flitted from ball to ball ... Fearing the inevitable cataclysm, we were determined to go down in a burst of splendour.' Yet the couture houses were still flourishing; Diana Vreeland described Paris in July 1939 as 'jammed with buyers – frantic, amusing, exhausting and glorious'. And in those final, feverish weeks of freedom, the entire city seemed to be celebrating; for as Janet Flanner observed in *The New Yorker*, 'There have been money and music in the air, with people enjoying the first good time since the bad time started in Munich last summer ... The expensive hotels have been full of American and English tourists ... French workmen are working; France's exports are up; her trade balance continues to bulge favourably; business is close to having a little boom. It has taken the threat of war to make the French loosen up and have a really swell and civilised good time. The gaiety in Paris has been an important political symptom of something serious and solid, as well as spirited, that is in the air in France today.'

All of which goes some way to explain why Chanel's decision to shut down her business in September was such a controversial one. She laid off her employees, aside from a skeleton staff to keep open the boutique only to sell perfumes and accessories (a decision that was to ensure that her property in Rue Cambon was not requisitioned by the Germans after their invasion of Paris). 'This is no time for fashion,' she declared; an announcement that seems in retrospect acceptable, perhaps even honourable, yet at the time was seen as an act of cowardice and betrayal.

Some of her detractors believed that Chanel was using the war as an excuse to punish her seamstresses for their involvement in the widespread strikes of June 1936, when she had been barred by a picket line from entering her own premises for several days. At one point in the negotiations, Chanel had made an improbable offer to turn the business into a workers' co-operative, on the condition that she could manage it; the proposal came to nothing, and the strike was settled. In her conversations with Paul Morand after the war, she gave her own bizarre version of the episode: 'In 1936, like everywhere else, we had a sit-down strike. (Whoever dreamt it up was a genius.) It was cheerful and delightful. The accordion could be heard playing all over the house.' Her seamstresses, she declared, were better paid than elsewhere, so the strike was not for money, but a heartfelt demand to see more of Mademoiselle: 'It was a strike for love, a strike for the yearning heart.'

Given the continuing success of the House of Chanel after the strike – despite mounting competition from Elsa Schiaparelli – it seems unlikely that Chanel would close her business out of revenge or spite, using the war to settle old scores with her employees. When interviewed in later life by her friend Marcel Haedrich, Chanel gave a far more simple explanation: 'I stopped working because of the war. Everyone in my place had someone who was in uniform – a husband, a brother, a father. The House of Chanel was empty two hours after war was declared.'

As it happened, Chanel chose this moment to cut herself entirely loose from her own brothers, Lucien and Alphonse; not that they had ever been part of her life in Paris. She had remained loyal to her sisters, although they were both long dead, and to her aunt Adrienne (now married to her baron and finally a respectable woman); but she had separated herself from her brothers, aside from supplying generous financial support, as long as they kept well away from her. In October 1939, Coco wrote a letter to Lucien, who was still living with his wife in the house near Clermont-Ferrand that she had bought for him a decade earlier. 'I am very sorry to have to bring you such bad news. But now that the business is shut down, here I am nearly reduced to poverty myself … You cannot count on me for anything so long as circumstances stay the way they are.' She sent Alphonse a similar letter, to the remote village where he lived in the Cévennes, and did not see either of her brothers ever again. Lucien died of a heart attack in March 1941, Alphonse after the war; and according to Edmonde Charles-Roux, when Alphonse's daughters, Antoinette and Gabrielle, came up to Paris in an attempt to visit their famous aunt at Rue Cambon, they were turned away, and never returned.

For a time, Chanel continued to live at the Ritz, as before, although Paris was becoming increasingly deserted. The editor of *Harper's Bazaar*, Carmel Snow, wrote in her final dispatch for the October 1939 issue: 'The city had become, almost overnight, an empty city. The taxis disappeared. All the telephones were cut off. You can walk for miles without seeing a child. Even the dogs – and you know how Parisians love their dogs – have been sent away.' Noël Coward, who was posted to Paris as a British liaison officer, reported that the Ritz was still open, and that Coco Chanel could be seen going into the hotel's air-raid shelter

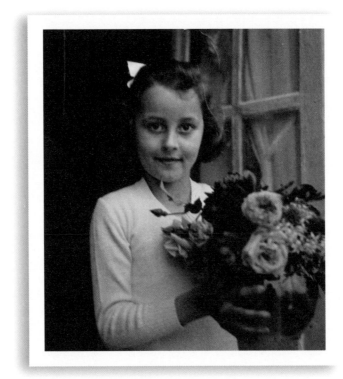

Above: Chanel's great-niece Gabrielle Labrunie.
Right: Chanel's dressing table in her suite at the Ritz. Pinned to the walls
are sketches of some of her designs and the photograph of her niece.
François Kollar, 1937.

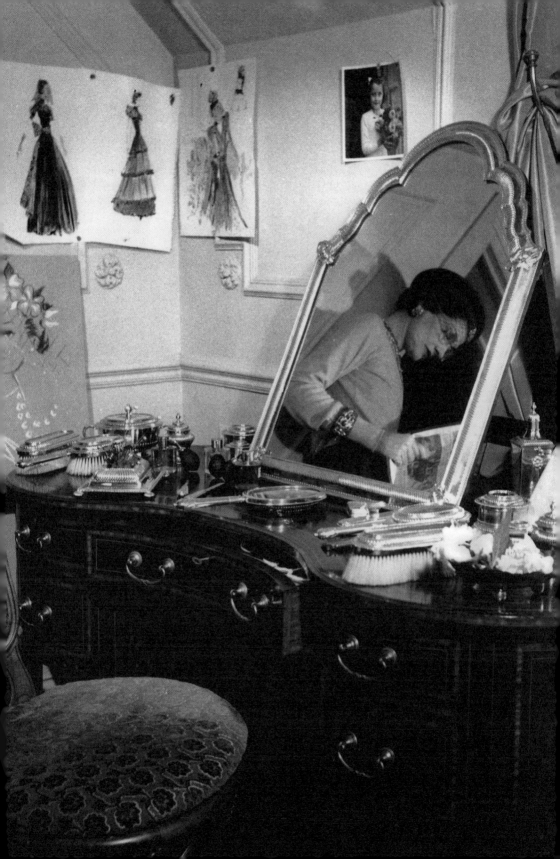

when warnings were sounded, followed at a discreet distance by her servant carrying her gas-mask on a cushion. Lady Mendl was also ensconced in the Ritz, along with several other socialites; as was Cocteau, in a room paid for by Chanel, and Elsa Schiaparelli, who had kept her business going. 'I wonder if people fully realized the importance as propaganda for France of the dressmaking business at this time,' wrote Schiaparelli in her memoir, *Shocking Life*, describing couture as 'the opposition of feminine grace to cruelty and hate'. Other fashion designers took the same view, including Molyneux, Lanvin and Lucien Lelong, the head of the Chambre Syndicale de la Couture (although Christian Dior, who worked for Lelong alongside Pierre Balmain, observed that the couture houses remained open 'as much to provide employment for thousands of workers as out of patriotic pride'). Schiaparelli's wartime collection remained as surreal as in previous years, when she had been inspired by Salvador Dalí, but all the more surprising given her declaration of its practicality: 'There was an evening dress camouflaged to look like a day dress. When one emerged from the subway at night to attend a formal dinner, one merely pulled a ribbon and the day dress was lengthened into an evening dress. There were the Maginot Line blue, the Foreign Legion red, the aeroplane grey, the woollen boiler suit that one could fold on a chair next to one's bed so that one could put it on quickly in the event of an air-raid driving one down to the cellar. There was also one in white which was supposed to withstand poison gas.'

But nothing withstood the German invasion of France in May 1940, and as the soldiers of the Third Reich approached Paris in early June, Schiaparelli joined the great exodus from the city. At the Ritz, Chanel packed her belongings into several trunks marked with her name, which she stored at the hotel, and paid her bill two months in advance. Her chauffeur had been drafted into the army, and she was advised by his replacement that it would be unwise to make her escape in her Rolls-Royce, so it was in her driver's own car that she left Paris. She was accompanied by several of her female employees, including a Madame Aubert, who had worked for Chanel from the very start, and had known her even before then, from the days when Coco emerged at Moulins. Somehow, the women made the long and arduous journey to the Pyrenees, to the house that Chanel had bought for her nephew André Palasse, close to where her former lover Etienne Balsan was living in quiet retirement. André had already departed, having joined the French army at the start of hostilities, and was soon to be captured as a prisoner-of-war and sent to a detainment camp in Germany. But his daughter Gabrielle clearly remembers her aunt's arrival in the Pyrenees. 'She came in the car with her maid, and a few other women – one of them was Madame Aubert – so it was quite a job finding places for all of them to stay. Auntie Coco had somehow managed to send on her entire gold dressing table set which had been given to her by my godfather, the Duke of Westminster, and that came to our house separately.' What seared itself most vividly onto her memory was Chanel's terrible grief upon hearing of the French surrender to Germany: 'She was already staying with us by the time the Armistice was signed – we listened to the news on the radio, and she wept bitterly.'

Gabrielle was 13, and old enough to understand the significance of the capitulation. The Armistice was signed on 22nd June 1940 in the forest of Compiègne, where her aunt had ridden Etienne Balsan's horses over 30 years before; the humiliating French surrender orchestrated by Hitler to take place in the very same spot where Germany had been forced to sign the previous Armistice in 1918, accepting defeat in the First World War.

As the summer passed, Chanel fretted to return to Paris, and eventually conceived a plan to make the homeward journey with another friend who had washed up in the Pyrenees, Marie-Louise Bousquet, whom she had last seen at Count Etienne's costume ball. The two women travelled first to Vichy, where the collaborationist French government of Marshal Pétain and Pierre Laval had established itself. 'Everyone was laughing and drinking champagne,' Chanel recalled, in conversation with Marcel Haedrich. The women were wearing flamboyantly big hats, and the seaside resort seemed to be in full swing. '"Well," I said, "it's the height of the season again."'

The hotels were so packed with guests that Marie-Louise had to sleep on a chaise longue in a linen room, while Chanel was given an airless attic garret. After a night of very little rest, they managed to replenish their supply of petrol, and set out for Paris, only to discover that the roads were blocked. Finally, after several detours, they ended up in the mountain spa resort of Bourbon-l'Archambault. The hotels were deserted, and Chanel was able to book a bedroom with an en-suite bath. There, she soaked away the dirt of the journey – 'the water was black when I got out,' she told Haedrich – but by the time she finally reached Paris, in August 1940, Chanel felt dirty again. Dirt was to be a recurring image in her subsequent account of what happened when she returned to the Ritz; indeed, it was how she characterised the entire era of the German occupation of Paris to Pierre Galante: 'That period was singularly lacking in dignity – it was a filthy mess.'

As soon as she approached the main entrance of the Ritz, she was confronted by the sight of German sentries at the door and uniformed officers in the lobby. The main part of the hotel, including her suite overlooking Place Vendôme, had been requisitioned for senior military personnel and high-ranking Nazis, among them Marshal Goering. (The hotel manager's wife would never forget the sight of Goering opposite the porter's desk, showing off his new diamond-studded baton by Cartier.) Chanel's story of what happened next varied slightly in different accounts, but she gave the most detailed version to Haedrich. An assistant manager informed her that she must go to see the German *Kommandatur*, to which she replied: 'What do you mean? All dirty like this? I must change …' She instructed the assistant manager to find her a room where she could wash herself. 'Then you go to the *Kommandatur*! Say that Mademoiselle Chanel has arrived. I'll go when I'm clean. I've always been taught that it's better to be clean when one is asking for something.'

After some negotiation, a small bedroom was found for Mademoiselle on the top floor of the Rue Cambon wing of the hotel – much lowlier in status than the Place Vendôme building, which was reserved solely for the Germans. The military were not permitted to pass into the Rue Cambon side, and nor could the civilian residents enter the Nazi-occupied section of the Ritz. Meanwhile, a small Resistance network was formed amongst a section of the hotel staff, which noted the movements of the Nazi leaders between Berlin and Paris.

Von Dincklage was not sufficiently senior to be billeted at the Ritz, and it may have been elsewhere in the city that Chanel encountered him again. But whatever the circumstances of that meeting, she had sought his help in arranging the release of her nephew, André, who was still detained in an internment camp. Spatz was unable to do this – a sign, perhaps, of his lack of influence – but nevertheless, Chanel embarked on her love affair with him at some point in 1941. Her maid, Germaine Domenger, who worked for Chanel from 1937 until 1966, was later outraged by suggestions that this relationship was tantamount to collaboration. 'Mademoiselle refused to re-open her couture house and work with the Germans!' she declared, in a letter she wrote defending Chanel from such accusations after her death in 1971. Twelve other couturiers remained open for business, including Balenciaga, Madame Grès and Lucien Lelong, who as president of the Chambre Syndicale resisted the German threat that all the leading designers were to be moved, along with their staff, to Berlin. The suggestion had been that Germany would become the centre of fashion in the New Europe, whereas Lelong declared that 'Paris's haute couture is not transferable, either en bloc, or bit by bit. It exists in Paris or it does not exist at all.' In the event, the designers stayed in Paris, but in doing so, were inevitably showing and selling couture to the wives and mistresses of German officers, alongside an unsavoury assortment of black marketeers, racketeers and collaborators.

Chanel, in marked contrast, led a quiet life, avoiding social contact with the Germans, apart from Spatz. He visited her at her apartment in Rue Cambon, rather than the Ritz (presumably to avoid the attention of more senior Germans, as well as to obey the rule that kept civilians separate from the military in the hotel). According to Germaine Domenger, who referred to Spatz as Baron von Dincklage, 'He was a gentleman ... Mademoiselle had first met him years before, in St Moritz ... He came often to see Mademoiselle at Rue Cambon, but we never saw him in a uniform ... I can swear that Mademoiselle never received any Germans, except Baron von Dincklage.'

Whenever they were visited by Chanel's closest and most trusted friends – Misia Sert, Serge Lifar, Jean Cocteau – she and Spatz openly declared their loathing of the war, and continued in their habit of speaking English to one another. They made several trips to La Pausa together, where they were contacted by Robert Streitz, the villa's architect; he was now a member of the local Resistance, and when he asked for Chanel's help in intervening on behalf of a friend, a physics professor who had been arrested by the Gestapo, she willingly agreed. Perhaps unbeknownst to her, the Resistance was also using the extensive cellars at La Pausa as a hiding place from which to send covert messages via a hidden transmitter, and its gardens as a staging post for Jewish refugees escaping from France to the Italian border.

But for the most part, Chanel behaved as if the Germans simply didn't exist. Marcel Haedrich – who was not afforded the opportunity of such lofty disregard, given his own detainment as a French officer in a German prisoner-of-war camp – nevertheless expressed some sympathy for Chanel's apparent refusal to acknowledge the enemy presence in Paris. Chanel would never have done business with Nazi dignitaries, he said, unlike Cartier, who sold jewellery to Goering: 'let no one think Mademoiselle Chanel would have spoken to him, or smiled. She did not see *them*, she declared, and I am sure she was telling the truth. "That did something to *them*," she told me, "when a woman who still has something left ignored *them* completely."'

And yet her avoidance was far from complete; Spatz, after all, was a German,

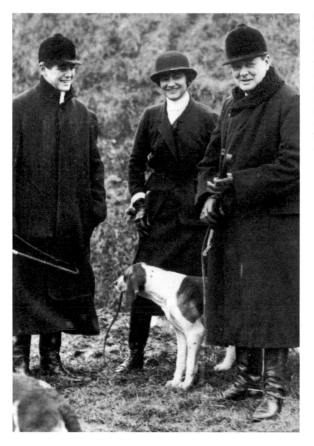

Left: Chanel, Winston Churchill (right) and his son Randolph (left) at the Duke of Westminster's French hunting estate, Mimizan, 1928.
Right: The opening lines from a private letter Chanel wrote to Winston Churchill during World War II.

however much he tried to keep a low profile during the Occupation. Nor was he the only German that Chanel had dealings with. A catastrophic error of judgement led her to become embroiled with another, far more senior Nazi officer; a relationship that would lead to a misguided trip to Madrid, the consequences of which were to prove markedly compromising. The catalyst for this appears not to have been Spatz, but a friend of his, Captain Theodor Momm, who had spent his childhood in Belgium, where his family ran a textile business, before returning to Germany. Momm was an army officer, possibly connected to the Abwehr, and sufficiently knowledgeable to have been assigned to Paris to supervise the local textile industry under German administration. When Spatz proved unable to get Chanel's nephew out of the prisoner-of-war camp, she turned to Momm for help (a painfully slow process, given that André was released only after four years' imprisonment in Germany). But at some point in

Hotel Ritz
Paseo del Prado
Madrid

My dear Winston

excuse me to come & ask
a favour from you
in such moments as
these. My excuse must
be that it is not for
myself — I had heard
for some time that Vera
Lombardi was not very
happily headed in Italy
on account of her being

Chanel's negotiations with Momm, as the war dragged on through 1943, a bizarre plan began to take shape: that she would act as a messenger to Churchill, and thereby initiate a peace process.

There were many extraordinary aspects of this implausible strategy – Chanel's total lack of political or diplomatic experience; the unlikelihood that the British would respond to such an advance – but perhaps the most obvious challenge was whether anyone in the German high command would consider it seriously. Yet when Momm went to Berlin with the proposal in the autumn of 1943, he found a receptive audience in the form of Walter Schellenberg, the Nazi chief of foreign intelligence. Schellenberg, like the Abwehr commander Wilhelm Canaris, was already searching for ways of covert negotiation with the Allies, despite the fact that to do so was to risk execution by Hitler, who had forbidden any such overtures. In retrospect, when Schellenberg was interrogated by the British after the German defeat, he indicated that he had hoped Chanel might at least give Churchill a message that senior German commanders were at odds with Hitler, and were seeking an end to the war. And his choice of the manner by which she would do so was significant: his strategy was to send her to Madrid to meet the British ambassador, Sir Samuel Hoare, with whom she was already acquainted. Schellenberg had long nursed an ambition to establish contact with Hoare – he had first conceived the idea in July 1942 – and was therefore swift to settle upon Chanel as the means to move forward. The mission was code-named Operation Modellhut ('model hat'); and for all the pantomime frothiness of the title, the participants appear to have embarked upon it with serious intent.

When Momm returned to Paris, the plan began to seem less clear; in part because Chanel now wanted Vera Lombardi to accompany her to Madrid. Vera was still living in Rome – her husband was in hiding in southern Italy – and needed German authorisation to travel to Paris, and thence to Madrid. Her version of subsequent events is at odds with Chanel's, and it is impossible to be certain which of them was giving the more reliable account. Vera described receiving a letter from Coco, delivered to her in Rome by a German officer, in which her former employer asked her to return to Paris to help her re-open the House of Chanel. She declined the invitation, and three weeks later was arrested as a British spy; for this she blamed Chanel, a charge subsequently levelled at Chanel by her biographer Edmonde Charles-Roux. But Chanel gave a different version, in which she had acted as a faithful friend to Vera, intervening on her behalf to gain her release from prison in Rome.

Whatever the correct interpretation of their motivations, the two women travelled to Madrid together; once there, Vera was refused permission to leave Madrid and return to Italy. Her claims that she was a loyal British subject, and that Chanel was an enemy spy, seem not to have been given much credence by the embassy staff in Madrid, nor by Churchill's staff in London. And when one examines the letter that Chanel wrote to Churchill from Madrid, it appears to be nothing more sinister than a straightforward appeal on Vera's behalf, to allow her to return home to Italy. Nor did it further the cause of Operation Modellhut, which was abandoned without ever really getting started. This was confirmed by Schellenberg's account of the plot to his British interrogators, although he adds a further layer of confusion by stating that it took place in April 1944.

In fact, Chanel attempted to make contact with Churchill in early January 1944. Germaine Domenger, who packed her bags for Madrid, appears to have known the specific details of Chanel's itinerary, and that of the British prime minister, who had fallen ill after the Tehran conference in December 1943: 'Mademoiselle went to Madrid in the intention of meeting her friend, Monsieur Churchill, who had agreed to see her when he came back from Tehran. She had taken with her Madame Vera Bate who had joined her at the Ritz in Paris. They left Paris together, and together went to the British embassy in Madrid. The ambassador there was Samuel Hoare. The meeting with Churchill could not happen – he was very tired after the Tehran conference, he cancelled his appointments in Spain, and went back to England after stopping in Cairo and Tunisia.'

Even so, it seems improbable that Churchill had ever agreed to meet Chanel in Madrid, and she did not refer to any such rendezvous when she sent him a letter via the British embassy there. The letter has survived, her handwriting firm on the Madrid Ritz's headed paper. She did not date it, but when it arrived in the office of Churchill's private secretary at Downing Street, it was accompanied by a note dated 10th January 1944 from a member of the embassy staff in Madrid. ('You may like to pass on to the Prime Minister the enclosed letter which we have been asked to forward by Mlle Chanel, who claims to be a personal friend.') She had addressed Churchill as 'My dear Winston', and most of the handwritten letter is in English, although she concluded it in French. In view of the accusations and counter-accusations that were to follow in its wake, the detailed contents of her letter are crucial:

'Excuse me to come and ask a favour from you in such moments as these. My excuse must be that it is not for myself – I had heard for some time that

Vera Lombardi was not very happily treated in Italy on account of her being English and married with an Italian officer.

'You know me well enough to understand that I did every thing in my power to pull her out of this situation which had indeed become tragic as the Fascists had simply locked her up in prison! To do this however I was obliged to address myself to someone rather important to get her freed and be allowed to bring her down here with me.

'The fact that I managed to succeed in this has placed her in a difficult position as the passport which is Italian has been visa-ed by the Germans and I understand quite well that it looks a bit suspect – But as you can well imagine my dear after 4 years of occupation in France it has been my lot to encounter many kinds of people!! How I would have pleasure to talk over all these things with you …!!'

At this point, she reverted to French, to explain that Vera wanted to return to Italy to find her husband, and that a word from Churchill would smooth out any difficulties in Vera's way. She hoped that his health had improved, and ended the letter on an affectionate note, along with a postscript that suggested she hoped to hear more news from his son, Randolph.

And there the matter might have ended. However, after Chanel was safely back in Paris, Churchill's office received further representations from Vera Lombardi. The first was a letter dated 19th February 1944, a plea that she had sent from the Ritz in Madrid to Bendor's elder daughter, Ursula, and which Ursula had forwarded to Churchill. 'I've written 3 times and wired 3 times to you and Benny to help me with Foreign Office and no reply. I can't understand it. It is a question of life and death for Berto [Alberto Lombardi] and they have kept me 2 months here. Could you should you get this get W. [Winston] or Anthony [Eden] to help me at once. I want only to return to S. Italy immediately please ask them to OK the permit of the passport control and give a recommendation to hurry. I can't understand as I am an exceptional case and escaped by miracle why they don't let me back en plus I can be useful there. And you can imagine what I am going thro not knowing if B[erto] has been caught or not …'

Churchill responded not to Vera, but to Ursula, with a telegram of brisk efficiency: 'If her husband is in enemy-occupied Italian territory we cannot interfere in any way. If he is in the liberated part of Italy he cannot be in any danger.'

On 8th August 1944, Vera sent another letter from Madrid, this time directly to Churchill. 'I've never dared write and bother you about this interminable and nightmarish wait here, to be allowed to repatriate after my escape from Coco and the Germans,' she began, and then did precisely that. Her husband had returned to Rome from southern Italy, having regained command of his regiment, 'or what is left of it', and had written to Vera in Madrid, saying that he had seen Randolph Churchill. According to Vera, Winston's son had sent the following message: 'Tell Vera to write immediately to my father and ask for his permission to go home to Rome. I am certain he will help her immediately.'

'It's no use writing you the history of my life,' she continued. 'You've known me so long … Since 1914 my war record was all right 7 medals etc. 16 years of hard work for Coco which was a great training and experience … She kicked me out in 1937. It was rather sordid and sad and I never saw her again until I was forcibly brought to her in Paris in December '44 [sic; presumably December 1943] by her orders and by the methods of her German friends and my jailers. I have written a report and given verbally all the information I can think of about the details of my imprisonment and kidnapping and I know no more. I found Coco very changed from seven years ago.'

Her presence in Madrid was, she said, the result of her outwitting Chanel: 'I managed to trick Coco into helping me to escape to here. No mean feat as she

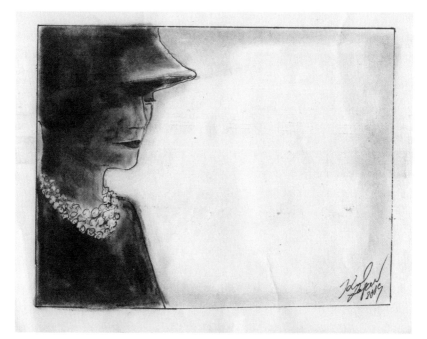

Chanel, by Karl Lagerfeld.

is pretty foxy even now. But I did it, and I naturally thought my personal difficulties were over.' Sadly, this was not the case, when she found herself, rather than Chanel, to be the object of suspicion: 'it couldn't [sic] occur to me after all I had been thro for my fanatically British attitude that I could be suspected by my own people of doing something traitorish. I can't believe it even now and beg to be allowed to defend myself. Before I was caught I had fought the Battle of Rome single-handedly with my only friend my dog Tiger beside me. Alberto on his side owing to my attitude poor thing was hounded from one hot spot to another all over the European battlefields. I can honestly say no hand was raised to help either of us ...'

Vera's plaintive story made no mention of her previous letter to Churchill in which she had urged him to befriend Mussolini; indeed, she now claimed to be the dictator's sworn enemy. 'I was on Mussolini's own private black list as the English wife of an officer who spread British propaganda all over the Italian Army. I want to tell you Winston, I should never have got thro without your example and little snapshot of you on Benny's fat horse.' Despite her claim to have been entirely alone and without aid, Vera had apparently managed to keep up with the news by listening to her radio 'at the dead of night ... hidden under a blanket. And Alberto's officer friends would creep in to cheer themselves up and get a little hope with the English news and stories about you and England.' There, beneath the blanket, she supplemented the news on the radio with her own reminiscences, to raise the morale of the poor Italian officers. 'They never tired of asking if it was really true I knew you well and you stood to us all as England, fair play truth and hope. One of our favourite stories was the one where you and Albert[o] and Benny ate spring onions together at Eaton. They adored that one and I always had to invent how many you had eaten and if you really liked them or had only done it to please Albert[o], because he loves them so ... These simple stories did more to raise the Italian Army's morale than you can ever imagine because you stood for Justice and Fairness, and that my England was something real after all.'

The other account of these events is that of SS-Brigadeführer Walter Schellenberg himself, as transcribed in the final Allied report of his prolonged interrogation after the war. Unfortunately, his testimony includes the obvious factual error regarding the date of the ramshackle mission; and he has Chanel coming to meet him in Berlin, but is curiously silent about her going to Madrid. It is possible, of course, that she made both trips – for there seems to be no good reason why Schellenberg would invent a meeting with her in Berlin. That said, no other evidence exists for her going to Germany, either in British intelligence records, or in French police files during the Occupation. The latter do, however, include the intriguing detail that Chanel was referred to by German security services under the pseudonym Westminster (which may have fuelled subsequent speculation that the Duke of Westminster was to some degree aware of Chanel's involvement in the abortive peace mission). The French police intelligence also noted that she was given two visas to travel from Paris to Spain, the first on 17th December 1943; the second on 16th March 1944.

If one is to believe Schellenberg, Chanel's only journey was to Berlin. She was originally brought to his attention, he said, through Theodor Momm and one of Albert Speer's functionaries, SS-Brigadeführer Walter Schieber. 'This woman was referred to as a person who knew Churchill sufficiently to undertake political negotiations with him, as an enemy of Russia and as desirous of helping France and Germany whose destinies she believed to be closely linked together.' On Schellenberg's instructions, Chanel was 'brought to Berlin and she arrived in that city accompanied by a friend, a certain Herr [Hans] von Dincklage'. Schellenberg told his interrogators that he believed that Dincklage might have had 'some working connection with the Abwehr', but he was unable to confirm this fully. When Schellenberg met Chanel – along with Dincklage, Momm and Schieber – it was agreed that 'A certain Frau Lombardi, a former British subject of good family then married to an Italian, should be released from internment in Italy and sent to Madrid as an intermediary. Frau Lombardi was an old friend of Frau Chanel and had been interned with her husband for some political reasons connected with the latter.'

The report of Schellenberg's interrogation continues: 'Lombardi's task would be to hand over a letter written by Chanel to the British Embassy officials in Madrid for onward transmission to Churchill. Dincklage was to act as a link between Lombardi in Madrid, Chanel in Paris, and Schellenberg in Berlin.

'Accordingly a week later Lombardi was freed and sent by air to Madrid. On her arrival in that city, however, instead of carrying out the part that had been assigned to her she denounced all and sundry as German agents to the British authorities … In view of this obvious failure, contact was immediately dropped with Chanel and Lombardi and Schellenberg does not know whether any communication was subsequently handed to Churchill through this woman.'

Long before Schellenberg's interrogation, Churchill's staff had gone to some trouble to establish their own view of the muddled affair, taking into account Vera's letter to Churchill, and a further representation made on her behalf by Lady Charles, the wife of the British ambassador in Rome, Sir Noel Charles. After several months of top-secret correspondence between senior officials in the prime minister's office, the Foreign Office and Allied Forces Headquarters, intelligence reports came to the following conclusions in December 1944: 'While there is no indication … that Mme Lombardi was sent to Madrid on a specific mission by the German Intelligence Service, it is equally clear that Mme Chanel deliberately exaggerated Mme Lombardi's social position in order to give the Germans the impression that if she were allowed to go to Madrid she might be useful to them. Mme Lombardi herself seems to have had some curious notion of trying to arrange peace terms.' It was also noted that while in Madrid, 'Mme Lombardi received letters from Rome by clandestine means.' Finally, while her exclusion from Italy was no longer considered to be necessary, she was deemed 'by no means anti-Fascist', and could not be 'completely cleared of all suspicion'; a view that was communicated to the British ambassador in Rome. He was warned that 'she is still under a cloud', and should be treated as such.

Meanwhile, Chanel herself had been questioned in Paris after the Liberation in August 1944 by the Forces Françaises de l'Intérieur (FFI). There has been much speculation about why she was quickly released, at a time when other women who had consorted with the Germans – '*les collaborations horizontales*' – were savagely treated, their heads shaved and their clothes stripped, before being paraded naked through jeering mobs on the streets, and in some cases, tortured and beaten. It has generally been assumed that Churchill somehow intervened on Chanel's behalf (although a lurid conspiracy theory has also circulated that links her release to the British Royal family, purportedly to prevent revelations of the Duke and Duchess of Windsor's unsavoury Nazi connections).

But according to her maid Germaine Domenger, the questioning was brief, and Chanel was released without the intervention of any powerful protector. Domenger was with Chanel in her room at the Ritz when the message came that two men were waiting to question Mademoiselle. She remembered that Chanel asked her the time – it was 8.30 a.m. – just as the men came upstairs to escort her from her room. 'They were perfectly correct, and asked Mademoiselle to come with them. She went to the bathroom to dress, and said, 'Germaine, if I don't come back immediately, ask Madame [at Rue Cambon] to tell Monsieur Churchill.' Germaine waited at the Ritz for a little while, in a state of high anxiety, but by the time she reached Rue Cambon, Chanel had already arrived there, having been swiftly released by the FFI. There had been no need for anyone at Rue Cambon to ring Churchill, at least according to her maid, 'because there was nothing very important with which to reproach Mademoiselle Chanel.'

The wife of the Ritz's manager – a woman who generally knew everything that had taken place in and around the hotel – was sure that Chanel had produced letters from Churchill, assuring her of his friendship and support, to dismiss accusations of collaboration. Even so, her circumstances in Paris remained dangerous. Malcolm Muggeridge, who had arrived in the city as a British intelligence officer on the day of its liberation, described it in his memoir as being in 'a virtual state of breakdown. The police, heavily tainted with Pétainism, if not collaboration, were lying low for the time being … By day, it was not so noticeable, though even then in places like the Palais de Justice and the prisons, which I had occasion to visit, there was total confusion; the judges having mostly disappeared or been arrested themselves, and the prisons being glutted with alleged *collaborateurs*, brought along by no one knew who, and charged with no one knew what. It was when darkness began to fall that one became aware of the breakdown; with no street-lighting, and the tall houses all silent and locked and boarded up, like sightless eyes. Inside them I imagined cowering figures, hopeful of surviving if they remained perfectly still and hidden. Then, as night came on, sounds of scurrying feet, sudden cries, shots, shrieks, but no one available, or caring, to investigate. It is unknown to this day how many were shot down, had their heads shaved, piteously disgorged their possessions in return for being released, but certainly many, many thousands.'

Muggeridge spoke with some experience, having spent several evenings with an FFI group that had taken over a large apartment formerly occupied by the Gestapo. Their leader was later discovered to have had a collaborationist record, and his second in command was 'probably a figure from the underworld'. Yet they operated with absolute authority, arresting and interrogating suspects, and even carrying out executions. 'If a door was not opened to them, they would batter it down; everyone cowered before them, and did what they were told … they behaved with horrifying callousness, arrogance and brutality, recalling a saying of Tolstoy to the effect that revolutionaries in authority always behave worse than those they replace because they come fresh to it.'

That Chanel was spared punishment was all the more fortuitous, given how many others were locked up in the notorious prison of Fresnes, where conditions were said to be worse after the Liberation than under the Gestapo. As an MI6 officer, Muggeridge spent a great deal of time 'trying to sort out the position of purported British agents who had been arrested as collaborators … For obvious reasons, their work for us had often necessitated their being ostensibly on good terms with the German occupation authorities, for which they now found themselves under the threat of severe punishment, if not execution.' In Fresnes, he encountered an extraordinary collection of alleged collaborationists, formerly eminent politicians and senior civil servants, dishevelled admirals and generals still wearing their medals and uniforms, diplomats, writers, actors, journalists, locked up with gangsters and prostitutes in squalid overcrowded cells in 'a kind of Beggar's Opera scene', where it was difficult to tell the difference between the innocent and the guilty. As Muggeridge brooded over what he witnessed in Paris, it seemed to him that 'everyone was informing on everyone else'; and that there was 'a great deal of working off of private grudges and envies. The truth is that under the German occupation everyone who did not go underground or abroad was in some degree a collaborator and could be plausibly accused as such. The barber who cropped the bullet heads of German soldiers, the greengrocer who sold them fruit, the waiter who served them meals, the whore who went to bed with them, the entertainer who sang to them, the clown who made them laugh, were all collaborating. I felt desperately sorry for the individuals

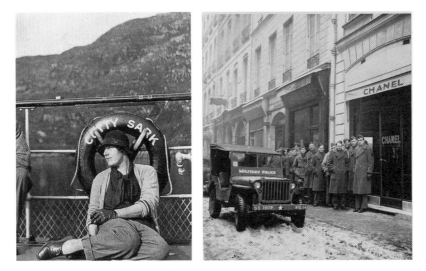

Left: Vera Bate on the *Cutty Sark*. Right: American soldiers queuing up outside the Chanel boutique in Rue Cambon to buy bottles of Chanel N°5, after the liberation of Paris. Serge Lido.

who were picked on for this *soi-disant* crime, especially when, as sometimes happened, I actually saw the pack going after their victim – shaving the head of some wretched girl … carrying some gibbering, trembling creature off to prison.'

Several of Chanel's closest friends teetered on the edge of the abyss in the purge that came to be known as the *épuration sauvage*. Muggeridge was aware that his counterparts in French intelligence had considered the case against Picasso. 'During the occupation years, it seemed, his Paris studio had been warmed – a rare privilege – and visited by German officers; such minutiae, as I was all too well aware … being collected, tabulated and seriously deliberated upon in that strange time.' Serge Lifar was initially banned for life from the French stage, having been the Vichy-appointed director of the Paris Opéra, a penalty that was then reduced to only a year's suspension. Cocteau managed to negotiate his way around the fact that he had accepted invitations to the ambassador's parties at the German embassy during the Occupation; and Marie-Louise Bousquet remained unscathed, despite having entertained 'nice Germans' at her weekly Thursday afternoon salons. Indeed, she flourished as the Paris editor of *Harper's Bazaar*, and was subsequently described by her friend Cecil Beaton as 'the brilliant Florence Nightingale of fashion'. But the film star Arletty did not escape retribution for her affair with a German officer. When she was arrested in early September 1944, a rumour spread through Paris that her head had been shaved and her breasts cut off; the truth was less hideous, and she was allowed out of prison to shoot the remaining scenes of *Les Enfants du paradis*.

During his time in Paris, Muggeridge had dinner with Chanel in her private apartment, and observed her with some fascination, in an encounter that was a curious combination of social visit and intelligence gathering for MI6. He had been taken to Rue Cambon 'by an old friend of hers, F, who had appeared in Paris, covered in gold braid, as a member of one of the numerous liaison missions which by now were roosting there'. His first impression of her 'was of someone tiny and frail, who, if one puffed at her too hard, might easily just disintegrate; her powdery frame collapsing into a minute heap of dust, as those frail houses had in the London Blitz. She seemed to have various pieces and shapes of shining metal about her person; like Earl Attlee in old age when he went to a ceremonial dinner, or one of the ancient men-at-arms at Windsor Castle who appear in breast-plate and armour at gatherings of Knights of the Garter. It seemed extraordinary that she should be able to support this extra weight.'

Yet as the evening progressed, he realised that for all the fragility of her appearance, Chanel was well able to defend herself. She gave no impression of uneasiness at the presence of an MI6 officer in her salon, and 'towards F she adopted an attitude of old familiarity, as though to say: "Don't imagine, my dear F (she addressed him by his surname), that your being dressed up in all that gold braid impresses me at all. I know you!" Nor had she, as a matter of fact, any cause for serious anxiety, having successfully withstood the first *épuration* assault at the time of Liberation by one of those majestically simple strokes which made Napoleon so successful a general; she just put an announcement in the window of her emporium that scent was free for GIs, who thereupon queued up to get their bottles of Chanel N°5, and would have been outraged if the French police had touched a hair of her head. Having thus gained a breathing space, she proceeded to look for help *à gauche et à droite*, and not in vain, thereby managing to avoid making even a token appearance among the gilded company … on a collaborationist charge.'

Muggeridge also observed how Chanel's past life in England was still present in her conversation: 'she and F reminisced about old times … I had heard that for a number of years she had been the regular companion of an English duke, and asked if she often saw Churchill in those days. Oh yes, she said, she knew dear Winston well, and used to play piquet with him, making a point, of course, of always losing, as otherwise he'd be in a bad temper.' Together, the three of them – the gold-braided F, the British spook and Mademoiselle – sat side by side on a soft sofa, in near darkness, dining by the light of two candles. 'The filet mignon was exquisitely tender, the red wine soft and mellow, the cognac silky, with other delicacies virtually unobtainable in Paris at that time, to all of which F did full justice, while Mme Chanel and I only nibbled …

'Even in this dim twilight, Mme Chanel seemed immensely old and incorporeal; I had the feeling almost that she might expire that very evening, seated between F and me, and we just tiptoe away, leaving her there with the debris of our meal – the coffee cups, the billowing brandy glasses, the cigarette ends, hers stained a deep red.'

Afterwards, Muggeridge tried to draft some sort of report on Chanel, but realised that there was nothing to say, except that he was sure 'the *épuration* mills, however small they might grind, would never grind her – as indeed, proved to be the case'. As he reflected upon his evening, he wondered whether a more rigorous agent might have discovered further details: 'how she managed to get to and from Spain during the occupation, whether she also offered free scent to the German troops, who were her clients, associates and intimates in those years. Alas, all I had done was to listen; fascinated, and even a little awed, at the masterly way she harpooned and skinned the braided F.'

As the weeks passed after the Liberation, the war seemed to recede from Paris, even though it was still continuing elsewhere. Bank accounts were unblocked, houses un-shuttered, women returned to the streets, the shaved ones now wearing wigs. The Germans had vanished, the GIs no longer crowded into the Chanel boutique for bottles of N°5, and Spatz's reflection was gone from the mirrored staircase, and his shadow from Mademoiselle's private salon. She had faced those who accused her, her cunning and courage undiminished, but when danger ebbed away, she was seldom seen at the Ritz or Rue Cambon. Mademoiselle Chanel had not disappeared altogether, but she had certainly retreated, and it seemed to some as if she might never come back.

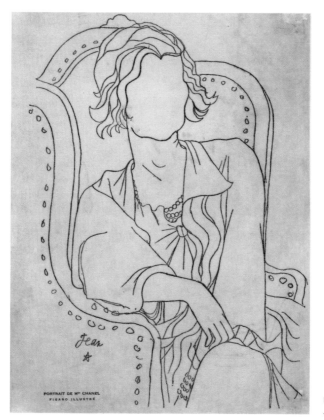

Portrait of Chanel, by Jean Cocteau, 1933.

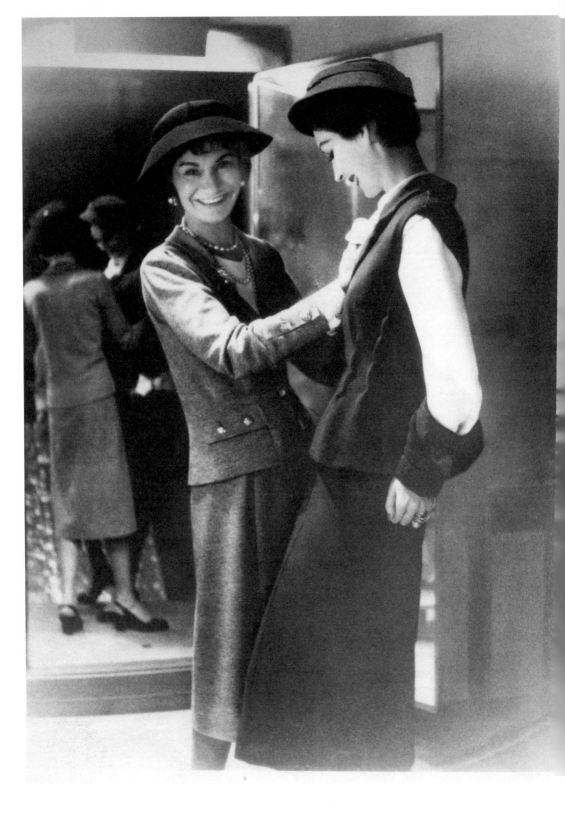

THE COMEBACK

On 7th July 1945, Hitler's former chief of foreign intelligence, Walter Schellenberg, was flown from Frankfurt to Croydon airport, on his way to several months of interrogation by the British security services. As his captors observed in their initial intelligence report: 'the plane which brought Schellenberg to England on a glorious summer day passed over Greater London.' It was Schellenberg's first ever view of England, and according to the accompanying British officers, he 'stared spellbound down on the giant living city. His eyes sought anxiously for the wounds inflicted on the centre of the British Empire. He could find no wounds, nor even scars. Giving up the hopeless search, he whispered: "I cannot understand – no destruction at all."'

If this account is to be believed, then Schellenberg cannot have looked very far; for amongst the many buildings destroyed during the Blitz was a monumental Bourjois factory in Croydon that manufactured beauty products, including those for Chanel. Built in 1934, it produced perfumes, talcs and soaps (over 600,000 bars a month) that were exported all over the world. Its strategic position – close to rail links, roads and airports, including three RAF bases – made the factory a prime target, and on 11th August 1940 it was badly damaged in a direct hit by the Luftwaffe.

At the time, Pierre and Paul Wertheimer, the owners of Bourjois and Coco's partners in Les Parfums Chanel, were arriving in New York, having escaped there with their wives and children from the German invasion of Paris. Both brothers had managed to make the perilous journey by sea, via Spain and Brazil; Pierre disembarked in New York on 5th August 1940, Paul a fortnight later. Despite the dangers of their journey amidst the chaos of war, the Wertheimers had also managed to keep their business interests afloat. Not only did the brothers maintain the production of Chanel perfumes in their factory on the outskirts of Paris, even as the Nazis made attempts to seize their assets (as they did those of other Jewish families), but the Wertheimers somehow retained control of their business empire.

This was despite the best efforts of the woman whose name was such a crucial element in the success of the perfumes, yet who felt her own financial interest in the perfume company to have been wrongfully diluted. And therein lies the key to the most troubling episode of Coco Chanel's history. Her legal manoeuvres against the Wertheimers were immensely complicated, but in essence she attempted to use the anti-Jewish laws of the German Occupation to oust her business partners; a strategy that proved unsuccessful, and gravely tarnished her reputation.

Since then, the question of whether this tactic was fuelled by anti-Semitism or pragmatism has continued to be raised in a debate that shows no signs of being definitively resolved. It is difficult to produce any firm evidence of Chanel making anti-Semitic statements – the accusations against her are rarely backed up by reliable sources; as with the bizarre encounter described in *Brando Unzipped*, a florid biography by Darwin Porter, which has Coco Chanel wearing blue jeans (an unlikely thought in itself) meeting Marlon Brando in Paris in 1949. Brando is quoted as saying, 'Chanel was the single most fascinating woman I've ever met. I detested every word that came from her mouth but was hypnotized by her … Even when she blamed the Jews for the weakened franc, she continued to be mesmerizing.'

A more authoritative account comes from Chanel's friend Claude Delay, who gives some sense of the contradictions inherent in Mademoiselle's professed lack of prejudice. 'She loved her Jewish doctor better than all her family,' and remained loyal to him, amongst others. '"I prefer my Jewish friends to lots of Christians, the St Cretin variety," she used to say. "There are the great Jews, the Hebrews in general, and the Yids. But all we've got are tramps …"'

Quite what Chanel might have meant by that final remark is unclear; and a similarly disquieting ambiguity is apparent in her comments to Paul Morand about

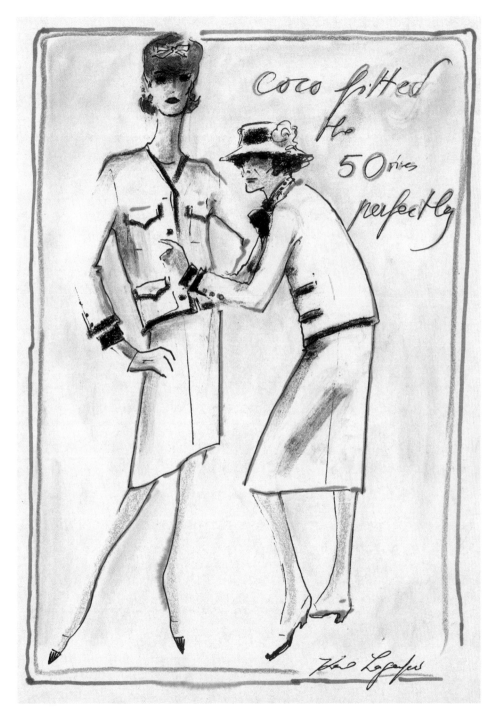

coco fitted
the
50ties
perfectly

Chanel fitting one of her 1950s designs, by Karl Lagerfeld.

Misia. These have subsequently been cited as anti-Semitic, although her true intent remains obscure. Misia was a Catholic, but one of Chanel's more irrational monologues about her friend concluded with the following curious observation: 'What allowed her to retain her Jewish soul were the Jews themselves.'

There is more clarity to be had from Boulos Ristelhueber, Misia's great friend (and Sert's secretary), whose diary during the first winter of the German Occupation gives some context to Misia and Coco's differing views. On 21st December 1940, Boulos recorded a 'rather sad lunch' with Jean Cocteau. 'At four o'clock called on Coco Chanel, so nice to me that she did me good. She has great hopes that her perfume business will soon be straightened out.' Six days later, he visited Misia, who was 'beside herself about all the anti-Jewish laws that turn Paris into a prison, the exact negation of what our city is. She is so right!' The following evening, he spent the evening at Misia's with Chanel and the Duc d'Harcourt, whose wife, Antoinette, was Jewish (a Rothschild). 'Coco goes into a long tirade against the Jews. The conversation is dangerous, given Antoinette's origins and the presence of the Duke. Fortunately she was sidetracked ...'

In fact, Chanel appeared to have no problem doing business with the most famous of Jewish dynasties, nor in socializing with them (an inconsistency that has often been perceived in the French and British upper classes). Her friends and clients included Rothschilds; indeed, Baroness Diane de Rothschild had been one of her earliest supporters, shopping at the Chanel boutiques in Paris and Deauville before the First World War, and Marie-Hélène de Rothschild has been credited as playing a part in persuading Chanel to return to couture in 1954. These and other paradoxical prejudices were to emerge in her conversations with James Brady, a young American correspondent for *Women's Wear Daily* in Paris, befriended by Chanel in 1961. 'She was a biased mass of contradictions,' he wrote, long after her death. 'If the vintages failed, the franc weakened. "C'est les Juifs. It's the Jews." Yet her closest friend was the Baroness Marie-Hélène de Rothschild. She complained that blacks smelled different and then rhapsodized about a certain black prizefighter. "That man and I ... how we danced."'

Brady did not damn Chanel for these remarks; nor deny what he saw to be good in her. 'She taught me most of what I know about fashion, much of what I know about life.' Yet unlike some others of her friends and admirers, he did not keep silent on the subject of her bigotry, in the hope that it would thereby disappear. For there is no escaping the ugly truth of her attempt to take advantage of an anti-Jewish regime; a fact duly noted by *Time* magazine, even as it named Chanel as one of the hundred most important people of the twentieth century, and by John Updike in *The New Yorker*: 'her attempted exploitation of the Holocaust was not becoming.'

That said, the possibility remains that Chanel's tactics against the Wertheimers may have had less to do with her own anti-Semitism than with her increasingly passionate belief that Pierre had done her an injustice by giving her only a 10 per cent share in the perfume company. Certainly, she had been engaged in sporadic skirmishes against the Wertheimers long before the Nazi invasion of France, in an effort to increase her income from Les Parfums Chanel. But she was further enraged by Pierre's arrangements for the company when he fled Paris in 1940, whereby the Wertheimer shareholdings were taken over by Félix Amiot, a French aeroplane manufacturer, in return for a putative stake in his aviation business. By signing Les Parfums Chanel over to Amiot, who was not Jewish (and therefore regarded by the Nazis as an Aryan owner, albeit one who would return it to the Wertheimers at the end of the war), Pierre hoped to protect the business from German requisition. But his actions also thwarted Chanel's efforts to have the company declared abandoned when he and his brother left France, and to seize control of it herself.

It is a measure of her adversaries' swift and adept tactics that they managed to outwit both Chanel and the Nazis. Yet the long-term consequences were not straightforward. Amiot was later accused of co-operation, if not collaboration, with the Germans, while Chanel perfumes were sold throughout the Nazi-occupied territories with as much success as in the Allied nations. The perfume company's wartime archives show that stocks of N°5 continued to be exported from Paris to the rest of Europe, along with Chanel's other leading scents: Cuir de Russie, Bois des Iles, Gardénia and N°22. At the same time, the Wertheimers were actively opposing Hitler from their position as businessmen in New York, as is evident from an advertisement taken out by Bourjois in the July 1943 issue of *Harper's Bazaar*, urging readers to buy war bonds in support of the Allied forces: 'Give us tank for tank, plane for plane, gun for gun – and we'll beat the Japs and the Nazis.' Bourjois also launched a patriotic new scent in 1942, Courage, which was packaged in the red, white and blue of the Union Jack and the Stars and Stripes, with an advertising campaign that declared it to be: 'A fragrance attuned to the times … stirring as martial music … reflecting the gallant spirit of today.' A subsequent advertisement evoked the mood of a Hitchcock spy movie, with a

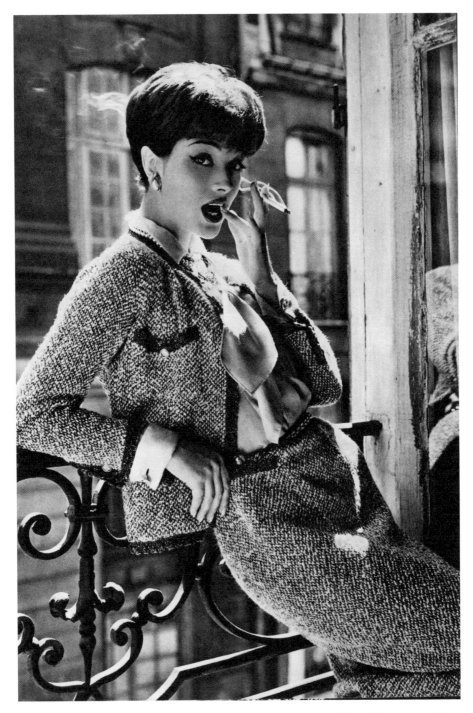

Chanel's signature suits from the 1950s onwards – as seen here on one of Chanel's favourite models, Marie-Hélène Arnaud (above photograph by Sante Forlano, and overpage by Peter Fink), and in sketches by Karl Lagerfeld (right and overpage).

black-and-white photograph of a woman looking over her shoulder at a shadowy man, and the strap line: 'It takes courage to be yourself.'

This slogan might have had an altogether different meaning for Coco, who became intent upon launching her own scents, labelled in bold red as Mademoiselle Chanel, to circumvent the Wertheimers. By 1946, according to her lawyer, she had succeeded in producing samples of perfumes that were good enough to rival those produced by Bourjois, naming them Mademoiselle Chanel N°1, N°2, and N°31. The lawyer was René de Chambrun, a not uncontroversial figure himself, as a loyal son-in-law of the French wartime prime minister, Pierre Laval, who was executed in 1945 as a Nazi collaborator. He had advised Chanel since the early Thirties, at the start of her first unsuccessful legal

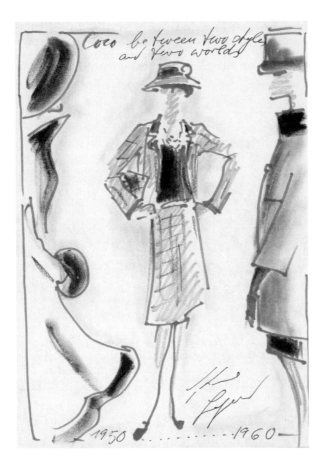

Coco between two styles and two worlds

1950 1960

battle against the Wertheimers. Chambrun had spent the war years with his mother's American relatives in the United States, but on his return to France, he continued to act for Chanel. When interviewed by Pierre Galante, the lawyer recalled that Chanel's perfume samples were sufficiently convincing to provoke a response from the Wertheimers. The brothers had by then invested massively in their US company Chanel, Inc., spending a million dollars on advertising alone; an investment that would have been undermined by a competing range from Mademoiselle Chanel. As Chambrun explained to Galante, Chanel had already sent samples of her red-label scents to 'her old friends Bernard Gimbel and Stanley Marcus [who between them owned the most powerful American department stores, including Saks Fifth Avenue] – people well-entrenched in the US perfume trade. A few days passed. Then one afternoon, Pierre and Paul

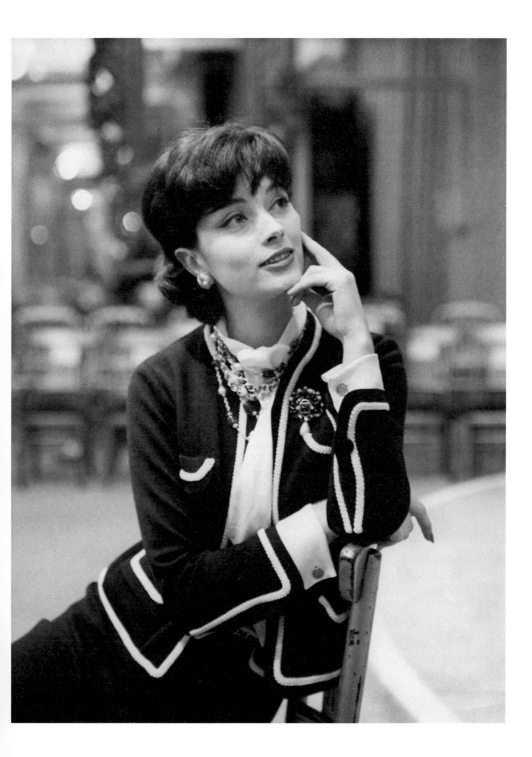

Wertheimer, accompanied by their entire management staff, burst into my office. "Exactly what does she want?" they asked in chorus.'

What Chanel got, after a meeting that went on into the early hours of the morning, was a deal that made her unassailably rich: 'After May 1947, Coco received 2 per cent on the gross royalties of perfume sales throughout the world, in the region of $1 million a year. She also received a sum calculated to cover past royalties.' In addition, the settlement gave Chanel the right to produce and sell Mademoiselle Chanel perfumes, but she never did so. Indeed, she was now wealthy enough to need never work again.

Yet without the defining schedule of her business – the regular couture collections that marked the passing of the seasons – Coco Chanel's post-war years seemed to slip and slide away from the grasp of commentators in any account of her history; an episode consigned to oblivion, an icy exile from the heart of fashion. Marcel Haedrich described her as 'entrenched in her Fortress Chanel'; Pierre Galante observed 'her retirement on the edge of oblivion and of history, cut off from the kind of life that had nourished her celebrity'.

But if time seemed to slow around her, she did not stay still, travelling constantly from La Pausa to the palace hotels of Lausanne, from Monte Carlo to Alpine ski resorts, occasionally alighting in London, New York and Paris (where her great-niece Hélène Palasse was temporarily installed with a governess in the apartment at Rue Cambon). In Switzerland she was reunited with Spatz, otherwise known as the Baron, who had found refuge there following the German retreat from Paris, and her nephew (and Hélène's father) André Palasse, whose health had never fully recovered after his wartime imprisonment by the Nazis. Chanel's loyalty to both her lover and her nephew in the aftermath of the war gives some indication of her ability (or possibly her need) to seek out a place of neutrality; and where better than Switzerland, with its pristine snows and glacial cleanliness, the purity of its air and crisp, clear skies? Chanel bought her nephew a villa, hidden amongst the woods above Lake Geneva; and continued to conduct a discreet affair with Spatz for several years. When their relationship ended, he moved to a Balearic island, although Chanel continued to send him a monthly allowance. According to Pierre Galante, 'Those who knew the Baron remember him as an impoverished, ageing playboy who nevertheless managed to keep up the pretence of wealth and fun-loving youth.'

Switzerland had also provided a refuge for Walter Schellenberg, who was seriously ill with liver disease. After his interrogation in London, Hitler's chief of foreign intelligence had returned to Germany for the Nuremberg Trials. Schellenberg later described his interrogation as harsh, telling a lawyer in Nuremberg that after the sessions in London, 'I was finished. Eight weeks in a lightless cell. I wanted to kill myself …' The final report into Schellenberg's testimony, written by MI5 officers, revealed something of his interrogators' frustrations: 'his incoherence and incapability of producing lucid verbal or written statements have rendered him a more difficult subject to interrogate than other subjects of inferior education and of humbler status.'

His wartime record was equally difficult to interpret; for Schellenberg had not only tried to initiate peace negotiations with the Allies (as was evident in the ill-fated Operation Modellhut) and thereby signal his disaffection with Hitler, but he had also been involved in the successful attempts to save thousands from concentration camps in the final months of the war. There were those who saw this as an act of pure self-interest, an attempt to rehabilitate his reputation in the certain knowledge of German defeat; others were more sympathetic, such as Count Folke Bernadotte, a Swedish diplomat who had negotiated the release of over 20,000 prisoners from German camps and who testified on Schellenberg's behalf at the Nuremberg Trials.

Schellenberg himself seemed confident that he would not be judged harshly by the Allies, at least when he was first interrogated in July 1945. An early intelligence report observed that he was 'facing his present plight as a prisoner in Allied hands in a spirit of complete realism. This does not mean at the thought of the fate that may befall [him] … The fact that Schellenberg seems to be possessed by a certain amount of good faith in Allied goodwill is due to his conviction that he has, ever since becoming conscious in 1940 that Germany had lost the war, been striving for a settlement with the Western powers and for an improvement of the lot of Allied nationals, soldiers and civilians in German hands …'

In the event, although Schellenberg first appeared at the Nuremberg Trials as a witness for the prosecution, he was later indicted for war crimes and found guilty. On 14th April 1949, he was sentenced to six years' imprisonment, but his time spent in custody from June 1945 was taken into account and set against his sentence. By this point, Schellenberg was judged too ill with liver and gall-bladder problems to be kept in prison, and was held instead in Nuremberg City Hospital. In March 1950 he was released under a medical pardon. As his health continued to deteriorate, so did his precarious finances. When he was well enough to write, Schellenberg worked on his memoirs (entitled, appropriately, *The Labyrinth*). The following year, in May 1951, one of his wartime contacts, Roger Masson, the head of Swiss military intelligence, arranged for him to come under the care of a local doctor in Switzerland (a Dr Francis Lang, who later wrote about his association with Schellenberg in his *Mémoires d'un médecin de campagne*). Lang covered his medical expenses for several months, but eventually, as these mounted, Schellenberg was forced to look elsewhere for financial help. Professor Reinhard R. Doerries – a leading authority on German intelligence and an expert on Schellenberg's activities – has recounted the subsequent events: 'Schellenberg contacted Coco Chanel and explained his dire financial problems. If the doctor remembered correctly, the lady of haute couture … arrived in a black Mercedes, curtains drawn, and gave Schellenberg about 30,000 Swiss francs. There are no other explanations from the doctor, other than the fact that during the war Schellenberg had been helpful to her and to others in the fashion world.'

Schellenberg died in March 1952, at the age of 42, and his posthumously published memoir made no mention of Coco Chanel. By then, Chanel had obliterated him from her own version of history, although Schellenberg was not the only omission. In the years following the war she had embarked on a number of attempts to write her memoirs, but none came to fruition. She had collaborated first with Louise de Vilmorin – an elegant novelist and Duff Cooper's lover when he was the British ambassador in Paris immediately after the war – and then with Michel Déon, who spent a month with Chanel at La Pausa towards the end of 1952. His task as her ghost writer continued during her sojourn at the Beau Rivage Hotel in Lausanne, but when he produced his manuscript based on her reminiscences, Chanel (who had employed Déon in the first place) decided against its publication.

Perhaps the most successful of the authors whom Chanel approached to write her memoirs was Paul Morand, a friend and fellow exile in Switzerland, who had served in the Vichy government. They had known each other for over a quarter of a century, since 1921, when Misia Sert had invited Morand to Chanel's New Year's Eve party at Rue Cambon, and the young writer had been so taken by the story of her romance with Boy Capel that he had used it as the inspiration for his first novel, *Lewis et Irène*, published in 1924. It remains unclear whether Chanel ever read his notes of their encounters at the Badrutt's Palace hotel in St Moritz; and the resultant book, *L'Allure de Chanel* (as slim yet pungent

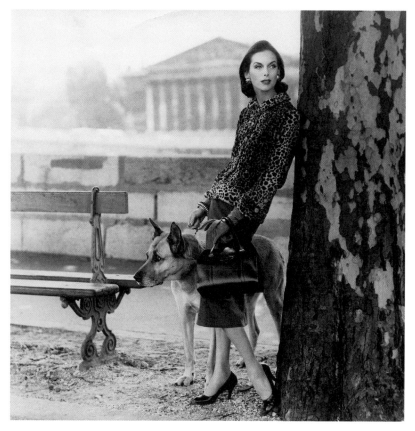

Anne St Marie in a Chanel jacket and skirt. Henry Clarke, 1955.

as its subject) was not published until the year of Morand's death, in 1976. But for all that Chanel chose to exclude from her conversations with Morand, his memory of her in 1946 gives a tantalising insight into her brooding fury and barely suppressed energies during her years away from the fashion business that had shaped her life, and bore her name.

'Chanel was Nemesis,' wrote Morand in his introduction to *L'Allure de Chanel*. 'The voice that gushed forth from her mouth like lava, those words that crackled like dried vines, her rejoinders, simultaneously crisp and snappy, a tone that grew more and more peremptory as age took its toll, a tone that was increasingly dismissive, increasingly contradictory, laying irrevocable blame … She felt both trapped by the past and gripped by time regained … [in an] age that was suddenly foreign to her, the de Gaulle years, and black bile flowed from eyes that still sparkled, beneath arched eyebrows increasingly accentuated by eyeliner, like sculpted basalt; Chanel, the volcano from the Auvergne which Paris was mistaken in believing was extinct.'

These were the years when her friends, as well as her enemies (who were sometimes one and the same), were passing away. Vera Lombardi died in Rome in 1948. Grand Duke Dmitri had finally succumbed to complications of his chronic tuberculosis in Switzerland in 1941; Chanel's other former lovers to whom she had remained equally close, Etienne Balsan and the Duke of Westminster, both died in 1953. As for Misia Sert, she and Chanel remained as inextricably linked as always, for better and for worse, throughout Misia's slow decline into blindness and drug addiction, which had accelerated after the death of her beloved ex-husband in 1945. According to Misia's biographers, Arthur Gold and Robert Fizdale, Chanel also used opiates – as had José-Maria Sert, Cocteau and many others in the gilded circle of Paris artistic society. But there were important differences: 'For Chanel drugs were harmless sedatives; for Misia their purpose was forgetfulness.' And in this pursuit, Misia became dangerously reckless, injecting morphine at dinner parties or while wandering through a street market. 'Once in Monte Carlo she walked into a pharmacy and asked for morphine while a terrified Chanel pleaded with her to be more careful. But carefulness was not in Misia's nature.' Eventually, she was arrested by the police and held overnight in a filthy police cell, before powerful friends intervened on her behalf. Thereafter, she travelled to Switzerland with Chanel to buy supplies; and it was after one such trip, on her return to Paris, that Misia died, on 15th October 1950.

Chanel sat beside Misia as she slipped towards death that night, and then returned the following morning, to prepare her friend's body for burial. She arranged Misia's hair, put on her make-up and her jewels, dressed her in a white dress, and surrounded her with white flowers; le deuil blanc for a dead queen or a long-lost girl; just as Diaghilev had wished for on his deathbed in Venice, 21 years before.

There were those at Misia's funeral who were dismissive of Chanel; who said that she had put too much rouge on Misia, that she had made her corpse look absurd; that Coco herself was skeletal. Yet Chanel remained indomitable; refusing to grow old and invisible or to wrap herself in a shroud of obscurity or penitence. She painted her lips crimson – a slash of blood red, like a wound or a challenge – and exaggerated her eyebrows in black, as if drawing her own portrait of her face. Some whispered she had undergone plastic surgery in Switzerland; that her features had been renewed, or distorted. But she still looked like a little black bull, unafraid and obstinate, challenging the lens of the camera. She was always photographed with a cigarette in her fingers or dangling from her lips; playing with fire, perhaps, or signifying that she possessed a light that would never go out.

'I have been a couturière, by chance,' she had declared to Paul Morand. 'I have made perfumes, by chance. I am now going to tackle something else. What? I don't know. Here again, chance will decide. But I am quite ready. I am not saying goodbye for long. I am not thinking of anything, but when the moment comes, I feel I will pounce on something that will be within my reach.'

As it turned out, Chanel swooped again on fashion, rather than anything else, whether by chance or intuition. Yet as was so often the case in her career, her timing was right. She had watched with barely suppressed contempt as Christian Dior launched his New Look in 1947; although her distaste was not motivated by the same impulse that had enraged some, who found the extravagance of Dior's fashion offensive after the strictures and suffering of the Occupation. 'People shout *ordures* at you from vans,' wrote Nancy Mitford to one of her friends, having ventured out in Dior finery onto the streets of Paris, 'because for some reason it creates class feeling in a way no sables could.' This was soon after a photographic shoot featuring Dior clothes had been brought to an abrupt ending, when outraged women shouted insults at the models, then attacked one of them, tearing at her outfit. In the wake of this assault, Mitford was only half-joking when she remarked, 'I know mine will soon be the same fate … Between the Communists and the ménagères one's life is one long risk.'

Chanel was neither Communist nor housewife, but she was infuriated by Dior's success in reintroducing the constrictive corsets that she had swept away in the First World War. 'I make fashions women can live in, breathe in, feel comfortable in, and look young in,' she had declared to Bettina Ballard in the Thirties, and 20 years later, Ballard witnessed her return to this manifesto. Ballard believed that Chanel 'went back to designing to escape boredom and to keep young'. Not that Chanel was ever going to look young again; for she was 70 when she launched her comeback collection on 5th February 1954. Nor did the choice of the fifth day of the month – her lucky number – do anything to soften the harshness with which she was judged by the French press.

But Chanel faced the critics with her lips and nails in brave warpaint, crimson as the dress that she had made the previous year for her friend Marie-Hélène de Rothschild out of a taffeta curtain. It had been an improvised evening gown, according to Marie-Hélène, but nevertheless a dazzling success; so widely admired that Marie-Hélène claimed that it was this red dress that had convinced Chanel to go back into business again. And when she did so, it was with full-blooded conviction, observed Bettina Ballard, who had returned to Paris to report on the show as the fashion editor of American *Vogue*. 'The French fashion press lay in wait for her first post-war collection, like cats at a rat hole,' observed Ballard, who was close enough to Chanel to know that she had worked on it tirelessly, despite being 'sick with a stoppage in her intestine. She sat at the top of her stairs, with a handful of close friends, watching the faces of the spectators in the mirrors, knowing that they had come with closed minds and venomous pens. The blast in the press the next day was blindly violent, as if the fashion writers could in some way deny the strength of this voice from the past by ranting and raving. Their attack only served to warm her fighting blood ...'

The reviews were savage enough to have felled a woman less sure of herself. Perhaps the French critics would have sneered at whatever it was that Chanel produced, as punishment for her wartime past; but when she revealed a collection that seemed to be a revival of the clothes that had once looked radical – easy, fluid, the very antithesis of Dior's corseting – they saw it as tired repetition, and therefore a failure to engage with fashion. *L'Aurore* dismissed the show as a 'sad retrospective', a resurrection of past fashions that dated back even further than Chanel's final collection in 1939, with 'suits in rather dull wools, in a wan black, matched joylessly with melancholy prints. The models had the figure of 1930 – no breasts, no waist, no hips.' *Le Figaro* was patronising: 'It was touching. You had a feeling you were back in 1925.' But the columnist in *Combat* was even harsher, hinting at the gossip about Chanel's facelift, and condemning her collection as the 'ghosts of 1930 things', in which the audience 'saw not the future but a disappointing reflection of the past, into which a pretentious little black figure was disappearing with giant steps'. The British newspapers were no less condemnatory: the *Daily Express* pronounced it 'a fiasco', the *Daily Mail* called it 'a flop'.

Bettina Ballard, however, remained loyal at American *Vogue*, despite the fact that her colleagues at French *Vogue* 'hated the collection, as did most of the press and buyers'. True, the designs were familiar, rather than revolutionary, yet

Ballard liked them for that, and stuck to her guns, with the support of her editor in New York. 'I photographed three full pages of Chanel models and *Vogue* backed up my fashion judgement by opening the March issue with them. The frontispiece showed Marie-Hélène Arnaud, a completely unknown mannequin, whom Chanel had created in her own image, leaning against the wall in a navy jersey suit with her hands plunged deep in her pockets, her tucked whitelawn blouse buttoned onto the easy skirt under her loose open jacket, her navy cuffs rolled back to show the white ones, and a navy straw sailor [hat] with ribbon streamers on the back of her head. I had owned practically the identical suit before the war and the whole look was as familiar to me as "Swanee River". I wanted this costume for myself – I had missed comfortable, reliably young clothes like this, and I was sure that other women would want them, too, if they saw them.'

But her support was not sufficient to make up for lost orders, and the mood in Rue Cambon was sombre, as it was in the perfume company, which had underwritten half the cost of the comeback collection. According to Pierre Galante, who subsequently interviewed the principal players in the drama, Pierre Wertheimer had taken the decision to back Chanel in her return to fashion, but some in the company were questioning the wisdom of this investment. He remained calm, even as scorn was heaped upon Chanel by the press, and a few days later, went to visit her at Rue Cambon, where she was working in the fitting rooms, although her fingers had seized up with an attack of rheumatism. She told him that she had to go on working, that she would go on; that she was not yet finished. So Wertheimer sat and waited, watching the woman he had known for three decades. At last, hours later, long after night had fallen, when she finally gave up the struggle to make her fingers do as she wanted, Wertheimer walked her back across the road to the Ritz.

In Galante's account of this episode, Chanel suddenly seemed to crumple into exhaustion for a moment, even as she declared her determination to Wertheimer: 'I am continuing, I shall continue. They'll end up by understanding.' To which Wertheimer replied, 'You are right. You must continue.' Chanel said nothing – silenced, for once, by him, speechless after years of bitter exchanges. Then she turned to Wertheimer, her business partner, before walking through the revolving doors of the Ritz, where the Germans had come and then gone. 'Thank you,' she said, and the unspoken peace deal was done.

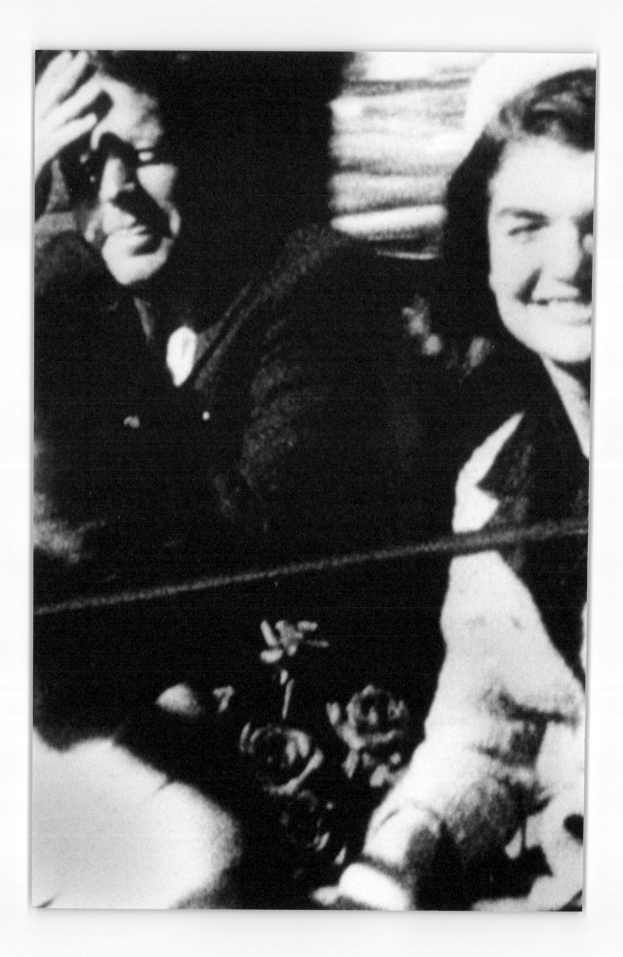

CELEBRITY CHANEL

It was America that celebrated the comeback of Coco Chanel; America that made her famous again, identifying her as a twentieth-century icon, making her face as recognisable as her legendary little black dress and pearls. And it was *Life* – the biggest magazine in America; not just a weekly chronicle of news, but a best-selling definer of fame – that took the lead in rejoicing in all that she represented. On 1st March 1954, the magazine ran a four-page spread on Coco Chanel, 'the name behind the most famous perfume in the world'. There was no mention of the war, none of the disapproval or scepticism that had ambushed her in Paris, simply wholehearted appreciation; as if the United States was far enough removed from the recriminations of post-war France to enjoy unadulterated Chanel. Like Bettina Ballard in *Vogue*, *Life* was enthusiastic about Chanel's revival of what it was that she had always done well. 'Her styles hark back to her best of the Thirties – lace evening dresses that have plenty of elegant dash and easy-fitting suits that are refreshing after the "poured-on" look of some styles ...'

In the following six months, the comfortable suits and dresses that Marie-Hélène Arnaud had modelled for American *Vogue* proved far more popular than anyone had predicted, and orders came flooding in from the United States. In New York, Bettina Ballard felt vindicated in her initial judgement when others in the fashion industry admired the navy jersey suit that she

sident John F. Kennedy and his wife Jackie, wearing a strawberry pink Chanel suit, allas (just before Kennedy's assassination), 22nd November 1963.

CHANEL 287

had ordered for herself from the comeback collection; in retrospect, she wrote, the clothes had taken on 'an uncanny timeless Chanel personality that defied the scoffers'. By the time of the second collection, *Life* was quick to endorse Chanel's achievement, and to perceive that what had been deemed a return to past glories was in itself shaping the future. 'She is already influencing everything,' proclaimed the magazine. 'At 71, Gabrielle Chanel is creating more than a fashion: a revolution.'

It seemed contradictory – and continues to do so, even with the benefit of hindsight – that staying still would be seen as a transformation. But as Bettina Ballard observed in 1960, 'The "Chanel look" remains exactly the same and precisely what women seem to want. Her extraordinary comeback in 1954 – a comeback that has endured – had far more to do with a real hunger that women had for the confidence-giving clothes that Gabrielle Chanel had always understood, always made, than any striking innovation that she brought to fashion. There was an unorganized revolt building up against the whimsy changes of fashion, many of which ridiculed the wearers, and Chanel came along like a messiah to be the leader of this revolt.'

But it wasn't simply the clothes that drew new generations of admirers. Even in old age, Chanel herself seemed to be her own best model, with her characteristic assortment of jewels glittering against a white silk shirt; her way of standing, which came to be emulated by legions of those who followed in her wake. 'She has invented that famous Chanel stance that looks as relaxed as a cat,' wrote Ballard, 'and has an impertinent chic; one foot forward, hips forward, shoulders down, one hand in a pocket and the other gesticulating.'

John Fairchild, who had arrived in Paris in 1955 to run his family business, Fairchild Publications, was equally impressed. As the European Bureau chief of *Women's Wear Daily* (and from 1960, its publisher), he was in a position of considerable power in the fashion industry, yet it took him four years to gain access to Chanel. She was, he later remarked, 'the Eighth Wonder of the World … the greatest designer in history … whose name was a household word throughout the world'. But when he was finally summoned to lunch at her apartment in Rue Cambon, she was self-deprecating, albeit with her characteristic sting. 'I am only a little dress-maker, trying to make women young and pretty. These other designers that do the pretty little sketches, the boys, they don't understand women, they don't know how they live. Their idea is to make them weird, freaks.'

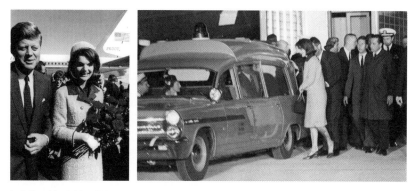

Left: President John F. Kennedy and his wife Jackie arriving in Dallas. Right: Jackie Kennedy beside the hearse containing her husband's body, on November 22, 1963, a few hours after he was assassinated. She is still wearing her Chanel suit, now stained with the blood of her husband.

Not everyone agreed. Although Christian Dior had died of a heart attack in October 1957, his house continued to flourish under the aegis of the young Yves Saint-Laurent; while Pierre Cardin and André Courrèges (who worked for Balenciaga until opening his own house in 1961) were fêted for their innovative Modernism. Nevertheless, women were responding to what it was that Chanel offered; which was, amongst other things, a way of dressing that was masculine in its unruffled dignity, while remaining true to its creator's idea of femininity. Just as she had appropriated the Duke of Westminster's clothes in the Twenties, and those of Boy Capel before him, so Chanel remained adept at combining a streak of androgyny with a decorative touch. It was not feminist fashion – it was not fashion at all, in its adherence to continuity – but there was something liberating about it. 'Elegance in a garment is the freedom of movement,' said Mademoiselle, in one of her oft-repeated maxims, a philosophy that she put into practice with her signature jacket. Lined in silk, and weighted with a fine chain sewed into the bottom seam to ensure that it hung with immaculate symmetry, Chanel designed each jacket to fit perfectly, and yet to be supple enough for a woman to swing her arms or put her hands in the carefully placed pockets. Some were in jersey, reminiscent of those she had introduced during the First World War, comfortable as a cardigan. Others were in tweed, soft as the ones she had borrowed from Bendor, and a reaffirmation of '*le style anglais*' that she had made famous, blending the style of an aristocratic Englishman with quintessentially Parisian chic. Thus the Chanel jacket was reborn in the Fifties, trimmed with grosgrain ribbon and gilt buttons embossed with the symbols for

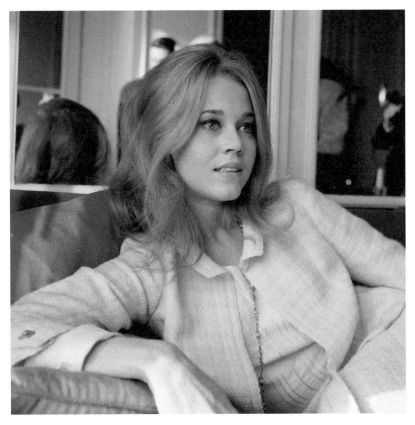

Jane Fonda wearing a classic Chanel suit. Kaye, 1965.

which she was renowned (a lion's head, to denote her astrological sign; a camellia, for her favourite flower; stars, as had appeared in her diamond collection and at La Pausa; and the famous double C logo).

To the jacket, she added a bag, equally redolent of her history and iconography. The 2.55 – named after its launch in February 1955 – used numbers as an ingredient in its mystique, coded clues to the past, which added to the perception of the bag as a classic, so desirable that it seemed its days would never be numbered. This was not the first handbag that Chanel had designed – that dated back to 1929 – but when she talked about the 2.55, the message was one of practicality, as well as heritage. 'I got fed up with holding my purses in my hands and losing them,' she explained, in reference to her original bag, 'so I added a strap and carried them over my shoulder.' And while

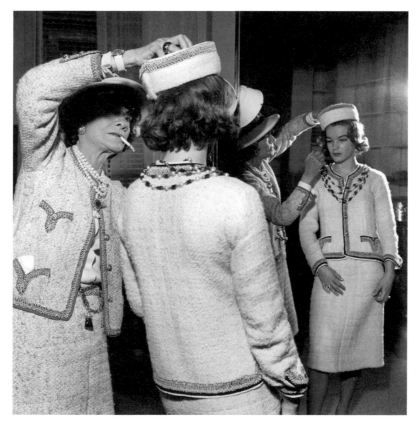

Romy Schneider being dressed by Chanel. Giancarlo Botti, 1960.

the stories of Chanel's history were ever more embroidered, the 2.55 became emblematic of her past at its most romantic, with the joys and sorrows of every archetypal fairytale. The quilted leather, or *matelassé*, was said to be an indication of her love of riding as a young woman, dating back to a time when quilted material was worn only by stable-lads. The chain that served as a shoulder strap was just as evocative: golden metal plaited with a leather cord, suggestive of horse bridles and harnesses, and also of the belts worn by the Catholic nuns who had educated her as a child. 'I know women,' she said, towards the end of her life, when the chain strap had become an instantly recognisable component of the classic Chanel bag. 'Give them chains. Women adore chains.' Perhaps she was being characteristically provocative; or possibly this was as close as she could get to honesty, to an admission that she had not yet rid herself of the bonds of her past, nor stopped yearning for the links that bind a woman to a man.

After the bag, she introduced another component to the essential Chanel look: two-tone slingback pumps that went into production in 1957, and in which she was frequently photographed. As with the jacket, they suggested a gentlemanly British tradition: the Duke of Westminster and his friends had worn two-tone shoes in white canvas and beige leather for playing golf, while the Prince of Wales was seen in similarly sporty versions in the Twenties and Thirties, giving royal approval to footwear that had previously been deemed a trifle too raffish for respectability. But Chanel's versions, beige leather tipped with black toes, were as flattering as they were practical. 'The black, slightly square toe shortened the foot,' explained Monsieur Massaro, then, as now, the shoemaker for the House of Chanel. 'The beige melted into the whole and lengthened the leg.' The heel was never too high to walk in, but with enough height to add a swing to the step. 'A woman with good shoes is never ugly,' commented Mademoiselle, adding another maxim to her collection. 'They are the last touch of elegance.'

As the elements of Chanel's style became globally recognised, her fame kept pace with that of her clients. Just as her first customers, in her earliest days as a milliner, had included actresses as well as socialites, so they did again, coming to pay homage to the oracle of Rue Cambon. She dressed the young French beauties – Romy Schneider, Jeanne Moreau, Anouk Aimé and Brigitte Bardot – and designed costumes for Ingrid Bergman in *Thé et sympathie* (a French version of a Broadway play, staged at the Théâtre de Paris in December 1956; the same month that Chanel also came up with the costumes for Jeanne Moreau in the Paris opening of *Cat on a Hot Tin Roof*). Moreau continued to appear in Chanel – in Louis Malle's film *Les Amants* in 1958, and two years later in Roger Vadim's *Les Liaisons dangereuses* – as did Romy Schneider, most notably in Luchino Visconti's *Boccaccio '70*. Indeed, both Vadim and Visconti took their young protégées to Chanel for inspection and reinvention; to be polished and dressed for the part. And Visconti already had much to be grateful for to Chanel: their friendship dated back to before the war, when the handsome young Italian was a visitor to Rue Cambon and La Pausa. She had introduced Visconti to the revered French director who was to become his mentor, Jean Renoir, (and Renoir himself had commissioned Chanel to design costumes in his pre-war films *La Bête humaine* and *La Règle du jeu*). The couturière's cachet in European cinema grew with her designs for Delphine Seyrig in Alain Resnais's *L'Année dernière à Marienbad*. Hailed by some as a haunting masterpiece of Surrealism, and damned by others as rambling and incomprehensible, the film (released in 1961) served as an undeniably elegant frame for the exactitude of Chanel's little black dresses, its meditation on symmetries finding expression in her designs, even if it were also questioning the premise of conventional form. But her appeal was to extend beyond Europe and its art-house directors: Hollywood royalty increasingly favoured Chanel, including Grace Kelly, Lauren Bacall, Elizabeth Taylor and Marlene Dietrich (who had first worn Chanel in 1933). The publicity in turn boosted the sales of the perfumes; though perhaps the biggest coup of all came courtesy of Marilyn Monroe. When the film star was asked in an interview what she wore at night, she replied – in an apparently unpremeditated line that did more than a multimillion dollar advertising campaign – 'Chanel N°5.'

While America embraced Chanel, it was no wonder that she spoke so warmly of its citizens when she met John Fairchild, at the same time as dismissing the

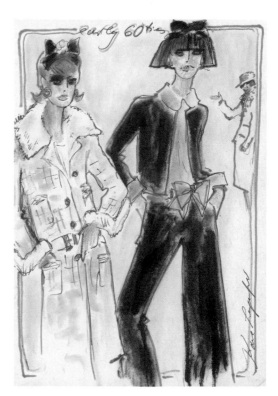

Chanel designs from the early 1960s, by Karl Lagerfeld.

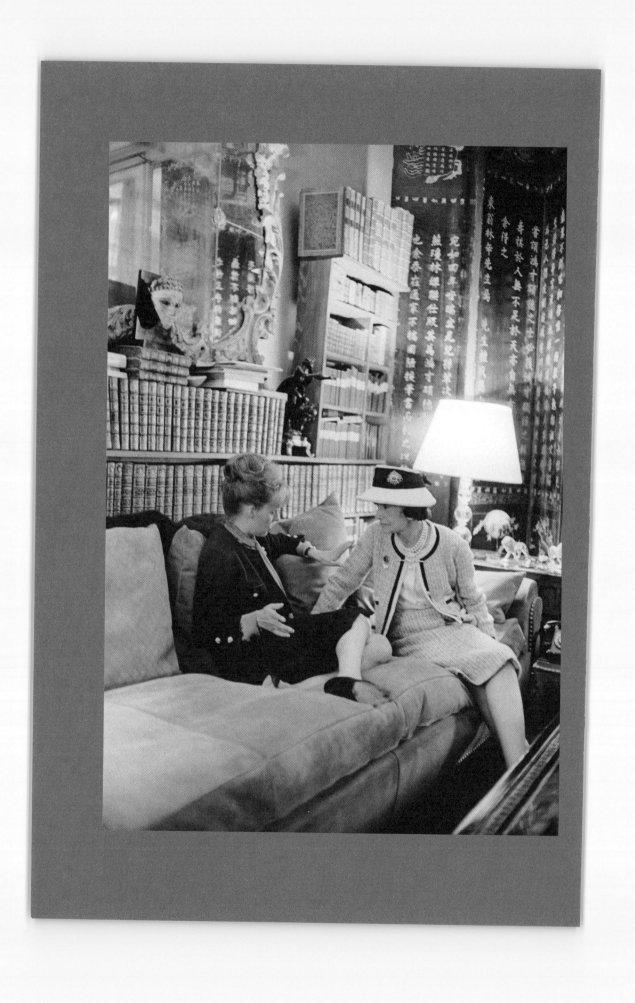

French, as if punishing them for the savaging she had received for her comeback collection: 'Chanel launched into a tirade against the French – how mean, how hard, how awful Paris was today. American women were the most beautiful. The Americans were the only ones who understood her.' They also honoured her; hence her trip to Dallas in September 1957, to receive a fashion award as the most influential designer of the twentieth century, from Stanley Marcus, the owner of the department store Neiman-Marcus.

On her way back from Texas, she was interviewed by Lillian Ross in *The New Yorker*, who seemed unusually smitten. 'We've met some formidable charmers in our time,' wrote Ross, 'but none to surpass the great couturière and perfumer Mlle Gabrielle Chanel, who came out of retirement three years ago to present a collection of dress and suit designs that have begun to affect women's styles every bit as powerfully as her designs of thirty-odd years ago did. At seventy-four, Mlle Chanel is sensationally good-looking, with dark-brown eyes, a brilliant smile, and the unquenchable vitality of a twenty-year-old, and when, giving us a firm hand-shake, she said, "I am *très, très fatiguée*," it was with the assurance of a woman who knows she can afford to say it. Since the Chanel look is causing such a stir these days, we took particular note of what its begetter was wearing: a natural-coloured straw sailor hat; a natural-coloured silk suit, with box jacket and straight skirt; a white silk blouse, with gold cuff links; low-heeled brown-and-white shoes; and plenty of jewelry – a pearl hatpin, pearls and diamonds in her ears, ropes of pearls about her neck, and, on her jacket, an enormous brooch of antique gold studded with rubies, emeralds and diamonds.

'"The brooch is of my design and the dress is nothing, *très* simple," she said. "The cuff links were given to me by Stravinsky, thirty years ago. The occasion? Admiration, of course – the admiration *I* bore *him*!"'

Chanel did not put a foot wrong in the interview with Ross – her answers, in English, were as well judged as her perfectly cut sleeves. Indeed, her performance was as graceful as the most skilled celebrity who knows how to shine in the limelight, without looking vain; her composure maintained even when Ross asked her why she had happened to be in retirement for so long. 'Her brown eyes flashed. "Never was I really in retirement in my heart," she said. "Always, I observed the new clothes. At last, quietly, calmly, with great determination, I began working on *une belle collection*. When I showed it in Paris, I had many critics. They said that I was old-fashioned, that I was no longer of the age. Always I was smiling inside my head, and I thought, I will show them."'

And so she did; pointing the way forward, even as she was mocked for looking backwards, with such success that now she was being copied in France. 'So much the better!' she declared to Ross, seeing imitation as the best form of flattery, a sentiment she echoed in another interview in which she damned her young rival Yves Saint-Laurent with faint praise: 'Saint Laurent has excellent taste. The more he copies me, the better taste he displays.' But the ethos that Chanel expressed in *The New Yorker* – both in the clothes that she wore and designed, and in her way of life, as an independent, self-reliant woman – seemed undeniably, uniquely, appealing. 'I must tell you something of significance. Fashion is always of the time in which you live. It is not something standing alone. The problem of fashion in 1925 was different. Women were just beginning to work in offices. I inspired the cutting of the hair short because it goes with the modern woman. To the woman going to work, I said to take off the bone corset, because women cannot work while they are imprisoned in a corset. I invented the tweed for sports and the loose-fitting sweater and blouse. I encouraged women to be well-groomed and to like perfume – a woman who is badly perfumed is not a woman!'

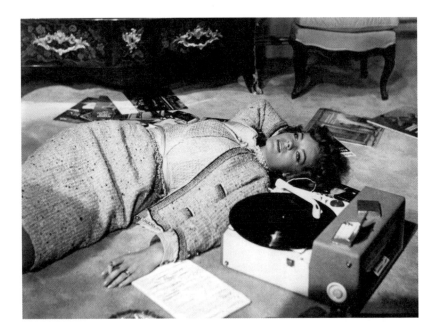

Romy Schneider dressed in Chanel, in a still from the 1960s film *Boccaccio '70*.

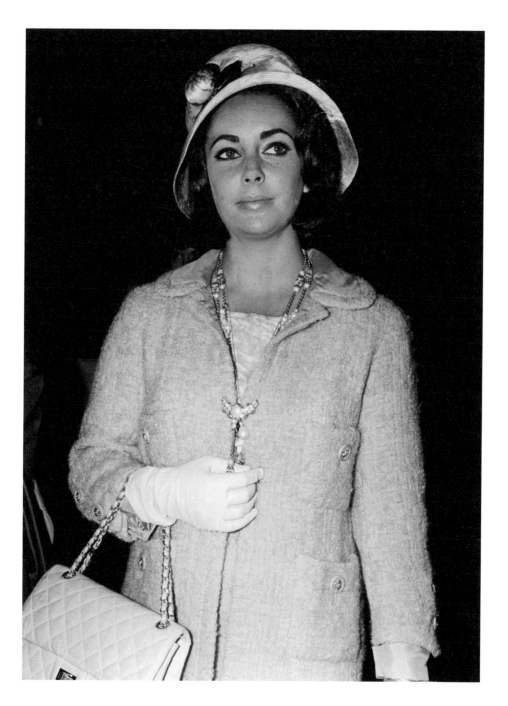

Elizabeth Taylor arriving in France dressed in Chanel, with a quilted Chanel handbag, 1962.

But there was more to being a woman than silk suits and scent. 'Women have always been the strong ones of the world,' she said to Ross. 'The men are always seeking from women a little pillow to put their heads down on. They are always longing for the mother who held them as infants. It is just my opinion. I am not a professor. I am not a preacher. I speak my opinions gently. It is the truth for me. I am not young, but I feel young. The day I feel old, I will go to bed and stay there. *J'aime la vie!* I feel that to live is a wonderful thing.'

What Mademoiselle Chanel did not choose to reveal to *The New Yorker* – nor to anyone else, aside from her great-niece Gabrielle, her own flesh and blood – was that in the end she had conceded some of her strength, giving up a piece of herself to a man more stalwart than others. And although she had not taken his name, he had taken hers, in a final sealing of a long and tumultuous relationship. In the winter of 1954, Chanel had gone to New York, accompanied by Gabrielle, for one last set of negotiations with Pierre Wertheimer. He was, by now, a man at the height of his power – described by *Time* as the 'King of Perfume', 'a lean and elegant Frenchman', wearing the emblem of the Legion of Honour in his buttonhole – and Mademoiselle Chanel had need of him. Gabrielle Labrunie still remembers the snows that winter – so deep that the city seemed silent – and the lengthy meetings that went on for several months. She stayed with her aunt for the entirety of the discussions, at the conclusion of which the Wertheimers agreed to buy out Chanel's business. In effect, they were to underwrite the couture house, gaining all rights to Coco's name, in return for paying every penny of her expenses, including her personal bills at the Ritz and elsewhere. Chanel kept creative control, and her royalties from Les Parfums Chanel, but gave up any involvement in the financial running of her company. Gabrielle believes that when her aunt finally signed the contract with the Wertheimers, she felt liberated, rather than constrained: 'She was free to do whatever she wanted.'

'*J'aime la vie!*' Mademoiselle had said to *The New Yorker*, the very model of an independent woman in her natural coloured suit; cut to her exact specifications, the epitome of the art of couture, yet suggestive of comfortable ease. Some years later, she still adhered to the merits of wearing beige, set against her trademark red lipstick. 'I take refuge in beige,' she told Claude Delay, 'because it's natural. Not dyed. Red, because it's the colour of blood and we've so much inside us it's only right to show a little outside.'

She also spoke to Delay about America: 'America attracted her, America, which had taken her father away and whose daughter she was by adoption.' Chanel's reminiscences included an anecdote about a visit to Stanley Marcus's ranch during her trip to Texas to accept the Neiman Marcus fashion award: 'There was a little short-horned bull just like me, with a wreath of flowers.' The bull was joined by another one, in a bizarre tableau of a wedding in Mr Marcus's garden; a peculiar story that Chanel repeated to Marcel Haedrich: 'A pair of unlikely newly weds suddenly appeared in the converging beams of a number of spotlights: a very young bull stuffed into evening clothes and wearing a top hat between his horns, and an equally young heifer in white Chanel with a long veil.'

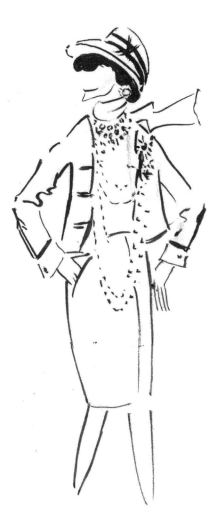

Chanel, by Cecil Beaton, 1969.

But she was amused, rather than offended; the star of the show in Dallas and in New York. For wherever she went, people wanted to know what she thought, what she wore, what the future of fashion would hold. If France had found her lacking, then in America, Mademoiselle Chanel's life still seemed full of promise; and her designs were worn by the most promising of women, none more so than Jackie Kennedy. In August 1959, Mrs Kennedy had appeared on the front cover of *Life*, in sharp focus in the foreground while her husband stood behind her, as if in a supporting role. 'A Front Runner's Appealing Wife' ran the cover line, beneath a photograph of Mrs Kennedy in pearls and a pastel pink dress. Inside, there were more pictures – Jackie on horseback, Jackie with her daughter Caroline on the beach, Jackie with her husband, Senator John F. Kennedy – and an accompanying, admiring piece: 'As the campaigning for the 1960 presidential election gathers steam, the U.S. is going to see more and more of one of the prettiest women to decorate a flag-draped speakers' platform … Hatless but stylishly dressed in clothes mostly of her own design, Jackie makes a graceful, refreshing appearance at teas, barbeques and factory visits.'

No mention was made of Chanel, nor of any other designer, but in fact Mrs Kennedy's clothes were soon to become a talking point in the Kennedy–Nixon campaign. She knew the political value of dressing down as a candidate's wife, aware that she should not be seen as extravagant; indeed, as she herself was to observe in a letter to Oleg Cassini, a French-born Russian-turned-naturalised-American who was to become one of her principal designers, 'I refuse to be the Marie Antoinette or Josephine of the 1960s.' Nevertheless, she was already a customer at Chanel, amongst other French designers, as was her mother-in-law; a vexatious issue, given that her husband had been cautioned by David Dubinsky, the powerful president of the International Ladies' Garment Workers' Union, that Jackie had to buy American.

By September 1960, when John Fairchild received an urgent cable in Paris from the New York office of *Women's Wear Daily* ('Send story Kennedy purchases in Paris couture'), he knew the significance of the request. 'We immediately started checking every Paris couture house. We found Jacqueline and Mrs Joseph P. Kennedy were important private customers in Paris … both Kennedys at Dior, Balmain, Grès, Rouff, Ricci, Griffe, Lanvin – and Jacqueline Kennedy, it was said, had bought heavily at Cardin, Grès, Givenchy, Balenciaga, Chanel and Bugnand.' Fairchild sent a cable back to New York with the news: 'The Paris couture reports that the two Kennedys together spent an estimated

$30,000 last year for Paris clothes and hats'; a figure that was, in Fairchild's opinion, 'not really a lot for elegant women'. But the reaction to the news was swift, as Fairchild noted: 'The Associated Press picked up the *Women's Wear Daily* story, reporting Jacqueline Kennedy had spent $30,000 for Paris clothes. The AP ignored the important fact that the $30,000 figure was for *both* Rose K. and Jacqueline K.

'Overnight the Republicans made the Kennedy Paris fashion sortie a campaign issue. The Republicans pictured Mrs Pat Nixon as the simple, hometown woman, in her simple old cloth coat. What they didn't say was that Mrs Nixon had been shopping at Elizabeth Arden, New York, where the prices were higher than Paris.' The story soon spiralled and spread; when Mrs Kennedy pointed out that her rival's dresses from Elizabeth Arden were every bit as expensive as her own Paris couture, Mrs Nixon's retort appeared in *The New York Times*: 'I buy my clothes off the rack and I look for bargains like all other American women.' Meanwhile, *Time* reported that Mrs Kennedy was upset about the stories of her Paris spending-sprees, 'devil-may-care chic', and of French couturiers keeping 'a Jacqueline Kennedy fashion dummy close by for fittings … "They're beginning to snipe at me about as often as they attack Jack on Catholicism," said Jackie, who also gets mail criticising her for her "floor mop" hairdo. "I think it's dreadfully unfair." That $30,000 figure was dreadfully unfair, too, said she … "I couldn't spend that much unless I wore sable underwear."'

On 8th November 1960, John F. Kennedy was elected president; a week later, his wife wrote a letter to *WWD*, pointing out the inaccuracies of press speculation about her supposed purchases for the Inauguration. Fairchild responded with an offer to publish a portion of the letter as the First Lady's 'Fashion Philosophy', which duly appeared on the front page of the magazine. 'When Jacqueline Kennedy moves into the White House she will wear only American clothes and she is looking forward to it … What fashion news can be expected from Mrs Kennedy in the next four years? She will not order a great many clothes. She does not believe a public figure can be photographed only once in the same outfit. She will wear simple and fairly timely fashions which will do hard work for her. She does expect interest to be taken in the "Kennedy Fashion Look" but is determined her husband's administration not be plagued with fashion stories of a sensational nature. Mrs Kennedy appreciates good clothes, and will continue to dress her type, but will strive to be appropriately dressed for official life. As a young and active woman, she simply does not have

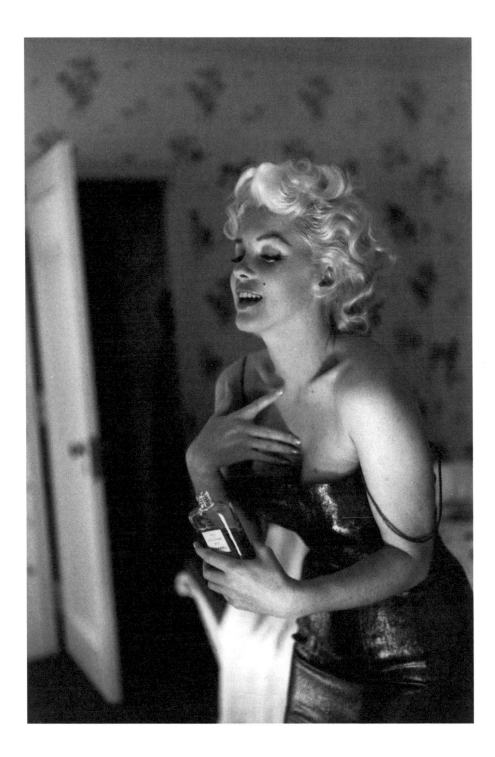

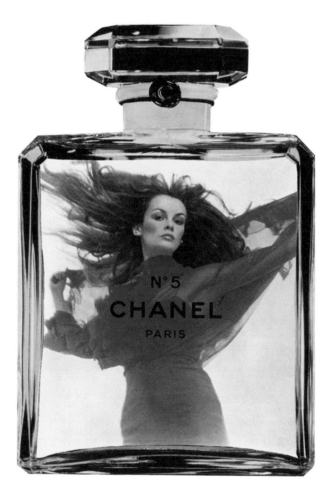

Left: Marilyn Monroe, who famously wore Chanel N°5. Ed Feingersh, 1955.
Above: Jean Shrimpton, photographed by Helmut Newton for the Chanel
N°5 campaign in 1971.

the time to be always shopping and besides this kind of extravagance has always been abhorrent to her.'

As it turned out, Mrs Kennedy did not wear only American clothes, despite the official insistence on her being seen to do the right thing; a role in which she was to play the patriotic young wife of a president who seemed to be unassailable in his position as the Real Thing. Behind the scenes, however, compromises were being made, in this and other matters. In June 1961, when she accompanied her husband on a state visit to France, Mrs Kennedy wore an ivory satin evening gown by Givenchy to a dinner at the Palace of Versailles. Such was the impact that she made as a Francophile – wearing French, speaking French – that even the austere de Gaulle was visibly charmed, prompting *France-Soir* to declare in a headline, 'Versailles at last has a Queen.' When the time came for the Kennedys to return to Washington, the president remarked in a press conference, 'I am the man who accompanied Jacqueline Kennedy to Paris.'

She also continued to add Chanel pieces to her wardrobe, albeit with some circumnavigation. The Chanel archive reveals that Mrs John F. Kennedy was a couture customer between 1955 and 1968, making regular orders before her husband became president, aside from 1957, when she gave birth to her baby, Caroline, in November. After 1960, she continued to buy Chanel, but in secret and via her friend Letizia Mowinckel (who pretended to be shopping for a cousin, supposedly a Sicilian noblewoman) and her sister, Lee Radziwill. A further diplomatic solution was reached, whereby Mrs Kennedy was able to acquire Chanel outfits sewn for her in New York by a dressmaking establishment called Chez Ninon. The garments were not fake or pirated, but made to order using materials supplied by Chanel in Paris. (Unlike other couturiers, Chanel never sold patterns, but adhered to what was known as the 'line for line' system, keeping as close as possible to the original design.) Mrs Kennedy did not save money by doing so – the prices at Chez Ninon were on a par with those at Chanel, with a suit starting at $850, and evening gowns running into the thousands – but she did save face, as an implicitly patriotic patron of an American dressmaker.

Thus it was that she came to be wearing a vivid pink Chanel suit (complete with fabric, trim and buttons from 31 Rue Cambon, but fitted at Chez Ninon) on 22nd November 1963, accompanying her husband to Dallas. It was not the first time the president's wife had worn the suit, of which the original had come from the Chanel autumn/winter 1961 couture collection. Mrs Kennedy had been seen in it on several previous occasions, including a visit to London in 1962, and it was said to be a particular favourite of her husband. In a subsequent interview with the writer William Manchester, Mrs Kennedy recalled how the president, shortly before their trip to Dallas, had for the first time in their marriage asked what she planned to wear: '"There are going to be all these rich, Republican women at that lunch,"' JFK told her, '"wearing mink coats and diamond bracelets. And you've got to look as marvelous as any of them. Be simple – show these Texans what good taste really is." So she tramped in and out of his room, holding dresses in front of her. The outfits finally chosen – weather permitting – were all veterans of her wardrobe: beige and white dresses, blue and yellow suits, and, for Dallas, a pink suit with a navy blue collar and a matching pink pillbox hat.'

When the First Couple arrived on Air Force One at Dallas's Love Field airport, Mrs Kennedy was given a bunch of red roses; the few surviving colour photographs show her looking radiant in the pink suit, the flowers in full bloom in her arms, the November sky blue beyond the wings of the aeroplane. Afterwards, riding beside her husband in an open limousine as the presidential motorcade travelled through Dallas, her husband asked her to remove her dark glasses because the crowd had come to see her face.

The vice-president's wife, Lady Bird Johnson, was following two cars behind the Kennedys with her husband, Lyndon Johnson. Later, she wrote in her diary that the sunlit streets were lined with people: 'One last happy moment I had was looking up and seeing Mary Griffith leaning out a window waving at me. (Mary for many years had been in charge of altering the clothes which I purchased at Neiman-Marcus.)' Then she heard a shot, and two more in rapid succession. At first, she thought these were the sound of celebratory firecrackers, but as her car accelerated, she heard someone say, 'Have they shot the President?' When they pulled up outside a hospital, she was hustled into the building by the Secret Service agents. 'I cast one last look over my shoulder and saw in the President's car a bundle of pink, just like a drift of blossoms, lying in the back seat. It was Mrs Kennedy lying over the President's body.'

After the president was declared dead and his body taken in a casket to Air Force One, wrote Mrs Johnson, she stood beside her husband as he took the oath of office on board the aircraft. Jackie Kennedy was also there, 'her hair falling in her face but very composed … I looked at her. Mrs. Kennedy's dress was stained with blood. One leg was almost entirely covered with it and her right glove was caked, it was caked with blood – her husband's blood. Somehow that was one of the most poignant sights – that immaculate woman, exquisitely dressed, and caked in blood.

'I asked her if I couldn't get someone in to help her change and she said, "Oh, no …" And then with almost an element of fierceness – if a person that gentle, that dignified, can be said to have such a quality – she said, "I want them to see what they have done to Jack."'

Jackie Kennedy kept the same suit on, still stained with her husband's blood, when Air Force One returned with his coffin to Washington, and did not remove it until early the next morning. When she finally changed out of the suit, her maid folded it and put it in a box. A few days later, the box was sent to Mrs Kennedy's mother, who wrote 'November 22nd 1963' on top, and placed it in her attic. Eventually, the suit was given to the National Archives for safekeeping, where it still remains, stored away from public view. It has never been cleaned.

Whatever else died with Kennedy's assassination, the Chanel suit survived, a shred of visible evidence from a split second when history was made, even as it appeared to fall apart. In the aftermath of the president's death, the bloodstained suit seemed emblematic of the ending of innocence, of a time before JFK's reputation was stained by the gossip about his infidelities and compromises; before the news of his affair with Marilyn Monroe had been made public, picked over and dissected in the context of her own unhappy end. And although it was kept out of sight, the Chanel suit lived on in photographs (the majority of them in grainy black and white); a troubling reminder of a lost era that was at first deemed golden, and then turned into something more tarnished. In retrospect, Mrs Kennedy's Americanised Chanel was never entirely uncomplicated, from the moment of its creation, even without the president's blood on it. Yet for all that, it served as a reminder of an age before Jackie Kennedy had become Jackie O, the haunting images of her as a grieving black-clad widow at her husband's funeral replaced by the photographs of her in a short white wedding dress with her billionaire second husband.

Whatever the painful associations, Jacqueline Kennedy Onassis did not stop buying Chanel. Even when her couture purchases became infrequent, and she turned instead to Courrèges and Valentino, she continued to wear the scent that Marilyn Monroe had made famous, dispatching a private jet from her husband's Greek island to Paris with a secretary on board to buy bottles of Chanel N°5 in the boutique at Rue Cambon.

Mademoiselle Chanel did not comment on the bloodstained pink suit, although several years after Jack Kennedy's death, she was sharp-tongued on the subject of his widow, telling James Brady at *Women's Wear Daily* that she disapproved of Jackie Kennedy wearing miniskirts: 'she wears her daughter's clothes.' The oracle had spoken, but afterwards, she worried aloud to Marcel Haedrich, the editor of *Marie Claire*, that she might have gone too far. But then Chanel reassured herself that she was right, as always. 'When one makes up one's mind to tell the truth, one has to go all the way.'

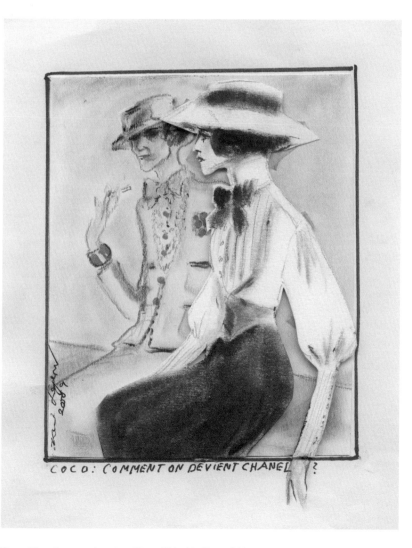

COCO: COMMENT ON DEVIENT CHANEL ?

'Coco: How does one become Chanel?', by Karl Lagerfeld.

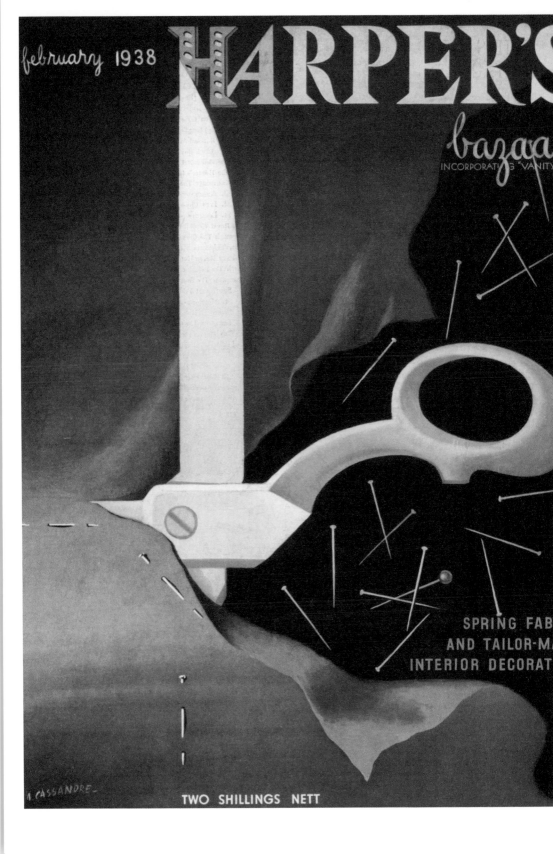

SCISSORS

When Gabrielle Chanel stepped into her realm at Rue Cambon, her assistant would hang a long white tape around her neck with Mademoiselle's special scissors threaded through it, like a ceremonial necklace. Other pairs of scissors were always within her reach – silver and gilt ones arrayed in her apartment and in rows on her dressing table at the Ritz; another on a plain white napkin on the bedside table, lying beneath an icon given to her by Stravinsky.

In old age, when Chanel was showing Claude Delay her gold boxes from the Duke of Westminster, she pointed out the coat of arms engraved on the top. If she were to mark her own emblem next to his, she said, 'I would add my scissors.' By this point, Chanel was never seen sewing – she had left that far behind her, back in her modest past as a seamstress, and before then, as a child of the orphanage – but she still wielded her scissors on a daily basis to shape and remake her creations. 'What you have to do is cut,' she said to Delay. The younger woman watched Chanel at work in her studio at Rue Cambon, surrounded by her staff, pinning and cutting the cloth on a series of models, working until all those around her were exhausted, taking apart a suit dozens of times, readjusting a hem, an armhole, or a sleeve until she was satisfied that it was perfect. As *Time* reported in August 1960, in an article that declared her to be the 'High Priestess of High Fashion', 'the surest touch in fashion is still Chanel's. She is no innovator for novelty's sake. She devotes her energies to barely noticeable refinements of detail of her suits and dresses, e.g., jackets are shorter this year, a little closer to the body. With scissors hanging from a ribbon around her neck and her four fingers firmly together in a characteristic Coco gesture as she pats a new suit in various places, she may say: "Make a pleat here, an intelligent pleat." One of this year's suits was changed 35 times after being made up before Coco was satisfied.'

As her hands moved over the model's body, her fingers feeling the flesh beneath the cloth and her scissors snipping, the tittle-tattle spread that Mademoiselle Chanel was a lesbian, that she touched her models in ways that she would never touch a man again. But those who knew her best said that her relationships with her models (including her favourites in the Fifties, a young Frenchwoman, Marie-Hélène Arnaud, and the Texan Suzy Parker) was a curious mixture of mothering and mentoring, rather than anything truly sexual. Bettina Ballard had experienced this herself, in her early years working for *Vogue* in Paris, and described Chanel as 'a sorceress', but one who seduced with words, to turn her protégées into versions of herself. 'She had, and still has, a strong proselytizing instinct. She likes converting people to her way of thinking, dressing, and living, particularly the young, who have a certain amount of hero worship for Chanel. I fell into this category immediately.' A quarter of a century later, Ballard saw the same process at work with Suzy Parker, who had been photographed on the front cover of *Elle* with Chanel, in a portrait that seemed closer to that of mother and daughter than designer and model. Certainly, when Suzy Parker had her first child in 1959, she named the baby girl Georgia Belle Florian Coco Chanel, and Mademoiselle became godmother to her namesake.

While the gossip about Chanel's sexuality continued, fuelled by an improbable story that she had been flirting with Jacqueline Susann, the best-selling author of *Valley of the Dolls*, she herself scoffed at the idea. As always, she was equally liable to dish the dirt on others. (Noël Coward noted in his diary for 29th November 1948: 'Lunched with Coco Chanel. Not a good word spoken about anyone but very funny.') But according to her friend Marcel Haedrich, Chanel was also hurt by the whispers about her sexuality. Shortly after her death, he wrote, 'I can still hear her bewailing a rumour about her that had to do with her supposed feelings about one of her models: "Imagine – me, now! An old lesbian! It's unbelievable how people dream up these things."' Haedrich sensed Chanel's vulnerability as she spoke, and the depth of her feeling of humiliation:

'It was shattering.' She also told him that she had given up on love altogether. 'Love? For whom? An old man? How horrible. A young man? How shameful. If such a terrible thing happened to me, I'd flee, I'd hide.'

If Chanel felt that to love a man in old age would be appalling, then her feelings about women were too complex to be easily categorised. Misia was dead, finally silenced, yet irreplaceable; for at the end of their long-running power struggle, there was no one left who had influenced Chanel, no one who had known her before her mask of fame had set hard. But she still knew how to control other women, how to remake them as she saw fit. Cecil Beaton, who sketched Chanel with her scissors hanging around her neck, had long observed her command over her clients and models, and her ability to turn them into androgynous creatures. 'She hated the way hairdressers set their clients' hair in tight waves like cart ruts,' he wrote, before her comeback collection, 'and would take nail scissors and crop the hair of her favourites herself. She then set about concealing their breasts and buttocks. Women began more and more to look like young men, reflecting either their new emancipation or their old perversity.'

Chanel continued to cut her models' hair – and her own, as part of the ritual of every new couture collection – but there was one exception to her rules: the ebullient, mercurial Suzy Parker. Bettina Ballard witnessed the designer 'pounding Suzy with words, which she seems to absorb through some process of osmosis. Suzy for a while worshipped at Chanel's feet every afternoon at five, learned to stand like Chanel, imitate her gestures, and wear her clothes with ease, but never went so far as to cut off her long, glamorous red hair, which Chanel deplored.'

What was it that Chanel abhorred about long hair? The mere sight of it was enough to make her lunge at a woman with her scissors, as Grand Duke Dmitri's sister learned to her cost. In her memoir, Marie described the savage cut that she had been given, without any warning: 'Before I had time to realize what she was doing, she had pulled out my hairpins, snatched up the scissors and was cutting off my hair by the handful.' The result was so unflattering that even Chanel was dismayed, 'but the damage was done.'

According to the ever-perceptive Claude Delay, Chanel's 'horror of hair was one of the things that survived from her childhood'. She told Delay on several occasions that her father hated the smell of hair; that he always asked when she had last washed hers (a story that seems unlikely, but not impossible). Her own hair had been short since she had cut it off as a young woman, but not hidden;

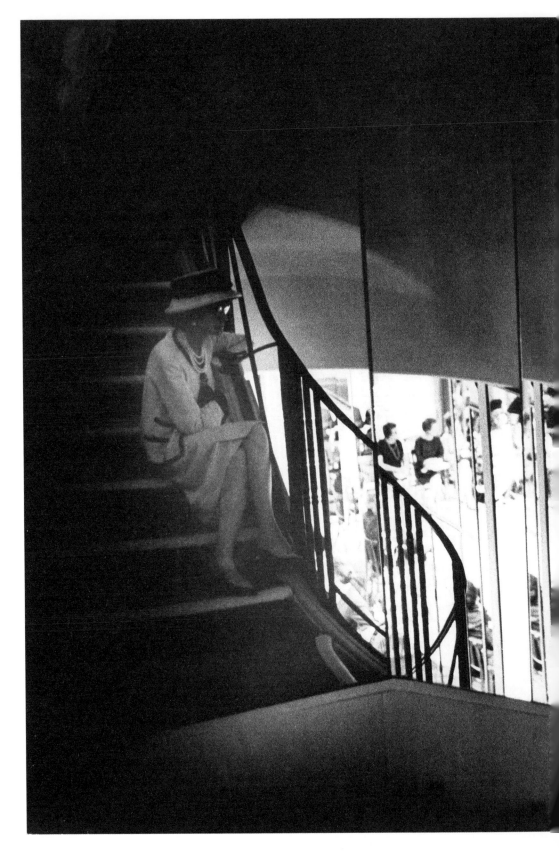

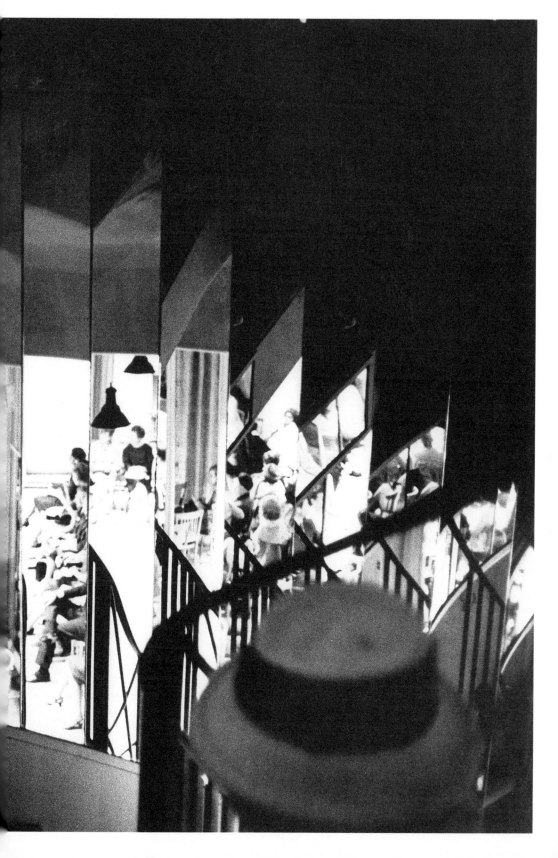

yet from the time of her comeback collection in 1954, Chanel was almost always seen with a hat on her head, the jaunty little straw boater of her youth. Some speculated she wore the hat to hide the thinning of her hair in old age; others that it was a way of concealing the scars of a facelift. But those who remained closest to her – Gabrielle Labrunie and Claude Delay – still saw the dignity with which she carried herself; the unyielding efforts to keep her proud head held high. Both of them were young enough to remain admiring of Chanel, at the same time as being sensitive to the older woman's vulnerabilities. Both saw her emotional scars, her loneliness, her sense of loss and failure at having never married, never borne children. After Gabrielle married and had her own two sons,

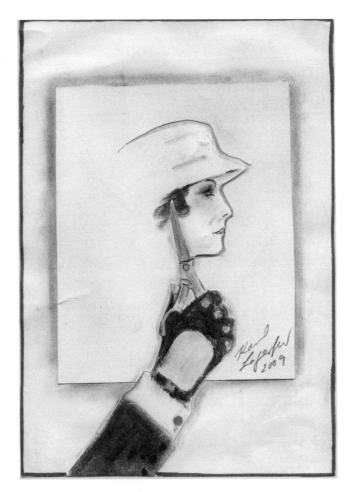

Chanel, by
Karl Lagerfeld.

Chanel spent time with them; never overly tender, she nevertheless gave them picture books, and took the trouble to talk to them, and to listen to their answers, in ways that she did not always do with adults. ('My son Guillaume remembers that she always wore a lot of make-up and kept her hat on her head,' says Gabrielle. 'One day, when he was at her apartment, a piece of crystal fell from the chandelier in the salon. He put it in the mouth of Auntie Coco's gold frog – last time I looked, it was still there …')

Sometimes, says Gabrielle, her aunt would tell her, 'A simple life, with a husband and children – a life with the people you love – that is the real life.' And yet Gabrielle could also see the manner in which Chanel had cut her own familial ties, to set herself free. 'She battled for her freedom, to escape from her childhood, from the suffering of Aubazine – and that was why she designed clothes that made women free. It was all a question of freedom – to be free to drive your car, to ride a bicycle, to walk to work, you had to be able to forget about what you were wearing. Forgetting is part of freedom – and so she was free to forget her past. And even if she did not forget it, she put her memories somewhere where they did not weigh too heavily on her – just like the clothes she made, that were so light that they seemed to weigh nothing at all.'

Claude Delay, her confidante, was similarly aware of what Chanel had cut out of her past; but while others have accused Chanel of lying in order to re-create history (and her own identity), Delay is less judgemental, seeing the revisions as Chanel's attempt to be true to herself. 'I remember Coco cutting bits out of a typed page of maxims she'd written and making them into thin strips for me. I watched the remains getting smaller and smaller. "That's how you arrive at a text." She exercised the same rigour towards human beings … Her rigour had far-reaching consequences: isolation, solitude.' There were times when Delay sat with Chanel in the apartment at Rue Cambon, long after everyone else had gone home, sensing the couturière's spirits sinking as darkness fell, scissors set aside. It was at these moments that Chanel would say that her life was a failure, that she had lost those whom she had adored; that there was nothing worse than being alone; that all that was left to her were dresses and coats. 'A woman who is not loved is no woman,' she said to Delay, 'whatever her age … A woman needs to be looked at by a man who loves her … without that look she dies.'

Yet still she went on, finding enough in the dresses and coats to continue; always moving on towards the deadline of the next collection, too stubborn to stop working on her own clothes, which were the essence of all those that she designed for other women. John Fairchild described having lunch with Chanel in her apartment ('veal roast with tiny peas, onions, carrots and potatoes – a spring garden on a silver platter'); but while he ate, she kept her scissors in her hands. 'Chanel started pulling at the threads on her jacket, snipping away as though she was making herself a new suit.' And still she kept talking, indomitable, 'her words shooting out like piercing machine gun bullets'.

Cecil Beaton found her equally animated whenever he visited her in Paris, as he often did, particularly after he began working on the set and costume designs for *Coco*, a Broadway musical based on her life with lyrics by Alan Jay Lerner and music by André Previn. In April 1965, Beaton was dispatched to Rue Cambon by the stage producer Frederick Brisson (who had first approached Chanel about the musical in 1954). Afterwards he wrote in his diary that the musical 'will probably never come to anything. But the fact that Chanel is still alive and in full sail is quite wonderful.' The House of Chanel was humming with energy and activity; more opulent than he had seen it before, entirely undimmed, like its owner. 'The mirrored palaces below were now heavily populated. The apartment upstairs more than ever filled with glitter of gold lacquer, ormolu and crystal … Chanel in oatmeal with facings of crimson and navy blue, looked thinner, but otherwise of an extraordinary girlishness. She was talking her head off to her staff …' And her monologue continued – 'rat-tat-tat' – as they lunched at the Ritz, her '*petite auberge*' across the road: '… was it to me that she talked? Or was she just talking for talking's sake? She did not really show much sign of judging whether I was present or not … Our heads became lower on the table and closer. Her eyes like pansies, with dark heavy lashes, her skin very clean and her aura delightfully perfumed, with hands that are like a peasant's. She kept fluttering a pair of gloves and I noticed that only the hands had become old.'

It took another four years for the musical to be staged, with Katharine Hepburn in the lead, playing Chanel in the run-up to her comeback at 70. According to *Time* magazine, in a preview of *Coco*, 'The plot is as simple as a Chanel suit: Yes, she'll open; No, she won't; Yes, she'll open; No, she won't; Yes, she'll open; Yes, she opens. Her collection is a flop with the Paris fashion world, but not (aha!) with the fresh-eyed buyers from across the Atlantic.' Lerner's script had Chanel reflecting on liberation ('A woman needs independence from men, not equality. In most cases equality is a step down'), and her self-determination as a couturière ('Everything is on sale but me').

Chanel at work with her scissors, making alterations to a model's dress. Shahrokh Hate

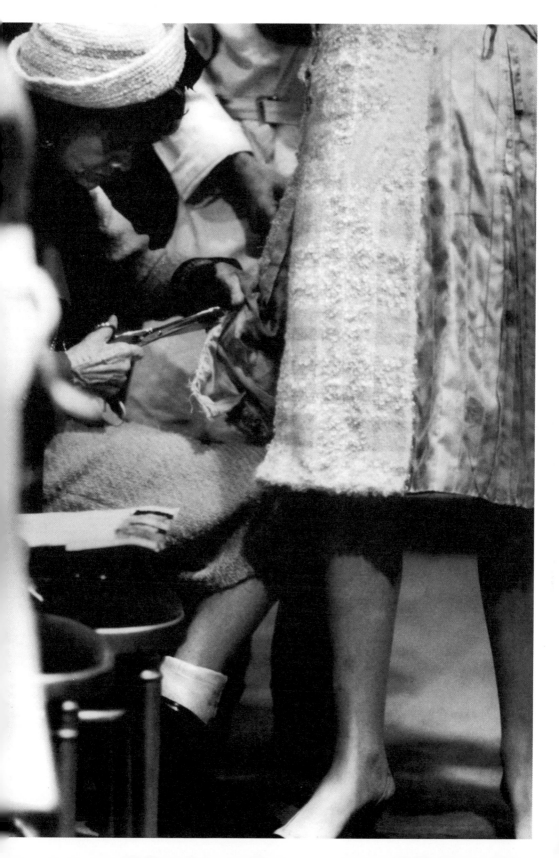

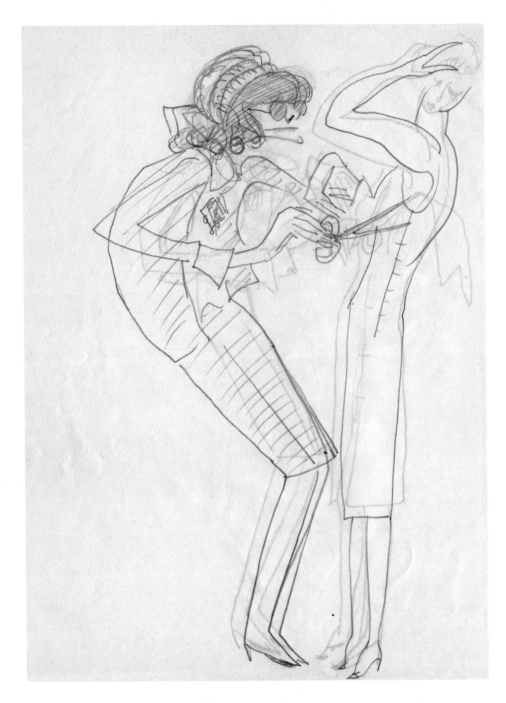

Cecil Beaton's portrait of Chanel at work, 1960.

Beaton noted some similarities between Hepburn and Chanel – the former talked as much as the latter, and sought company to 'keep loneliness at bay' – but thought that this was not reflected on stage. 'She [Hepburn] does not give any suggestion of Chanel herself, is in fact K.H. as ever, but it is a remarkable tour de force, full of vitality and emotion.' The final days before the opening were fraught – 'I find K.H. in her Chanel hat feeling that the stars had stopped in their courses because she had cut her hair' – and at one point, Hepburn threatened to cast aside Beaton's costumes in favour of her own original Chanels. Despite his exasperation with the demanding leading lady, Beaton was nevertheless unable to conceal his admiration for Hepburn's couture garments from Rue Cambon: 'They are impeccably made. Real works of art.'

After a great many arguments, Hepburn agreed to wear Beaton's costumes, and the two became sufficiently friendly (albeit only temporarily) to have a conversation alluding to Chanel's supposed lesbianism, and the rumours concerning Hepburn's friendships with women. On 1st November 1969, Beaton observed in his diary that Hepburn was unhappy about a scene in which a young actress appeared alongside her as a Chanel model and muse, with her hair styled in a similar way to Coco's. Veering between irritation and amusement, Beaton reported that Hepburn had said to him, 'she must not have her hair cut in a bang like mine. That would be too lesbian and we can't introduce that element into the play. As it is there have been rumours about me, because I have some very good friends like Laura Harding [the American Express heiress, to whom Hepburn was close for many years] and we wear trousers. Oh, it's been said millions of times, and Chanel too, she's had that reputation.' Beaton remained unconvinced: 'I told K. that I did not for a minute believe that C. had those tendencies (lots of women fell for her romantically, passionately, doggedly) but Chanel was far too unrelenting against homosexuality in men to have those feelings about women. She spent her later years inveighing against pederasts, saying that they had ruined fashion by purposefully making women look foolish. "Is that so?" said Kate … and the rattle voice was at it again.'

By the time the musical opened in December, Beaton was alternating between black depression, rage with Hepburn ('a rotten, ingrained viper'), and bursts of malice about various others. (After having dinner with Jacqueline Kennedy Onassis, he wrote in his diary that 'Jackie looked quite hideous, square-faced, fat-cheeked, double-chinned, with old hands, her hair worn in straggles and her body disguised in a sort of Barbarella cowboy suit.') His fears that the musical would be badly reviewed proved to be true – and his designs came in for particular criticism – but it nevertheless proved reasonably popular, and ran for 329 performances.

As for Coco Chanel herself: she was suffering even more than Beaton. Having agreed to go to New York as guest of honour for the first night of the musical, she had designed a white sequin gown to wear. She told Delay that she was touched by the reverence and affection she received from Americans: 'When you're badly treated, America comes to your defence.' But she was also terrified about the prospect of the trip, and of seeing a version of herself on stage. Interviewed in Paris by *Time* just before *Coco* began previews, she said that she had loved Lerner's *My Fair Lady*, and therefore had confidence in him: 'I was convinced that Lerner was incapable of doing anything vulgar.' Even so, she expressed some doubt that audiences would find anything very interesting in her story: 'My life is rather boring, I would say. But we'll see.' Chanel's uncharacteristic note of uncertainty was evident too when she talked about the casting of Katharine Hepburn in the lead. 'She's very very expensive, you know,' she remarked to *Time*, as if that might be sufficient to confirm Hepburn's impersonation of her; but then added, 'I'd always thought of her as such a gendarme type – so sure of herself.' *Time* noted that 'Hepburn had characterized herself as "the stevedore type",' and then quoted Lerner's conviction that the actress and couturière were very much alike: 'In essence, they're similar. Both women are extraordinarily independent and vulnerable and feminine.' And both were consumed by a fierce work ethic: 'Look at Chanel at 86,' Lerner points out, 'still pinning and ripping'; while Hepburn was equally committed, 'totally immersed' in her role, the first to arrive in the morning for rehearsals and the last to leave at night. 'The only time she panics is when she's left with nothing to do.'

A week before Chanel's departure from Paris, disaster struck, when her right hand was paralysed in what appeared to be sudden, inexplicable nerve damage. Her triumphant return to New York was cancelled, and she was rushed instead to the American Hospital in Neuilly. Delay found her there in bed, 'her hand hanging down inert'. A priest had arrived earlier, Chanel said; she had woken up to discover him looming at her bedside. 'Too soon,' she snapped, and sent him away. The January collection was awaiting completion at Rue Cambon, and even with her right hand limp, unable to hold her scissors, nothing was going to stop Mademoiselle Chanel from returning to her studio. Her white sequinned evening dress was put aside unworn, but still, there was more work to be done.

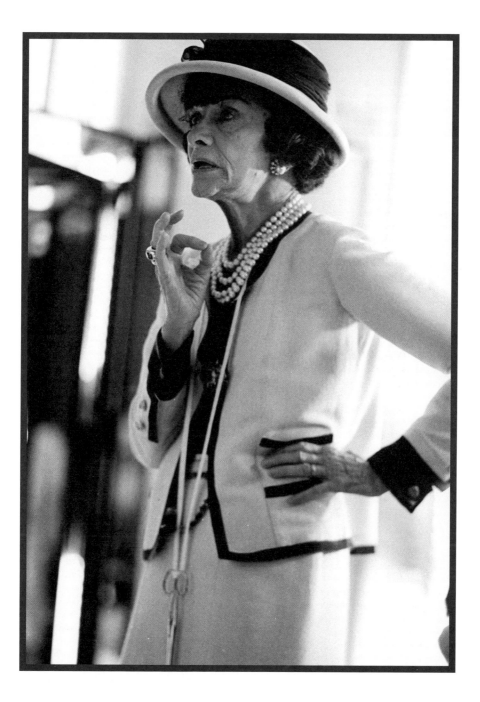

Chanel at work. Douglas Kirkland, 1962.

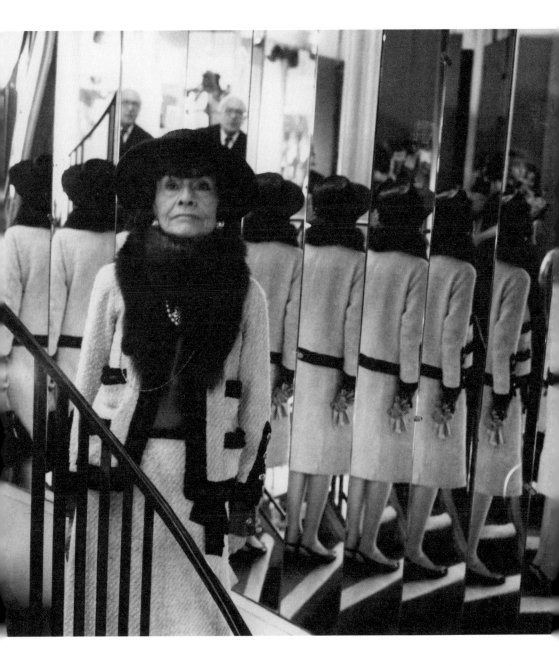

LA GRANDE MADEMOISELLE

You could search forever for the whole truth about Gabrielle Chanel, and never find the last of the missing pieces; for when she cut up her history, she scattered it all around, losing some details, hiding others, covering her trail. Sometimes, you feel you might just catch up with her: in the apartment at Rue Cambon; or in her upstairs studio, where Karl Lagerfeld now reigns, although her name still remains on the door, as if barring anyone else from entering. The sign is just as she left it: '*Mademoiselle – Privé*'.

There is a manor house in the French countryside, an hour or so by train beyond Paris, where Gabrielle Palasse-Labrunie lives; a quiet place, hidden behind high stone walls and solid wooden gates. Madame Labrunie is in her eighties now, but her face still contains clear traces of the girl she once was; the young girl carrying a bouquet of white flowers in the photograph that her great aunt kept pinned by her dressing table at the Ritz. In those outlines – the high cheekbones, the arch of her eyebrows – you can see why one of Chanel's oldest associates (Madame Aubert, who had worked for Coco since the business launched in 1910, and had known her even before then, in Moulins) was so startled by the sight of the young Gabrielle coming down the staircase

...nel on the mirrored staircase (the photographer and his camera are ...ected behind her head). Cecil Beaton, 1965.

CHANEL 323

at Rue Cambon that she told her, 'You look just like Mademoiselle as a girl, you could be her granddaughter …'

Now, Gabrielle Labrunie lives alone, but Mademoiselle is all around her. In her bedroom, there is a photograph of Chanel as a young woman, before she had cut her hair off; the long dark locks plaited and pinned up on her graceful head, her neck held with such elegance that you can see why Cocteau christened her the Black Swan. In the living room are rows of bookshelves filled with Chanel's first editions – some signed by the authors, including Paul Morand and Pierre Reverdy – and her furniture still stands solid on the floor: a Coromandel screen, a console table from the entrance to the apartment at Rue Cambon, an eighteenth-century Korean cabinet given to Coco by Boy Capel. Most striking of all is what looks like a hand-carved black sculpture above the fireplace; the same one that Chanel treasured on the mantelpiece in her salon. 'It's a meteorite,' explains Gabrielle, 'that came down to earth in China. It was given to my aunt, by someone who told her, "You cannot buy that which comes from the sky."' As she speaks, she rests her hand on the meteorite, just as Chanel used to do. She pauses, and then continues, 'Nobody can possess her spirit – she was the embodiment of independence and freedom. Nobody could buy her, and she is not for sale.'

Then Gabrielle leads me along a corridor, to a simple room with a wooden wardrobe on one wall. She opens the door to the wardrobe, gestures inside, and says, 'These are her clothes. You can try them on if you like.' There is a coat the colour of autumn leaves, made of the softest tweed I have ever touched, with carved lions on the gilt buttons. I slip it on, and see a reflection of myself in the wardrobe looking-glass; when I turn, the coat swings with an easy fluidity. It feels like wearing something that weighs almost nothing; yet it seems to mean everything now, coming out of its hiding place after so many years in the darkness of the cupboard. I take off the coat, stroke the wool before shutting it away again, and put on a cream jacket trimmed with black braid, its narrowly cut sleeves elongating the arms, flattering the curve of the body, yet comfortable enough for me to raise my hands above my head. Then there is a fur-collared jacket in a pale natural-coloured wool, just as Mademoiselle recommended to others, but lined with a Japanese silk print, its black calligraphy unintelligible to my Western eyes, yet perfectly proportioned, repeated in minute detail over and over again. I slide my hands into the pockets – 'The pockets are meant to be used,' Gabrielle reminds me, 'just like the buttonholes, never a button without a buttonhole, everything has its purpose' – and find a pair of ivory-coloured gloves inside. I take them out, and a faint scent emerges. 'Chanel N°5,' says Gabrielle, with a smile. 'Her gloves, her perfume – still here ...'

I wish I could tell you that her scent still lingers in her rooms at the Ritz, but that would not be the truth; although when I stayed there, I could smell it on my own jacket, after spending a day within the perfumed air of Rue Cambon. I was not sleeping in the Coco Chanel suite that overlooks the Place Vendôme – its gilded grandeur a reminder of Chanel's pre-war years at the hotel, when the Duke of Westminster visited her here, as did Churchill and the Prince of Wales – but in the accommodation that she inhabited after the German invasion of Paris, and where she chose to remain in peacetime. It is a modest bedroom on the sixth floor, with a view of the garden and the rooftops of Rue Cambon, its door just across the corridor from the little lift that rises from a discreet side

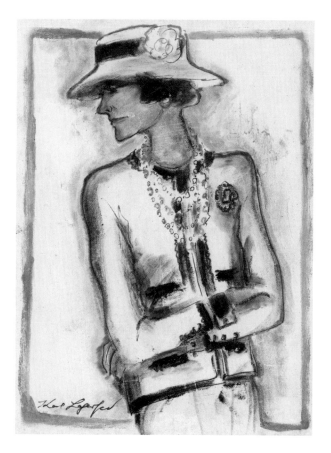

Chanel, by
Karl Lagerfeld.

entrance of the Ritz. Now, the room is decorated in pale shades of peach and blue, with splendid brocade curtains framing the windows. Only the ceiling remains white, but if you lie on the bed looking up at it, you see where it has been painted over many times before, and it is possible to imagine how the bedroom might once have looked, when the walls were plain white, just as Mademoiselle wanted them; white walls to match her white sheets; everything simple and austere as a nun's cell.

Here she lay, night after night, alone as she grew older, albeit beneath the same roof as others; the Ritz a kind of secular monastery where the rich found refuge in the consolations of its quiet order; although Chanel's rest was often disturbed. As a winter's afternoon turned to dusk, not so long ago, I sat in this bedroom and listened while Claude Delay talked to me of what had taken place within these walls. Mademoiselle had occupied the room, and another alongside linked by an inner door, with her bathroom en suite, just as it is now. The wallpaper and upholstery are new, and the taps in the bathroom have been changed into faucets in the shape of gold swans. But the view from the window is the same as it was when Chanel was here, black crows and gulls circling

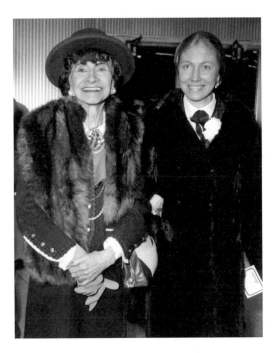

Chanel with her friend
Claude Delay, 1970.

above the rooftops, flying towards the Jardin des Tuileries and the river Seine, as the pale winter sunlight dwindles into darkness, the sky turning from blue to rose to grey. 'I often found her alone here,' said Delay, 'sitting at her dressing table, gazing down into the garden, looking at the chestnut trees. She was still so slender, thin as a girl in her white pyjamas, her eyebrows washed clean of their black makeup, her jewels put away beneath a chamois cloth, a silk scarf tied around her hair. "One shouldn't live alone," she'd say. "It's a mistake. I used to think I had to make my life on my own, but I was wrong."'

Mademoiselle Chanel – la Grande Mademoiselle, as she became known by the press, like the famous royal cousin of Louis XIV – was still attended by a retinue: a butler, François Mironnet; a maid, Céline, whom she called Jeanne (the name of a previous maid and also of her mother); her secretary, Lilou Grumbach. Sometimes François took off his white gloves and sat down beside her to eat, to keep her company; or played cards with Lilou in the room adjacent to Mademoiselle, while she was falling asleep. She gave François the key to her safe, told him that he could be a jewellery designer, as Paul Iribe had been. On Sundays, when she was often melancholy, Chanel asked her chauffeur to drive her to the cemetery, Père Lachaise. None of those she had loved were buried there, but still she walked among the graves, just as she had done as a child in another time, another place.

But she always came back to her quiet white bedroom at the Ritz; and when the day ended, when there was no one left for her to talk to, she would take her scissors from their place on the bedside table, cut her pills from their foil covering, and then give herself her nightly injection of Sedol, a form of morphine that she had relied upon for many years to help her sleep, ever since she had witnessed the death of her lover Iribe. The ritual was not a secret: Claude Delay witnessed it, the phial of drugs taken out of a small metal box in the bedside drawer, the syringe carefully sterilised in surgical spirit. 'I never saw her do the injection in haste,' says Delay, 'except when she was in the last stages of fatigue, or it was very late.' Eventually, the young woman came to believe that Chanel's dependency on the drug was more complicated than a physical addiction: 'her injection was a substitute for love … Sedol was her last defence against the night – the ultimate and solitary penetration.'

Yet the sleep it brought was not that of dreamless oblivion. In the darkness Chanel was troubled by nightmares, unbidden terrors, sleepwalking; sometimes she would rise from her bed, take her scissors from the bedside table, and sit in front of the mirror of her dressing table, cutting at her pyjamas, jabbing and slashing at the cloth. She would awake suddenly, scissors in hand, shocked and frightened at what she had done to herself; or sleepwalk into the bathroom, turning on the taps to wash her hands, over and over again. Her maid was instructed to lock the doors to the bedroom, in case Chanel's somnambulism sent her out into the hotel corridor, but she did not want her scissors to be kept from her, whatever the risk to herself.

There were nights when she slipped in the bathroom or fell from her bed. She told her friends that she preferred not to call a doctor – that would be too undignified – and so she tended to treat her wounds herself. Marcel Haedrich remembered seeing her cuts and bruises, and her explanations of how she was able to mend these injuries, without any help: 'She had brought together the fragments of broken skin on her nose to join them again. "With precision," she said, making the same movements: "like this, one bit against the other, almost to the millimetre."' Very occasionally, after a fall or another unsettled night, she mentioned her father to Haedrich, in connection with her childhood sleepwalking; the briefest of references, which nevertheless seemed designed to reassure her of past tenderness. 'Her sleepwalking came up again,' noted Haedrich, who had come to regard Chanel with a mixture of sympathy and frustration. 'When she was only six, her father used to put her back into bed when she got out. "Very gently, in order not to waken me," Coco said. "I was very scared. I would stretch out my hand and cry: '*He's* there! In the dark!' My father would say: 'No, no, don't be afraid, *he* isn't bad, *he* won't do anything to you.'"'

Lying awake in the darkness of Chanel's bedroom at the Ritz, I remember this story, and wonder who '*he*' was, and whether she still feared him, three-quarters of a century after her father had gone. I reach out to turn on the bedside lamp, but there is an electrical quirk, the lights seem not to be working, and the hairs on the back of my neck are prickling, as if there is crackling static in the room. I close my eyes, and see an image of Chanel within these walls, her sanctuary, as Delay had described her to me earlier today: red lipstick wiped away with a clean cloth, white face-cream, but eyes still black and glittering, like dark pools. I think of the scissors that glinted beside her bed, and the sterilised syringe of morphine, and of the surgeon's knife that remade her face in Switzerland, before her comeback, after the shadow of the war. I imagine Chanel closing her eyes at night, after she had injected herself with Sedol, seeing the white ceiling and the white walls turning to black, as the drug soothed her into brief oblivion. As I drift towards sleep myself, the walls dissolve into shadows, the dividing door between this room and the next gently rattles; I hear a murmur of voices, and the sound of footsteps in the corridor, or is it inside my room?

On the day before her death, 9th January 1971, Mademoiselle Chanel was still working, even though it was a Saturday, furiously racing against the clock to finish her latest couture collection. The following morning, she was forced to remain at rest; even the formidable Chanel could not insist that her employees go to work on a Sunday. Claude Delay came to visit her at the Ritz at one o'clock, where she found her sitting at her dressing table again, applying her make-up, carefully drawing on her dark eyebrows and red lipstick, examining her reflection in the mirror.

They lunched together downstairs at Chanel's usual table – 'out of the way', where the couturière could watch the others in the restaurant, without being watched herself – and then, long after the room had emptied, the two women finally left for an afternoon drive. The car drove them up the Champs-Elysées – 'crammed with a gloomy crowd', remembers Delay – and through the streets of Paris, while a wintry sunshine finally emerged through the mist. Chanel told Delay that she hated the setting sun, that she should have worn her dark glasses. By the time the car had brought them back to the Ritz, the sun had disappeared, and a full moon was rising. Delay said goodbye, and as Chanel disappeared through the door of the Ritz, she called out that she would be working again at Rue Cambon, as usual, the next day.

Mademoiselle Chanel took the lift back to her bedroom on the sixth floor, where her maid Céline was waiting for her. She was tired, she said to Céline, and lay down on her bed, still fully clothed, not wanting her maid to undress her. At about 8.30 p.m., she suddenly cried out to Céline that she couldn't breathe, asking her to open the window. The maid rushed to her mistress's bedside, trying to help her, as Chanel was struggling to give herself her injection. Céline broke the phial of drugs, and then Mademoiselle pushed the syringe into her hip. 'You see,' she said to Céline, 'this is how one dies.'

The next morning, Chanel's body lay in her white bedroom at the Ritz; her maid had dressed her in a white suit and blouse, and tucked her hands beneath the linen sheets. 'She looked very small,' says Delay, 'almost like a little girl taking her first communion.' The funeral service was at L'Eglise de la Madeleine, the grandest church close to Rue Cambon, famous for its monumental portico of stone colonnades. Her coffin was set beneath the statue of Mary Magdalene,

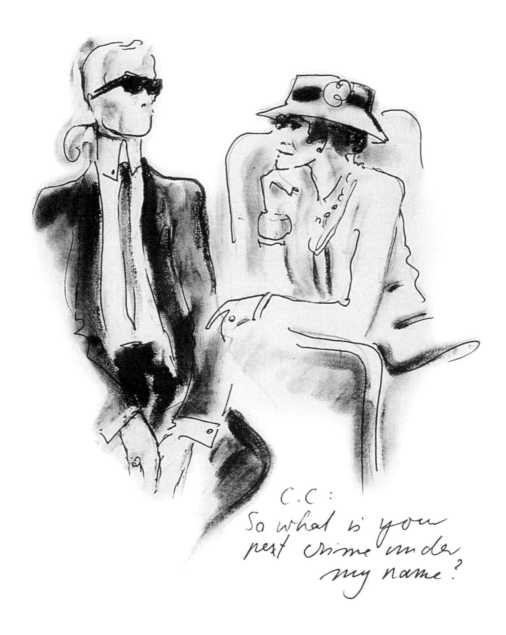

Imaginary dialogue between Chanel and Karl Lagerfeld, drawn by Karl Lagerfeld.

C.C: Are you not tired of Chanel?

KL No, only of the question...

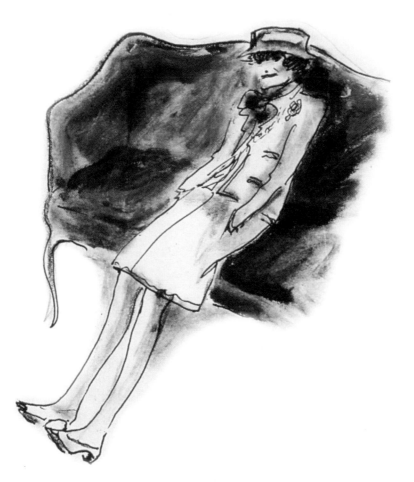

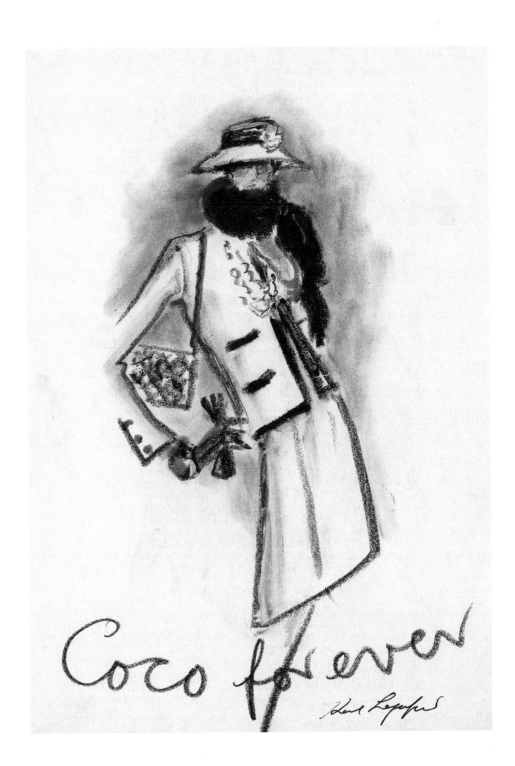

Coco fforever

Karl Lagerfeld

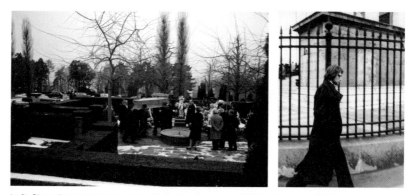

Left: Chanel's burial in Lausanne, Switzerland, January 1971. Right: Yves Saint-Laurent leaving Chanel's memorial service at L'Eglise de la Madeleine, Paris.

and covered with white flowers – camellias, gardenias, orchids, azaleas; some formed into a cross, others in the shape of scissors – except for a single wreath of red roses. (Diaghilev, the great impresario, would have approved; as would Misia, with her instinct for the making of drama and myth.) Yves Saint-Laurent came to pay his respects, as did his fellow couturiers, Balmain, Balenciaga, Courrèges. So many of her friends and lovers were dead – she had outlived Pierre Reverdy by a decade, and Cocteau had died over seven years previously – but Serge Lifar was at the church, along with Jeanne Moreau, Salvador Dalí and all of her models, a long line of them, wearing immaculate couture. Two weeks later, the same models appeared in Mademoiselle's last couture show, in ivory tweed suits and white evening dresses; many of those in the audience found their eyes drawn to the steps at the top of the mirrored staircase, where Mademoiselle used to sit, hidden from view; still hidden from them now.

She was not buried in Paris, but in Switzerland, as she had requested, in the cemetery at Lausanne. There is a headstone with five lions carved on it, her name above the dates of her birth and her death, and a simple cross. But the grave itself is covered with white flowers, rather than a heavy tomb. 'She did not want to be buried beneath a stone monument,' says Gabrielle Labrunie. 'She'd said to me, "I want to be able to move, not lie under a stone."' Madame Labrunie pauses, and then she says, 'You know, if you want to be close to a person who has died, you'll never find them in a graveyard.'

In Switzerland, in the long winter of 1946, Gabrielle Chanel had told Paul Morand that she was 'free as a bird'. Thirty years later, as Morand himself

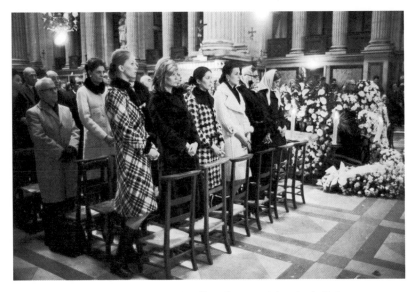

Models from the House of Chanel attending Chanel's memorial service in Paris.

approached death, he transcribed her words, in his book *L'Allure de Chanel*. 'Nothing was written by me,' he wrote in the preface, 'it was all by a ghost, but a ghost who, from beyond the grave, kept up a frantic gallop ...' These then were her last words to him: 'I would make a very bad dead person, because once I was put under, I would grow restless and would think only of returning to earth and starting all over again.'

On the top floors of 31 Rue Cambon, the lights in the workrooms are still burning bright through a winter's night, scissors snipping as a new haute-couture collection is being finished for the coming spring. Mademoiselle's apartment lies undisturbed beneath them; the door closed, the curtains drawn, silent in its darkness. But the moonlight finds a way in and is reflected in the silvery mirrors; so that the pale engravings on the Coromandel screens are visible, a feathered white phoenix clearly distinct on one of the panels in the hall, rearing above the flowering stems of ivory camellias. On the other side of the looking-glass doors, the mirrored staircase is quiet; no one treads its carpeted steps. When the couture collection is completed at last, close before the cold dawn rises above Paris, the lights are turned out, and shadows slip down the stairs. Then, as morning comes, the House of Chanel will open again and set to work once more.

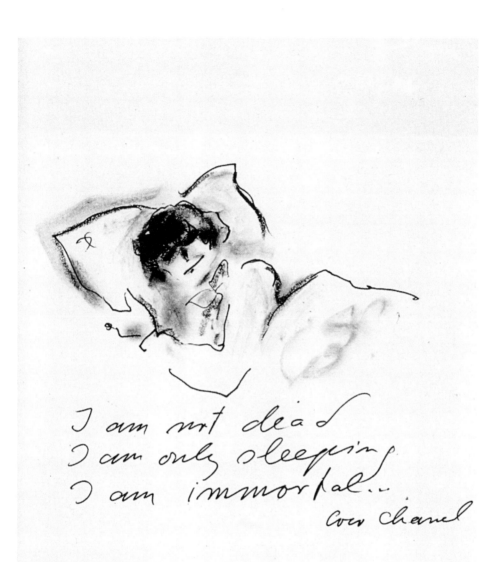

I am not dead
I am only sleeping.
I am immortal...
Coco Chanel

Chanel, as imagined by Karl Lagerfeld.

PICTURE CREDITS

BIBLIOGRAPHY

Biographies of Coco Chanel etc.

Baudot, François, *Chanel*, Assouline, 2003

Charles-Roux, Edmonde, *Chanel* (tr. Nancy Amphoux), Jonathan Cape, 1976

Delay, Claude, *Chanel solitaire*, Gallimard, 1983 (tr. Barbara Bray, Collins, 1973)

Galante, Pierre, *Mademoiselle Chanel* (tr. Eileen Geist and Jessie Wood), Henry Regnery, 1973

Greenhalgh, Chris, *Coco and Igor: A Novel*, Headline Review, 2002

Haedrich, Marcel, *Coco Chanel: Her Life, Her Secrets* (tr. Charles Lam Markmann), Robert Hale & Co., 1972

Leymarie, Jean, *Chanel*, Editions d'Art Albert Skira, 1987

Madsen, Axel, *Coco Chanel: A Biography*, Bloomsbury, 1990

Morand, Paul, *Venices* (tr. Euan Cameron), Pushkin Press, 2006

—— *The Allure of Chanel* (tr. Euan Cameron), Pushkin Press, 2008

Wallach, Janet, *Chanel: Her Style and Her Life*, Mitchell Beazley, 1999

Miscellaneous

Acton, Harold, *Nancy Mitford*, Gibson Square Books, 2004

Auster, Paul (ed.), *The Random House Book of 20th Century French Poetry*, Vintage, 1984

Ballard, Bettina, *In My Fashion*, Secker & Warburg, 1960

Barthes, Roland, *The Language of Fashion*, Berg, 2006

Beaton, Cecil, *The Glass of Fashion*, Weidenfeld & Nicolson, 1954

—— *The Years Between: Diaries 1939–44*, Weidenfeld & Nicolson, 1965

Beevor, Antony, *D-Day: The Battle for Normandy*, Penguin, 2009

Beevor, Antony and Cooper, Artemis, *Paris after the Liberation: 1944–1949*, Penguin, 2007

Bryer, Jackson R. and Barks, Cathy W., *Dear Scott, Dearest Zelda: The Love Letters of F. Scott and Zelda Fitzgerald*, Bloomsbury, 2003

Capote, Truman, *Portraits and Observations: The Essays of Truman Capote*, Modern Library, 2008

Cocteau, Jean, *Journal, 1942–45*, Gallimard, 1989

Daisy, Princess of Pless, *Daisy Princess of Pless by Herself*, E. P. Dutton, 1928

Davies, Mary E., *Classic Chic: Music, Fashion, and Modernism*, University of California Press, 2006

Dior, Christian, *Dior by Dior* (tr. Antonia Fraser), V&A Publications, 2007

Doerries, Reinhard R., *Hitler's Intelligence Chief: Walter Schellenberg*, Enigma Books, 2009

Doerries, Reinhard R. (ed.) *Hitler's Last Chief of Foreign Intelligence*, Frank Cass, 2003

Dolin, Anton, *Last Words* (ed. Kay Hunter), Century, 1985

Dorril, Stephen, *Blackshirt*, Penguin, 2007

Dwight, Eleanor, *Diana Vreeland*, William Morrow, 2002

Ewing, William A. and Brandow, Todd, *Edward Steichen: In High Fashion*, Thames & Hudson, 2008

Fairchild, John, *The Fashionable Savages*, Doubleday, 1965

Fane, Julian, *Memories of My Mother*, Hamish Hamilton, 1987

Field, Leslie, *Bendor: Golden Duke of Westminster*, Weidenfeld & Nicolson, 1983

Flanner, Janet, *Paris Was Yesterday: 1925–1939*, Virago, 2003

Gilbert, Martin, *Churchill: A Life*, Pimlico, 2000

Gold, Arthur and Fizdale, Robert, *Misia: The Life of Misia Sert*, Macmillan, 1980

Griffiths, Richard, *Fellow Travellers of the Right*, Oxford, 1983

—— *Patriotism Perverted*, Constable, 1998

Harrison, Michael, *Lord of London: A Biography of the 2nd Duke of Westminster*, W. H. Allen, 1966

Higham, Charles, *Mrs Simpson: Secret Lives of the Duchess of Windsor*, Pan, 2005

Leese, Elizabeth, *Costume Design in the Movies*, Dover Publications, 1991

Loelia, Duchess of Westminster, *Grace and Favour*, Weidenfeld & Nicolson, 1961

Manchester, William, *The Death of a President: November 1963*, Harper & Row, 1967

Marie, Grand Duchess of Russia, *A Princess in Exile*, Cassell & Co., 1932

Mitford, Nancy (ed. Charlotte Mosley), *Love from Nancy: The Letters of Nancy Mitford*, Sceptre, 1994

Muggeridge, Malcolm, *Chronicles of Wasted Time*, Collins, 1973

Mulvaney, Jay, *Jackie: The Clothes of Camelot*, St. Martin's Press, 2001

Norwich, John Julius (ed.), *The Duff Cooper Diaries*, Weidenfeld & Nicolson, 2005

Payn, Graham and Morley, Sheridan (eds), *The Noël Coward Diaries*, Da Capo Press, 2000

Poiret, Paul, *King of Fashion* (tr. Stephen Haden Guest), V&A Publications, 2009

Reverdy, Pierre, *Prose Poems* (tr. Ron Padgett), The Brooklyn Rail Black Square Editions, 2007

—— *Coffret en 3 volumes*, Gallimard, 2007

Ridley, George, *Bend'Or, Duke of Westminster*, Robin Clark Ltd, 1985

Ross, Alex, *The Rest Is Noise: Listening to the Twentieth Century*, Harper Perennial, 2009

Schellenberg, Walter, *The Labyrinth*, Da Capo Press, 1999

Schiaparelli, Elsa, *Shocking Life*, V&A Publications, 2007

Smith, Sally Bedell, *Grace and Power*, Aurum Press, 2004

Soames, Mary, *Clementine Churchill*, Doubleday, 2002

Soames, Mary (ed.), *Speaking for Themselves: The Personal Letters of Winston and Clementine Churchill*, Black Swan, 1999

Spotts, Frederic, *The Shameful Peace*, Yale University Press, 2008

Stravinsky, Igor, *An Autobiography*, Calder & Boyars, 1975

Swanson, Gloria, *Swanson on Swanson*, Michael Joseph, 1981

Trevor Roper, Hugh, *The Last Days of Hitler*, Pan, 2002

Updike, John, *Due Considerations*, Penguin, 2008

Vickers, Hugo, *Cecil Beaton*, Weidenfeld & Nicolson, 1993

Vickers, Hugo (introduction), *Cecil Beaton: The Unexpurgated Diaries*, Phoenix, 2003

—— (intro), *Beaton in the Sixties*, Phoenix 2004

Vickers, Hugo (ed.), *Cocktails & Laughter: The Albums of Loelia Lindsay*, Hamish Hamilton, 1983

Vreeland, Diana, *D.V.*, Da Capo Press, 2003

Walsh, Stephen, *Stravinsky*, Pimlico, 2002

Wheeler-Bennett, John, *The Nemesis of Power*, Macmillan, 1954

INDEX

ACKNOWLEDGEMENTS

This book could only have been written with the help of many others. Coco Chanel's niece, Gabrielle Labrunie, and her friend, Claude Delay, were very generous in sharing their memories and insights. I am also hugely grateful to Karl Lagerfeld, whose knowledge and understanding of Chanel is unrivalled, and to all those at Chanel who provided erudition and expertise: in particular, Marie-Louise de Clermont-Tonnerre and Cécile Goddet-Dirles, for invaluable wisdom in Paris, and Jo Allison and Julie-Anne Dorff for advice and friendship in London. Marika Genty, Patrick Doucet, Marie Hamelin, Julie Deydier and Odile Babin at the Chanel Conservatoire in Paris were exceptionally kind and meticulous in answering my innumerable questions; as were many others in the Paris headquarters, including Jacques Polge, Amanda Harlech, Sigrid de l'Epine, Elsa Heizmann, Veronique Perez and Laurence Delamare. I am equally grateful to Olivier Nicolay at Chanel UK, and all in his London team, including Sarah Brooks, Zoe Evans, Phily Keeling, Nathalie Rumpf and Mighela Shama.

I was able to enjoy unrivalled access to the Grosvenor family archives and would like to express special thanks to the Duke of Westminster KG CB OBE TD CD DL for making that possible. Andrew Riley and Sophie Bridges guided me skilfully through the Churchill archives in Cambridge. Nicholas Coleridge gave me access to the Condé Nast archives, where I was helped by Bonnie Robinson. Gavin Fuller and Lorraine Goodspeed provided much support at the *Telegraph* library, as did Luci Gosling at the Mary Evans library; while Chloe Batt assisted with research at these archives and others. Matthieu Goffard opened doors into the history of the Ritz Paris; Jennifer Graesser kindly allowed me to visit her at Rosehall, as did George and Sarah Lopes in Sutherland. I was made welcome by Soeur Laeticia, Lucile Casadesus, Didier Rovoal and Jean-Louis Sol in Aubazine. Malene Rydahl regularly provided solace and comfort in Paris.

Hugo Vickers was an inimitable guide to the Cecil Beaton papers, and a great deal else besides. I am also indebted to Sally Bedell Smith for sharing her detailed knowledge of Jackie Kennedy and the Kennedy White House; to Gilberte Beaux, for historical information about Ernest Beaux and the Beaux family; and to Richard Griffiths for his scholarly investigations into the European Right and British fascism in the 1930s. Anna Murphy, my editor at *Stella*, has been unfailingly supportive; likewise the editor of the *Sunday Telegraph*, Ian MacGregor.

I could not have been better served by the editorial team at HarperCollins: thanks to Carole Tonkinson for her remarkable patience and insight; Victoria McGeown for her faultless eye for detail and design; and to Jennifer Barth, Patrick Budge, Caroline Hotblack and Anna Gibson. I am grateful, as always, to Maggie Phillips, Linda Van and Charlie Campbell at Ed Victor Ltd; and to Ed Victor himself, who never lost confidence in me, even when I lost confidence in myself.

Many thanks, too, for encouragement and perceptive suggestions: Jessica Adams, Sam Baker, Sophie Dahl, Adam Phillips, Polly Samson, Alexandra Shulman, Harry Wyndham, Lucy Yeomans. To my mother, Hilary Britten, and my sons, Jamie and Tom MacColl: thank you, always, for everything.

And Philip Astor: a rigorous critic who read and corrected each draft of manuscript; my companion on the serendipitous trail of Coco Chanel, from Cape Wrath to Cap Martin, without whom I would have lost my way ... *je t'embrasse.*

HarperCollins*Publishers*
77–85 Fulham Palace Road,
Hammersmith, London W6 8JB

www.harpercollins.co.uk

First published by HarperCollins in 2010
This edition 2011

10 9 8 7 6 5 4 3 2

A catalogue record of this book is
available from the British Library

ISBN 978-0-00-731899-5

Printed and bound in China by
South China Printing Co. Ltd

Mixed Sources
Product group from well-managed
forests and other controlled sources
www.fsc.org Cert no. SW-COC-001806
© 1996 Forest Stewardship Council

FSC

FSC is a non-profit international organisation established to promote the
responsible management of the world's forests. Products carrying the FSC
label are independently certified to assure consumers that they come
from forests that are managed to meet the social, economic and
ecological needs of present or future generations.

Find out more about HarperCollins and the environment at
www.harpercollins.co.uk/green

Art & design director Patrick Budge